HIGH PRAISE FOR
MARIE BRENNER'S

HOUSE OF DREAMS

"SUPERIOR!"   *Time*

"ENGROSSING . . .
Brenner deals out the complexities
so ably that one can understand—almost—
how this family, willfully and spitefully,
refused to fulfill its destiny."
New York Daily News

"FASCINATING . . .
Captures the grace of this wonderful family
as well as the flaws that shattered it . . .
A remarkable book about remarkable people"
Louisville Courier-Journal

HOUSE
OF
DREAMS

THE COLLAPSE OF
AN AMERICAN DYNASTY

MARIE BRENNER

AVON BOOKS ◆ NEW YORK

Grateful acknowledgment is made to the following for permission to reprint previously unpublished material:

Alanna Nash for permission to quote from interviews with the Bingham family.
The Arthur and Elizabeth Schlesinger Library on the History of Women in America, Radcliffe College, for the use of letters in the Mary and Barry Bingham Collection. Reprinted by permission of Mary and Barry Bingham.
University of Louisville, Oral History Center, for their permission to use excerpts from taped interviews.

AVON BOOKS
A division of
The Hearst Corporation
105 Madison Avenue
New York, New York 10016

First Avon Books Printing: March 1989

AVON TRADEMARK REG. U.S. PAT. OFF. AND IN OTHER COUNTRIES, MARCA REGISTRADA, HECHO EN U.S.A.

Printed in the U.S.A.

K-R 10 9 8 7 6 5 4 3 2 1

For Ernie Pomerantz and Ann Arensberg

The House of Dreams.

In a tiny, quiet village,
Up a narrow, crooked street,
There's a quaint old-fashioned
      cottage
Standing in a garden sweet.

Such a dear old smiling cottage
With the hollyhocks in bloom,
Bending shyly towards the window
Peeping through into the room.

Such a cheery, cosy cottage,
Dreaming through the
          summer day
Of the many happy people
Who have come and gone away.

How you loved those bygone people,
Knew their secret joys and fears,
All their heartbreaks
          and their pleasures,
All their smiles and all their tears.

Surely ghosts walk in your
          garden
'Neath the silent silver moon
'Mid the scent of blossoms
          faded
In a dear forgotten June.

Then, should I disturb
          their dreaming
Drive them from their
          garden sweet?
I must turn and softly hasten
Down the narrow crooked street.

          Barry Bingham

Our family history is as convoluted as a Greek drama. . . .
Certain things happened that shouldn't have happened, which
led to other mistakes being made, which in turn doubled back
and bred fresh mistakes.

GAIL GODWIN, *The Finishing School*

Sweet curly head, safe in your bed, reaching to hold my hand
Surely you know, I love you so
Someday, you'll understand, dear.

"Baby Eyes"
Lyrics by Barry Bingham

Prologue

It was impossible to think of Barry Bingham without his wife, Mary. Even now, on a chilly January day in 1986, as Barry came into the grand house for lunch, Mary walked a bit more quickly through the halls to greet him, to search his face for any new information or insight. "Hello, Barry darling," she said, as he came over to kiss her cheek, and there was nothing casual in her greeting. When she called his name in her fine Richmond accent, she held on to the last sound as if she didn't want ever to let it go: *Ba-rah.* Mary was eighty-one years old. Her face had the supreme confidence of all women with great marriages, not a hint of discontent or bitterness in her expression or manner. In old age there was a faint line of sadness, but that was perfectly understandable. However passionate she was about her husband, she had lost her two favorite sons in the most tragic of circumstances. She could never mention her youngest son's name without tears.

Mary and Barry Bingham often had lunch together. After fifty-five years of marriage, they were still each other's best friend. Now in the midst of the family catastrophe brought on by their decision to sell their communications empire—the Louisville *Courier-Journal* and *Louisville Times,* their television and radio station and printing plant—Mary and Barry were even closer. And on this rainy day in January Barry had driven as always the fifteen minutes from his office at the Louisville *Courier-Journal* to his home just out of town, riding along the vast Ohio River, which separated Louisville from Indiana, until he reached the handsome stone pillars that marked the road to Melcombe, the Bingham estate. "The family is in disarray. It is absolutely shredding," Mary said soon after Barry walked into the house.

The Binghams sipped sherry in the library and waited for Carolyn, the black cook, to announce lunch and to serve a full three courses in the dining room all the way through to fingerbowls and dessert. The fingerbowls were always used. But now lunch was over; Carolyn had been complimented on her Kentucky ham

1

and Mornay sauce, and the fingerbowls had been put away. The
house was so damp from the rain that it was actually cold—bone-
chilling, in fact—which was how Mary and Barry liked it, very
English, with what they considered proper ventilation.

"May I serve the coffee now?" Barry asked Mary with a
smile as he got up from the table and moved gracefully around
to help her with her chair. He took Mary's arm with great tenderness, not because she was incapable of walking without help
but because after all these years of marriage he still adored her,
and these niceties of behavior—serving coffee to her, escorting
her from the dining room—were part of the very fabric of their
existence. They walked out of the dining room together, passing
a cabinet of porcelain treasures, into a hall that led to the library.
On a table was a large photograph of Franklin Roosevelt, the
patron saint of the household, inscribed affectionately to Judge
Robert Worth Bingham, Barry's father and the Bingham family
patriarch.

The Binghams came into a small room with peach-colored
walls where the single fire in the house sputtered fitfully. Mary
settled into a wing chair by the fireplace and arranged her slim
legs in front of her. She was dressed beautifully in a tapestry
jacket of velvet and brocade, a beige cashmere sweater, a narrow
black skirt, black stockings and, on her tiny feet, kid shoes with
grosgrain bows. Although she appeared as delicate as lace, she
wasn't. She still had a disciplined body, faultless posture, me-
ticulously cared-for silvery blond hair, a creamy skin and a beautiful mouth now hardened into an expression of determination.

"One lump or two?" Barry Senior asked with a silky voice
as he picked up a cup and saucer made of bone china that the
cook had arranged for him on a tray. Strangely, Mary didn't
answer but let the question hang in the air, as if her attention
had wandered. She had come near the end of a life that she had
tried to control perfectly, only to discover that nothing had turned
out the way she had planned. After all these years of marriage,
she knew Barry was being polite, exhibiting the impeccable
manners that she had fallen in love with when she first met him
at Harvard. But this day his dance of etiquette seemed to play
on Mary's nerves. Suddenly, her eyes filled with tears and she
sat up even straighter in her chair. "I am eighty-one years old.
Barry is seventy-nine. We don't have much time left with each
other. I certainly hope our children will come to our funeral,
but I cannot predict with any certainty how any of it will turn
out." For the first time that day Mary looked her age. She turned
to gaze at her husband, who in the face of this outburst had
frozen by the tray, demitasse in hand. And then Mary cried out
with that mixture of fervor, need and feminine confidence that
only Southern women ever seem to master in the presence of a

powerful man. "Barry, I cannot imagine that our problems with the children will ever heal! I cannot imagine why Barry Junior cannot reconcile himself to our dilemma! I cannot see why Sallie is raging at me so! Barry, what have we done to make our children come to this terrible state of affairs?"

"We can only hope," Barry Senior said. "And, of course, be quite firm with our decision." His words came fast, maybe a bit too fast, and then he walked over toward the window of his jewellike library and stared out at the storm. The library at the Little House, as they called this cozy Italianate villa on the grounds of their grand estate, was a small room with bookshelves filled with editions of Faulkner, Dickens and Trollope. Across from the fireplace was a chintz sofa that needed refurbishing and several chairs that had seen better days. This was their interior landscape, the setting of their daily lives: vaguely uncomfortable rooms, good pictures, great books, family photographs in tarnished frames, a genteel paradise right down to the chill in the air and a vague smell of must that permeated the house like the odor of old currency.

"I do so hope the rain will not bring up the tulips before our May visitors arrive," Barry Senior said as he stared out the window in the direction of the Big House, the large Georgian mansion up the driveway where his son Barry Junior lived. Barry Senior's voice was so smooth and clear that it was chilling, although he meant only to avoid a scene, not to show his wife any disrespect. It was impossible to know what he was really thinking. Unlike Mary, Barry was almost incapable of showing any emotion except pleasure. At most, when he was upset, he would be quiet or subdued, but usually he could walk into a room and light it up with his smile.

The Binghams were a family that appeared to have everything: immense prestige, intelligence, power, heraldic ideals, a vast fortune and the very real desire to use their money and power to improve the world. And yet the public virtue, money and power could not save their newspaper empire, prevent the deaths of two of their sons, or stop their three surviving children from turning on one another—and in their older daughter's case on her parents—with fury. The Binghams' friends were stunned by the suddenness of the explosion in the family, for their lives had always appeared so smooth and grand, with a perfection that was seemingly impenetrable. "When I was growing up in Louisville, the Binghams represented everything that was dignified and patrician," Diane Sawyer, the CBS reporter said. But for all their public composure, Mary and Barry suffered a tremendous void at the center of their lives. "The Binghams," a friend said, "were supremely elegant, grand and intelligent, and yet they were completely mysterious. I think their children understood them least of all."

1

It was Paris, it was June, the war had been over for four years and life was wonderful, so wonderful that years later, when he was an old man living amid the wreckage of his family and his family's newspaper empire, Barry Bingham often spoke of this perfect summer of 1949. His life had been glorious then, the world had opened up to him. The disasters of his childhood had been smoothed over years before, and now anything seemed possible for this splendid aristocrat. Bingham was forty-three years old, known in his hometown of Louisville, Kentucky, for his extraordinary charm and blond good looks, his money and power, but most of all for his immense dignity. His wife worshiped him and his five children thought of him as a hero, and he really was a hero that marvelous summer of 1949.

Bingham was an important man in Kentucky, the proprietor of his family's distinguished newspapers, the Louisville *Courier-Journal* and the *Louisville Times*, and President Truman had just put him in charge of the Marshall Plan for France. He was to work with his country's foreign policy greats, Averell Harriman and Dean Acheson, administering the distribution of American foreign aid to the French. Bingham was filled with pleasure at this appointment and a bit nervous about the responsibilities he had taken on. Running a Louisville newspaper was one thing, doling out foreign aid from Paris with the awesome Averell Harriman was something else again. Still, he welcomed the challenge. He was about to embark on an intoxicating time when everything around him seemed golden and preordained.

Newspaper owners and publishers often served the country in this era. They used their papers to become factors in society, to launch themselves, to catch the eye of the president. These were the great days of newspapering. There was no television that anybody paid any attention to, you could listen to the radio, but you read newspapers for *news*. Publishers were the equivalent of statesmen, and newspaper people were often appointed to serve as cabinet officers or as ambassadors. Barry Bingham's own father, Judge Robert Worth Bingham, had been appointed by Franklin Roosevelt to serve as his ambassador to Great Britain in 1933.

Now it was 1949 and his son was in Paris for this remarkable job with the Marshall Plan during the first real postwar tourist season. As Bingham walked down the graceful boulevards he loved so well, he marveled at the fine displays in the shops on the Faubourg St.-Honoré. It had taken four long years, but France was beginning to recover from the devastation of the war. Bingham was pleased to see that the Germans had not stripped all the wine cellars he remembered from years before. One of his first letters home to his wife, Mary, mentioned the champagne supply, for Barry Bingham took pleasure in noting vintages, food, even what kind of flowers a hostess had planted in her gardens. Hostesses adored him; he was masterly at dinner parties, and could amuse anyone near him with just the right story, his fine appreciative deep laugh, his perpetual bonhomie. He dressed beautifully—pin-striped suits, fine shoes, very Savile Row. His friends were just as polished. He was a people collector on first-name terms with Adlai Stevenson, Douglas Fairbanks, Jr., Lady Astor, Hedda Hopper and Noel Coward. But he was careful never to drop names. Only in private did he ever speak of ''Adlai,'' ''Doug,'' ''Nannie'' and ''Noel,'' or of ''Larry'' and ''Dottie,'' meaning Laurence Olivier and Dorothy Parker. He had a caviar voice, part Harvard, part Ashley Wilkes, and used expressions such as ''tay,'' a current café society term that meant elegant, and ''Oh, boogey!'' when he was annoyed. Although he was from Kentucky, Bingham moved between continents and worlds with total self-assurance, a rich man's son who had gone to Harvard and who later often came to New York to see his friends ''Dottie'' and ''Noel,'' Alexander Woollcott, the round-table wit, or Robert Sherwood, the playwright. Unlike them, he was not brittle, but he could be dismissive, and at times a bit cold. On the surface, he seemed a perfect gentleman, somewhat of a romantic about the South and the Lost Cause, and certainly sentimental about his grandfather Bingham, a North Carolina colonel who had stood proud at Appomattox. Bingham had that same Confederate bearing, the civility and the thoughtfulness of the beau ideal. Anyone who visited the publisher's office at the *Courier-Journal* was shown his prized possession, his grandfather Bingham's charred Confederate flag.

Everybody noticed his manners. They were almost feminine, and so exquisite that he seemed to come from a different time. In public, he did everything possible never to offend or to say an unkind word. He inevitably offered a departing guest ''the convenience of the house,'' as if he were a character in an Edith Wharton novel. In Louisville he was still called "Mr. Bingham" or "Senior," as a mark of respect. Some people thought Bingham was a dandy, a period piece, yet he could command a room with his ability to tell stories and his clarity of mind. Bingham had a jaunty, optimistic façade. With his china blue eyes, his round lips and his neatly coiffed hair, Bingham was so handsome he was actually pretty. The name Barry suited him perfectly, so much better than his real first name, which was George. But only Mary and his closest friends ever called him Barry; for everyone else it was "Mr. Bingham."

The *Courier-Journal* reporters often complained that when they encountered him in a hall, he rarely greeted them, almost as if he didn't notice they were there. That made sense too, for despite the charm and the civility, Bingham could be surprisingly remote. Sometimes when he was spoken to, he didn't answer—strange behavior for a newspaper man. He seemed to resist direct talk of any kind. Some of his reporters believed that the coldness and the detachment came from the responsibilities of his job, the awesome weight he felt being a liberal newspaper man in the border South. This position in which he found himself—the lone hero fighting the good fight—was a frequent topic of conversation around Bingham. He surrounded himself with other aesthetes and loyalists, and, as he said within the privacy of his family, he "wouldn't dream of playing golf with the Republicans at the Louisville Country Club."

But imagine. At this time in his life, the summer of 1949, he was the hardworking heir to a fine Kentucky newspaper, still proving himself, really, and he had managed to get himself appointed to replace the immensely distinguished David K. E. Bruce in this spectacular Paris job. Although his liberal credentials were impeccable, he was still a small-town publisher from Louisville and he would be working with Harriman, Acheson and Bruce himself, who had been appointed the new American ambassador to France. Harriman, Acheson and Bruce were the best the State Department of 1949 had to offer, "the wise men" who represented the fine egalitarian ideals that Bingham himself stood for. Bingham would report directly to Averell Harriman, who was in Paris to administer the Marshall Plan.

A reporter met Barry Bingham just after his arrival in Cherbourg and interviewed him in French. Bingham knew that his French was pretty bad, but the reporter was taken with his charm and wrote of Bingham's *"silhouette élégante et sportive."* Bingham was wearing a red handkerchief in the pocket of his gray flannel jacket, a festive touch that he was sure had inspired the adjective "sportive" in the paper. An entire army was at the

Queen Mary to receive him: press, the American consul, French diplomats. Within minutes of his arrival, he was whisked off to the countryside to inspect new freight cars manufactured in France. As part of the Marshall Plan, his job would be to help rebuild the French economy from its debacle caused by the war. On his way into Paris, through the Normandy countryside, he stared out the window of his train marveling at what he saw. There on the grassy banks that sloped down toward the train tracks were the fields of daisies, poppies and wild foxglove that he remembered from the invasion of 1944. Bingham had come in with the American press after D-Day. "The whole country-side was punctuated by blossoming hedgerows, the feature of the landscape that made the fighting so desperate in that part of the 1944 campaign," he wrote, but now it was utterly peace-ful, there was no war, no need for camouflage. Four years later Bingham noticed with delight the "magnificent herds of cattle in the greenest of fields," as if there had never been the slightest ruffle in the land.

When he arrived in Paris, he set up at the Lancaster Hotel on the Rue de Berri and wrote home to his wife, Mary, as he always did, every detail of his crossing, his arrival, each shading of his thoughts, the smallest conversations, the slightest details. Writ-ing to Mary was his way of staving off the desolation he felt at not having her share his joy, even in the first few weeks. His pain at being separated from her was a sensation so intense, he wrote to her, "that it hurts physically." But he did take some consolation in being able to report his joy at being in Paris again. And, of course, Mary and the children would soon be joining him.

Barry Bingham always associated Paris with his wife. How he loved her and depended on her for every little thing; she understood him perfectly and always had. Mary was a Southern girl, a real Daisy blonde without a pore on her face that anyone had ever noticed and so fragile she weighed barely a hundred and sixteen pounds. It annoyed her tremendously when friends told her how much she looked like Clare Boothe Luce because she hated her conservative politics, but in fact the two blondes did look very much alike: the same sharpness beneath the good features, the same flawless clothes. Although Mary was origi-nally from Richmond, she was by no means a classic Southern belle. She was far too much of "a bluestocking," as she called herself, by which she meant she was an intellectual, an oddball in the atmosphere of genteel Richmond, where she had been reared in a family that was "terribly well born but living in rather reduced circumstances." Mary spoke in formal phrases just like Barry's, as if they were actors in a comedy of manners.

Now, in 1949, the former Mary Caperton of Richmond, Virginia, had five servants and rarely entered her own kitchen. She was served breakfast in bed. She spent summers in Chatham on Cape Cod and winter ski holidays at North Conway in New Hampshire. She was dressed by Mainbocher and Piguet, wore tea gowns to dinner at home, and was photographed by the society photographer Dorothy Wilding. She was the kind of person who "carried on correspondence" with educators, clergy and botanists. In fact, after one lengthy exchange with a New England lilac grower, he was moved to name a new species the Mary Caperton Bingham lilac. Mary loved the word "arriviste," which she used only half jokingly. She was the mother of five children and the mistress of Melcombe, the Binghams' vast Louisville estate. The former vice president Henry Wallace had played tennis on her courts, and she had entertained Eleanor Roosevelt at a dining table that seated eighteen and was set with golden Limoges and vermeil. The table was so wide and so grand that you could hardly hear the person across from you, but you could look to the mantel, straight into the harsh gaze of Mary's ancestor the Earl of Egmont. Mary was a fabulous hostess, known for her food, her sauces, the butter and heavy creams that permeated almost every morsel that came out of the Melcombe kitchen. When Mary ran Melcombe, the fires were always burning in the hearths and the gloomy house was warmed by the intoxicatingly rich smells that wafted from the kitchen. In France the family would laugh because the chef complained that "les Binghams" ran through ten kilos of butter a week. But Mary never overlooked the smallest detail in providing striking touches at her parties. At that dinner for Mrs. Roosevelt, she had made sure there were two Negro guests, a local doctor and his wife, and that her downstairs maid, Ollie, was forewarned that "the colored lady coming was arriving for dinner with the First Lady and should be brought into the front door, not taken around to the kitchen." That same night Mary also made sure that Mrs. Roosevelt went out to the kitchen to greet their cook, Cordie, and Lizzie Baker, who had been Barry's nurse when he was a child and who was so arresting a figure, a real Southern mammy, that Cecil Beaton had once insisted on photographing her as an example of a vanishing way of life.

Despite all this marked imperiousness, Mary had a delightfully naughty streak that often shocked her husband and her children; she loved to talk about sex, who was having affairs with whom, the more illicit the better. In private, she referred to her love life with Barry as their "midnight feasts." In Chat-

ham in the summers Mary and Barry liked to swim nude together at North Beach. The sensuality they shared would remain
all their lives. Even when they were in their seventies, long after
Paris, they once took a group of their college-aged grandchildren
and friends on a nude midnight swim off a Chatham dock at Mill
Pond. "I can't believe your grandparents. . . ." one of the
friends said to a grandchild. "Granny and Grandy are free spirits. Just like they were in the 1920's," the Bingham grandchild
replied matter-of-factly as he looked at Mary and Barry bobbing
happily in the moonlight.

For a Richmond girl, Mary was surprisingly liberal, a classics
scholar who had gone to Radcliffe, although her web of preju-
dices was subtle and Byzantine. "We called our coloreds the
'dear nigs' because we loved them so," she said, and she meant
this with humor and affection and absolutely no condescension
or disrespect. If you pressed her, she might tell you that the only
"coloreds" who should truly be equal are those that had gone
to college, and preferably Harvard. Her son Barry Junior thought
his parents were "limousine liberals," but they were liberals in
Louisville, which was not a small thing. Just after the war a
Time correspondent had come to Louisville and, upon encoun-
tering Mary, described her in a memo to his boss, as "a doll-
like blonde" who "looks like a Park Avenue socialite but who
has a tough, keen mind behind her beautiful facade." She was
credited with being the power behind the newspapers, and she
and Barry had that rarest of marriages: they were a closed corporation, no one came between them.

Years before, when they were still young, Mary had to flee to
Paris when Barry had taken his time proposing to her. It had
taken Barry three long years to propose to Mary after he got out
of Harvard, but finally he did, sending a series of maudlin letters
to Paris to get this cool Radcliffe bluestocking to come home. It
wasn't hard to do: marrying Barry was all Mary had ever
dreamed about. She was madly in love with him and took the
first ship out of the chill of that Paris winter of 1931 back to
New York, where Barry waited for her on the dock with his arms
filled with jonquils.

In private their judgments were severe; they loved to laugh at
middle-class pretension. From the boat on its way to France,
Barry wrote Mary fabulous accounts of the hordes of "pretty
horrifying" Americans come to Paris in this first postwar season. He didn't know how he was going to survive the boat ride,
he wrote Mary, what with the anti-Semitic remarks he heard
from all the nobodies on the *Queen Mary*. "Those with dark
hair and especially those with German names hasten to make
cracks about the Jews so as to establish their own Aryan claims."
But he had endured them on the boat and smiled pleasantly at

their gaucheries, for he was always pleasant, no matter what his private thoughts. Besides, he could see it both ways. "I must say there are some pretty dreadful Jewish girls in mammoth shorts and their papas who look like the cruellest of Grosz cartoons, but the snobbism with which they are viewed by second-generation Germans is enough to make you gag. Maybe it was this bad in the 20's and 30's, and I am only beginning to notice it more, or it may be that this first real post-war tourist season has brought out all the termites in our society." He didn't mean to sound even vaguely anti-Semitic, of course. He was just showing the class bias that was natural in this era. Besides, the Binghams judged everyone in private, their children, friends, the reporters at the paper, intimates, strangers. In the privacy of his letters Barry shared his disdain with Mary, and only Mary, for both the anti-Semites and their targets, because they had a perfect understanding between them, as if they were two halves of the same whole.

He italicized each detail in his letters home. He couldn't wait to write her about running to the Quai d'Orsay to meet with the French foreign minister, "a delightful old boy with a most humorous and ugly face." He wanted Mary to know everything; that his office around the corner from the Place de la Concorde had a balcony with double doors; that his suite at the Lancaster was replenished daily with bowls of roses and pink hydrangeas; that he was awakened not by his beloved childhood mammy, Lizzie, as he had been at home in Glenview, but by a red alarm clock and a Basque waiter who brought his breakfast to him on a tray. He wanted Mary to see the fine displays that he was seeing in the shops on the Faubourg St.-Honoré. When he first arrived, he had marveled at the roses, and in the second fortnight—that was the word he used—he had taken such pleasure in the representations of the fables of La Fontaine. How he wished the children could have been there to see the town mouse and the country mouse sipping tea at their dear little table in the shop window on the Right Bank.

Within days of his arrival he received a message at his hotel that the Duchess of Windsor was "still strangely interested" in the Binghams of Louisville. The Duchess of Windsor was a distant cousin of Mary's and, according to Mary, "was always quite good about family." Wallis, like Mary, also grew up in reduced circumstances but with appropriate ties to proper Southern lineage: the Daughters, the Dames and "the Montague line." When Barry's father, the old Judge, had been the ambassador, Mary and Barry had gone to parties in London with the Prince of Wales and the former Wallis Warfield, so Barry was delighted that the duchess was determined to keep up the relationship, even though his father was long dead.

Certainly, Bingham had not wanted to spend his entire life running the family newspapers. His vision was global, and so were his ambitions. At the end of World War II, stuck in Guam doing Navy public relations work, he wrote Mary, "I don't want to spend the next twenty years simply hurrying back and forth to the office, with no pattern for making my time contribute toward the goal of social usefulness which I know is the only thing which would bring satisfaction to either of us in the long run." Like his father before him, he had used his editorial page to gain favor and influence. He was in Paris because he had crusaded for the Marshall Plan again and again, publishing editorial after editorial in the *Courier-Journal*, until he landed this terrific job. Although Bingham was deluged with paperwork and Marshall Plan financial reports, he had every intention of enjoying himself in Paris. He wrote to Mary that he admired Dean Acheson's "insouciance" about his work, an insouciance that he was sure came from confidence. "His good humor in the face of intolerable responsibilities has made me feel that I must not lose all perspective in relation to my comparatively minute duties." And so when the Windsors issued a dinner invitation almost upon his very arrival, off he went to their mansion in the park.

At first he didn't know what to make of this strange little couple in their French exile.

Wallis was floating around in a huge white skirt (with something above), looking well-preserved and speaking in a terribly affected half-British whine. But she made herself pointedly agreeable to me, and I found myself on her right at dinner. She mentioned several of the guests she had invited "for me," and made it clear that I was supposed to be the central point in her arrangements. She talked all through dinner about the Montague family, but mainly about the Duke's having had to give up the throne, how he had been misjudged, and how he was beloved in England. . . . She wound it up with this comment: "He really is quite the nicest little man I have ever known. You see I have been married three times, and I have stayed longer with him than any of the others."

After "the fabulous dinner and much champagne" the Duke came over and sat with him. "He asked if I was still living in Louisville, and when I said I had lived there all my life he exclaimed, 'Oh, then you must be alright on the *nigger* question.' " Barry could not believe what he was hearing. The Duke of Windsor, of all people, was taking off on "the niggers" as if he were a member of Louisville's River Valley Club. And so, sitting in Paris, Bingham found himself in the same position he often did in Kentucky. He was the political outsider among the social elite, his liberal credentials suspect, forced to defend the New Deal, the Roosevelts, "the nigs," as he called them, and the Jews. "[The Duke] then started criticizing Mrs. R., with old-fashioned comments on the Eleanor Clubs, etc. I rather rudely said that I thought he must have been seeing the wrong people in America, and that I thought Mrs. R. a great woman. He seemed astonished and said the 'niggers' had given him trouble in Nassau," he wrote Mary. While it was no surprise that the Duke of Windsor was hardly Martin Buber in terms of his love of humanity—after all, like many English royals, he was at first quite sympathetic to Hitler—Bingham was not about to offend him, not with all those dinner parties to come. Rather than arguing, he stayed late at the party and wound up, convivial to the end, singing show tunes. "I found myself doing duets of old Gershwin numbers with him, locked arm in arm. He has a way of peering up at you with that prominent blue Hanoverian eye, like an anxious bird looking out of a nest. Still worse, I was eventually forced to do the Charleston, which they seemed to think an accomplishment."

His days were filled with meetings, briefings with foreign ministers, tours of agricultural projects, press conferences for the Anglo-American and the French papers. As a newspaper owner, Bingham knew how to answer reporters' questions and would, when interviewed, inevitably toss out a remark that was a gem of modesty. "I've got a lot to learn," he told a reporter. "[This work] promises to be the most complicated and interesting assignment of my life." In Paris he was no longer the detached observer of world events that he had been as a newspaper man. He was in the very center of things, learning about the four-power conference from Dean Acheson, lunching with Averell Harriman, meeting on the state of the French economy with Harriman and the finance minister of France, worrying about the Palestinian negotiations, which were being observed by his very own publisher of the *Courier-Journal*, Mark Ethridge, a well-known Southern liberal.

Although he was having a terrible time finding suitable accommodations, he managed to strike his usual light tone in his letters home. He wrote to Mary that the sumptuous villas that were described to him turned out to be little more than mazes of neglected servants' rooms, priced at hundreds of thousands of francs. Bingham always concerned himself with money. Although the Binghams of Louisville owned vast properties in Kentucky, most of their cash was in the newspaper, and Bingham was going to try to get by on his salary of $17,500 a year. He talked to his children about scrimping and saving, missing summer camp. He hoped that his friends in Paris, such as the Harrimans, would turn up something respectable for the family to live in, and for the summer anyway he planned for Mary and the children to remain in Cabourg on the Normandy coast. He hoped to visit them "once in awhile," he joked with a reporter from the *Herald Tribune*.

Barry had the best intentions toward his children. He could just imagine, he had written Mary from Paris, the children's anticipation as they crossed over on the boat for their year in Paris, for it matched the eagerness he felt at the prospect of arriving in his red Buick convertible in Le Havre to pick them up when the boat docked. He could just see, he had written, the excitement of twelve-year-old Sallie and seven-year-old Jonathan, the somber resignation of Nursie, the Kentucky farm woman who was the children's nanny, and three-year-old Eleanor's "wide-eyed examination" of her new surroundings. He was less sure about the reactions of his oldest sons, Worth and Barry.

Worth, in particular, was an enigma to him, for he was intensely masculine, more so than his father had been at any age, and somewhat wild, called "Worthless" by his classmates from the moment he had been in boarding school. The year before, at age sixteen, he had been kicked out of Exeter for drinking. His father had been beside himself, in his way, about this prank, since both Barry Senior's sister and brother were sodden alcoholics. However, his way of coping with Worth was to avoid discussing the episode. He allowed Mary to discipline him, as he always did. Mary's idea of discipline was to tell her oldest son, "I hope we have not let you down." The school suggested he consult with a psychologist, which Worth did. This, of course, was never discussed openly in the family. Even his own brother, Barry Junior, had never been told that Worth consulted with anyone, much less that the psychologist quickly realized that the boy's relationship with his father was problematical, at best. Barry Senior had written Mary that he was "optimistic" that this drinking episode, the strange wildness, so terrifyingly like his Uncle Robert Bingham's, as if it were a family trait, was to be the last of its kind. He hoped that one of the good Swiss boarding schools would take the boy for his senior year of high school and straighten him out. Worth had been placed on the waiting list at the fashionable Le Rosey, which was a very good sign, he was sure.

At age fifteen, Barry Junior, the next son, was less difficult. Although his mother had been convinced through his childhood that Barry was "lazy," "fatter" and "vague," as she used to write her husband during the war, Barry Senior had a soft spot for this second son, his namesake, who was very much in his brother's shadow. He had reading problems and had missed his father terribly for the four years he had been away during the war. His father used to say that Barry's sensitivities and droll sense of humor reminded him of the way he himself had been as a child, as did his second son's physical frailties and eagerness to please.

In the main, however, he was highly satisfied with his children and, like all parents, wildly hopeful about their promise. He and Mary were so in love with each other that their children, he believed, could only turn out blessed. Barry and Mary were sure that their brood, especially the two oldest sons, had everything it took to uphold the very special birthright of the Binghams of Louisville, and like the little aristocrats that they were, the Bingham children were imbued with a sense of their responsibilities to carry the family forward, to extend the web of their power but to help others, and never to put themselves forward in any way that was either flashy or second-rate. Their mother's favorite word was "appropriate," and she applied it to schools, curricula, religion, friends, potential partners and mates. "Do you really think a girl who puts a spoon in a fingerbowl is appropriate?" Mary once asked Worth about his teenage girlfriend. On the first floor of the *Courier-Journal,* old Judge Bingham had inscribed the family credo: "I have always regarded the newspapers owned by me as a public trust, and have endeavored so to conduct them to render the greatest public service." And now the Binghams of Louisville were to have a year in Paris, as a confirmation of their special mantle and their desire to serve the commonweal. That was what Mary considered "appropriate" behavior, to be at the very vortex of achievement, entertained by diplomats and royals.

Freeze this moment: Barry Bingham waiting at the dock in Le Havre, watching for his wife and children to come off the boat, searching for Mary's lovely blond hair and petite frame, so in love, knowing that his responsibilities in Paris would seem less of "a boogery," as he had written her, once she was there. Mary and Barry would revel in their time together in Paris, so busy that they would complain later they hardly saw their children the entire year, and "time's wingèd chariot," as they called it, would fly by.

Freeze the Binghams of Louisville, right here in Le Havre, before the tragedies, bitterness and betrayals that would befall them in later years. They walked off the boat, Mary running to Barry, with the children bringing up the rear as if they belonged to another family, Worth Bingham once told a friend. But Mary and Barry were thrilled by their reunion, thrilled to be in France and in each other's arms. "Take some advice from

a very old lady,'' Mary Bingham told me one day long after
Paris, in the winter of 1986, that terrible season when the mag-
ical family had been torn apart by death and rage, when the
publishing empire was up for sale, when the great house near
Louisville had become a cold relic, and the Binghams' dreams
had finally run out. ''Always remember I told you this. After
a while in life enough things happen to you and you learn to
just go numb.''

2

But Mary and Barry still had each other, even now when they were old and their family was shattered. On that gloomy day at their grand house outside Louisville, Paris was a faraway memory. Memory was all they had, a lifetime of memories, images, the photographs in silver frames, photographs everywhere in their halls. The Binghams were rich and soon would be a lot richer, but their power would soon be gone, except locally, as would their dreams. Even so, Barry Senior kept saying that there was no reason in the world not to try to go on as always.

It was an extraordinary time for the Bingham family. The family's newspapers, printing plant, and television and radio stations were up for sale. Twenty-three hundred jobs in the Bingham companies were suddenly at risk. The family was a shambles, the children fighting with the parents and among themselves. After decades of controlling Louisville's only morning and afternoon newspapers, the Bingham ownership was about to end. Old Judge Bingham's credo about the newspapers being "a public trust" would become the motto of another ambitious publisher. With the end of the Bingham dynasty, Mary and Barry Bingham's hopes for their children would also come to an end. Still, one had to hope that there would be some healing, Barry Bingham kept saying on this dreary day. *We must let some time pass.*

Time and place, knowing when it was appropriate to react and how to do so, a sense of what was appropriate—the Bingham family had cared about these things a great deal. The Binghams' "place" in the world, their importance, had been a part of their legacy and their reputation, and now the family would be a mere footnote in American history, or so Barry Senior said. They would be remembered for their differences, their scandals and their tragedies. The Binghams' three surviving children, Barry Junior, Sallie and Eleanor, had seen to that. They were going this way and that like shuttlecocks, and had fought bitterly over the control of the family companies, particularly the *Courier-*

17

Journal. "It will take time to get over these things," Barry Senior said. "The question is how to repair the damage we can for the next generation. There is nothing much worse than an inherited family feud." His tone was eerily detached.

On this rainy day, Barry Senior, old now but still elegant, was in curiously optimistic spirits, for that was his style, grace under pressure, no matter what. But even Barry Senior found it hard to be graceful in the midst of a terrible family crisis that had been all over the national news. The *New York Times* had bannered his problems under the headline "Sale by Binghams Marks End of Era in Kentucky Journalism." As the fairy-tale world he and Mary had presided over had collapsed, reporters at the hotel bars in Louisville were wondering why. "I worked for the Bingham papers because when I woke up in the morning I felt my life was about something," one reporter said. The collapse of the $475 million Bingham publishing empire also meant the failure of the liberal ideals that had sustained the Bingham family and the *Courier-Journal* reporters for almost seventy years. The newspaper had been called the South's Guardian and its green-and-white delivery trucks and three thousand vending machines had distributed the Binghams' editorial vision to all 120 counties of Kentucky, even to the most remote areas of Appalachia. On the day Barry Bingham Senior announced that his newspapers were up for sale, clusters of reporters gathered around one another's desks and wept openly. The publisher of the paper, fifty-two-year-old Barry Bingham Junior, cried too. His dreams and his life had been wrecked by his father's announcement, and far worse, he had no idea why his father was selling the newspapers. "I thought my father always told me the truth, but now I'm not sure," he said. Although Barry Senior knew that his son and his forty-nine-year-old daughter, Sallie, were hardly speaking to him or to each other, he appeared oddly calm. "Mary and I will get through this dread time together as we always have," he said. "With our complete and abiding faith in each other."

Barry Senior had survived a hellish childhood by his ability to transcend nightmarish events, such as the one that now confronted him. When Barry was seven years old, he was on his mother's lap when she was fatally wounded in a car crash. The accident had left him temporarily unable to walk and practically mute for a year. Four years later, in 1917, his father, the Judge, was all but accused of murdering his new wife, Barry's stepmother, Mary Lily Flagler Bingham, who happened to be the richest woman in America. Although Barry's father was never officially charged, the news stories of this scandal captivated the country during the autumn of 1917. Mary Lily's wealth had come from her first husband, Henry Flagler, who had been John D.

Rockefeller's partner in Standard Oil and who developed Palm Beach, Key West and St. Augustine. He owned most of Florida and left Mary Lily Bingham $100 million in property, stocks, jewelry and cash, an enormous sum at the time. When she died, eight months after she married Bingham, she left her new husband $5 million in a handwritten codicil that would soon be challenged in court. The Judge survived this probate hearing, and soon after he collected his $5 million he bought the *Courier-Journal* and the *Louisville Times*. For years thereafter, right down to the present, the Judge's reputation remained vaguely sinister, despite his good works, his public acclaim, his intimacy with presidents.

After these horrifying events, young Barry's father shipped him off to a New England boarding school, Middlesex School, where as a Southerner he was perfectly miserable, often ill and homesick. But he survived Middlesex and went to Harvard, where he acquired the mannered personality of a dandy, and a fierce loyalty to his father, who by now had begun to live down the scandal of Mary Lily's death and the handwritten codicil. Although his older brother and sister had come from the same background, only to become drunks and misfits, Barry was able to conceal the trauma of his mother's death and the horrific Mary Lily Bingham scandal beneath a cool exterior that was nothing short of miraculous. Barry was a survivor. "God knows what would happen if you scratched the surface of my father, what is lurking under his skin," his daughter Eleanor told me. Even as an old man he cannot recall the awful events of that dreadful year of 1917, although he was eleven years old then. For that matter, he would unfailingly avoid whatever unpleasantness arose not only in his own family but in most situations. As an adult, Barry was so theatrically genial, so warm-spirited and bluff that he might have been a public relations man, and in fact during the war he was.

Based in London with the Navy for much of the war, Bingham briefed correspondents from Navy headquarters in Grosvenor Square. He took reporters into top security areas and into Normandy with the invasion. He was fabulous at this job (more grace under pressure), organizing the tours for the *New Yorker* writer "Joe" Liebling, for John Steinbeck, for Hemingway. The reporters liked to hang around Barry's desk at the Navy press office; it must have been the greatest city room of all time. What's more, there were nightly cocktail parties, speeches on the BBC, country weekends at stately homes. Barry had a marvelous war. It was everything he loved, the access to power, the social web and even good theater. Nothing seemed to bother him, not the buzz bombs, not the blackouts. He often wrote to Mary about his weekends at Cliveden with the Astors, his dinners at a chic club called The Ivy with "Larry" Olivier and Vivien Leigh, never mentioning a bomb or a body in any of his correspondence except in the most casual way. "I was not telling her anything that would be disturbing," he said.

This was all part of the unwritten code of upper-class life, Southern style. One never spoke an unpleasant word or "needlessly worried," as Barry said, anyone in the family. Better to deny, to shroud any controversial or painful episodes of the past. One had morbid interests, but they were usually in other families, of course, never in one's own. The capacity for denial, in the Bingham family in particular, must have stretched all the way back to the undying romanticism with which the colonel and countless other Southerners of a similar disposition viewed the Civil War. In this code the Lost Cause was not lost as long as one remained a gentleman. Candor was not for gentlemen, nor were emotional displays or confrontations. The notion of chivalry came down finally to simply not telling the truth, if the truth wasn't pretty. It was fine to criticize, to be vicious even, but never directly, always behind someone's back. Outwardly one had to be gracious, for appearance was all. The Bingham children accepted this code unquestioningly, at least until everything fell apart and they stopped speaking to their parents and to one another.

The family knew there were certain powerful taboos where Barry Senior was concerned, that you never brought up his mother's death or the threat of murder charges against the old Judge. What's more, his own children had never seen him cry, not even on the two worst days of his life: the first, in March 1964, when his twenty-one-year-old son, Jonathan, had climbed a utility pole and was electrocuted, and then two years later, in July 1966, when his oldest son, thirty-two-year-old Worth, the star of the family, was killed in another freak accident while vacationing in Nantucket with his wife, Joan, and their two young children. The death of two sons within two years, and from Barry Senior not a tear that anyone except perhaps Mary and one intimate friend ever saw. And so, as an old man standing at his library window, having buried two sons without breaking down, Barry Senior was not going to indulge in a pathetic display just because his family was breaking up, the murder allegations about the old Judge were about to be dredged up again and his communications empire was being turned over to strangers. As Mary wept about her children and wondered if they would appear at her funeral, he turned to her and said with only the slightest tremor, "My heavens, the tulips are always so lovely at Derby time."

* * *

For years the Binghams of Louisville had been talked about reverentially, with the kind of respectful whisper used to describe great churches and symphonies. The Binghams owned the newspapers, WHAS (the local CBS-TV affiliate), a radio station and a printing plant called Standard Gravure, which printed Sunday magazine supplements for themselves and other publishers, including the publisher of *Parade,* but their importance to the state arose from far more than their being the proprietors of a reasonably profitable communications company. They were obsessed with their role as newspaper proprietors. The Binghams saw themselves as *editors;* it wasn't just money they cared about—money was the least of it—and for a time the papers returned only 2 percent profit to the shareholders. When times were good, the newspaper ran almost without budgets or any kind of real financial plans. The newspaper was a monopoly; the ad revenues were high. For many years the Binghams didn't have to plan, and they talked about their newspaper in the loftiest terms. They said they were news shapers, they cared about the issues, and it was their responsibility, they believed, to employ reporters and editors who shared their view of the world and could interpret events for the *Courier-Journal* readers. Although there were many people in Kentucky who thought the newspapers were "judgmental" and did not cover the state as well as the local weeklies, the Binghams were unfazed by such criticism. "We tried to convey the notion of noblesse oblige," Mary Bingham said. It was as if the Binghams had a missionary fervor to serve the commonweal. Barry Senior was known as Mr. Louisville. The Binghams were Kentucky kingmakers; you ran with or against the *Courier-Journal.* They created senators, governors, mayors. Once in the late 1950's, two of Barry's close friends decided they wanted to run for governor. Barry called a meeting. "*You* will be governor," he reportedly said to the future governor, Bert Combs, "And *you* will be lieutenant governor," he said to the future lieutenant governor, Wilson Wyatt. The Binghams did so much for the state that although people sometimes wondered what their motives actually were, there was hardly a person in Louisville who wouldn't tell you that the Binghams had brought Kentucky into the twentieth century.

They presided over a backward state that was traditionally near the bottom in everything, including per capita income and literacy, so it was easy for the Binghams to cut a wide swath, wider than they would have in a more privileged environment. Through the crusading of the *Courier-Journal,* the Binghams were responsible for saving much of eastern Kentucky from the strip miners, the mentally ill from Kentucky's grim institutions, and downtown Louisville with its charming pressed red brick façades from real estate developers. The Binghams, as one Lou-

isville executive put it, "had a finger in saving everything in
Louisville. Children, buildings, the ballet, the symphony, even
the Dutch elm trees." Mary Bingham had personally brought
bookmobiles into the entire state, reading teachers into the illit-
erate hills of Appalachia, and Negroes, as she called them, into
Louisville's restaurants. She wrote many of the editorials for the
Courier-Journal during the war. She had a subtle mind and an
indomitable will, and she and Barry made sure that the *Courier-
Journal* pushed for every Democratic presidential candidate and
every cause dear to liberal hearts.

In private, Mary and Barry Bingham often compared the *Courier-Journal*'s reporting with that of the *New York Times*. Before
World War II, Arthur Sulzberger, the owner of the *Times,* had
been slow by the Binghams' standards about advocating America's intervention in the war, while the *Courier-Journal* had
pushed America's entry into the war from the first moment. Even
Barry's father, old Judge Bingham, when he had been Roosevelt's ambassador, had warned against Hitler, had predicted that
there was a war on the way. But the *Times* had been extremely
conservative about the war. Barry and Mary were obsessed by
this flabbiness. In June of 1941, as Barry trained for his Navy
assignment, he was taken to a dinner party at Adlai Stevenson's
house. He was delighted with the group assembled, which included the first Mrs. Ernest Hemingway and Adlai Stevenson's
sister, "a fine ugly intelligent woman." The latter was a friend
of Arthur Sulzberger and his wife, Iphigene, and she regaled the
guests with news of a recent dinner in New York when the French
playwright Henri Bernstein had said to Sulzberger, "Arthur,
what is the matter with the *Times?* You must not think that by
taking a mild policy you will escape the wrath of the Nazis, if
they ever control this country. If Hitler captures America, you
will be the first Jew in New York to be persecuted, and there is
no escape for you in being pusillanimous. The Nazis see through
that and only punish all the harder." All of this fine gossip Barry
immediately wrote home to Louisville along with the Sulzbergers' reaction. Sulzberger was "thunderstruck" and his wife,
Iphigene, was "angry at such an assault." But perhaps, Barry
wrote to Mary, "It may have sunk in on them."

The *Courier-Journal* had never been pusillanimous or weak-
willed about anything the Binghams believed was right and
proper. It was a marvel of a newspaper, all the more so because
it came out of Louisville, a Jell-O and Velveeta town with a
population that never exceeded three hundred thousand people.
By the 1970's Louisville's downtown was deserted. The living
was inexpensive and good. The town moved slowly and thrived
on gossip and social pleasures, and had qualities of both its
neighboring regions, the Midwest and the South. "This town,

from its beginnings, was kind of a loose town. There was a lot of New Orleans in it. A river town. *Pleasuring* has always been a part of life here,'' a local newspaper man once told a *New Yorker* writer.

For years Louisville had prosperous factories and strong unions. In 1974 it had around a thousand manufacturing firms and was the world's largest producer of bourbon whiskey and a major center of tobacco, but it also had vast factories that turned out electrical appliances, neoprene, bathroom fixtures and air-filtration equipment. For decades, but no longer, General Electric, International Harvester, Brown & Williamson Tobacco, Philip Morris, and B. F. Goodrich all thrived in Louisville. But by 1984 International Harvester was gone, General Electric had cut back considerably, the bourbon and tobacco industries had declined. Louisville's nickname became Strike City.

Thanks to the Binghams and the single new major industry in Louisville, the Humana hospital corporation, there was fine culture, an arts center, theater and ballet. Louisville had its own orchestra, dance company, the distinguished Actors Theatre (which staged the yearly Humana Festival), chamber music and a Bach Society. Even so, the only time Louisville truly came alive was in May during the Kentucky Derby. The *Courier-Journal* was an extraordinary newspaper for such a town—a talent pool, an oasis of civility. For the Binghams the *Courier-Journal* was a plantation to rival what the Ford Motor Company meant for the Fords of Grosse Pointe. "I am so tired of having these young Negro reporters that we train come work for us, stay a year or two, and then leave for the *New York Times*," Mary said. The *Courier-Journal* was a family business, but it was also the only local paper, and it covered big stories and small stories, right down to the Kentucky State Fair and the Louisville yard sales. Once, before a Kentucky State Fair, an editor named Bill Cox rode a buffalo through the city room into his boss's office. "I just want you to know I am thinking Fair," he said.

For sixty years the newspaper had sponsored statewide farm awards. The *Courier-Journal* had begun the National Spelling Bee. The daughters of the family complained about defending the paper's editorials at local cocktail parties, for this was small-town Southern life. Everybody who mattered knew everybody else, and you couldn't avoid that, or stop going to parties, not in Louisville. Through the years the paper had won eight Pulitzer prizes and had kept over three hundred people—an extremely high number—in the city room to cover the state, almost as many reporters as the *New York Times* needed to cover the entire world. The C-J, as it was called in the family, had eleven re-

porters and an editorial writer to cover the legislature, which
met for only three months every two years.

The newspaper was at Sixth Street and Broadway in downtown
Louisville, across the street from a bank, and two blocks away
from the venerable Brown hotel, a local landmark, but its editorial position was so fixed while Barry Senior was running
things that the block where the C-J was located was often called
Red Square by the local wags. But the Binghams didn't care and
they didn't answer to anybody: that was the power of being your
own boss, of keeping a newspaper private. The Binghams were
so grand that, for a time, they were beyond caring what anyone
in town thought of them. They moved in a different sphere,
globally, internationally, and they almost seemed to take a per-
verse pleasure in the times that the crackpots drove around the
driveway of their Georgian mansion, shouting obscenities at
them, or when the windows of the newspaper office were
smashed in 1975 at the height of the busing crisis. They were
used to being attacked and called "the Commie Binghams" as
they often were from church pulpits and in the legislature in
Frankfort. They were such snobs that they enjoyed these assaults
tremendously. Yet there were hints that beneath the façade, all
was not so smooth. Once when Barry Junior was on an airplane
in the early 1970's, a local congressman handed him a circular
that reprinted a 1917 speech accusing the old Judge of murdering
his wife. But that's what you lived with if you were a Bingham.
You ignored scandal, you served principles. When the locals
would become outraged at something that had appeared in the
paper, it was Barry Bingham they called, not the editors, for
everyone in Louisville knew that the Binghams listed their telephone number in the directory and you could call them about
anything, even to complain about your newspaper not being delivered; that's the kind of people they were.

Of course the Binghams were listed in the Louisville directory; that was part of their mystique, the belief in the public
trust. Their willingness to be accessible to the community was
what had earned them the adoration of most people in the state:
Imagine. They list themselves in the telephone book. At the height
of their power they were often quoted in the *New York Times* on
political matters and likened to the Kennedys both for their liberal beliefs and for the tragedies they had endured. Their ideals
were forged long before the desperate times of the Depression,
when the intervention of the government had been a godsend, a
necessity, and they hadn't varied much from their early New
Deal beliefs. Although the name Barry Bingham was not a
household word like the names of other great publishers—the
Sulzbergers, the Chandlers of the *Los Angeles Times,* or the
Meyer and Graham families of the *Washington Post*—the Bing-

hams' newspaper had, until recently, frequently been on the list of the ten best newspapers in the country. The Binghams served on "boards" and "foundations," nominated Pulitzer candidates and Harvard presidents, and reported to the White House on foreign affairs; this was their world, very Harvard, very inbred. And now it was all over. It was difficult for them to accept that the golden age of family newspaper ownership was over too. "Mother and Daddy just lived too long," Barry Junior said.

The Binghams in their day presided over upper-class Louisville as if they were monarchs, and they looked down on the old tobacco and whiskey families they socialized with occasionally. Dinner invitations to their great house, Melcombe, were coveted. There wasn't a Kentucky politician who didn't crave an audience at one of these evenings to try to impress Barry Senior with his credentials.

Melcombe was hardly a house, but an English-style country estate of forty acres designed at the turn of the century for a Louisville flour magnate named Charles Ballard, who wanted to impress the town with how rich he had become. Melcombe was a mansion of thirty or so rooms, a gloomy red-brick pile with little architectural distinction and charm, huge and oppressive in scale. The entrance was a forty- by forty-foot gallery that the family had used for dances in happier times, a vast space decorated with Victorian settees from the flour magnate's collection; immense gilt mirrors, one from James Monroe's White House; and oversized Venetian gondola lamps that the Judge had once bought in a moment of Italian madness and shipped back to Glenview. At the door were seven-foot-high gilt candelabra topped with masses of dried flowers that looked as if they hadn't been changed since Eleanor Roosevelt's visit. The whole house felt that way, as if it inhabited its tenants, not the other way around. Even in the attic, there was room after room of old toys and clothes. Sallie Bingham had saved almost every dress from her childhood as well as all her dolls and would never give one toy or dress to her nieces saying, "Those things are meant for my daughter." But Sallie never had a daughter, only sons, and the toys in the attic remained untouched and covered with dust.

There were three formal reception rooms, which were closed off in the winter by the original paned glass doors. Each room was so large, so oversized, that the ceilings had several crystal chandeliers. The same portraits had hung on the walls for decades.

There were formal gardens, stables, kennels, an Olympic-sized marble swimming pool, and an amphitheater designed by the man who built the New York Public Library. Sallie Bingham, the older daughter, used to stage adaptations of *Hamlet* for her high school friends in the amphitheater, the folly her grandfather had ordered up when he became a new millionaire. Almost immediately, Judge Robert Worth Bingham had renamed his estate Melcombe, after the town of the Binghams' English forebears.

When the old Judge, as he was known, bought Melcombe, he brought new money, scandal, a new history, ritual, rules and a birthright for the Bingham family. The real estate and the house on the hill were the first steps toward respectability for the Binghams and were a means of launching them. So much so, that over the years an elaborate protocol was established in the family about who could live where on the Bingham estate and when, as if they were English aristocrats passing titles. When a Bingham son was brought into the newspaper, he could assume residency in the Little House. When he was named publisher, he became the occupant of the Big House. It had worked this way for Barry Senior, who first moved into the Little House when he started working for his father. He took over the Big House when Aleen, the Judge's widow, finally decided to give up her claim to the house five years after the Judge died. By then the war was on, and Mary had a terrible time getting rid of Aleen's dark walls and taffeta curtains. "You could come in here in the middle of a summer day and not be able to see," Barry Junior said. "That was how dark it was." Barry's brother Worth demanded the Little House as his birthright when he was named assistant publisher in 1962, but he was killed before he could take over the full job. His younger brother Barry Junior stepped in after Worth's death in 1966 and took over the Big House in 1971, when *he* became editor and publisher of the *Courier-Journal*. The retiring publisher moved down the hill to Little Melcombe, as the Little House was formally called, and although the two publishers lived a stone's throw from each other, nobody in this family ever dreamed of dropping in on one another without first calling. There was always an excuse, a reason for a visit: flowers picked, presents delivered, gestures of civility. For years Mary's Piguet ball gowns had been languishing in the attic of the Big House, packed away in a box, but Edie Bingham said, "My daughters and I wouldn't think of taking them out and looking at them without discussing it with her first. It would be inconceivable that she would allow her grown granddaughters to unpack them, much less to try them on." In fact, everything the Binghams of Louisville did was so planned and so studied that the idea of a public scandal, like the one that finally destroyed them, was unthinkable.

The Binghams dealt with crisis badly. Crisis demanded spontaneity and intimacy, and maybe even displays of anger or grief. There were no rules to cover how to behave in the midst of a public mess, no protocol, no memos, five-year plans or lawyers' letters, which is how the Binghams often communicated with one another. Barry Senior often marveled at the Kennedy family, and would come home from dinners at Hyannisport and tell his grandchildren, "The Kennedys actually push each other about on the arms and then hug. Think of it!"

But the Binghams were cold and correct with one another, even in a crisis, and so, on January 8, 1986, Barry Senior and Mary invited their son Barry Junior and their daughter Eleanor to the Little House. Barry Senior was ready to announce "the dread decision"—whether or not to sell the empire. He had specifically chosen the week after New Year's for his announcement. He was fed up with the war that had been going on among his children. For two years Barry Junior, Sallie and Eleanor had been sabotaging one another. Although on the surface their problems were about business—who was going to control the newspapers and how—their real conflict went deep into the past. "We vied with each other for our parents' love," Eleanor Bingham said. "It was hopeless how we were pitted against each other."

For many years the children had focused on their business disagreements, which stood for everything else that was troubling them. As the publisher, Barry Junior resented his sisters' influence as company directors and forced them to resign from the board. He was tired of trying to run a huge company with their questions, complaints and what he believed to be their stupidity. "Sallie looked at our profit-and-loss statement for years and finally said, 'If the company is only in debt five thousand dollars, why can't we just pay it?' She was so inept that she didn't realize all P and L's drop the last three zeros," he said. "My brother is a terrible businessman," Sallie said. Sallie's sister, Eleanor, agreed. "I could not live in Louisville if Barry ran the newspaper," she said.

Eleanor and Sallie wanted their money out of the business. Personality differences played a tremendous part. The two sisters, who were at times allies, believed their brother Barry was "dreary and rigid," according to Eleanor, as well as "pathetic and dull," according to Sallie. "The newspaper under Barry Junior had a pompous and moralizing vision that is infuriating a lot of people in Louisville," Eleanor said. For that matter, Eleanor's husband, Rowland, was furious that Barry Junior ignored him. Rowland was highly sensitive, a young architect who had yet to find success. "I don't know why I couldn't make Barry my buddy," Rowland said. "Barry Junior takes the notion of freedom of the press a little too seriously." For his part, Barry Junior believed that his sister Eleanor was "unmotivated," that Rowland was "someone I have nothing in common with," by which he meant that Rowland "did not make enough

money to live decently and has . . . been trying to run Eleanor's
life.'' Furthermore, he believed that Sallie was ''an intellectual
snob,'' ''a failed writer who was trying to find herself by cre-
ating havoc at the Courier-Journal.'' Barry, Eleanor and their
parents were all in agreement that Sallie was ''narcissistic'' and
''desperate for attention.''

To make this morass even more depressing and complicated,
Sallie, Eleanor and Mary were united in their contempt for Barry's wife, Edie, who they were convinced was ''stiff-necked,''
''dreary,'' didn't have a decent cook and committed gaucheries
like giving a yearly square dance. ''Edie is a cloth-coat moralist
who hides her diamonds in the vault,'' Eleanor said. A local
politician named Harvey Sloane and his wife, Kathy, in particular, reportedly encouraged them in this belief, as did the two
men who ran the Humana hospital corporation who did not like
the way Barry Junior ran the newspaper. Although Worth's
widow, Joan, was in the family, she was outside the main orbit.
Mary sometimes referred to her by her full name, ''Joan Bingham.'' She lived in Washington and was closer to Barry Junior
and Edie than to anyone else, but was still quite fond of her
former in-laws, whom she spoke to frequently. ''I have been
fascinated by Mary and Barry for almost thirty years and I will
never truly understand them,'' she said. Barry Senior and Mary
agreed that Joan had done a superb job raising Worth's children,
Clara and Rob, who had distinguished themselves at Ivy League
schools. But Sallie had mostly ignored Joan, and now Eleanor
was cold to her too. ''Joan and I used to be close, but not
anymore,'' Eleanor said. ''She is obsessed with having her son,
Robbie, take over the newspaper.'' What was significant about
all these unguarded comments is that they were made without
any hesitation to me, a reporter, but apparently never directly to
the family members themselves.

There was a fortune at stake. Analysts had placed the value
of the Bingham newspapers, radio and TV stations, and printing
plant at close to $500 million. Although Barry Junior had the
title of publisher, his parents still controlled the business. At
fifty-two, he was, in effect, their employee. ''We will have
Christmas as always and then I will announce my intentions,''
Barry Senior told his children in December of 1985.

The holidays arrived, presents were delivered, the grandchildren assembled at the Big House as usual. Christmas was always
particularly special for the Binghams because Mary's birthday
was Christmas Eve and it was expected that all differences be
put aside for the celebration. Although Sallie fled Louisville with
her family for the holidays, she saw to it that her mother received
a lovely gift, signed by the children. From Washington, Worth's
widow, Joan, sent bridge pads in leather boxes. Then she left

for the Orient to visit her daughter, Clara, who was working with refugees in Hong Kong. Barry and Edie sent Mary and Barry Senior a case of wine, demitasse cups, and a handmade bedcover. Mary gave her son Barry an electrically heated bird-bath. And then, after New Year's, when all the thank-you notes had been dutifully sent and received, Eleanor and Barry Junior were invited to the Little House on January 8 at 10:00 A.M. Sallie did not appear. As Eleanor and Barry Junior waited they were served coffee in the peach-colored library. Barry Junior sat on the faded chintz sofa. He wore his usual ancient suit and crooked bow tie and he looked, Eleanor remembered, "as if he were going to jump out of his skin."

"Junior," as the reporters called him, was tall, oppressively thin, and had a handlebar moustache that sprouted from his upper lip into two waxed points, like tiny spears. He had survived Hodgkin's disease some years earlier, and his mother was convinced that his personality had changed as a result, that he had become constricted and introverted since his disease. "A terrible rigidity came over the darling little boy that he was," his mother said. Before his cancer and the death of his brothers, Barry Junior had been, at times, as graceful and witty as his father, but at this point in his life Barry Junior's expression was grave and without humor, his eyes so sad that he looked as if he were carrying the woes of the family on his thin shoulders; here was the dutiful son. The other Binghams could dazzle a table with their verbal abilities or their intellects, but not Barry. He was a man of character and principles. "I don't believe in hyperbole," he said. But this day in the Little House, even raucous Eleanor Bingham, who loved to outrage her friends and family with her antics, was totally subdued.

Eleanor was a handsome woman who dressed at times like a rock star—sequins, tie-dyes, leopard prints. She had pale skin and hair that she wore in a Buster Brown cut, like a little girl, a childlike quality enhanced by the lack of makeup and her spontaneity, as well as her clothes. She loved to call herself "the family hippie" and for a time she truly was, but now she cruised around Louisville in her husband's black Porsche like a Big Chill girl come back to the fold. Eleanor breast-fed her infant sons at the River Valley Club or at the Hard Scuffle race at the height of the Louisville social season. Once she even brought the former yippie Abbie Hoffman, an old friend, to be her houseguest and to sit in the *Courier-Journal* box at the Kentucky Derby. While her older brother prided himself on doing what the family expected of him, Eleanor took pleasure in the opposite. Flotation tanks, meditation, training superbabies at the Better Baby Institute in Philadelphia, religious reawakening by walking on hot coals—Eleanor and her husband, Rowland, had either tried

these spiritual quests or were in touch with those who had. But
Eleanor was a loving mother, a woman of such enthusiasms that
you could hear her laugh across the room at a party. "Eleanor
wants everybody to love her," her sister, Sallie, said. Certainly
as a grown woman, she was so warm that she became her parents' favorite child. "To think we almost didn't even want to
have her!" her father said. "And now she is the child of our old
age." But Eleanor's wonderfully bohemian nature was limited
to affairs of the spirit. Eleanor and Rowland were extravagant:
They once instructed a *Courier-Journal* executive to rent a private jet to whisk them to the Dominican Republic. They used a
friend's corporate plane to take their baby furniture to the Cape;
and one summer, they rented *Washington Post* executive editor
Ben Bradlee's East Hampton house for thirty thousand dollars
for the month.

The children shared certain physical traits: long faces, a prominent jaw, pale hair and skin, and their mother's look of total
determination. Even so, their personalities were as different as
if they had come from different families, especially Sallie, who
was not in the room that day but who was a presence there
anyway, Eleanor said. "You couldn't get away from it," Barry
Junior said. "She started it all."

Sallie, almost forty-nine years old, the mother of three sons,
was a writer and what the French call "a princesse eloignée"—
a faraway princess. She seemed to be real, she talked with utter
logic and precision, but she lived so much in her own world that
it was hard to know her. According to her mother, much of what
Sallie had to say was "an utter phantasm, destroying in the extreme and pathological." Sallie, tall, with faded blond hair, gentle eyes and prominent teeth, was thin and liked to dress in long
flowing skirts, lacy tights, fringes, billowing scarves and elaborate shoes—Bloomsbury in Louisville. She had a gracious manner and was highly organized, the kind of woman who saw to it
that her doilies were neatly lined up in the kitchen drawers.
Although she could give the appearance of utter kindness, she
was capable of unusual behavior, such as leaving on her refrigerator door a schedule of financial punishment for bad behavior
of her children: a hundred dollars deducted from their trust funds
if they were caught with drugs or drunk again. Like her parents,
Sallie always expressed herself more effectively on paper than
she did in direct conversation. Her father liked to remember that
as a child she disappeared each night after dinner and sat at her
desk to turn out stories and fill journals. Once she composed an
entire book of poems and sent them off to her beloved father
when he was away at war.

She went on to Radcliffe, published short stories and an early
novel, won awards and married young. At times Sallie seemed

shy, but she was capable of such self-absorption that it frightened her family and friends. "Sallie is a failed writer because she has no compassion. She will destroy anyone for her career," her mother said. She had a novelist's imagination and would say anything about anyone in the family for the shock value alone. From time to time, she told friends that some people in Louisville speculated that her father was a homosexual. What Sallie may have been repeating was a persistent Louisville rumor for which there was no evidence and which could have been started maliciously by Barry's political enemies.

In recent years Sallie had become an ardent feminist. Sallie's rage was such that even after the family collapsed, she went on a public rampage against her father. She sent dozens of letters to book editors around the country accusing him of attempting to suppress a book about the family as well as arranging a Pulitzer Prize for a favored reporter. Though she seemed determined to destroy her family's reputation, the most Barry Senior could say was, "After we are gone, I am afraid that Sallie will be consumed with guilt and vain regrets."

Although the meeting in the Little House was nominally about the family newspaper, the tension in the drawing room reflected years of family misery. Sallie seemed convinced that the very air her family breathed might be lethal. Until Sallie Bingham was forty-eight years old, her father had never told her he loved her, and when he finally did, it was her husband who gave him the idea. This sign of Barry's affection was such that soon after her father said, "You know I love you," Sallie announced the fact on national television. "He told me . . . that he loved me," she told Diane Sawyer on *60 Minutes*. "I don't understand," Mary Bingham said to her children one day. "You are all so rich, so talented, so good-looking, why can't you be happy?"

And so, in the Little House that first week of January, Mary and Barry Bingham walked into the living room together, like royalty, Eleanor remembered. There were no tears, of course, not in the Bingham family; no begging their children to mend their ways, no asking for forgiveness, no wondering where they had gone wrong. Mary and Barry stood near the fireplace, suitably grave but exquisitely dressed. This was, after all, an occasion. Barry Senior was wearing a three-piece suit; Mary, a designer dress. Eleanor remembered being frozen in her chair, unsure of what was going to happen next, as if she were a small child and not the thirty-nine-year-old mother of two sons.

"This is the hardest decision I have ever made in my life," Barry Senior said. Eleanor remembered thinking that despite the pouches under his eyes her father was surprisingly calm. His voice was steady, as if he might have been holding a Navy press conference in Grosvenor Square. "I have decided that the only way to proceed is to sell the companies. There is no going back on this decision. Eleanor, I know how unhappy you will be because you wanted to run WHAS. Barry, I know you will find something else to do with your life.''

As Barry Senior's voice filled the living room his son turned as pale as a statue. His father had just fired him. ''Won't you just look at the numbers again on the spread sheets? I can show you this is completely unnecessary,'' Barry Junior said. ''I will look at them this afternoon and we will meet again tomorrow,'' Barry Senior said. But his tone was definitive; there was no going back. Eleanor remembered being unable to look at her brother, such was her glee at her father's decision. She had exactly what she wanted. The company would be sold and she would get all of her money out. She had no feeling whatever about the family newspaper and neither did Sallie. What they couldn't stand was the way their brother was running it.

Finally, at the Little House that January day, Barry Junior looked up and said with a shaking voice, ''I disagree violently with what you are doing and I am going to prepare my own statement.'' Then he walked out of the Little House and up the driveway to the Big House, a spectral figure on a chilly, wet morning. The next day Barry Junior showed his father his statement. ''How dare you say I am 'irrational,' '' his father said. ''People will think I am senile.'' Mary railed at her son, ''We gave you and Edie the best job in Louisville and the two of you have acted like martyrs.''

One day later statements by both ran in the *Courier-Journal*. Barry Senior wrote:

> My father spoke of the newspapers he owned as a ''public trust.'' My son Barry has conducted them since my retirement 14 years ago in that same spirit of dedication to high standards. He has placed his own mark on the product with force, yet with a sensitive understanding of the obligations attending monopoly ownership.

Barry Senior was careful to cause no offense. Barry Junior had no such qualms.

> The decision . . . to sell all family-owned companies is in my opinion both irrational and ill advised. While my father has kind words to say for my stewardship, his decision to sell all the companies I have managed clearly indicates that he holds other family members' personal interests and priorities at a higher value than my service to the companies. It is difficult not to view this action as a betrayal of the

traditions and principles which I have sought to perpetuate. It fails to meet any standards of fairness I can comprehend.

On the day these statements were published Barry Bingham Senior parked his wife's small blue Ford in the *Courier-Journal* parking lot as he always did, near the dozens of green-and-white *Courier-Journal* trucks. (*Just the things you want to know, all rolled into one. C J Everyday,* a sign on the trucks read.) He walked into the lobby of the seven-story limestone building with its diorama of Kentucky heroes. Daniel Boone, Henry Clay leaning on his cane in the bluegrass, John James Audubon. Near the elevators were even more symbols of the newspaper's importance—bronze plaques of Pulitzers won, glory years in *Courier-Journal* history, all the way back to 1826, when the Louisville *Focus* began.

The paper was as inhabited with ghosts as the Big House, such ghosts as Henry Watterson, the most famous editor of his era, who had stood next to Lincoln at his inauguration; "Skeets" Miller, who won a Pulitzer in the 1920's when he crawled into a coal mine to interview a trapped miner. There were Kentucky folk columnists who printed the news of every two-headed billy goat in the state; a food editor who kept a bottle of bourbon in her desk and who knew one hundred ways to cook Kentucky ham; editorial writers who exchanged letters in ancient Latin. A block away at WHAS, the Bingham TV-Radio headquarters, there were DJs and newsmen and more ghosts, such as Tom "Cactus" Brooks, who in the early days of TV had a famous show called *T-Bar-V.* "No one would care a bit if we were a button factory," Barry Bingham said. But the *Courier-Journal* wasn't a button factory. It was a collection of journalists who loved gossip and feuds and searching for warts. There were Nieman fellows, Kentucky history experts, sportswriters, horse people, environmental specialists, night men, deaf-mute printers, guild organizers, cafeteria workers, drunks, gamblers, secretaries, accountants and editors who believed, as one said, "that working at the *Courier-Journal* had been a rare privilege and an honor." Later, Barry Senior would marvel at how reporters he had never once greeted had come up to him that day with tears in their eyes and touched his sleeve.

The *New York Times* carried the story of the sale on page one and devoted seven thousand words to the Bingham family's history in the business section of the Sunday edition. There were page-one stories in the *Washington Post* and the *Los Angeles Times* and shorter takes in every other major newspaper in the country. The *New York Times* series "The Fall of the House of Bingham," by Alex Jones, would win a Pulitzer Prize, and where most people would have been chagrined by this exposure, Mary and Barry were thrilled that their story had won yet another award. Selling the empire was the least of it. Except for Barry Junior and Joan, each Bingham wanted the last word. "I will not allow Sallie to speak for this family," Mary said. "I think we all decided, 'Oh well, let's just say it all,' " Sallie said.

The Binghams, too, devoted a lot of space to their own story, including a special magazine supplement that ran in the *Courier-Journal* with Mary and Barry's eerily cheerful faces on the cover, photographed in a pink light, a distinguished couple who had borne their tragedies with grace and yet who had managed through their very goodness and devotion to each other to contribute mightily to the Bluegrass State. No wonder the editors dispatched their reporters to Louisville. No wonder *60 Minutes* sent Diane Sawyer, a Louisville girl. But Diane Sawyer, and the other reporters, came back from Louisville strangely depressed. Something was terribly wrong with this family, the coldness beneath the warm surface, the clinical attitude toward its own collapse, the imperial standards. The reporters' reactions mirrored what the children had experienced. "It was so damn subtle," a family member said. "Everyone sought their [the parents'] approval and no one ever really got it."

The attraction of the story was not the astonishing heretofore untold original Bingham saga—the death of Mary Lily and the $5 million codicil. Nor was it the Binghams' devotion to the state, the nation and the world. The true fascination of the Bingham story was the strange power of the marriage of Mary and Barry Bingham, a union so tight, so closed, that nobody could so much as approach it, not even the Binghams' own children. Mary and Barry survived the loss of their two favored sons in terrible accidents, a double tragedy that no parent could truly recover from, by retreating more deeply into their own marriage. At the same time, they increased their already heavy commitment to public causes. Their three surviving children were grieving too, but however decent their intentions, Mary and Barry's capacity for empathy seemed limited primarily to their own suffering. The family grew increasingly unable to reach one another, until finally the only way they could communicate was through a terrible public scandal by talking to reporters who, though virtual strangers, suddenly found themselves bearing witness to the most heartbreaking private moments, such as the lunch I had in the Little House that damp January afternoon. These chilling scenes and revelations in front of reporters would be repeated again and again, and Mary in particular would shed her tears easily with strangers, but not with her own children. In the end, it would be impossible for Mary and Barry to have any form of catharsis or even clarification with their son Barry or their daughter Sallie. "It is a question of pride," Mary told me. In the end, it would be impossible for Barry Senior, with his distaste for unpleasantness, ever to tell his surviving son why he had taken the newspaper empire away from him. "How will I ever be able to go on with my life unless I know what I did wrong?" Barry Junior asked his family.

Tragically, Mary and Barry would remain as mysterious to their children as they were to casual acquaintances, so locked together that even in old age with their family in ruins, they were interested almost entirely in each other, their faces still lit with romance, free of bitterness or disappointments. "Our children may resent the enduring longtime happiness of our marriage," Barry Senior said. "There never has been a question for me about who comes first in my life and where my loyalties lie," Mary said. "It was always Barry. He was first. *Always.*"

3

"I can remember at just what point . . . I saw you across the street, bareheaded in that coon skin coat and fashionably unbuckled galoshes and just how you looked when you came across the street to speak to me, and the very smell of the slush and melting snow—and how wonderful every moment of my life has been since then because you have been the very heart and core of it. . . ." Mary wrote to her husband almost twenty years after they met. All their lives Mary and Barry shared a feeling of divine intervention about their union, as if their very meeting had been predestined. They met in Cambridge when they were sophomores. It was March of 1926. Barry was twenty; Mary was twenty-one. The attraction was instant and made perfect sense; they were both Southerners, beautiful and blond, and far away from home. Although it was springtime, there was still snow on the ground. When they met and fell in love, "Barry was so striking and handsome and Mary so exquisite-looking and pale that we all thought there couldn't have been a more suitable couple," a classmate remembered. Through their life together, Mary would provide the strength and direction that Barry needed; Barry would provide for Mary the financial security and refined sensibility she was determined to have. Neither would ever truly dominate the other; rather, they became like a single being.

It was a wonderful moment to be in love. The times were euphoric; it was the Jazz Age, the Roaring Twenties. There was never going to be another war. Speakeasies and bathtub gin were plentiful and a new kind of freedom was in the air. "We all drank so much," Mary said. "It was our rebellion against the pernicious government and Prohibition." Imagine Harvard in the springtime of 1926: the sleek varnished shells with their oarsmen gliding by on the Charles, young men and women walking beneath the elms, the Glee Club serenading couples as they sat on the steps of the Widener Library at twilight. That March day Barry Bingham, with his slicked-back blond hair and his

36

pretty features, decided not to study his Romantic poets or Shake-speare's sonnets but to head for an audition of a play called *A School for Princesses*, a creaky vehicle that the Radcliffe Drama Club had scheduled for their spring show. At the audition at Whitman Hall, he saw an acquaintance, a Radcliffe redhead named Rhodita Edwards and a friend of Mary Caperton, who was trying out for a part. It was Rhodita who actually introduced them. *Mary, may I present Barry Bingham. Barry, this is my friend Mary Caperton.*

He was young for twenty, fine-boned, sensitive, overprotected by his father and his older sister, Henrietta. He had dropped out of Middlesex during his senior year and had come back to a languid Louisville, where he and Henrietta had run a literary bookstore called Wilderness Road, which their father had kindly financed. Louisville then was filled with easy pleasures—roadhouses, fancy-dress parties, and during racing season an atmosphere, as one old Louisvillian put it, "of constant gaiety punctuated by the cries of black boys running down Third Street towards Churchill Downs." The black boys sold fried chicken from baskets at the track, where Barry's father had a private box. You could go to the theater at Macauley's on Walnut Street, eat at the Brown Grill and take in the Saturday movies. For a teen-ager who had never had much fun, the Louisville of 1923 must have been a kind of paradise, especially with a wild older brother and sister drinking to divine excess in the Big House and a father pleased with his new money and newspaper. The Mary Lily scandal, now six years behind them, was receding into memory.

Although he had sent Barry away for most of his childhood, the Judge sympathized with his younger son, who had seen his mother die and then contracted tuberculosis, severe asthma and chronic hay fever. Barry was a frail child and had to be sent to his father's hometown, Asheville, in the North Carolina mountains, where Thomas Wolfe came from. Barry was raised there by his aunts Sadie and Mary. What he needed was mountain air. The Judge built a sleeping porch on his sisters' house so Barry could toughen up by sleeping outside. "Like Christopher Robin, I 'wheezled and sneezled' throughout my childhood," Barry wrote. His adored Aunt Sadie raised him, and then he was sent into the depths of New England for his education while his father went on with his life.

His older brother, Robert, and sister, Henrietta, at home in Louisville were hardly positive influences. Young Barry was said to be dazzled by the glamour of Henrietta and Robert, their wonderful clothes and free-spirited ways. His brother was hand-some and such a fine tennis player that he almost made the Davis Cup team. But he was weak, what his brother would later call "high-strung." Once when he was drunk, he had driven his car into the foyer of the Big House. Another time he appeared in the amphitheater during a musicale completely naked with an urn on his head. One Christmas before Barry went to Harvard, Barry staged a pageant in the vast foyer of the Big House as a present to his father. "Wouldn't you like to be in this?" Barry reportedly asked Robert. "Oh, sure," said Robert. At the end of the performance as Aleen and the Judge's guests clapped politely, Robert stepped over the footlights and the audience was able to see that he was once more completely naked, except for a top hat, shielding himself with a trough of horse manure.

At this time, Henrietta, with her piercing blue eyes and raven hair, was in the full bloom of her sexuality, so glorious to look at that the Bloomsbury artist and writer Doric Carrington called her "a Giotto Madonna." Henrietta was bisexual, and she had already had a public flirtation with Carrington, Lytton Strachey's companion; and the director John Houseman. Houseman wrote in his memoirs that he was madly in love with Henrietta from the first unforgettable moment he saw her. She sat "on top of a piano in a purple velvet dress and played the saxophone." When she wasn't in Louisville, she spent much of the year in England, riding to hounds and going to parties with the Bloomsbury group, who nicknamed her the Kentucky Heiress. Henrietta's friends were the Sitwells and Lady Colefax, who viewed her as an exquisite salon pet with money to burn.

She had fallen into this louche existence her freshman year at Smith when Mina Kirstein, her English teacher, convinced her that she should drop out of college and head for the pleasures of London with her as a companion, which Henrietta was pleased to do. Mina's younger brother was the distinguished poet and critic Lincoln Kirstein, who would become the collaborator and friend of Balanchine and later start the New York City Ballet. With Robert and Henrietta as Barry's role models, the Judge did not have much hope for his younger son either, but he urged him to take the Harvard boards. Miraculously, considering his Louisville life, he passed.

Mary Caperton was prettier, blonder and more feminine than most of her classmates. She had class. Her mother had made sure of that, poor as she was. Mary was at Radcliffe thanks to the oddly named scholarship "Distant Work," which meant it was for qualified poor girls who came from far away, and she always claimed the distinction of being the first girl from Richmond ever to attend Radcliffe. "It was considered far more ladylike to go to Bryn Mawr," Mary said. It was her immense discipline and her ability to focus on her studies that got her to Radcliffe, no small accomplishment. There were seven children in the Caperton household—six girls and Arthur, the oldest.

Mary was the fourth child, and not the favorite by any means. She was not as pretty as her sister Helena, her mother's namesake and favorite, nor as good a dancer as her sister Harriette, and she wasn't as cheerful as her sister Sara. Although she was good-looking, with her small features and golden hair, Mary disdained her sisters' vanities and shallow ways. Like Barry, she had a passion for the theater. Also like Barry, she was very much a Southerner and had grown up with the same hard lessons of vanquished pride, the specter of Civil War memorials, geriatric veterans invited for Sunday dinner, and the endless parades of cripples up and down Monument Avenue celebrating another battle of the Lost Cause.

Like the North Carolina Binghams, Mary's family had once been distinguished. Her mother's grandfather was, as she liked to say, a Montague, the founder of the Richmond German, the dance that set the tone in Virginia, and her mother's father was the dean of Dromore, a prominent figure in the Anglican Church. But Mary's mother had committed a most egregious sin for a Southern girl: she married beneath herself. Mary's father, Clifford Randolph Caperton, who, Mary said, "came from a West Virginia farm family of some repute," was the nephew of a Civil War hero, Major Robert Stiles. He was handsome, overly sensitive and perhaps too weak to cope with poverty.

As a child Mary Caperton rarely had a new dress. She lived in hand-me-downs from her sisters in a small house the neighbors nicknamed "the cabbage patch." The sisters rummaged through one another's drawers, stole one another's stockings, mended gloves, and worried about keeping up appearances.

It was Mary's mother, Helena Lefroy Caperton, who kept the family together. A small woman with immense energy, her neighbors said she resembled "a small Pekinese dog she used to have." What they meant was that Munda, as she was nicknamed in the family, had an intense, twitchy nervousness. She also had a regal manner. "One must marry rich," she often told her daughters. She was, moreover, a writer of frothy magazine pieces and gothic regional folktales full of marvelous humor— "florid thrillers" her future son-in-law would call them. Thanks to the Montague connection, she was obsessed with genealogy, and for a time, to earn extra money, she organized the Richmond social register. "That was always considered such a curious occupation. Because we all knew everybody and certainly didn't need such a book," a Richmond matron said. But Munda was a snob, a self-styled social arbiter, and loved to tell everyone how she had spent her own childhood between Ireland and Virginia. "By the time I was seventy-five I had crossed the Atlantic forty times," she said.

She published dozens of articles in the popular glossy maga-

zines of the day, as well as two books. Dorothy Parker, whose
husband came from Richmond, wrote an introduction to one of
them, a favor presumably to her mother-in-law, as well as Mary
and Barry. Once in New York, Mary wrote to Barry that Dottie
had given her a look that meant, *What could one do?* when Mary
thanked her for writing her mother's introduction. Mary remarked that writing this introduction was "the only nice thing
Dottie ever did in her life."

The introduction was masterfully opaque:

> These are curious tales to come from the pen of a gentle,
> pretty, Richmond lady, the mother of a son and six daugh-
> ters. I do not know the words for Mrs. Caperton's stories.
> They are strange, swift, tense, emotional . . . all these. But
> there is more about them. There is a wildness, a fierce rush
> of drama, a long spreading terror, a passionate champion-
> ship of the lovely and the innocent and then a sudden cu-
> rious tenderness. No. You see? I told you I could not find
> the words to describe them.

Munda's stories were as florid as her son-in-law had said. "All
the voyage he sat beside silver pall and burning candles, as the
great ship swept towards New York. It was the last and only
honor he could do the woman who had loved him enough to die
for his happiness." In this collection, Munda wrote a Virginia
period piece called "The Doctor's Story," of which Barry wrote
to Mary, "the handling of the Negro problem must have made
Dorothy Parker raise her blue eyebrows pretty high."

She was obsessed with finding the right husband for her
daughters, although she had no means of providing them with
the proper trousseaux, much less the china and the silver, that a
well-born Richmond girl needed for her dowry. "My mother
would throw up her hands and say, 'All these girls, who will
provide their drawers and petticoats?' " Mary said. Helena
sprinkled her motherly bromides with Latin phrases. When her
daughters fought over stockings, she would cry, "Oh you girls
have no sense of *teum et meum.*" For that matter, Mary's grandmother was so rigorous that she made "insistent and pious
reference to the Latin roots of any words we used. . . ."

The Capertons' small brick row house was at 1510 West Avenue, a few blocks from the grand houses on Monument Avenue, with its procession of Civil War heroes on their immense
bronze horses riding forever to glory. The lessons of pride were
everywhere, even on Monument Avenue, where all Virginia
schoolchildren learned that the eternally loyal General Lee, on
his faithful Traveller, faced south. "The dead hand of the Civil
War hung all over my childhood," Mary said. The six blond

Caperton girls, popular and surrounded with beaux, were convinced that they would have to make their debuts "on the sidewalk." They kept their refrigerator stocked with gardenias and not much else. Mary seemed to despise the atmosphere, so much so that all through her life she would dislike what she called "ladies' pursuits," the lunches, gossip and "hen parties," as she called them. When she became a mother, she seemed not to feel as close to her daughters as she did to her sons and used to describe the birth of males as "accomplishing a boy." Barry Senior appeared to share her bias, for in a prominent place on the wall in his office at the newspaper were individual portraits of his three sons, but not of his two daughters.

Mary escaped the chatter and the poverty of "the cabbage patch" by reading her way through the Richmond library. "I was stopped at the formation of the vegetable mold in Darwin's *Origin of Species,*" she said. When she was a teenager, she moved out of West Avenue and into the home of Louise Burleigh, the director of a local Richmond theater. Miss Burleigh was a Radcliffe graduate who had moved to Richmond and saw so much promise in Mary that she helped her prepare for her Radcliffe boards. She was a mentor to Mary, convincing her that her place was in the highest stratum of achievement. But when Mary left, she escaped more than her vain sisters. "I believe I was rather deeply upset and depressed even as a pre-adolescent child by the rather grim financial difficulties we were always facing at home, and by the consequent tension and misery that marked the definitely tempestuous relationship between Father and Mother," Mary would later write.

Munda's husband, an advertising manager in Richmond, made no impression on any of Mary's school friends. An acquaintance of his said, "He was almost never there. I always thought he was a traveling salesman." In fact Mr. Caperton had been the manager for a small company called Whitehead & Hoag, which sold promotional badges, banners and crystaloid signs from a one-room office at a local bank. Earlier, he had been a Western Union telegraph operator. Whitehead & Hoag went out of business during the Depression, and after that, Mr. Caperton is listed in the Richmond city directories as an "advertising manager" but without a company affiliation. Mary called him "a sweet man" and politely changed the subject when his name was mentioned. In 1939, after his daughters were long grown, Caperton stepped in front of a trolley and was killed. "The theory in Mother's family was that he committed suicide," Barry Junior said. But the subject of Mr. Caperton's death, like the awful death of Barry's mother or the Mary Lily Bingham scandal, was simply never discussed.

Helena Lefroy Caperton instilled in her daughters a remarkable self-confidence. She reminded them that her mother's family went back to the "Burgesses of Virginia," and this ensured Helena's place, much to her delight, in the Colonial Dames of America. Helena's panache had given her daughter Mary the illusion of great class and confidence, qualities that no doubt attracted Barry to her that March day and would win over old Judge Bingham, who adored her on sight. "The Judge could not believe that Barry had stumbled into someone with such brains and common sense," Joan Bingham said.

Of all the girls Barry could have met, Mary was particularly adept at knowing how to please him, an ability that was the very essence of a Southern girl—to look at a man with adoring eyes, to appear to make him the pivot of her existence. The Civil War had taught its daughters to treat their men as heroes, to permit them their illusions of the Lost Cause, never to allow them for a moment to believe that they had failed. Mary went to Miss Virginia Randolph Ellett's School for Girls, where "Miss Jennie" taught her girls how to be proper young Southern ladies, but the headmistress was unusual in that she believed all her girls should go to college and even sent her students' papers to a Harvard professor to be corrected.

But Miss Jennie's curriculum had a handy way of skirting reality, and certainly the disaster of the Civil War. "American history was never taught," Mary said. "We memorized the Plantagenets." Miss Jennie drilled her students in Greek and Latin. Mary's rigorous training made her uncompromising about education, and what she learned from Miss Jennie affected everyone around her. She lived in her own world; she did not suffer fools on the subject of education, and this intolerance would cause her children and grandchildren problems in later life. When her son Barry was ten, she wrote to Barry Senior about her displeasure with the children's schools. "I feel deeply that [Barry] might much better be learning something about the Greek city states and the downfall of Athens in the thorough and uncompromising way in which [my teacher] Miss Lulie Blair taught it to me when I was ten."

On Robert E. Lee's birthday the girls would chant, "Who is the greatest man? Robert E. Lee! Who is the greatest person? Miss . . . Blair!" Her classmates, the daughters of Richmond's best families, included Mrs. Leslie Cheek, the daughter of the noted historian Douglas Southall Freeman, who was the biographer of Robert E. Lee. "We were taught to be tremendously thoughtful, to never start a letter with 'I' for example. We were taught to be as attractive as possible, we were being trained in the role of being a fine wife and a mother. The Capertons had such an energetic mother that perhaps they had the idea of a larger possibility not thought of by the rest of us," said Mrs.

Cheek. The Richmond of this charming era was still governed by the customs of the Old South. Many of the streets were still lit with gas lamps and shaded by magnolia trees. You could walk down Monument Avenue to St. James's Episcopal Church and the Commonwealth Club or take a trolley out to the new Country Club of Virginia to have dinner in Jeffersonian splendor. In the summertime good Richmond families put away their rugs and brought out special straw mats, and replaced the silver with crystal because they believed it looked cooler. A Negro would call out from his wagon, "Watermelon! Ten cents!"

When a member of a family died, the tradition was to spend the night in the same room with the dead body wrapped in linen burial sheets. Every family had its secrets—its closet alcoholics, its kleptos—but there was always the obsession with appearances. No proper girl was ever married without silver; what is more, it had to be the right silver: old, impossible to clean, with as much ornamentation as possible, such as acorns and rosebuds. Twelve "covers," as place settings were called, were considered a bare minimum. The Capertons were classic upperclass Southerners. They were ancestor worshipers, and, for all their enlightenment, thought that whites were better than blacks. Their racism was specific. The writer Florence King once explained the notion deftly: you could be an archsegregationist and still believe that Marian Anderson should be allowed to sing at Constitution Hall. In this argument, Negroes would be welcome at libraries and the theater because their desire to go would make them, by definition, superior beings. This was known in the South as "the consciousness of kind."

Helena impressed her grand plans on her daughters and used her journalism to prop up the Capertons' reduced circumstances. In 1933 she wrote an article for the *Ladies' Home Journal* called "Care and Feeding of Sons-in-Law," a surprisingly revealing statement of her intentions.

I imagine there can be no greater humiliation to a mother than to see a cherished daughter marry unworthily. When it happens, it is to a certain extent the fault of the mother. . . . "You are a very ambitious mother, are you not?" I have had this said to me in varying tones, running the gamut of superiority, disapproval and envy. Of course I am an ambitious mother. Would I be worth my salt if I were not? Is the best too good for our daughters? Is there anything more *infra dig* in demanding the superlative in husbands than in striving for quality in housing, food and education? . . . I do mean that the beginning of success is to insure in the girl a high opinion of herself. The higher the personal estimate, the less danger there is of her taking a second-best matrimonial bet.

Helena's closest friend from childhood was Nancy Langhorne, later to become famous as Lady Astor, who came from similar circumstances in Richmond but who made a brilliant marriage to Waldorf Astor and became the mistress of his great English estate at Cliveden. All through their lives "Nannie" Astor and Helena remained close, so close that during the war one of Mary Bingham's more onerous duties was to send Lady Astor's clothes from Henri Bendel to Barry, through the service maintained by Parcels for the Forces, so that he could deliver them on his weekends at Cliveden. In their correspondence, Barry and Mary referred haughtily in code to Nancy Astor as "Mother's old school friend," though they deplored her Tory politics. Mary frequently complained about the clothes-buying task. "I have sent off the printed silk to the old school friend. It is a navy and white dress and jacket of the same material, and I do not think it looks as if it cost $139.90, as it did. . . . I just hope she will not return them in a rage."

Helena was determined that her daughters would somehow do well. One of them would marry a stockbroker from an old Louisville family, but another became a nightclub dancer. Two others married well, but Arthur, the only boy, would die in a plane crash after the war. Mary, however, triumphed, walking off with an ambassador's son, and her mother would bask in her reflected glory, able at last to hold up her head to Nannie Astor and her sister, Irene Langhorne, who had married the illustrator Charles Dana Gibson. Of all her daughters, Mary, the bluestocking, had taken her mother's lessons most to heart. "In all contacts encourage the best," Helena Caperton had written in the *Ladies' Home Journal*. "At a coming-out party, for instance, my hand is bowed over by one hundred and fifty young men. Five of these I consider eligible. Five out of more than one hundred. Among these five there is one of whom I think 'You perfectly delicious creature, though you are unaware of it, we are destined to become much better acquainted.'"

Though he eventually succumbed, Barry resisted for years the efforts of both Mary and Helena. He had his first taste of real freedom and was studying hard enough to graduate as a magna cum laude, but he also must have been pained when he was not elected to one of the Harvard social clubs. It is impossible to know for certain why Barry wasn't asked to join a club other than the Harvard Dramatic Club, but at Harvard in that era there was a natural bias against Southerners, which no doubt affected him. But the real reason that Barry was excluded was probably the scandal surrounding his father. The gossip about Mary Lily's death had traveled the social circuit from Newport to Palm Beach just eight years earlier and probably ruined his chances for the right club bid. Although Harvard was filled with Trotskyites and scholarship boys from Boston Latin, it was the blond dandies of the clubs who were the social arbiters. A rich Southern boy as sensitive as Barry Bingham would have suffered from not being asked to join a club, for there was no question that the elite social life at Harvard in the 1920's revolved around these clubs. It was just before this period that the rumor spread through Cambridge that Franklin Roosevelt was such a liberal because the Porcellian Club had rejected him years before. Although "the Porc" set the Harvard social tone and was the club of Saltonstalls, Cabots and Lodges, the Binghams for whatever reason were not yet prestigious enough for their son to get the nod. "I had no part of club life at Harvard," he said. "Almost no one from Middlesex did." Yet as an adult, Barry clearly enjoyed club life to such a degree that he belonged to several clubs in Washington, London, New York and, of course, Louisville. Mary and Barry would become trustees of Harvard and Radcliffe, and would help determine who would be on the Board of Overseers, but all their lives they remained harsh about the Porcellian Club and the Harvard cliques, as if they could not forgive the exclusion. In their voluminous correspondence they referred to blond elitists as "pseudo-Porcs," but years later, when Worth Bingham went to Harvard he became an enthusiastic member of the Delphic Club, known as the Gas House and campaigned to get his younger brother a bid.

Mary and Barry, however, often acted in plays together at the Harvard and Radcliffe drama clubs and after performances went to dances at Brattle Hall, where "hip flasks passed behind the scenes, some holding our own home-made gin, a prohibition concoction with raw alcohol for kick, glycerine for smoothness, juniper drops for flavor." When he was just a freshman, Barry took the lead in a satire of college life called *Brown of Harvard*. The following year he starred as Harlequin in an adaptation of *The Love for Three Oranges*. The Judge publicized his youngest son's achievements. "Barry Bingham Wins High Grade At Harvard," the *Louisville Times* reported, and mentioned his leading roles in the Harvard Dramatic Club.

Their passion for amateur theatricals would always remain. Mary and Barry acted in Louisville theater, attended play-reading groups, and invested in Broadway plays, such as *'night, Mother*, by Marsha Norman, who came from Louisville. Barry took such pleasure in the theater that after the family had collapsed and his relationship with Barry Junior and Sallie was in ruins, he acted in a benefit performance of *The Tempest* in Louisville, as if to recall a more peaceful time in his life.

Certainly, Mary and Barry were happy in Cambridge. They walked around Fresh Pond, took some of the same courses, and often went into Boston to dance at the Ritz Roof. They were at the Ritz Roof so often, Mary once wrote, that "the orchestra leader, Ruby Newman, gave us a theme song which he would play whenever we appeared. It was called 'Beat on the Big Drum, Baby's Awake Now.' " Although the parietal rules were still strict at Radcliffe, Mary and Barry would linger on the porch at Bertram until the house mistress would tap on the window and say, "Ten o'clock, Mary dear."

Barry once wrote to Mary about the joy of their years at Harvard:

. . . the late afternoon, with the lights on in the Merle and the Coop and the Splendid, and the wintry dusk closing in with feeling of snow to come, and the wonderful chance of seeing you, my darling, on the Radcliffe side of the square as I used to come across from Massachusetts Hall. Wasn't it grand for us to have those Cambridge years together, so that we can remember the same details about college. I wish all our dear children could have such luck as I have had, my precious, instead of falling in love with some mopheaded fool as I'm afraid Worth in particular may do.

There was no question but that at Radcliffe Mary Caperton came into her own. "These were among the happiest years of my life," she once wrote, recalling the "luxurious" Sunday breakfasts of popovers and fish balls served in her room, and her "intellectually dazzling" studies of Shakespeare and Thucydides. She always had a passion for the school, and, as a trustee, took a firm hand in choosing its presidents. She would encourage her own daughter Sallie to go to Radcliffe, as well as her granddaughters, Worth's daughter, Clara, and Barry Junior's daughters, Emily and Molly. When her grandsons Barry Ellsworth and Rob Bingham chose Brown over Harvard, Mary was horrified that Brown had no required courses. She wrote Rob Bingham a harsh letter, in which she said words to the effect that "anyone who can choose his own education certainly doesn't need one. Attending Brown is irresponsible in the extreme." Radcliffe meant so much to Mary that years later, when Barry was donating his papers and those of his father to the Library of Congress, Mary insisted that hundreds of her private letters be sent to Radcliffe to the Schlesinger Library for women's studies.

* * *

Graduation time, June 1928. Mary and Barry were making plans, but they didn't include marriage. Mary was leaving for Greece after graduating with honors and winning the Charles Eliot Norton Fellowship to study classics in Athens at the American School of Classical Studies. Barry wanted to be a writer, and, in the style of the period, was heading for the Paris cafés, traveling at times with his sister and Edie Callahan, their close friend from Louisville. Edie was an intimate and a confidante of Mary and Barry, as well as of Henrietta; she was the perfect companion—wonderfully musical, a good sport with an insatiable thirst for champagne and a large inheritance from a father who had been a prominent Louisville businessman. For years it was commonly believed in Louisville that Edie Callahan and Henrietta Bingham were lovers. Certainly, they were the closest of friends. Barry was their frequent traveling companion, which might have given rise to the long-standing Louisville canard of that era that he was not interested in women.

Barry's graduation from Harvard was marked by his father and Aleen's arrival on their private houseboat from Louisville. The Judge entertained in high style with dinners and cruises for all of Barry's friends. "I was brought onto the houseboat to meet the Judge and he couldn't have been more charming to me," Mary said. "And then the dear Judge took us all down to New London for the boat races." But Barry was not about to settle down, not with Henrietta luring him to Europe and parties with her famous friends. Who wanted to get married? In Europe nobody thought of Judge Bingham, as some still did in Louisville, as a parvenu and possibly a society murderer. The Binghams were just one more rich American family. Barry's father now owned a thirty-thousand-acre plantation in Georgia where he hunted birds. Later, he would build a lodge called Pineland. Each summer he went to Scotland and later bought his own hunting preserve, Guthrie Castle, where he bagged grouse with his neighbor, the financial speculator Bernard Baruch. For Barry, the pull was irresistible. All the rich Harvard boys sailed for Europe; Henrietta was in London, Edie Callahan was on her way, Mary was going to Athens. "In Paris, we sat around the cafés and drank all day with all the other Americans and I don't think I spoke a word of French the whole time I was there," Barry said.

Henrietta's influence over her younger brother appeared to be powerful. They were united by the traumatic childhood they had shared, the murder allegations against their father, and their mother's death, which they had witnessed together. When Barry left for Harvard in 1924, Henrietta had taken off from Louisville as well. She had gone back to London to be with Mina Kirstein, and it was Henrietta's intention to be psychoanalyzed by Freud's disciple Ernest Jones. The Judge was more than willing to indulge this. It was in London that Henrietta, young, beautiful and an heiress, met Lytton Strachey.

"Both these girls were beautiful in different ways," a Bloomsbury historian once wrote of Mina and Henrietta. "Mina was highly intelligent, something of a blue-stocking; Henrietta had nothing to say for herself, but managed by her meaningful silences and her husky singing of negro spirituals to a guitar, to break many hearts belonging to both sexes." Her most literary conquest was Strachey's own girlfriend, Doric Carrington, who wrote that Henrietta "sang exquisite songs with a mandoline, southern state revivalist nigger songs. She made such wonderful cocktails that I became completely drunk and almost made love to her in public. . . ." Strachey was homosexual as well, but he and Carrington lived comfortably together in Ham Spray, their rambling country house, which was inevitably filled with the Bloomsbury crowd of the day; Maynard Keynes, Virginia and Leonard Woolf. In this world, Henrietta was, as Barry would say, "hardly an intellect, more like a good-time girl," and Henrietta and Carrington started a relationship that resulted in secret afternoon meetings in a house in Knightsbridge that Henrietta had borrowed from a friend. In the summers Carrington grew morose that Henrietta had other obligations to her "father and brothers" and would leave for Scotland to join Robert, Aleen, Barry and her father for the grouse shooting. The Judge desperately wanted to be accepted. Scotland, then and now, was easier than England to penetrate if you were rich. It was also away from the provincial judgments of Louisville society.

The Binghams stayed in Scotland as much as they could, and when Henrietta left in 1924, to be "engulfed in her father and brothers," Carrington wrote, "I am glad I knew her, as I did know her. It was an experience and I feel I have known the strange possibilities that some women are capable of." It goes unrecorded what old Judge Bingham made of Henrietta and her carryings-on, or of Robert and his drunken states "of utter disintegration," as Barry called them.

Certainly, the Judge was not sure about Barry's prospects either. He wondered whether "[I] could get along very well in a strange organization because I was still, I guess . . . a fairly shy, immature boy of my age," Barry said. When Barry graduated from Harvard and told his father he wanted to travel and to write a novel, the Judge was pleased to indulge him. The papers were making money, and Barry and his brother and sister had the good luck to be young, rich and careless at the height of the 1920's. "It was a period of euphoria," Barry said. "Everybody was out to have a good time. . . . Some of my friends quite literally went out of college in 1928 saying that before they were thirty years old they would be millionaires . . . maybe they would

retire and live on a yacht. . . . It looked as though the world
was just designed for that.''

With his father's blessing and all the money he needed, Barry
took off for Europe with Henrietta. Even as an old woman, Mary
could hardly bear to mention Henrietta's name. ''Do we have to
talk about her?'' she said with contempt. She was, Mary seemed
to believe, possessive of her younger brother and her father, who
were the only two men she had ever truly loved. Henrietta was
the kind of person, John Houseman wrote, whose ''curious
glamor . . . shed over us all,'' and Barry, when he was young,
adored her.

Although Mary didn't worry about other women taking Barry
away from her, she must have had a formidable adversary in
Barry's own sister. Henrietta seemed afraid to let Barry have a
life that excluded her. Henrietta was very alluring. The British
writer David Garnett marveled at her appearance. He called her
face ''the perfect oval of a Buddha . . . her straight, dark hair
was parted in the middle; long black eyelashes shaded her bril-
liantly blue eyes. She spoke with the warm, caressing voice of
the South, drove a car really well and understood its mecha-
nism, . . . and never at any time read a book unless forced to
do so.'' As a young man, John Houseman became so obsessed
with Henrietta that he wrote ''there was hardly an hour of my
days and nights that was not permeated and colored by dreams
of her. . . . I find it impossible to separate the memory of the
real Henrietta Bingham, with whom I . . . finally lost my vir-
ginity in a seaside hotel with a crystal chandelier and red damask
walls . . . from the fantasy of her that I created. . . .'' He wrote
''yearning letters'' to her, as did another one of her ardent suit-
ors, John Mason Brown, the drama critic who was originally
from Louisville. But Henrietta was tied to her father and brother.
In fact, there are those in the Bingham family who believe it was
Henrietta's hold on Barry that stalled his marriage to Mary.

Until Henrietta died in 1968, Mary dealt with ''Miss Natt,''
as the family called Henrietta, as carefully as one Mafia don
deals with another. Mary wrote to Barry:

> I have tried hard to examine the hard core of my resentment
> and bitterness toward her, and I am not very proud of the
> primary source of it which I believe is fear—fear of her as
> a nihilistic and destructive force in our lives. This fear is
> very primitive and simple, I suppose. It rises out of the
> conflict that always seems to go with Natt and me, even
> when you are away—a conflict that is revolting to me. What
> increases my own feeling of revulsion and enmity is the
> conviction that this condition, too, has been provoked and
> augmented as just another of Natt's idle and destructive

emotional adventures . . . through which she would like to
make yet another show of power as she used so mercilessly
to do in her relationship with Papa.

For years, when Henrietta would visit Glenview, she would
get, as Mary said, "into an awful sodden state of drunkenness."
She would then stay up late and talk to her nieces and nephews
about her friends the Prince of Wales and Noel Coward. Her
nieces and nephews thought she was as fascinating and romantic
as anyone could possibly be, their very own Auntie Mame. For
a while she lived in New York in a Park Avenue apartment with
cupboards full of Limoges and drawers full of Georgian silver,
although she had run through most of her inheritance when she
was still young. Barry paid his sister's expenses and complained
about it frequently, perhaps as a way of appeasing Mary. Miss
Natt was the Bingham family's eccentric; her influence was
strong.

In 1980 Sallie Bingham wrote an autobiographical play called
Milk of Paradise, in which Henrietta was transmogrified into a
character called Aunt Jane, Barry Senior became Robby, and
Mary a forbidding character named Alice. In the first act Aunt
Jane has come to the immense house for a visit and is talking to
the children's nurse, justifying her presence.

Robby and I used to roll down the hill, below this house.
Side over side, hands and heels hitting; your neck clicks,
you think your head's going to roll off. Lie at the bottom
and laugh, pick leaves and sticks off each other. . . . Maybe
you know what happened when we quit rolling down the
hill. . . . I said to Robby, Let's take a week off from this
heat, this waiting, those dresses of Alice's with the puritan
collars. Let's go to Hatteras like we used to when Papa was
alive, let's go to Hatteras and roll in the waves. . . .

"Robby and I used to roll down that hill to the river. . . . We
were close. But I was the one who left, in the end. . . . He met
your mother and forgot about everything else," Aunt Jane tells
Missy, the character who stands for Sallie, in *Milk of Paradise.*

4

Eventually, Mary would win Barry, but it took her three long years. Mary always seemed to hate this period in her life, the longing for Barry, the indecision on his part, the worry. "I wanted you too badly then to be happy without you, and you were too busy growing up and making your own decisions to have me," she later wrote to him. It is easy to imagine Mary's panic over possibly losing Barry to the outside world. Certainly, Mary seldom discussed with her children the delay in her courtship or her vulnerability, as if it were yet another family secret. "Did my father wait years to propose to my mother?" Barry Junior asked. "I never was aware of that." And yet, paradoxically, although she rarely talked with her own children about the rough spots in her courtship with her beloved Barry, she donated hundreds of their most intimate love letters to the Schlesinger collection for any interested historian to read. The early love letters clearly detail the indecision on Barry's part. But the later ones are so intimate that Mary might have been trying to prove how very much a man Barry truly was and, more important, how physically and emotionally devoted they were to become to each other.

What could twenty-five-year-old Mary Caperton have been thinking about her future through the winter of 1929 and spring of 1930? Four years had passed since the audition at Whitman Hall and their romantic nights on the Bertram porch. Just before the stock market crashed, Mary came back to Boston and took a publishing job with Little, Brown, the publishers, as an editorial assistant, living on Irving Street on Beacon Hill, while Barry, having traveled through Europe with Henrietta, came back to Asheville and Louisville to work for his father. Earlier, he had visited Mary in Athens with Edie Callahan as chaperone. "She was hardly much of a chaperone," Mary said. "Edie drank more champagne than anyone I ever knew." But now Europe was behind them, her parents had no money, and she was stuck In Boston without Barry at the beginning of the Depression.

51

Barry was determined to finish the novel he was writing, a dreary and "turgid effort," he later said, "a study of a child who is illegitimate." "I just poured everything into it the way young writers tend to do. I overwrote terribly. I wrote very much in the manner of other writers that I admired at that time. . . ." The narrator was a nine-year-old boy, the illegitimate son of an illegitimate mother. "I suppose that little boy was in some degree myself," Barry said, "because I was remembering impressions I had from that age, and what I was thinking about older people and their lives." He finished his novel, but it was never published and now he says, "I keep it on a high shelf underneath lock and key."

By the winter of 1929, however, as Louisville began to feel the effects of the stock market crash, Barry was brought home by his father and put to work at WHAS, the family radio station, which the Judge had started in 1922, the fifteenth CBS affiliate, "a strong station, one of our first when we were struggling," William Paley, the chairman of CBS, said. WHAS was a highly sophisticated radio effort of the day, broadcasting concerts and live serials. Barry's job included everything from sound effects to writing copy for the symphonic selections. For over a year "we wrote a lot of letters and there wasn't much else going on between us," Mary said. Barry lived in Louisville, Mary in Boston. Their letters were coy, filled with evasions, descriptions intended to impress the recipient with lavish details of parties. They wrote like two people fencing with each other. Mary's anger at Barry was positively elegant. She disguised it with subtlety. Just after Christmas in 1929, perhaps in an attempt to dazzle Barry with her literary abilities, she wrote to him in the style of Fielding, thanking him for his rather impersonal Christmas presents of bourbon and roses. Her Radcliffe friend Connie Templeton had spent Christmas with her on Irving Street, and Mary seemed determined to make Barry realize what fun they had had without him.

Mistress Constance Templeton has Cheered me by her company during the holiday season which has been marked by the usual number of Candles, Plum Cakes, Roasted, Boyled, and Baked Meats and Pyes of many kinds, also tumultuous and indecent noyses. The bottle has been pushed about Briskly, but, as the Ancients had it, *Nunc est bibendum,* so I feel no guilt in honestly confessing that last night we were both in our Altitudes and saw two-a-Moons. Indeed, such was our hilarity that we were perforce dragged off to Bed, being conveyed thither by Henry Smith, a Physician of some Repute . . . a True Gentleman who Unbuttoned us with all respect and Tenderness and put us between the Covers in

our Shifts. We are even yet a little Feavourish, due to im-
bibing Mint Juleps made after your receipt from the Contents of a Truly excellent Bottle of Bourbon the gift of an
Admirer.

Mary ended this lengthy letter by informing Barry that she would
not be going with him on a trip to Europe, even though he had
found an adequate chaperone:

It would, I confess, give me some pleasure, but I cannot
Risk appearing fantastick and wrong-headed, and I have
resolv'd to settle down seriously to the Business of Life, and
not to be Thwarted and Turned aside by such Dissapations
and Gayities as would present themselves on a Jaunt Abroad.

By February of 1930 Barry was well into his new job at
WHAS, "crowded into a cell-like room, with two huge desks,
a coat rack, a telephone and one small prison window set high
in the wall, not barred, but effectually obliterated by soot."

With a musical dictionary close at hand I devise flowery
phrases about each number on the concert programs, and
the more dripping the style, the more pleased are the office
force. More than ever I regret having missed that grand snap
course on the history of music, but I go on regardless of
my total ignorance and fling out technical phrases to startle
the greatest impresario.

He was twenty-four years old, and showed little sign of the
man he would become. He wrote to Mary:

After two weeks of work, these are my opinions: the worst
feature is the lack of time for the amenities of life, reading,
writing letters, and all that; the best feature is having so
many small tasks to overcome and pass beyond, with the
accompanying sensation of accomplishment. The people in
the office are all nice tacky people in spectacles who are
embarrassingly obliging to me. One or two are amusing in
the sort of way that you can never describe, and I chortle
to myself half the day over the mannerisms of the "artists"
who come in to broadcast.

Barry was set up comfortably in Louisville in the Little House,
which was at that time called Fincastle.

I've been in my own house ten days now, and very nice it
is, with nigger Lizzie at the stove and my old college fur-

niture in the living room heavily disguised in Fortuny materials. There was no heat in the house the first morning when I got up, the thermometer stood at two below zero, and I couldn't button my shirt for the stiffness of my fingers but things have gotten adjusted since.

He came home to a fire, and, he wrote Mary, he was "taking one or two drinks but not a third on week nights." The Judge had just built his hunting lodge at Pineland and was spending months at a time in Georgia with his beagles and his hunting cronies from Louisville. But Barry was hardly lonely. His Asheville aunts often came and stayed with him at Fincastle. Additionally, Mary's mother was often in Louisville to visit her favorite daughter, Helena, and her new stockbroker husband. The mother might have had a dual purpose for her visits, and made sure to call on Barry each time she arrived. Sometimes she brought Mary's youngest sister, Melinda, to meet the eligible Louisville boys. Barry wrote to Mary that "all the little boys who used to rush her are away at school, so I don't know what kind of time she'll have. If only there were something in Louisville corresponding to the Gypsy Bar, I feel that Lena and your mother and I could have a grand time just among ourselves." The letter was affectionate, but hardly ardent. "I do hope you're still enjoying your job, and that you are, as I am, filled with health and good spirits. All love, my very dear, dear, Mary," he wrote.

Mary tried every feminine wile. She knew how to flatter, and wrote to him that she felt his book should be published. She told him she had sent it to an editor at Houghton Mifflin for consideration and that this was a particularly good time there because of Oliver La Farge's Pulitzer for *Laughing Boy*. She wrote to him about subjects she knew would fascinate him, the upcoming Kentucky Derby, for example. "I'm in such a swivet about the Derby—I agree with you about Gallant Fox, at least I don't think for a minute that he is capable of winning both the Preakness and the Derby, and nobody will tell me whether he is a good mudder, and I suppose it will rain on Saturday." She was also determined to let Barry know she wasn't in Boston sitting at home. "Last night I went to the Cocoanut Grove, and sitting at the next table were all the Stones, as marmoset-eyed as ever. . . . I fell into quite a bad humor and instead of getting benign, got waspier and waspier as I sunk into my cups and the evening wore away." And, she reported, she had seen Barry's best friends, Francis Parks and Warren Buckler, part of the "Nantasket group," who had been to cocktails at her apartment.

That April he cabled Mary that he was arriving on the Bingham houseboat and would be coming to Boston possibly with

Edie and Henrietta. How furious Mary must have been that Barry
needed to travel with this entourage, but she never showed the
slightest hint of pique. Barry came to Boston and then took the
train with Henrietta to Baltimore, where he attended the very
social Hunt Ball. There was a seated dinner for three hundred,
where the champagne and whiskey "flowed in torrents." Henrietta didn't need a constant supply, since she kept a flask of
bourbon in her handbag and was "tippling out of that after dinner."

There had been, he reported, the Hunt Cup race, cocktails, a
dinner, everyone drunk. He even wrote to Mary about a married
woman who was flirting with him as the band played "Happy
Days."

> Fortunately, the girl was a swell dancer, and we drank some
> champagne, and things got more and more complicated un-
> til somebody came up and snatched H. and me away to
> another party. This was the best of all, a Country Club
> brawl with good music. We finally left at seven o'clock on
> a lovely blue morning and drove back to town, leaving a
> large crowd still raging at the dance.

Barry's letters were filled with descriptions of madcap parties,
"blotto" cousins, drinking, more drinking, passing out. Over
Derby weekend of 1930, he didn't spare her a detail.

> The Derby weekend itself was better than I have ever seen
> it. Henrietta and I severed all ties with the family. . . . A
> nigger cook called Mary Lizzie came in for the weekend,
> and she was always to be found standing in the kitchen,
> ready to fix some nice soothing scrambled eggs. . . . We
> had Laurence Callahan, our blotto cousin from Chicago,
> and a swell married lady . . . staying with us. . . . They
> shared a quart of whiskey, discussed sex in all its manifes-
> tations, and stayed up till four o'clock in the morning. . . .

He wrote to her on his father's stationery—"Robert W. Bingham, President & Publisher, The Courier-Journal, The Louisville Times." And then, in the same post-Derby letter, he announced his summer plans, which had to be far more upsetting
to a love-struck twenty-five-year-old girl than any of the Derby
parties:

> The family are [sic] going to Scotland, but H. and I see no
> excuse for our joining them. According to present plans, I
> will stagger off the ship at Cherbourg, go to Paris to join
> Edie for a couple of days, and then she and I will set off in

a penny parlor for Hamburg, where Henrietta will meet us
in her car. From there we will drive to Sweden. There is a
grand Exposition going on in Stockholm this year, and the
whole place sounds very cold and bracing and blonde, just
my idea of a swell place for the summer. After ten days or
so of drinking Swedish Punch, we plan to cross back into
Germany and motor to Munich, where the great big Wagner
operas will be in progress, and from there to Salzburg to
see the Rhinehart *[sic]* Festival. By that time it ought to be
grand autumn weather in the Alps, and we might go to the
Tyrol for a few days. Doesn't that sound like a wonderful
plan? And not a breath of hay fever in the entire trip. Edie
is already chanting something about "there's a Ritz in Buda
Pest," and she seems to think that we will float down the
Danube and end up in the Crimea or some such unnatural
place. . . . Please write soon, my dear, and let me know
how the world wags from your point of view.

It was time for desperate measures on Mary's part. A month
later Mary attended a wedding in Richmond and invited Barry.
Something happened during that Richmond trip that began to
move Barry closer to her. Did they make love for the first time?
He wrote to her that his "brains are addled" and he "can't
forget . . . the moments alone with you in the suffocating but
grand vacant apartment . . . and all through [the weekend] your
unforgettable way of looking up at me. It was confused in just
the right degree, a really perfect weekend. . . ." He wanted to
see her in New York at the Plaza before he sailed and was trying
to stay cool in the Louisville summer heat with "the cheering
thought of seeing you soon to make my wilted spirits as crisp as
a fresh lettuce leaf."

Of course she rushed to New York to be with him even before
he set sail. Later she would say, "Barry was just young. He
needed to grow up." As Barry sailed for London that August
he wrote to her from the *Mauretania:*

My dearest M., I've just been standing on the bow, and the
weather is lovely and blue and cold, just the kind of day
that inspires us to such maudlin rejoicing. It makes me think
of you so damn much, just as practically everything else
does. . . . When I left you on the dock, I felt so miserable
that I wanted to go and shut myself up somewhere, in a den
of roaring beasts by preference. As I staggered up the gang
plank, I saw my family planted firmly nearby. . . . It all
seems very colorless and drab after the two days with you.
I miss you so intensely at night that I feel bitterly alone,
almost as though I were lying in a grave.

Mary dearest, Arriving Aquitania. Mary dearest, Good night, darling. I love you, Mary dearest. Cable Guthrie Castle. Dearest Mary. Dearest. Telegrams, salutations, love messages, from Barry to Mary, and still no proposal came. Four months had passed since their Richmond weekend. By the end of October 1930 Mary Caperton had to have been discouraged, and ready to play her final card. She would leave America and stop waiting for Barry.

Barry dearest, I have just cabled Zora Stephens that I would come over and spend the winter with her in Paris. I had a letter from her last week asking me to come, and as life in Boston doesn't seem particularly exhilarating, I think I might as well give the L.B.& Co. the air and take to my heels. . . . I don't know how long I shall be abroad. My plans are very indefinite. I shall probably come home in the spring unless I can find something to do in Paris and like living there and don't get a violent case of flag-waving homesickness.

I wish I could see you. I feel very far away from you and it makes me feel sad and strange. I wonder whether you like your job and how ''The Successful Calamity'' went, and if you are happy. I love you, Barry darling.

Another man might have taken the first train to Boston, but not Barry. His response was totally in character. He decided to make the best of it.

I don't know what to say, or write, or even to think, for the most numbing sense of loneliness came over me when I read your letter last night. Of course from any rational point of view, I am bound to think that you are exactly right in going over to stay with Zora. You have gotten all there is to get out of Boston, and probably out of Little Brown too, and the opportunity to have a grand winter in Paris is much too grand to pass up. . . . Maybe you'll be able to walk in the Parc Monceau sometimes, and see the drifts of fallen leaves, and the children with their unbelievably short clothes, and the nursemaids reading six franc romances in paper covers. It will all be lovely, of course. But I can't help feeling the sense of loneliness for you that will haunt me all winter.

He would be grieved by her absence, but he loved his new job. His father had made him a police reporter. He was out of WHAS into a tougher world, learning about life.

The reporters themselves are a race apart, and I think they are all together the most likeable people I have ever met. . . . Most of the reporters are mildly drunk all the time, and they are all foul-mouthed in a genuinely imaginative way. Did you ever see or read *The Front Page*, that Ben Hecht play? It is the bible of the reporters' room, and they all seem to feel that the good old rowdy traditions must be kept up.

I've gotten fairly used to seeing "floaters" dragged out of the river, and dead farm boys lying in dried blood, but I must say my gorge rose yesterday when I was sent to get a statement from a man who was dying from burns. He had somehow set his whole body on fire, and my darling, he didn't have any face left. I had to lean over his bed and ask him how it happened. He slowly, slowly opened his eyes, which had no lashes and almost no lids. I could see his tongue move, but he couldn't speak.

If this was the Judge's idea of how to turn his son into a man, it was a good one. And Mary's decisive action upset Barry tremendously.

I've been rambling on all this time, trying to think of a lot of things, when there is really only one thing in my mind. That thing will be in my thoughts so constantly while you're gone that it will be my most familiar companion. It's that I love you, and I'm going to miss you like hell.

He sent her roses to say good-bye. "Mary darling," his card, engraved with his name, read, "I've been at Fenway Court looking at the violets under the Giorgione, and any kind of flowers now seem pretty inadequate to set before beauty. These are an attempt. For my darling, with all my love."

From the M.S. *Lafayette*, Mary wrote to Barry:

Darling, I am so glad you will miss me, but, my sweet, I don't think I would have seen you this winter if I had been in Boston. I feel that you are naturally and necessarily so engrossed in what you are doing that nothing else matters very much just now. But I do hope you won't forget me, or let me get too out of touch with your life. I want to see you so much. Barry darling, you must know now that I shall always love you, and that I have meant and do mean every word that has passed between us on that subject. You must know that. . . . And whether I am in Paris or any where in the world doesn't really matter because my . . . deepest feelings are always bound up in you, and do love me darling, because I feel that I am *really* yours, and that I can't help it, but I hope that you feel something like this, too.

Now it was Mary's turn to torment Barry with her activities: "I saw 'Three's a Crowd' before I sailed, and darling, you must see it, it's almost as good as the first Little Show, and is terribly bright and smart and fast and has that Saks-Fifth Avenue feeling." She thanked him for his roses, which "were perfectly lovely and lasted longer than anything else, and I think it was so well organized of you to have a card with a real message in your incredibly regular and deliberate handwriting in the box."

Years later Mary would explain she went to Paris because she "wanted to do something with my French" and "my friends knew everyone," and that was always her explanation. Whether her friends believed her or not, this guise was a superb cover. All her life this strange winter in Paris would mean more to her than any of the more festive times she would spend there, its malaise would cling to her. She did a great deal of walking, in "the queer, pearly gray cold weather," she wrote to Barry years later, thinking of him, and "wishing that she could be any where that he was."

And then, Francis Parks, Barry's close friend and traveling companion, was killed in a car crash. The accident happened two weeks after Mary left, in late November of 1930, after the Harvard-Yale game. For Barry this was an immense tragedy, and he suffered intensely. "Francis was my first friend who died," he said years later. "And, as with any first death, it had a profound effect on me."

Barry was filled with questions about his own life, about how he had been spared a similar fate. For the first time in his letters he showed a glimmer of insight, questioning Francis's maturity as well as his own. For Francis Parks, like Barry, had a Jazz Age foppishness. He had gone to St. George's and then to Harvard, and had been active, along with Barry, in the Harvard drama club. He was theatrical, a bit effete and, like Barry, wanted to be a writer. All his life Barry saved a letter Francis Parks had written him just before he died, the only letter from a friend besides Edie Callahan that was donated to the Schlesinger Library:

I have had so many ideas for novels lately that I can't know which to begin. Terrible dilemma, I believe I shall do them all concurrently, a chapter a day on each, finish them all at once and frightfully annoy the five or six best publishing houses in New York by having each of them announce about the same time the year's best seller and finding out that their competitors are also announcing a best seller by the same author.

When Francis was killed, he was carrying a letter from Barry in his pocket. This unexpected detail, along with the atmosphere in the Parks house in Springfield, the "lugubrious luncheon" and the "passionately chaste New England day," Barry described to Mary in a letter. "I feel very queer about his death, but somehow not at all sad. He never had to grow out of a phase which I think of as the college phase. . . . I'm going to miss Francis badly. . . . I had the feeling about him that if I ever wanted terribly to kick over the traces, he might break loose too and help me."

In this reflective mood he moved even closer to Mary:

I have written you all this depressing stuff because my one chance to get it straight is to share it with you. Now I have some more vital things to say in my awkward and blundering way. I realize that I've been a troublesome lover, my dearest Mary, a very unsatisfactory one, and it may be that you have spoiled me with your unspeakably lovely sympathy and understanding. But oh my darling, don't forget me this winter. If ever you have felt that I love you, feel it a dozen times magnified now. I have been such a damn fool on so many occasions, I have had growing pains and such flashes of a funny kind of wildness at times in these years. . . . I'm happy and sad all at once as I write this, because I feel it so deeply that it gets all mixed up with all my emotions. Let me be more explicit. I can't ask you to be true to me, because I think that is an unfair thing to demand under the circumstances. . . . For God's sake please don't think of our love as a thing that has been. Don't, don't, please. I am looking entirely toward the future, and God willing, we have hardly reached the beginning of a great love.

It began then, the inexorable union of Mary and Barry, and it seemed to be based on a perfect understanding. Barry knew that Mary had been reared with dreams of grandeur, and Mary certainly understood that Barry had to be protected from his family scandal. To most of their friends Mary appeared tougher than Barry. Someday her children would believe that she dominated the family, but their relationship was extremely subtle and complicated. They appeared to understand each other's frailties and kept each other's secrets. It seemed to some of her friends that all her life, even at the end, Mary had moments when she actually acted as if she was terrified of losing Barry, as if she had never outgrown the insecurities of her courtship. However flinty

she could be, Barry was her weakness. She could be so possessive of him that her own children would suffer from it. In the
dreadful winter of 1986 she railed against her daughter Sallie.
"I will not allow Sallie to believe she can drive a wedge between
Barry and me," she told me, as ferociously as she must once
have railed against Henrietta. But Barry was devoted to Mary
and "wouldn't hear a word against her," his longtime editor,
Mark Ethridge, used to tell friends. Mary's passion had rescued
him from the epicene world of Henrietta and Edie Callahan,
after all. But there was no doubt that Mary and Barry genuinely
loved each other. Mary came home from Europe in March 1931.
He proposed to her that afternoon at their favorite speakeasy,
the Gypsy Bar, and the first person to learn of their marriage
plans was George, the bartender, who "opened a bottle of champagne for everyone in the room," Mary said.

Almost immediately, Mary and Barry left for Richmond to
tell her family, who were "overjoyed." Mary stayed on to plan
a June wedding while Barry returned to Washington, where he
had been sent to work in the *Courier-Journal* bureau. In love at
last, Barry wrote to her,

> It is so obvious that life for me is only real in the fullest
> sense of the word when I am with you, when I can take
> your hand in mine and hear your voice so comfortingly
> close. . . . I still have with me the assurance, as warm as
> firelight and as luminous as the stars on a dark night, that
> we are doing the right thing that all our lives and all our
> natures stamp as indubitably right. . . .

The *New York Times* announced the engagment, and Barry
was surprised at the reactions:

> I continue to be amazed and delighted by the way that ev-
> erybody who knows us feels about this event, which I
> thought would hardly be recognized by the world as the
> perfect thing we know it to be. Literally everybody seems
> to be struck with the romantic aspect of the thing to such
> an extent that they look positively rosy and sentimental when
> they speak of it. I had no idea how the world really reacts
> to a love affair.

Barry was soon obsessed with Mary—what she was eating for
breakfast and if it was "roe herring and batter bread" or how
she would look sipping orange juice on the porch of the country
club with her sister Sara. At last Barry had a family that was
warm and adored him, a future mother-in-law who was original,
cultured. For her part, Munda was so thrilled to have him that

the celebrations went on for weeks. Barry wrote Mary, "I feel an even greater and more warming assurance of our future joy in each other. Despite all that has been written and said throughout the course of time, I consider that being in love is the most underestimated thing in the world."

Mary was entering an exotic new world as well, the Louisville paradise that would transform her life. She would have servants to command and almost unlimited resources at the height of the Depression. The Judge loved to spend money and had extraordinary style. Once Mary wrote to Barry about a certain summer night in 1931: it had been so hot that "Papa," as Mary called the Judge,

> in his frenzy of heat-driven restlessness, ordered Loubelle to go to town to get Aunt Margaret's harp and, with every nig on the place up and sweating, had that . . . harpsichord put in the theatre so that a little impromptu musicale could be had. . . . The result was a performance of, 'O Believe me if all those endearing young charms,' with many flourishes and much style. . . . We laughed . . . at the thought of what went on in Loubelle's head while he was speeding to Cherokee Park on this midnight errand to move the harp.

Mary and Barry were filled with plans for their glorious future. He had written to Henrietta in Europe, urging her to come back for the wedding. He had asked Robert to be his best man. He told his mammy, "nigger Lizzie," and her response was the "most satisfactory" because she burst into loud laughter and said, "Does Miss Sadie know?" Barry bustled about calling travel agents that "father" had recommended for their honeymoon abroad. They planned to go to Sweden and Iceland because of Barry's love of the northern climates. He could hardly wait to go to the Stockholm restaurants or to see the fjords.

> Doesn't the phrase wedding journey sound old fashioned, almost like the Grand Tour? Since we are to have one together, I think it is a noble expression. . . . Well, if I can stop babbling long enough, I'll finish my story about making the reservation. . . . Mr. Franke wanted to know, it seemed, just who "the other party" in the stateroom would be. . . . I started to say, "Miss Caperton." . . . I shouted into the phone "It will be Mr. and Mrs. B.B." The words sounded incredibly pleasant to my ears, and I'm sure the stenographer got the idea. . . .

Like anybody in love, they were sure that life would stay the same forever.

I want you to be identified with everything that has ever
been in my life, so we can seem to have some common
memories long before the first time we first met at Whitman
Hall, God bless its ugly old frame. . . . I have flashes now
when I seem to remember something you have told me about
your childhood, just as though it had happened to you and
me together. I'm sure there must have been a bond between
us, even in the days when we did nothing but lie in the sun,
and were afraid of the dark and the johnny seat. . . .

Five years after their first meeting at Harvard, Barry Bingham
and Mary Caperton were married at 4:30 P.M. on June 10, 1931,
at the very correct St. James's Episcopal Church of Richmond.
Mary was attended by her sisters and "wore a white satin gown
made on severe lines with long sleeves and a long train from the
waist. Her tulle veil, which fell to the end of her train, was
covered with a cap and veil of old Limerick point lace that had
belonged to her grandmother and was sent from England for the
occasion," the *Courier-Journal* reported in a two-column story.
Barry's brother, Robert, did not attend, but Henrietta and Edie
Callahan did. Barry's groomsmen came from Boston, New York
and Louisville. Before the wedding one of Mary's family challenged the Louisville groomsmen to a cockfight, and the cocks
rode to Richmond on the wedding train. The Judge reportedly
paid for the wedding, the trousseau, the china and Mary's silver.
It was the best investment that the old Judge ever made, but
Mary never got over her shame about the silver, nor forgot its
importance to her. The silver would remain in the Big House as
part of the Bingham legacy. But as the family dreams collapsed
in the winter of 1986 Mary, an old woman estranged from her
only surviving son, demanded that he return the Judge's silver.

5

It was a fabulous match, the kind of marriage that inspires jealousy and awe, a union of passion, understanding and intimacy. When Mary and Barry married, they found a haven in each other, a way to wipe out the past and move forward into the future, as if their childhoods had been a haze of unreality and the only reality they found was in being together. Their pleasure in each other was obvious to everyone who knew them.

The bedroom seemed to be the center of their world. Each morning Mary held court in their "lovely bed," as she called it, the sunlight streaming in through the upstairs windows in the Big House. Mary wore layers of chiffon and satin to bed and embroidered bed jackets, and received children, servants and visitors while propped up with a breakfast tray. Barry would be nearby, reading the paper, reclining on a chaise. Their bedroom door was always firmly shut until 7:45 A.M., when their children were allowed in to say good-bye before they left for school. Sex permeated the household. Barry liked to talk about coming back from the war and "scooping Mary out of the bathtub throwing her down on the bed." There were plenty of taboo subjects in the Binghams' world—beginning with Mary Lily Flagler—but sex was not one of them. In Sallie's plays and stories, daughters are sometimes obsessed with a mother's "spasms," did she have them or did she not? All her life Mary would confide in her children about Barry's sexuality. She told her daughters not to breast-feed their children, as she had not breast-fed hers, because she didn't want her exquisite figure to change. Mary once wrote to Barry about her deep annoyance with the Episcopalian service and "St. Paul's passionate puritanism, so full of loathing for the decent lusts of the human flesh." Another time, she wrote, "the greatest joy in life for me is giving something to you (from your breakfast tea, to those high moments of our whole togetherness, lovely and shared, yielding and yielded in all the senses and all the mind and heart)" and "about the heart shaking delight of all of both of us touching and knowing each

64

other in lovely nakedness, and the peace and beauty of going to sleep with you there and waking up with you still there.''

And yet, with all this intimacy, they lived a lie. The lie was that Barry's father had been a great and perfect man. Right to the end, Mary and Barry tried to protect Judge Robert Worth Bingham's reputation as if their lives depended on it. At age eighty, Barry Senior was willing to come to New York in a snowstorm to obtain information from reporters who he found had learned about the old allegations that his father might have been a murderer, but he couldn't walk up his own driveway to make peace with his one remaining son. He reportedly spent over $75,000 hiring lawyers to stop the publication of a controversial book about his father written by a journalist named David Leon Chandler who had previously published a biography of Henry Flagler. Chandler's thesis was that Judge Bingham had conspired with a Louisville doctor to fail to give Mary Lily Bingham proper medical treatment, which led to her death. Chandler also theorized that the Judge had given Mary Lily syphilis. Although there was no real evidence of murder or syphilis in Mary Lily's death, there was ample proof of the Judge's neglect of his dying wife. If he was not guilty of murder, he was certainly guilty of murderous indifference.

Understandably, Barry was so apprehensive that this murky history would become public knowledge again, as it had during the horrible autumn of 1917, when he was eleven years old, that he determined that Chandler's book would never be published without major corrections. As his son Barry Junior attempted to come to terms with his father's rejection and the loss of his career, Barry Senior virtually ignored him and could talk of little else except his ''deep distress'' over this possible blight on his father's reputation.

Although he had always revered his daughter, Barry Bingham now railed against Sallie for helping Chandler with his book. ''She told me David Chandler was a reputable journalist,'' he said. ''How could she have done this?'' Although his father had died fifty years earlier in 1937, Barry Senior could barely bring himself to speak to his daughter Sallie because ''of the deep distress she has caused him by listening to servants' gossip about the grandfather she never knew,'' Mary explained. ''Sallie would destroy anyone around her if it meant she could be recognized as a writer,'' her father told me. ''Why does Father care so much?'' Sallie asked her mother, according to Mary. ''It all happened so long ago.'' As if she were determined to avenge Mary Lily, Sallie publicly accused her own father of suppressing information about the Judge's role in Mary Lily Bingham's death in 1917. She then announced that she would write her own version of the family history. In the three-page letter severely attacking her father that she sent to book editors and censorship committees, she wrote, ". . . if this intimidation proves successful in Chandler's case, it may also prove successful in the case of . . . my own. . . ."

"Barry Senior is more outwardly concerned [about his father's reputation] than he was when his sons died," his lawyer, Gordon Davidson, said. "I mean, he worshiped his father. I think he put him in sainthood." However vigorous a liberal publisher he once had been, when it came to Chandler's attack on his father's reputation, he was ruthless, perhaps as ruthless and indifferent as his father might have been in his treatment of his second wife, Mary Lily. "What my father has done is shocking," Barry Junior said. "It is the death of all our principles." But Barry Senior was compelled to take drastic action, for maintaining the fiction of his father's exemplary character must always have been at the center of his life.

Mary and Barry, two people who adored each other, interpreted their family history without a shred of ambivalence. They publicly never joked about themselves, the Judge's new money ways or cavalier behavior and didn't find it amusing when people in Louisville did. Once in the 1960's, Richard Harwood, who was then with the *Louisville Times,* wrote a speech for a local historical society about how the Judge first made his fortune. It was a study in the mores of the nouveaux riches and Harwood was proud of his research. One night at dinner Harwood told Mary about it, and she turned, he remembered, from a warm companion to ice. "It was clear she was not amused," Harwood said.

Mary was not the kind of woman who nagged or probed her husband, and she would never have asked, "Could your father have murdered your stepmother?" *Just suppose.* She never would have said, *Let's find out.* "Jaunty-jolly," his children called him. Even at eighty his face was remarkably youthful, as if no hard facts had ever intruded. "My father never once spoke to me about my stepmother and her death," Barry Senior said. "Perhaps I should have asked him. But I never thought about it and he never brought it up."

A less compassionate view might suggest a strong relationship between the Binghams' sanctimony, their devotion to public service, and their need to live down the scandal about Judge Bingham. Surely Barry had to believe the best about his father, for to entertain any other notion would have mired him forever in sordid tragedy.

The Judge, Mary said, was the most "marvelous man in the world." "He was a most proper, courtly, very conventional man," Barry Senior said. "He cared so much about doing good." There was much evidence in the public record to back this up. Exemplary deeds. Stories in the press. He helped the tobacco farmers, although he tried to grab more than his fair share of credit; he guaranteed a failing bank during the Depression, although part of his motivation might have been a desire to humiliate the owner; he worked for women's rights, Negroes, the poor. He closed saloons and supported Prohibition. Like many a socially ambitious man before him, he was a passionate Anglophile, which led one opposition newspaper, the Louisville *Herald Post,* to call him "Lord Bingham." But he did warn against Hitler and urged America's intervention to stop him.

For years, the *Courier-Journal* extensively reported his meetings with presidents, his good works, his appointments to commissions. In small-town Louisville, controlling the newspaper as it did, the Bingham family made its own reality. The Judge was a collector of memorabilia; he saved everything, including a draft of a note he once wrote in 1894 to the mother of his first wife. But there is hardly a scrap of paper about his life from 1917 to 1919. Even the Louisville Coroner's Archives have no record books for the entire year of 1917, although there are detailed case records for 1918.

One would speculate that such papers were destroyed, sanitized by someone in the family, perhaps the Judge or his son Barry, although Barry denies this. "I don't know how to account for that. . . . There were never any papers that I know of. They never existed. The only things that came into my hands were the things that were left after my father died. And those I turned over in two batches. One to the Filson Club, our local historical society, and one to the Library of Congress." The Filson Club historian, however, is convinced that someone "weeded out" documents before they came into the hands of the Filson Club, as he later told Barry Bingham's own lawyer. Whatever happened, the documents are lost, leaving only hearsay and gossip, a vague sense that something sordid had happened long before. "My father believed in helping others," Barry would often say, and "My father was a monument of noble patience." Small towns and big towns, the same code applies. Money fuzzes memory and changes the rules. The Judge had the money and the power and the devoted son to gloss his reputation, at least for a time.

Mary and Barry even had a special vocabulary of superlatives to describe the Judge, as if it was impossible to say his name, Bob Bingham, without prefacing it with a string of adjectives: "the wisest," "the most generous," "simply charming," "the most decent and upstanding individual who ever lived." In public, Mary could not even bring herself to call him anything but "the Judge" in the most hushed tones, as if she were discussing John Marshall or Charles Evans Hughes. Once, during the war, she railed against her sister-in-law, Felice, married to Barry's older brother, Robert, because long after the Judge died Felice had the audacity to refer to him as "Father." She wrote Barry about this shocking breach of manners, this egregious intimacy—such disrespect!

At the very least, the Judge was an inattentive parent and a political opportunist, and as riddled with weaknesses and secrets as anyone who begins with nothing and winds up rich and powerful. Certainly, he was careless with those who loved him. Even so, Barry often said, "My father was the most wonderful man who ever lived."

If the Judge buried his second wife under irregular circumstances and if two of his children, Robert and Henrietta, were hopeless drunks, what matter? He was an important man, in touch with presidents and appointed to committees, quoted in the *New York Times*. Mary emphasized the work with Roosevelt, what the Judge had done for the Kentucky tobacco farmers, the Democratic party and the "dear nigs," as she called them, and just like Barry, she appeared to believe that every word of what she said was true.

And yet there is some evidence that Barry Bingham might have understood the complexities of his father's character better than he let on to anyone except Mary—including his own children, who grew up with the myth of the Judge's impeccable character. During the war, Barry once wrote to Mary commenting on an unusual private meeting she had had with Franklin Roosevelt. The occasion took place just after the 1944 Democratic convention. Roosevelt, whom the Binghams supported vigorously, was trying to explain to Mary Bingham why he had thrown his then vice president, Henry Wallace, off the 1944 presidential ticket. His explanation was feeble, and Barry said that "the drama reminds me of Papa on the defensive."

> The effort to divert the conversation into extraneous but acceptable channels, the marvelous front that is erected against criticism, the artful avoidance of issues while seeming to accept the policy of a free and open discussion—all these seem to me the marks of an honorable and righteous soul caught in a trap of embarrassment and guilt. . . . I must say I can feel a little more sympathy with this sort of dishonest behavior because of the strong comparison it makes in my mind with similar situations I can remember through the years at home.

Barry was a tireless organizer of his father's memorabilia and papers. In 1974 he presented each of his three surviving children and his daughter-in-law Joan with a slim green scrapbook that contained letters to the Judge from Calvin Coolidge, Herbert Hoover, Woodrow Wilson and FDR. The letterheads were impressive: The White House, embassies, the Associated Press. Presidents writing to Louisville to discuss agricultural reform or, in the case of Woodrow Wilson, to thank "Major Robert W. Bingham" for a birthday message. "I am very proud of having such friends as are everywhere organizing for the creation of the Foundation." If Woodrow Wilson erred in calling Bingham "Major," Coolidge and Roosevelt would get his title right. The Judge donated money to their campaigns. He made sure that the presidents were aware of his editorial page and of himself, the new publisher of the *Courier-Journal*. It was to be the means of winning back his respectability.

The letters in Barry's scrapbook were historical curiosities of the second class, the kind of document a president writes to a Kentucky newspaper publisher whom he wants to keep in line. "Dear Judge Bingham, thank you for the editorial in the Courier-Journal." That from Calvin Coolidge. A tribute to Judge Bingham from a prominent Louisville rabbi as well as a congratulatory note from the Judge's friend Josephus Daniels, a North Carolina publisher who was then ambassador to Mexico. Daniel's wife, Addie, was a relative of the Judge's and Daniels remarked with familial pride, "That was a very beautiful picture all the papers carried of Henrietta when she was presented at court." From a far-flung cousin, a family tree. Illustrious twelfth-century Binghams. Intimate letters from Roosevelt, his worry about the war.

Page after page, all addressed to the Judge: letters from Joseph Kennedy, another tireless Roosevelt supporter and Bingham's future successor as ambassador, about his young son Jack. "Jack is far from being a well boy and is giving me great concern with the result that my time for the next six months will be devoted to trying to help him recover his health with little or no time for business or politics," he wrote in 1935. Barry included a story about his father from the Associated Press, and a thank-you note from Roland Hayes, the first black singer in America to be taken seriously as an artist.

The Judge wore a pince-nez like Woodrow Wilson, whom he resembled. The photograph is in the scrapbook for the family to see: portrait of a father as statesman. His delicate hands are clasped together. The Judge had been handsome when he was young, before his hair thinned and his features had hardened. Bingham had come a long way in his life, longer than he had ever dreamed he would travel, although a family cliché has it that he once swore that he was determined "to own a newspaper, to marry rich and to become the Ambassador to the Court of St. James."

Another letter in the scrapbook is from the Judge to Margaret Mitchell. The occasion was the publication of *Gone with the Wind*. For the Judge, like most Southerners, reading *Gone with the Wind* had been so overwhelming that a few months before he died of Hodgkin's disease he typed a four-page letter to the author, because at last someone understood what had driven him, what had driven all of them, the Binghams, the Capertons, the vanquished sons of the South:

Dear Mrs. Mitchell,
. . . the peak of my rejoicing comes from the realization of what you have done for the younger generation in the South; my children, all the heirs of our traditions throughout our sections who have learned what they might have never known, and whose lives must be exalted, whose spirits inspired, by the grim but noble background which is theirs.

I know it all, because I was born into it, in 1871. My earliest memory is of clutching my mother's skirts in terror at a hooded apparition, and having my father raise his mask to relieve me. Then he went out in command of the Ku Klux in our district. . . . He was at Appomattox, and came home, lousy, ragged, hungry, and barefooted to the wreck left by Sherman. . . . My mother was Melanie to the last emotion, but very beautiful, outside as well as within. . . . My elder brother, my mother's first child, died in infancy, because no doctor could come, no medicine could be obtained. "God damn the Yankees," all of my blood who survived said, too.

I know every phase of it all; the poverty and the pride, the gentility, the gracious manners, the romance, the preservation of dignity and high and generous humanity in rags and semi-starvation.

My father was hunted with blood hounds by Kirk's raiders. When he turned his face homeward from Appomattox, he had nothing except the remnant of the battle flag of his regiment. . . . I have it to pass on to my son and my son's son.''

The flag always hung in Barry's office at the *Courier-Journal*, pressed under glass, charred. But though the Judge's son was a publisher, a newsman, he never sought the truth about his father, even when his longtime publisher Mark Ethridge discovered that Mrs. Flagler might have been a drug addict and certainly was a drunk. For years, neither Ethridge nor Barry ever talked to a member of Barry's stepmother's family, the Kenans, about the past, even though they were prominent North Carolina people and easy to locate. The University of North Carolina has a Kenan library and a Kenan stadium, in fact. Thomas Kenan is a distinguished North Carolina lawyer and the amateur family historian. He has always had a box of family papers, which, he said, "raised many suspicions about the Judge and my great-grandmother Mary Lily Kenan Flagler."

The documents in the scrapbook begin in 1922, although the Judge was born in 1871. Barry did not paste in any boyhood letters, nor a single clipping from the Judge's days in Louisville politics. In Barry's scrapbook, there is no evidence that the Judge had ever married a fabulously rich widow in one of the great society weddings of the era, or that he had been involved in a scandal concerning her strange death. No page-one headlines about a suspicious death or a body stolen from a grave. "I've never read all the papers that are on file at the Filson Club," Barry Senior said. Barry's history of his father begins with the documents of a rich man's life—coronations and plantations. Barry's vision of his father appeared to be so singular that the family theory was not that he was hiding something, but that he didn't have a clue as to what had come before.

6

Asheville, North Carolina, 1892. It was and still is a spa town, set in a plateau in the Blue Ridge mountains, surrounded by pine trees, with waters guaranteed to cure. Asheville was simple then, nothing like Hot Springs or White Sulphur, with the grand hotels like the Homestead and souvenir stands. The setting was glorious, all that mountain air, with so lovely a climate that the town was considered a superb place to recover from tuberculosis. Invalids, called ''lungers'' by the locals, flocked to Asheville. NO CONSUMPTIVES TAKEN was often written on the signs in front of boardinghouses.

The rich were discovering Asheville, too. George Vanderbilt, a grandson of Cornelius, built a château there in the style of Louis XV on his eight-thousand-acre estate. Splendid hotels, such as the Grove Park Inn and the Battery Park, had opened. In the years to come, Thomas Wolfe, who came from a poor family in Asheville, would immortalize the town in *Look Homeward, Angel*, but in 1892 Asheville was just starting to come alive. That was lucky for young Bob Bingham, as he was called, for he had just dropped out of the University of Virginia and had come home to teach at his family's school.

His father and stepmother ran the Bingham School, a military academy, which had been in the family for three generations, a respectable school run by a respectable family. Bob's father, Colonel Robert Bingham, doted on him, the only son to survive to adulthood. As a young boy in the 1870's, he often rode with his father through the school grounds. It was unclear why young Bob left the University of Virginia and came back to Asheville, though he had been a rather wild young man who had made the most of his good looks and his name. It was also unclear why he had switched to the University of Virginia from the University of North Carolina.

Bob's best friend at the University of Virginia was a young medical student named Hugh Young, who became the most famous urologist of his day. Young would invent Mercurochrome,

72

preside at Johns Hopkins Hospital and become a leading authority on prostate cancer and venereal disease. He traveled with General Pershing to France during the First World War, treated Diamond Jim Brady, and was asked to operate on Pope Pius XI. But what was far more significant was that Hugh Young treated Woodrow Wilson and was accused later of lying to cover up the President's complete debilitation after his strokes. Dr. Young, like Bob Bingham, adhered to a gentleman's code—you protected your friends—and much later Bingham, after he was accused of the murderous neglect of his second wife, would benefit immensely from Young's loyalty.

In 1940 Young published his memoirs and described his first meeting with Bob Bingham:

> On the football team . . . at the University of Virginia a dashing figure was the right end—a tall, handsome, dark athlete, Robert Worth Bingham of North Carolina. . . . I was trying for the team, and we soon became fast friends. His father was the celebrated Colonel Bingham who commanded North Carolina troops in the Civil War, and as my father had commanded Texans, we quickly formed an offensive and defensive alliance against the Virginians. . . .

It was Young's belief that his friend dropped out of school for financial reasons; ". . . he had to go to work." Perhaps his father, the Colonel, didn't feel his son was serious enough about his studies. Young wrote, "Bob's good looks soon won the favor of the great college vamp, a Mrs. Du Bose, a grass widow who had a fine stable of riding horses. Bob was soon elected to ride with her over the mountainous bridle paths of Albemarle, much to our envy."

The Bingham School was prestigious and the Binghams were considered intellectuals, Civil War heroes, with a former governor of the state Jonathan Worth in their family tree. They didn't have money, of course; their money had gone to Jefferson Davis—one hundred thousand dollars in Confederate bonds. But they were gentry. Though the Binghams owned slaves, they were supporters of the antislavery societies, and they prided themselves on their association with the faculty at the University of North Carolina.

The Binghams had lost everything in the Civil War, and Colonel Bingham's experience seared him, as his son explained to Margaret Mitchell:

> . . . hundreds of his fellow prisoners starved and froze to death; he was exchanged and returned to his regiment; he was at Petersburg, in command at the point where the

explosion which formed the crater came. His men held the breach and killed over two thousand negro troops who had been made drunk and pushed into the crater by white Federal troops behind them. They rolled their bodies into the bottom of the crater, scraped a few inches of dirt over them and held that charnel house against all assaults for six weeks. . . . My grandfather Bingham's barns were burned under the direct supervision of the carpet-bag Judge Albion W. Tourgee, and three thousand bushels of wheat destroyed, the first crop made after the surrender. . . . my maternal grandfather was John Milton Worth, who, with his brother, fought the carpet-baggers and scallawags to the death. Two of my mother's three brothers were killed. The one surviving was a small child.

When Bob Bingham was born in 1871, the war was barely over; the Klan was trying to protect white property owners, and murders, violence and whippings were the norm. The nether land of the New South shaped Bob Bingham's character. It was a society of creeds, myths and historical rationalizations. Bob's father, Colonel Bingham, exemplified the New South mentality with his chivalry and devotion to the Lost Cause. But he also exhibited the dark side of the Southern character, self-deception and provincialism. In *The Hills Beyond,* Thomas Wolfe seems to have drawn on Colonel Bingham as the prototype for his Southern headmaster, Colonel Theodore Joyner. Joyner's academy, Hogwart Heights, was a "neo-Confederate" academy modeled after the Bingham School. Wolfe wrote:

When he first decided to restore the place he thought he could resume his career at the point where the war had broken in upon it, and things would go on as though the war had never been. . . . For the war was a heroic fact that could not be denied, and it now seemed . . . the South had been gloriously triumphant even in defeat, and that he himself had played a decisive part in bringing about this transcendental victory.

In a curious way, the war became no longer a thing finished and done with, a thing to be put aside and forgotten as belonging to the buried past, but a dead fact recharged with new vitality. . . . And under its soothing, otherworldly spell, the South began to turn its face away from the hard and ugly realities of daily living that confronted it on every hand, and escaped into the soft dream of vanished glories— imagined glories—glories that had never been.

Theodore himself became the personal embodiment of the post-war tradition, a kind of romantic vindication of rebellion, a whole regiment of plumed knights in his own person.

The cadets often saw old Colonel Joyner "being conveyed through the streets in an old victoria, driven by an aged Negro in white gloves and a silk hat. The Colonel was always dressed in his old uniform of Confederate gray; he wore his battered old Confederate service hat, and winter or summer, he was never seen without an old gray cape about his shoulders." Much as Bob Bingham would, "Silk" Joyner, the son of the schoolmaster in Wolfe's novel, left his father and Hogwart Heights behind to make his fortune beyond Asheville.

But not yet. In 1892 it was the Gilded Age, even in Asheville, North Carolina. Young ladies carried parasols, listened to Sousa marches at band concerts, read the brand-new Sunday funnies and romance novels, and marveled over the new telephones. The Northern rich wore their five-hundred-thousand-dollar necklaces, summered in Newport, wintered in St. Augustine, and later in the new resort of Palm Beach. But their Southern equivalents rarely traveled the Palm Beach–Newport circuit. Instead they stayed with their own kind in Southern spas like White Sulphur Springs. North or South, the upper classes emphasized good manners, strict propriety, but lived in a social atmosphere of hidden intentions, sighs and glances. Bob Bingham was handsome and perhaps a bit fast, but he was very much a young man of his time.

By the time he went to college at Chapel Hill, Bob Bingham was a fervent Democrat, captain of the football team, a fine debater, and a member of Alpha Tau Omega. But popularity, good looks and football were not enough. He was still a schoolmaster's son, another well-born Southerner with no cash.

Certainly, he wasn't good enough for the pride of the Kenans, Mary Lily, whose North Carolina family was far richer and more prominent than the Binghams had ever been. Mary Lily was four years older than Bob and had gone to school with his older sisters, Sadie and Mary. The girls had gone to a genteel establishment called the Peace Institute, a two-year college in Raleigh. A school like this was "a kind of elegant country club for Southern maidens," Thomas Wolfe wrote, "a sanctuary where they could wait till marriage or early spinsterhood claimed them, and meanwhile could fill their empty heads, not with any smattering of conceivably useful knowledge, but with vicious triviality, gossip, and the accepted rituals and mannerisms of their own grotesque, aborted little world." Born snobs taking in "the dreary drivel" of "Southern Charm," Wolfe wrote.

The Kenans had always been well-to-do. Mary Lily's father

was a customs agent in Wilmington, North Carolina, but their money went back to plantations in Kenansville, where there were over a dozen slaves working in the main house alone. Mary Lily was petite but voluptuous, just over five feet tall with thick brown hair that reached her waist.

Bob Bingham first met Mary Lily Kenan at a commencement dance in Chapel Hill. David Chandler in his book theorized that they had a sexual liaison and took secret trips together. But the facts of this flirtation are not clear. "It is awfully hard for me to imagine. In the first place she was three or four years older than he was. Very unlikely that he at that age, at that very early age, would have a love affair with a proper young lady," Barry Bingham said. "She was by no means a tramp. She was a person of good family, good reputation. It would be unheard of." According to Thomas Kenan, "Mary Lily and Bob had hardly done much more than say hello in those years. She was a virgin, and very proper and they knew each other only slightly. She came from a strict Presbyterian upbringing and each time Bingham courted her, the parents came along." Certainly, the social mores of the era would support Thomas Kenan and Barry Bingham's version of Mary Lily: these belles were rarely unchaperoned. A girl who was less than pure was a pariah.

There is no way of knowing whether Mary Lily was nevertheless ready to defy her upbringing and these stringent sexual mores. Clearly, something happened, if not between them, then to Bingham alone, because Bingham, the star of his University of North Carolina class, dropped out of school the year after he and Mary Lily had known each other and wound up at the University of Virginia. Years later, his son, Barry, would explain that his father had gone to Virginia to read the law.

"We had what could be called an affair then," Mary Lily told the *New York Evening Journal* twenty-five years later, when she and Judge Bingham, both of whom had lost their mates, finally became engaged. But "in those days, an affair did not mean what it means today," Thomas Kenan said. "It was more like a romance, just the way it was in Victorian literature. There are simply no letters, no documents to back up any kind of real sexual relationship." Even to use the word "affair" in 1916 to a reporter from the *Evening Journal* was bold language, implying as it did stolen kisses, the glimpse of stocking, the exchange of intimacies that were considered unladylike in the extreme.

Whatever went on between them was brief. Mary Lily was destined for riches, grandeur and international position. This son of a schoolmaster could never have given her that.

* * *

In 1891 Mary Lily was back in Kenansville, and Bob Bingham would soon be out of the University of Virginia without a degree, ignominiously back home in Asheville, teaching Greek and Latin. That year Mary Lily went to Newport. Bored in Kenansville, Mary Lily set off with her family for the fashionable resorts. The Kenans' objective was to find Mary Lily a suitable husband, and Kenansville was not the proper place to look. They took her to Newport, which was a tremendous leap for a Southern family. "Even when I was growing up, nobody would have thought of Newport," Mary Bingham said. "We looked down on Newport. All those *arrivistes."* But the Kenans had friends there, the Pembroke Joneses. That summer in Newport, Mary Lily had the great fortune to be taken up by this glamorous couple. Although originally from North Carolina, the Pembroke Joneses had moved to New York. They were grandly social, and lived in a mansion at 5 East Sixty-first Street. The distinguished architect John Russell Pope was their son-in-law.

In 1891 the social-climbing Mrs. Pembroke Jones was a Newport hostess who spent three hundred thousand dollars on dinners and dances alone. Mary Lily loved frivolity and adored the excesses of Newport life. She was taken up by the Joneses immediately, and became a social star, a voluptuary with a Southern drawl. It was through the Joneses that Mary Lily met a girl her own age named Elizabeth Ashley, who happened to be the niece of the railroad and hotel magnate Henry Flagler. That summer while Bob Bingham went into exile in the North Carolina hills, Henry Flagler, a self-made wildcatter and Rockefeller's partner in Standard Oil, as' well as a developer who was settling the Florida wilderness, took a new interest in the welfare of his niece and her new best friend.

He was sixty-one years old. Mary Lily and Elizabeth, who were twenty-four, were bored upper-class girls with nothing to do. No doubt they were thrilled to be invited to travel with Flagler in his private railroad car, awed by watching him plant palm trees in a swamp called Palm Beach, and by his building the railroads into Key West, Miami and St. Augustine. To be with the head of this great company was surely intoxicating.

On the Flagler train it took thirty-six hours to get from New York to St. Augustine. There was a staff to wait on the girls, and as Flagler's railroad cut through the jungles of Florida that he owned the passengers could marvel at Flagler lemon trees, acacia and eucalyptus until they pulled into his town of St. Augustine. Here was Flagler's Moorish city. He had built the stores, the roads and the architectural jewel, the Ponce de Leon Hotel, where Mary Lily and Elizabeth set themselves up in an immense suite, with special lady's maids to unpack their trunks and arrange their taffeta gowns in the wardrobes for the nightly balls.

During the day there were promenades on the boardwalks. It was a dazzling life, especially if you were young and vapid and interested in social advancement. Gossip, parties, more gossip about the parties at the next day's lunches, who wore what, the excesses of this new-money life, bathing at the beach. *We are here with Mr. Flagler.* No one could dream this tale and yet it happened; what's more, it was respectable. Flagler was well married, and if that wasn't enough, he maintained a mistress in New York.

No doubt he liked having young girls around him, especially when one was his niece and safe from any hint of scandal. For her part, Mary Lily must have been exhilarated. Flagler's vision was grand. When he first arrived in 1889, Palm Beach was an island occupied by twelve people and surrounded by swamps. On one side was the ocean, on the other Lake Worth. He filled in the swamps and built the Royal Poinciana. The hotel could take two thousand guests, and the best suites rented for a hundred dollars a night. Such was the grandeur of the Royal Poinciana that the staff had its own orchestra. At the height of the season more than a hundred private railroad cars would pull in to Flagler's hotel, and if he wasn't in Miami or Key West, supervising the building of his railroad, there would be the white-haired Flagler himself with Mary Lily and his niece.

Of course, the inevitable gossip started. His wife, Ida Alice, had become literally mad. She imagined that the Czar was trying to contact her through her Ouija board. She attacked a doctor with scissors. Perhaps she was driven crazy by the constant presence of these young girls, watching the seduction going on before her very eyes. For her part, Mary Lily was growing more and more attached to her benefactor. Flagler gave her necklaces and gifts that made the gossip columns. They were always together, Flagler and Mary Lily, Flagler and Mary Lily with his niece. Years passed and Mary Lily, unmarried, was still with Flagler. The pride of the Kenan family was getting the reputation of a tart. "Obviously, he cared a great deal about her," Thomas Kenan said. "But she was always chaperoned. The only thing that happened was that he gave her jewelry. And that was what got into the newspaper accounts of the time."

Mary Lily spent a lot of time by herself. She learned the hard lessons of being attached to a man of power and position, that she came second to business. She began to drink. "She had a very low tolerance for alcohol," Thomas Kenan said. "Two glasses of wine could do her in." But the glamour of her life, circa 1894, seemed so grand, who could think of the price.

Autumn, 1894, Asheville. Eleanor Miller, a young woman from Louisville, arrived for a holiday with her parents. Her father was suffering from melancholia and the doctors had suggested he stay in the soothing mountain air. The Millers were staying at the Battery Park Hotel, where one night Bob went to a dance on the porch, and in that restless bit of wandering his luck began to change. Eleanor Miller was twenty-three and an heiress; everybody called her Babes. Her father owned iron foundries that built steamboat and pump engines, and prospered to the extent that his money still supports her descendants almost a century later. She was rather good-looking, as petite as Mary Lily Kenan, with curly hair and "a piquant face," as Barry said. Her grandchildren have her to thank for their prominent jaws and squared-off faces, the so-called Bingham chin.

Besides the ironworks, Samuel Miller owned one of the largest houses in Louisville, a mansion with turrets, gables and a tower, where in 1910 his grandson Barry Bingham would watch Halley's Comet whiz through the sky. By 1894 Bob Bingham must have been bored in tiny Asheville, after two years of teaching Latin and Greek. He soon began to take Eleanor Miller around.

In 1895 Samuel Miller was fifty-six years old and had spent the previous summer in Colorado to take a cure. There is no evidence of how Miller regarded Bob Bingham's courting Eleanor, but there is little doubt that Eleanor's mother, Henrietta, did not like her daughter's beau. "My father and grandmother had a very cool relationship," Barry said. "She was a stern and forbidding person." Some months after he arrived in Asheville, Miller invited one of his daughters to visit him. Miller drove to the station to pick her up, and in a moment of dementia, as the train roared into the station, raced from the carriage and "fell between the cars," Barry Senior said. He was killed instantly.

Eleanor and her mother returned to Louisville in deepest mourning, and Bob spent another summer in Asheville, presumably reading about the heiresses having a fabulous time at Henry Flagler's new Palm Beach playground. Then he reportedly heard that a friend from his university days, William Davies, was moving to Louisville.

It was then that Bob wrote to Eleanor's mother to ask for permission to become engaged to Eleanor, borrowed money and left for Louisville. Eleanor's father was dead and Bob was persuasive. Eleanor and Bob were married in May 1896 with his future law partner, "Dave" Davies, as his witness and best man. "It was a great big church wedding and my aunt Katie Callahan sang a solo," Barry Senior said. The *Courier-Journal* reported that the ceremony took place at Calvary Episcopal Church at 8:30 P.M. and "was attended by a large and fashionable crowd. . . . After the ceremony a wedding reception followed at the home of the bride's mother. . . . At the home, the decorations were unusually tasteful and elaborate. . . . Kurkamp's orchestra played throughout the evening.'' Thus was Bingham rescued from Asheville, the Colonel and the grave of the Confederacy.

7

Bob Bingham took to Louisville immediately, although at first the town did not take to him. Outsiders were not trusted in turn-of-the-century Louisville. Louisville's population was about two hundred thousand when Bob and Babes married at the dawn of a new century. Anything was possible: the vote for women, flying machines. Unlike the Deep South, Louisville was prosperous, and had not been so badly affected by the Civil War. Employment was high. The signs of progress were everywhere. The Louisville Country Club had just opened off the River Road and the *Louisville Times* had hired its first woman reporter.

Bob Bingham's new family was even more prosperous; the iron from the family foundries was shipped all over the country. The L&N Railroad linked Kentucky to southeastern America, the Ohio River ws a major Midwest shipping route. At the turn of the century Thomas Edison's light bulbs replaced Louisville's gaslights, and the new electric interurban trains cut through the countryside making it easy for anyone who wanted to live in these new "suburbs" to work in town. Even the nationally known editor of the *Courier-Journal*, Henry Watterson, was a regular commuter.

Watterson was the most famous editor in America at this time, a leader in the New South movement to bring industry and pride back to the region. "I remember being taken to see him when I was a young boy and he scared me with his white flowing beard, his eye patch and his fierce expression," Barry Senior said. "He looked like he came out of a Grimm's fairy tale."

Watterson's protégé at the newspaper was a young reporter named Arthur Krock, who would later become a political columnist on the *New York Times*. Even then, or especially then, the *Courier-Journal* was an exemplar of American journalism, and its editor, called Marse Henry by one and all, was suited to his job. The son of a Tennessee congressman, Watterson, as a child, had known two ex-presidents, John Quincy Adams and Andrew Jackson. During the Civil War he edited a Confederate newspaper, but later, as a reporter, Watterson stood by Lincoln when he was inaugurated. After the war he moved to London, where he met Charles Darwin and Thomas Huxley.

But Watterson was an editor, and not an owner, although he did have a small amount of *Courier-Journal* stock. The owner of the paper was Walter Haldeman of Louisville, and he gave Watterson free rein. "Everyone assumed that Watterson was the owner," Barry Senior said, "because the paper was just completely associated with him and you never heard a word about the Haldemans." But the Haldeman family made the *Courier-Journal* modern. The building had one of the first Linotype systems in the country.

More important, Haldeman always backed up his editor. Watterson wrote time and again against the Ku Klux Klan. For Louisville, he was an enlightened Democrat, not doctrinaire. In 1896 Watterson was against the movement toward free silver and in favor of an unpopular stringent monetary policy. He even ran an anti-silver campaign in the *Courier-Journal* headlined "No Compromise with Dishonor!" which cost so many advertisers and subscribers that the paper almost closed. But however free he was at the turn of the century, with one generation of the Haldeman ownership backing him up, he would feud with the next one. And when Bob Bingham took over, he would soon be gone.

Meanwhile, Mary Lily and Bob were moving unknowingly but inexorably toward each other. No doubt mutual friends were keeping them informed of each other's life: *Did you hear that Bob Bingham was trying to get into politics in Louisville?* He was living in his wife's huge house with a mother-in-law who didn't like him, forced to share a bath. It is easy to imagine the scene: *Mr. Bingham,* as she might have called him, *have you finished shaving?* Eleanor and Bob's first child, a son, was born in 1897, eleven months after their wedding, and they named him Robert. Henrietta was born a few years later, in 1901, and named after Babes's mother.

A few years later Bob and Eleanor were still marooned with their two babies and his mother-in-law in a large gray limestone house on Fourth Street in a good section of town that is now called Old Louisville. The Miller house had four stories, turrets and a mansard roof, and a huge attic, where Barry used to play. But in the style of the time, it was designed with only one bathroom at the top of the stairs on the second floor. "The bathtub, rearing its massive bulk on iron claw feet, seemed as big as a swimming pool to me. The stairway itself was lit by a stained glass window which cast colored prisms onto the carpet, an optical hazard which made my grandmother pluck up her long skirts

and peer attentively before her as she bustled up or down,"
Barry once wrote.

Bob enrolled in an accelerated program at the University of
Louisville Law School, graduated in 1897 and started work at a
law firm that eventually dissolved. He had borrowed $2,500 from
his grandfather to get married and invested a bit of it in real
estate. Then his best friend, Dave Davies, came back to Louisville in 1899 from the Spanish-American War and they set up
the law partnership of Bingham and Davies.

Like most American cities, Louisville at the turn of the century was wide open, running on graft. Labor was cheap, easy
to exploit, and a man's vote could be bought and sold for pennies. Bribes and brawls were common. John "Boss" Whallen
ran the Democratic organization of Louisville from the Bucking-
ham Theater, a burlesque house, which delivered women and
whiskey to the voters. Many of the customers were employees
of Kentucky's largest employer, the L&N Railroad, who were
ready to give up their votes for bourbon and the pleasures of
Boss Whallen's fleshpots.

"To call my father a politician is such a strange misnomer to
me, because he did have a rather brief career in political life
early on. But he was just not a politician, in the sense of seeking
office," Barry Senior said, although his father's history would
suggest the opposite. In those years Bob Bingham was a young
man on the move. He called himself a reformer and favored
Prohibition and Sunday closings of saloons. Even so, no matter
how high-minded one was, city politics, with its payoffs and
bosses, was not considered fit employment for anyone with pretensions to refinement. It was, on the other hand, a fast way to
make a financial score.

By 1901 Bob Bingham, who had earlier been a Republican
poll watcher, was making speeches for Boss Whallen's Democratic candidate for mayor. In 1902 he suggested his own Democratic candidacy for Congress to Whallen, but was rejected.
But in 1903 the county attorney of Louisville resigned and eleven
candidates sought the appointment, a highly desirable position
given the opportunities for graft. Bingham got the job and then
had to have his position ratified in the election of 1904. He wrote
a friend that he believed he would "surely win." The Whallen
machine endorsed him and he won handily. As county attorney,
he became a man of stature.

In 1905 Bingham was county attorney during one of Louisville's typically corrupt elections. Ballots were burned, the opposition candidates were beaten up, and Republicans were kept
away from the polls by force. Although he called himself a reformer, Bingham, as county attorney, could do little to stop this
violence. His jurisdiction was the county, not the city, and the

two governments, then as now, were not merged. The 1905 city election was challenged, and then, in 1907, thrown out by the Kentucky Court of Appeals. The governor of Kentucky appointed an interim mayor and picked his man right from Boss Whallen's machine. The new mayor was County Attorney Robert Worth Bingham.

At the Louisville *Courier-Journal*, Watterson endorsed the appointment, although tepidly, and in a cartoon on the front page of the *Louisville Evening Post* Bingham stood with his hands in his pockets, looking young, well dressed and powerful. The portly Henry Watterson stood by his side. "Come on now. Be a good mayor and accept these suggestions that Bill and I have cooked up," the Watterson character says. The headline reads: "The Circumstances Under Which the Courier-Journal Will Support Mr. Bingham." He served only four months, but in that time he enforced a Sunday closing law for the saloons and made some attempt to clean up the police force, the meat inspector's office and the Water Works. His reforms did not impress Louisville, but they did weaken the Democratic machine. In the election of November 1907 the Republicans won overwhelmingly.

The reformist political ideals of the Bingham family were forged during these first years of the century. As mayor, Bingham fought patronage and tried to ensure honest elections. When he exposed a previous mayor who had taken a city horse for his own use, the man committed suicide, and the *Courier-Journal* blamed Bingham. For a time Bingham's primary enemy in town was the great Henry Watterson, a conflict that neither man would forget.

Bob Bingham later ran on the Republican ticket for judge in the Fourth District, Court of Appeals. "This fight here must be made," he said, because "Louisville is in worse condition than it has ever been, and unless there are some left to fight for better things here, the city is doomed to years of base and contemptible servitude." He urged the Republicans and Democrats to "throw off the yoke of political machines." He praised Theodore Roosevelt and was later invited to the White House to meet him. Although the machine won the election, the governor of Kentucky appointed Bingham to the Jefferson Circuit Court, the last political office he would ever hold in Kentucky. He was now and forever after "Judge Bingham."

Although later in his life the Judge was considered a liberal, during this period he exemplified middle-class Progressivism, a popular reform movement of the era, perhaps because he had been unable to find success in the world of machine politics. Bingham, however, along with Louisville's other Progressives, supported the notion of helping the needy, and Bingham personally donated money to the YMCA, the Salvation Army and the Kentucky Anti-Tuberculosis Association, among other causes. He believed in education for Negroes and often spoke to Negro groups. He settled labor disputes and lobbied for child labor laws. However, as a Kentucky historian remarked, "Pro-Southern politics and sympathy for the 'lost cause' of the Confederacy dominated Kentucky culture after the [Civil] War." Bingham, a young, ambitious lawyer married to a rich girl, would not have wanted to violate the harsh racial mores of the era, however decent his intentions. His liberalism was yet to come.

Bingham was making terrific progress, but nothing as grand as the success of Mary Lily, who had now become a tabloid heroine, and would soon be Mrs. Henry Flagler. In 1901, when she was married in splendor in the family's mansion in Kenansville, the press had to be held back by the Kenansville police. Flagler had a new road built to her house and brought down private trains filled with New York friends. The Kenan house was repainted for the occasion. It was the society wedding of the year, if not the decade, and the newspapers reported that her wedding gifts from Flagler were a block of stock in Standard Oil, a two-hundred-thousand-dollar necklace consisting of 111 pearls and an oblong diamond clasp, a certified check for $1 million, and "a palace to rival the greatest in Europe." That was Whitehall, the Palm Beach mansion that is now the Flagler Museum, so named because it was built of marble, the Taj Mahal of America, as the tabloids wrote. The second Mrs. Flagler and the State of Florida had made all this possible for Mary Lily. Ida Alice Flagler had become certifiably insane. As a favor to Henry Flagler, the most powerful man in the state, Florida had changed its state laws to make insanity grounds for divorce. Flagler had divorced Ida Alice just ten days before he married Mary Lily.

How Bob Bingham, making his ascent in small-town Louisville, must have been astonished to read about Mary Lily. Here he was mired with two children at his mother-in-law's, trying to fight the Democratic machine. The description of Whitehall must have been cause for envy. The newspapers were filled with details of the gold leaf and the cloisonné work, the seven different kinds of marble and the golden damask walls, as well as the Louis XV ballroom, billiard room and fourteen guest chambers, each with double doors and each decorated in a totally different style. The mistress of the house was never seen in the same dress twice, a fact that was later noted in the *Guinness Book of World Records*.

8

There is a remarkable photograph of Eleanor Miller Bingham with her younger son, Barry, in her arms. Barry, who had been born in 1906, wears a sailor suit, white high socks and knickers. His blond hair is brushed neatly to the side, his hand is in his mother's lap. Her dress is muslin and lace, with embroidery at the throat, which showed her fine bosom and tiny waist. No six-year-old child ever looked happier or more at peace than young Barry, even under the harsh lights of the primitive photographer. He had one leg tucked under him—a casual, boyish pose caught forever in a Louisville portrait studio, circa 1912. It would be one of the last portraits ever taken of Barry and his mother. In the spring of 1913 she went to Asheville to pick up Robert, who was already attending the Bingham School. "If anything happens to me, please take care of the children," she reportedly told her sister-in-law, Sadie Bingham Grinnan.

There was no reason for young Barry not to have looked secure in the photograph with his mother. Till then, his childhood had been a dream. He was the son of "the Judge," a powerful man, the former mayor, who was greeted on the street by one and all, "Good morning, Judge Bingham." *What a fine child little Barry is getting to be.* Barry could visit him at his office at the local courthouse, a vast and imposing stuccoed-limestone building with a rotunda that must have seemed to him the size of a baseball field. He was, moreover, the youngest child, and a boy. His mother was rich, and the family lived in a new house by a large park. Barry could see from his room the beech trees, the creek and the open vistas of Cherokee Park.

Barry's mother was considered a beauty. His aunt Sadie once wrote to him in a nostalgic mood to tell him of a Charleston ball she had attended with his parents around 1912:

In the dim past, your father and mother and I went to visit Harrison Randolf and attended a St. Cecelia Ball. On sight . . . [the] president of the ball chose your mother for his

86

partner which was considered there a greater honor than
being elected president of the United States. I wish you
could have seen her then, so lovely, brilliant and delightful.
All four of us got tight on champagne so plentiful that it
seemed to be drawn up in huge buckets out of unfailing
wells.

Once at his grandmother's country house just outside of town
in the Pewee Valley, his mother hopped on his tricycle. "Here
I come lowly riding on my ass," she called out to Barry's startled father and grandmother. "My mother had the most delightful sense of humor," Barry said.

But most of his memories focused on his grandmother's house
in town. The house at 1236 South Fourth Street was a citadel of
security, a child's paradise. There was a speaking tube into which
he could whistle to the cook, Sarah, in the kitchen, and an attic
filled with relics, including Grandmother Miller's dressmaking
dummy. Barry could hide in the circular tower, play billiards at
the table that stood, he remembered, "like a heavy animal risen
from its wallow." At his grandmother Miller's house he wasn't
lonely, and he remembered it with longing:

It was not only that the neighborhood teemed with boys and
girls, and that some of their elders were of the understanding sort who kept red-and-white striped peppermints in a
paper bag or cookies in a jar for their neighbors' children. . . . Such rambling old houses, though intimately familiar, yet retained a slight feminine air of mystery in their
depths, as though a secret room might still be found at the
edge of a well-known corridor.

He was a gentle boy, protected by his mammy, Lizzie, and
his mother. During the war Mary wrote to Barry:

Lizzie has been puttering around my room reminiscing in
her wonderfully comforting way . . . how on your fifth
birthday you refused to entertain any of your contemporaries and invited (to what must have been the best party in
the world) all the servants, including your grandmother
Miller's cook.

Just before his sixth birthday, in February of 1912, the family
moved into town and took a suite of rooms at the Galt House,
which was particularly grand. Charles Dickens had stayed there
in 1842, and the hotel was a marvel of chandeliers and coal
fireplaces in every room. The Judge had moved his family into
town because the Cherokee Park house was being repaired.

Barry, at six, was enthralled by the visits from the bellmen, the maids, the waitresses. He had the joy of spending his birthday cosseted in that fine hotel. These were the happiest times, the part of his childhood he can recall easily. He remembered mostly

> having my father and mother come to kiss me goodnight on their way to one of those spectacular parties. . . . They were in full evening dress. My mother smelled deliciously of perfume, and she wore fresh flowers which seemed to me utterly remarkable at that snowy season of the year. My father looked courtly and grand in his white tie and tails.

> Bending over my bed they gave me the feeling that they were poised on the threshold of a wonderful world of bright lights, music and laughter. In case I should feel lonely when they left, they explained that they would be right downstairs in the same building all evening. With that assurance, I was able to wake up once in a while during the night and imagine them nearby, yet floating on a wave of glitter and gayety.

If anything happens to me, take care of the children. It was April in Louisville, 1913. Eleanor's brother, Dennis, who had chaperoned her in Asheville so many years before, took his wife, Luci, his sister, Barry and Henrietta for an afternoon drive. They drove west of Louisville, along the Brownsboro Road toward the Pewee Valley, on their way to Barry's grandmother's country house, driving over oak-shaded roads that curved through farmland. Seven-year-old Barry was asleep in his mother's lap in the backseat. Henrietta sat in the front seat with Dennis and Luci. One of the young Callahan boys, Franklin, was in the car as well. Although it was sunny when they left town, Barry would always think of this day as rainy. At an intersection called O'Bannon Crossing there was a small cluster of country stores, including O'Bannon's Grocery, a low Greek Revival building with four columns. The farmers did their shopping at O'Bannon's at the intersection of LaGrange Road and Collins Lane. The grocery sat beside the Interurban electric tracks, which ran along the Old LaGrange road.

Dennis stopped the car at O'Bannon's to wipe his eyeglasses. No one in the car saw the coming train. The buildings blocked the view of the track; rain and the noise from the automobile engine might have muffled the sound of the speeding train. Dennis drove across the tracks just as the train crossed the intersection. It was possible that Barry was the only person in the car who saw the train coming at them. He couldn't scream, couldn't react, didn't react. All he remembered was the glare of the headlight of the approaching train. It happened very fast. "I heard my mother scream," Barry said. The car was almost across the

track when the train smashed into its rear end with such force
that Dennis and Eleanor were knocked out, Eleanor's skull was
severely fractured, Dennis was bruised, and Henrietta and Barry
were thrown from the car. Barry said:

> I was seven years old, I was in the car, I can remember it.
> It was a horrible memory when I saw that street car bearing
> down upon us. . . . My mother was sitting in the back hold-
> ing on to me. It was raining and I can remember seeing this
> terrible glaring light. I think my mother's screams must have
> awakened me. I probably had been dozing myself, and then
> suddenly I was aware of this crash. . . . The next thing I
> woke up and I am in a strange room in a strange house. . . .
> I came out of it with a considerably injured spine. I was
> thrown free. My mother was unconscious. She died two
> days later. . . .

According to Barry's daughter Eleanor, "It was terrible, I think
Daddy literally couldn't say a word he was so traumatized, he
was struck mute. And my grandfather, which was typical of that
era, thought that something in his spine was responsible. As if
it were a physical problem, not mental. Can you imagine? They
thought if he stayed in bed he would be perfectly okay in no
time." Barry said, "I couldn't walk for many months. They had
to keep me in bed, and I can remember the pain of trying to
take two steps." Not only did he lose his speaking voice and his
ability to walk, but he was on the verge of contracting tuberculosis and asthma. His father sent him to the mountain climes of
Asheville to Aunt Sadie to try to cure him. "It took a long time
to pull him together," Eleanor said. "At least this is what Mother
has always told me. Finally, he began to speak after about a
year." Throughout his life, however, Barry could never confront
the horror of this event, much less talk about it with his children.
If pressed, he would discuss it only in the blandest, most detached terms, as he discussed every other painful family experience.
    "My sister was crying uncontrollably," he said. "I was young
enough, so it wasn't quite so devastating to me as perhaps it was
to my sister, who was quite a bit older. . . . You know, children
are awfully resilient. I got ahead once I was back on my feet. I
was probably too young to take in how completely devastating
it was."
    What he now needed was a mother, a strong woman who
could bring a frail child around, and one day he would marry
one. But in Asheville he was shielded from the harsh verities of
his loss by the two aunts who reared him and who were good
Southern women who stressed life's niceties. The Judge remod-

eled his sister's Asheville house so that Barry could sleep on a
new outdoor porch. Barry would always be devoted to these
aunts, particularly to Sadie, whom he called Zaddie and who
had no children. The ladies were obviously delighted to have a
small boy in their care. Sadie was the nurturer; Mary was a bit
more austere. Their effect on him was powerful. Hardly a
Christmas passed at Glenview that Zaddie wasn't there. She lived
a very long life, dying many years after the Judge, and all through
the war she was a character in the voluminous correspondence
between Mary and Barry. Aunt Mary became fatally ill in 1931,
just as Mary and Barry were engaged. "I wish you could have
known her," Barry wrote his fiancée.

> She was a brilliant and majestic personality with a wit that
> was sharp and devastating. . . . When I was a little albino
> baby, I would have crying spells for some reason, about
> going to the bathroom. I have a vague recollection of being
> afraid of the johnny, with the swirl and gush of what seemed
> like an infinite expanse of water. On those occasions, Aunt
> Mary had to be called in, and I immediately performed
> without further protest.

He was luckier than Henrietta, who was sent away to school.
Barry, at least, wound up in a loving household of women, which
may not have done much for his sense of reality but most assur-
edly saved his life and perhaps enhanced his inherent gentleness.
He was, as his father had been before him, a Bingham at the
Bingham School. His grandfather was still alive and a man of
privilege and position, yet when Barry talks about his childhood,
he rarely mentions his father or his grandfather. Instead he talks
about the women who dominated him.

Asheville to Louisville, Louisville to Asheville, he was
bounced back and forth. Besides his aunts and his older sister,
Henrietta, who smothered him with affection, Barry was close
to a Louisville teacher who would often read to him as the other
children went out to play. Additionally, a teenager named Sophie
Alpert became his lifelong friend. Ten years older, she was his
brother Robert's girlfriend and would be called in to be with
little Barry "because his mother had just been killed in a terrible
accident," she explained. "We used to read together. He used
to write poems and I used to illustrate them." He was a shy,
understandably immature child. His love of solitary pursuits,
especially poetry, led him to be active in the Aloha Club,
a children's literary section that ran in the Sunday *Courier-
Journal,* run by another strong woman called Aunt Ruth by
her charges. Aunt Ruth introduced Barry to the newspaper.
". . . all the kids used to come in there to see 'Aunt Ruth' once

a week and sit in her office, and she'd give us cookies and cocoa and talk about things . . . I think it gave many of us the feeling that writing was something that we could really get hold of and that you'd get a little recognition for," Barry said.

The Judge received close to eighty thousand dollars from his wife's estate, but he had substantial debts. He moved from Cherokee Park into the second floor of a modest house on Burnett Street in Old Louisville. "I think he had no heart for living in that house which he and my mother had built together," Barry Senior said.

Mary Lily Flagler's life had changed dramatically as well. In an eerie coincidence, in the same month that Eleanor died, Flagler, at eighty-three, fell down a flight of stairs at Whitehall and broke his hip, an accident that would be fatal. Two weeks before Eleanor was killed the front page of the Louisville *Herald* showed the "Latest Photograph of Dying Millionaire" Flagler in a wheelchair on the boardwalk in Palm Beach. "Henry M. Flagler, the aged multi-millionaire, who is dying at his home near West Palm Beach, Florida," the caption read.

Flagler's condition was big news around the country. His life had been filled with controversy, deals and activity, even at the end. With Mary Lily by his side, he spent the last few years of his life fighting to get the railroads into Key West. He died two months after his accident and willed almost everything to Pudgy, as he called Mary Lily. Her twenty-two years as his companion, half as mistress, half as wife, earned her $100 million, every bit of it tax-free. All the properties, most of the Standard Oil stock, the railroads, the mansions, the art, waterworks, newspapers, hotels, the Miami electric company. Flagler even left a provision that his executives would run things for five years until Mary Lily learned the business. She was the richest woman in America.

The newspapers took to Mary Lily Flagler, who was just the froth that the American public craved. When the Germans sank the *Lusitania* in 1915, it was Mary Lily who made the news again. Her cousin Owen Kenan, a doctor and a ladies' man, had been on the ship and survived. When the story broke, the file photograph that the papers used to illustrate the tragedy was Mary Lily and Owen standing on the Poinciana dock. She was a genuine tycoon, perhaps the first independent female multi-millionaire.

Two years passed. Mary Lily was a lonely widow. She closed Whitehall, moved to New York, and spent a great deal of time with her niece Louise Wise, a teenager who was photographed in the tabloids slathered in fur boas looking smug. "My niece,

Louise Wise of Cincinnati, will be my principal heir," Mrs.
Flagler announced.

The Kenan family has always believed that the Judge finally
sought out Mary Lily in order to pay his debts. "She was so
lonely," Thomas Kenan said. "There is no question in anybody's mind that Bob Bingham plotted to get Mary Lily's money
and that he wasn't going to stop until he had it. He just played
on her misery and she fell for it." Barry, all of nine years old,
was in Asheville that summer staying with his aunts when Mary
Lily checked into the Grove Park Inn. "Mary Lily came to
Asheville for the climate," Barry said. "And when she was
there she realized that my aunts Sadie and Mary were around."
Soon his father came to Asheville too. The couple didn't waste
a second. Mary Lily cabled her family that she "had never been
so happy," Thomas Kenan said.

They began to keep company. The Judge went to New York,
stayed in Mary Lily's summer retreat in Westchester and at the
Plaza. Mary Lily reopened Whitehall. The following summer
the Judge and Mary Lily stayed at the Greenbriar Hotel in West
Virginia. It was not known who was paying the bills for the
Judge's frequent trips, but through his association with Mrs.
Flagler he was soon catapulted into Newport, Fifth Avenue and
Palm Beach, the world of heiresses and titles, balls and fingerbowls. When the newspapers discovered him, they romanticized
this small-town politician. As Mary Lily Flagler's beau, he be-
came "a reformer."

It was not, however, the easiest of courtships. The Judge's law
partner, Stanley Sloss, was called in to mediate. "I remember
lots of long-distance phone calls between Mary Lily and my
father," Sloss's daughter said. "There were a lot of negotiations. . . . I knew something was going on, but I couldn't tell
what. He was convincing her that she should marry him [the
Judge]. He was courting her for him. I would say my memory
of it was he had a hand in it."

The Judge soon began to act the great man around town again.
In the spring of 1916 he took part in a benefit performance of
The Trojan Women, mounted in Cherokee Park by the wife of
the editor of the Louisville *Post.* The Judge played Menelaus,
the king of Sparta, and his friend Dave Davies portrayed the god
Poseidon. Davies's beard was so magnificent that when young
Barry, at age ten, watched Davies and his father rehearse at the
park, he would "shiver when I beheld it." For weeks, Barry hid
in the grass near the theater and watched the leading citizens of
Louisville, the drama critic John Mason Brown, the future senator Thruston Morton, the teachers and the politicians cavorting
on the stage. Even Barry's sister, Henrietta, was allowed to dance
in the Ball Dance of Nausicaa and Her Maidens. Years later

Barry wrote about this production of *The Trojan Women* with complete recall: "Yet as the spectators moved away across the lawn . . . in the late afternoon light of that June day, the only shadows that fell across the scene were those cast by the stately trees that stood around the amphitheater. To the audience, the war already raging in Western Europe must have seemed almost as remote as the siege of Troy." A year later Barry and his father would also be under siege.

The Judge's engagement was announced at the beginning of November 1916. The New York *Herald* headlined the story as "Mrs. Flagler's Romance": "Mrs. H. M. Flagler to Be Married on November 15." In a two-column story, the readers of the *Herald,* as well as the *New York Times,* the *Evening Journal* and the five other newspapers, were treated to every glorious detail:

Congratulations poured in upon Mrs. Flagler yesterday. "One of my friends said to me," she observed to a friend, " 'Why, this is not a very brilliant match, is it?' 'Yes it is,' I replied to her. 'It is of the heart and what can be more brilliant than that?' "

In a gush of excitement she confessed to the *Herald* reporter,

"You see, we had what you might call 'an affair' then, but our paths took us in opposite directions. In later years he married and three years ago Mrs. Bingham died. We met again when guests of a mutual friend at Asheville, North Carolina, about a year ago. Now Mr. Bingham's son Robert Jr. is a fine young man of twenty years, just about his age in the old days, and he is a student at the University of Virginia, as he was then."

With that, the bride-to-be pointed to a portrait over the mantelpiece, a study of a lovely young girl. "And she is?" the reporter asked.

"That is a picture of Miss Louise Wise, my dear niece. . . . She is the youngest member of our family circle and will eventually inherit the responsibilities that now rest upon me. Great wealth brings responsibilities to those who possess it—responsibilities to others who have capabilities, but whose horizon is narrowed through a want of proper means. It was Mr. Flagler's idea that wealth should bring as much happiness to the greater number, and it has been and will continue to be my duty to follow his principles. And Miss Louise Wise is one of many young women I know, or know of, who is as capable or more capable than most men are in making wealth do the greatest amount of good.''

The groom was described in the most glowing terms: a reform politician, a former mayor, a judge, all very impressive. The *New York Times* reported portentously that when he was appointed, "Mayor Bingham at once instituted a crusade against the saloons, took the Fire and Police Departments outside of politics and in general carried out reform work.''

Just before the ceremony the Judge agreed to Mrs. Flagler's trustees' demand, renouncing any claim to her $100 million or the Standard Oil stake. Mary Lily gave $125,000 to a hospital in St. Augustine, but the Judge was not shortchanged. Her wedding present to her new husband was $50,000 in cash. She also paid his real estate and stock debts and provided him with a yearly income of $50,000, the dividends from $695,000 in Standard Oil stock.

The wedding was small and in perfect taste. The bride wore gray satin, white lace and her two-hundred-thousand-dollar pearls. The Pembroke Joneses gave the wedding party, but it was hardly lavish. The ceremony was held at 4:00 P.M. and the guests numbered only about fifteen. Although the wedding took place just before the Thanksgiving school holiday, the Bingham children were not invited. In fact, only Bob's best friend, Dr. Hugh Young, and Bob's sister Sadie were there to represent the groom. The Joneses had so few people gathered on East Sixty-first Street that they brought in screens of vines, palms and chrysanthemums to make their rooms seem smaller. The only member of the wedding who dressed extravagantly was the heiress apparent, Louise Wise, in full-length white broadcloth, trimmed in narrow bands of white fox. She carried pink roses and wore a hat of white satin and fur, the *Herald* reported.

The newlyweds spent their honeymoon in the Flagler railroad car en route to Louisville that night, and two days later the richest woman in America moved into a modest suite at the Seelbach Hotel—a small bedroom and a wood-paneled living room with a fireplace. The suite cost five dollars a night and was reportedly paid for by the bride, who would not live to celebrate her first anniversary.

9

The persistent controversy over the odd events surrounding the death of Mary Lily Flagler Bingham still haunts Barry Bingham. More than a half century after his stepmother came back to Louisville as a bride, Barry remains so fearful that the scandal over Mary Lily's mysterious death in 1917 will resurface that at age eighty-one he instructed his lawyers to try a novel copyright defense to prevent the publication of David Chandler's book, which was filled with facts and speculations about the Judge's possible role in Mary Lily's demise.

There is no question but that when the Judge married Mary Lily Flagler she was hardly the Lillie Langtry pictured in the tabloid press but an alcoholic and perhaps also dependent on morphine. By 1917 there were sanatoriums all over the South for problem drinkers, yet Judge Bingham never sought decent treatment for Mary Lily's addictions. Instead he isolated her in a mansion in Glenview just outside Louisville under the care of unqualified doctors who Mary Lily's family believed overdosed her with narcotics.

Despite Barry Bingham's denials, there is simply no rational explanation for the way Mary Lily was allowed to die: Judge Bingham's closest friend was the renowned Dr. Hugh Young, who presided at Johns Hopkins in Baltimore, where the Judge, so concerned with his own health problems, often went for the slightest stomach ailment. Furthermore, Mary Lily's immense fortune could have brought any specialist to Louisville, had the Judge been inclined to do so. Instead, when Mary Lily developed heart problems, perhaps because of her morphine addiction, he turned her over to a local dermatologist. He did not even call in a qualified specialist from a larger city, such as London, where the first work with electrocardiography was being done. Although there is no substantial, much less conclusive, evidence that Bingham actually murdered Mary Lily, the events of her first and only year in Louisville leave little doubt that the Judge was dangerously irresponsible toward a very sick

woman, unable to care for herself. The scandal remains common
knowledge in Louisville to this day. It was extensively reported
in the newspapers of 1917, and even mentioned in Congress when
Judge Bingham was nominated for ambassador to the Court of
St. James's in 1933, but Barry Bingham has always maintained
that he knew little about it—yet another instance, and in this
case a tragic one, of his refusal to confront or even acknowledge
painful truths about his family.

Christmastime, 1916. Mary Lily's misery quickly became apparent. She was a stranger in a new town, marooned in the small
Seelbach suite, spending her days looking at suitable houses to
rent. The Judge was away from Louisville for days at a time,
seeking business with his newfound celebrity. Mary Lily's unhappiness was more than the normal depression that comes in
every marriage when the tedious rigors of daily life set in. The
mood in the Bingham household was ominous. "Their marriage
went sour almost immediately," Thomas Kenan said. "She
wrote home to Kenansville how unhappy she was, how the children were treating her with nothing but pure hatred."
   From the beginning, Mary Lily alienated the Judge's two oldest children, Henrietta and Robert, who by this time were hardly
children; Robert was already at the University of Virginia and
Henrietta was finishing boarding school at Stuart Hall in Staun-
ton, Virginia, and would soon be starting at Smith. Not only
had Mary Lily excluded them from her wedding, she excluded
them from her new will as well. Though Louise Wise and Henrietta were only three years apart, Henrietta was barely mentioned in the endless news stories about Mary Lily and the Judge.
Henrietta was Cinderella, a footnote at the bottom of the columns, while the anointed heiress, Louise Wise, was photographed in large fur hats all over the tabloid press. It would be
easy to imagine Henrietta's jealousy and justifiable rage. She
would soon be a gorgeous party girl, why wasn't she brought to
New York to socialize with the Pembroke Joneses? But Barry
Senior denied that a problem existed between Henrietta and Mary
Lily. "I just don't know how to account for the fact that we were
not at the wedding. I do think that it is a rather strange point
that I had never thought about until recently," Barry said.
   Mary Lily, who never had children, did not understand the
possible hazards of taking a sixteen-year-old girl's father away
from her. Henrietta Bingham was wildly possessive of her father, Mary Bingham always said, much like Sallie in the next
generation. What's more, Henrietta was forced to read each detail of her new stepcousin's future "responsibilities of great
wealth." *Henrietta, did you see the paper? Henrietta, do you*

know this girl, Louise Wise? Henrietta, you are going to the wedding, aren't you?

A few years later, the Judge's third wife, Aleen, would be shrewd enough not to repeat Mary Lily's mistake of alienating Henrietta. In the 1930's, when Aleen Hilliard Bingham lived in London as the wife of the ambassador, she made sure that Henrietta stayed in the residence too, even though it meant dealing with Henrietta's odd ménage, her close friend of the period, Helen Jacobs, the renowned tennis player, who lived in the house at Prince's Gate as well. "Aleen always acted as the hostess," Helen Jacobs said, "but she was kind enough to allow Henrietta and me to live together in the residence. It was a glorious time."

But what could Mary Lily, at age forty-nine, know of the devilish ways of a jealous sixteen-year-old girl? Her entire life had been spent as a coquette, the child bride of a much older man. "The letters started coming from Louisville almost immediately about how depressed Mary Lily was," Thomas Kenan said. "She railed against her stepchildren and said that they had been perfectly dreadful to her. She said that she had never experienced such hate. In the letters, she was distraught."

"I was the first person in Louisville who ever met her," Sophie Alpert said. "Judge Bingham asked my cousin Sophie Rogers and me to meet them at the Seelbach when they came here to live. She was a very sweet woman. She took me in her bedroom and showed me all the presents she had for the children. She was kind of like a little old lady and very quiet. I never saw her again, except they had a great big garden party when they had the Belknap house. Of course the children weren't here. They were all away at school."

The presents on the bed. This scene is a part of Bingham family history. The story has it that Mary Lily, set up at the Seelbach for Christmas, ushered in her stepchildren to show off the display of presents she had bought for them. Henrietta and Robert were older teenagers, hardly toddlers, and long past the presents-on-the-bed stage. Like all family histories, the presents-on-the-bed story has variations: in one, Henrietta and Robert throw the presents around the room; in another, Henrietta is at Stuart Hall and when she heard about the presents—and her father's remarriage—she destroyed her room.

There is no debate, however, on the subject of how little time Barry spent with his new stepmother. Although the Judge first began seeing Mary Lily in the summer of 1915, Barry met her only twice, and then very briefly. "I was eleven years old. She was a small, white-haired lady with dark eyes. I think she struck me as a pretty, slightly buxom, matronly lady." Although Barry's dear friend Sophie vividly remembered seeing the presents, Barry denied that any presents ever existed. "This was a piece

of Louisville gossip at the time. . . . I can only say it couldn't
have been true in the sense that I would have been so conscious
of it. If presents were sitting on the bed, I would have been avid
to get at them.''

If Mary Lily had filled three suites with presents, the reactions
would probably have been the same. From Barry, the Southern
"good boy," denial and refusal to engage in controversy; from
Henrietta and Robert, hostility fueled by rage and jealousy. It was
not that Mary Lily did nothing for her stepchildren. What she did
was probably inadequate. She gave Henrietta a lovely coming-out
party that Christmas at the Seelbach, but there was no matched set
of pearls to offset the fact that Louise Wise was getting all the
jewelry. Still, the dance was written up in the *Courier-Journal*,
which was some small consolation. Mary Lily's theme was a Louis
XV garden, and from the three main chandeliers the hostess had
hung large French baskets "filled with pink Killarney roses and
stevia from which fell a shower of pink tulle and dew drop tulle at
the end of which were butterfly bows." Mary Lily spared none of
the Flagler dollars to achieve "the appearance of fairyland," as the
Courier-Journal phrased it. Smilax covered the walls. Roses, bay
trees, blankets of stevia were brought in for the occasion, but all of
it had little effect on the guest of honor. "Henrietta . . . was thoroughly unappreciative of everything she did for her," said Ellen
Barret Wood, whose mother was a close friend of the future Aleen
Bingham. "My husband . . . said he never saw such a party in
Louisville for young people. She had champagne—oh, you never
heard of such a party. Favors, very expensive favors for everybody.
This was for Henrietta, and of course, she was hateful to the old
lady and so was Robert. . . . And I think to accept so much from
someone and then be so ugly is bad." Sallie Bingham always believed that just after the deb party, Henrietta went to her father and
told him that she had been spying on Mrs. Flagler and that she was
convinced Mary Lily was "a drunk and a drug addict." Barry said,
"There is not a word of truth in that," and her mother added that
"Sallie is a creature of her fantasies."

Spring holidays, 1917. Mary Lily and the Judge were at Whitehall. Henrietta and Robert, who loved nothing more than parties, spurned Mary Lily's invitation to stay at America's Taj
Mahal. "I don't think anybody at the time was thinking about
the idea of going to a place that nobody had ever been to before,
and which we'd never even heard of," Barry said. "I didn't even
know there was such a thing in those days. And I don't think
either Robert or Henrietta had the smallest interest in going to
Palm Beach. . . . We just didn't live in the era in which Palm
Beach or that kind of social life played any part." Whatever the
explanation, Barry and his brother and sister didn't go south.

The Judge took their side. He left Palm Beach and went to Asheville and Louisville to be with his children. In doing so, he may have been exacting a kind of revenge, punishing Mary Lily for the harsh terms of her will where he was concerned. Soon after Mary Lily and the Judge married, he voluntarily signed a statement affirming that her will would leave him nothing. However lavishly Mary Lily was providing for her cooks, Florida hospitals and the Kenan cousins, she wasn't giving anything to the Judge or his children. Why the Judge chose to reaffirm his omission from the will is a puzzle, though it is not unreasonable to suppose that he was trying to save face by pretending that this onerous contract had been *his* idea.

Almost seventy years later Barry Bingham was still putting forward this theory about his father and the Flagler millions:

He didn't want her money. . . . She had written a will before she married my father. After she married him, he realized that her will would still carry on, and that she would be automatically leaving him half of her estate. . . . My father did not want half of Mary Lily's money, but under the law of the time, a wife could not exclude her husband from her estate. . . . He insisted that she republish the will . . . and that my father specifically agree in writing to waive his dower rights.

Did Barry believe this? Did he imagine that his father, without funds, turned to Mary Lily and said, "I don't want your money." He had already accepted money as a wedding present. He took stock, rode on the train, let her pay the bills at the Seelbach, and order up the roses and the stevia for Henrietta's party. "My father was so noble that he didn't want anyone in Louisville to think that he had married Mary Lily for her money," his son said. And what about allowing his wife to pay the bills? "Well, she had a great deal of money. Why shouldn't she have been the one to pay. . . ." Barry Senior said. His father was too proud to provide his children with any of the Flagler money for education or their future, but he was not too proud to have Mary Lily pay the household bills.

By spring the Judge and Mary Lily took possession of Lincliffe, an immense stucco-and-stone Georgian Revival mansion in Glenview set on the bluffs high above the Ohio River. Lincliffe had been built for a hardware magnate named William Belknap, one of the richest men in Louisville. Known around town not by its formal name but as "the Belknap place," Lincliffe had three stories, an oak-paneled library and study, and bedrooms and baths to spare. Plenty of room for children to come and visit, even to live, but still none of them, not even little Barry, came home. Besides, the Judge was back in politics. That year he had declared he was running for Louisville country commissioner in the November election.

By the summer of 1917 Mary Lily was no longer the "happiest woman in the world," as she had once written to cousin Owen Kenan. She was in a terrible state, but unfortunately for the Judge's reputation she never stopped writing letters home. The Kenans began getting frequent letters from Louisville. "They were remarkable because she was so sad and depressed," Thomas Kenan said. "Nobody knew what to do about it. Mary Lily used to write things like, 'I have been so very sad that Bob has said I should start going to a doctor. Now I go twice a week and he has been giving me a shot of something, a medication, and then I feel very good indeed until it wears off." Mary Lily, depressed and given to drinking bourbon, might have discovered the joys of morphine. Morphine and cocaine were often prescribed for depressed women, often for chronic headaches, and were a superb panacea for the boredom brought on by feelings of female uselessness. In this era, morphine and laudanum, an opium derivative, were easily obtainable at drugstores. It is easy to imagine Mary Lily, unhappy in Louisville, turning to drugs. Mary Lily would soon become as isolated by her addiction as she had been by her riches. She was a celebrity and a freak, distinguished by money she had done nothing to acquire. Her money became her jailer and her definition. Ignored by her stepchildren and with few friends in Louisville, Mary Lily had no personal resources to prevent her self-destruction. She was like many women of that class—Sunny von Bulow is the most recent and obvious example—who simply have no reason not to sink into torpor. "She was a sad case," Barry said about his stepmother.

That summer of 1917 was as usual hot and muggy in Louisville. For once, Mary Lily did not leave for her summer house in Mamaroneck or Newport. The Judge did not go to Asheville to see young Barry. In June, just after they moved to Lincliffe, the Judge and Mary Lily had a housewarming party, as was the custom at the time. A string band came from Lexington, and the entire grounds, according to the *Courier-Journal,* were strung with red Japanese lanterns. A new silent movie was shown on a screen set up in the garden. By this time Mary Lily was in the care of Dr. Michael Leo Ravitch, a guest at the party, who soon would move into the house.

Ravitch would be the shadow figure in Mary Lily's death; a Russian immigrant, a dermatologist who had been trained in Moscow, he and the Judge had become friends years earlier, when Bingham had been in politics. Although Mary Lily was being treated for depression and heart problems, it was Michael Leo Ravitch, a skin specialist, not a heart specialist, whom Bingham called in to treat her. Even stranger, Ravitch brought two assistants to help him. One, Sol Steinberg, was just out of medical school and Ravitch's own brother-in-law; the other, Walter Boggess, was a diagnostician. Mary Lily could buy and sell hospitals, and yet, ailing in Louisville, she was being treated by inexperienced doctors. "You wonder why her family didn't insist on bringing a heart specialist in, if that was the case," Barry Senior said. "Or why she didn't ask for one herself." The theory in Louisville was always that Dr. Ravitch was Mary Lily's drug supplier, a theory supported by the rumor that after Mary Lily died, Ravitch reportedly collected a fifty-thousand-dollar fee and a new Packard car from Judge Bingham and then, several years later, moved to Chicago. "Everybody knew Dr. Ravitch left town. He either got drugs for her or I don't know what— something underhanded, and left and never came back. . . . There were lots of veiled stories. I couldn't vouch for any of that. Well, I know the whole thing with Dr. Ravitch, but it was something that wasn't discussed openly," the daughter of the Judge's former law partner said.

June 19, 1917. What really happened to Mary Lily Bingham on this June day in Louisville will always be a mystery, although a few facts about her activities are known. For one, she went to see Dr. Ravitch and would have been driven into town from Lincliffe. Whether she went to Dr. Ravitch for a morphine shot, there is simply no way to know. It is know that when she arrived at Ravitch's office, she attended to more than medical matters, for on this day Mary Lily in the doctor's office signed a hand-written codicil leaving her husband $5 million. The codicil was presented to her for signature by Bob Bingham's close friend and lawyer, Dave Davies, who happened to appear at Dr. Ravitch's office that day too. Was Mary Lily surprised to see him? Had she planned this meeting or was she ambushed? The answer is lost to history.* Whatever happened, Mary Lily signed a primitive legal document on Ravitch's letterhead witnessed by Davies and Ravitch. The strange codicil still exists: "I give and bequeath to my husband R.W. Bingham, five million ($5,000,000) dollars to be absolutely his, and he shall have the option at my death of taking this from my estate in money or in such securities as he and the administering authorities of my estate may agree upon with respect to market value." It was written clearly by

---

*Later at the probate hearing Davies said "someone" called him that day and told him Mary Lily wanted to meet him at Ravitch's office. But he couldn't recall who that "someone" was.

someone and then signed "Mary Lily Bingham" in a zigzag
line.

Barry Senior has always maintained there was nothing unusual
about this procedure, as if signing away $5 million was a pas-
time routinely undertaken in the presence of a dermatologist. No
one can do more than speculate about what happened at the
doctor's office, as Mary Lily's own family later did. Desperate
for morphine, the unhappy Mary Lily might have arrived for her
shot to be greeted by her husband's friend Dave Davies. *Hello,
Dave, what a surprise to see you here.* Did he tell her: *Sign this
or there will be no morphine?* Later, Davies would testify under
oath that Mary Lily had asked him to write a codicil earlier, but
if that was so, why was this one written in haste on a doctor's
letterhead? Why wouldn't she have signed it at Davies's office?
"As I have always been told, this codicil was something my
stepmother wanted to do," Barry later explained neutrally, re-
luctant as always to acknowledge that something was askew.
"This was what Mary Lily wanted," he said, although he didn't
know Mary Lily and, like her own family, could only wonder
about her motives.

In early July the Judge bought three lots at Cave Hill Cemetery
with room for eighty-eight bodies. During the same month he
might have been thinking of making another substantial investment, perhaps even acquiring the *Courier-Journal*. Certainly, he
was representing the owner, Walter Haldeman, in litigation with
his relatives. The Haldeman family, in a bizarre foreshadowing
of what would happen years later, was battling over control of
the *Courier-Journal* stock. At the same time, Henry Watterson
was feuding with Walter Haldeman's son, who was about to be
named publisher. But if he were to buy it, the Judge would need
$1 million, more than Mary Lily had so far given him.

By this time Mary Lily was suffering terribly. The *Courier-
Journal* discreetly reported that she was afflicted with heart
problems at her home off the River Road. She was attended by
nurses. Moreover, Dr. Ravitch was now staying in the house,
and the nurses reported to the Kenan family, according to
Thomas Kenan, "that he was overdosing Mary Lily on morphine."

July 12, 1917, was a typically hot and humid day. A detective
report later ordered by the Kenan family stated that Mary Lily
collapsed on her bed with a heart attack. There is no doubt that
the Judge and Mary Lily were having marital problems, possibly
exacerbated by Mary Lily's addictions. He had written for advice
to her minister, George Ward, and Ward had later replied to

Bingham: "Would it do any good for me to write her just a casual letter?"

What is known and what is circumstantial about Mary Lily's next days now becomes murky. The house was stifling, not a breeze stirred off the Ohio River at night. The nurses complained about the heat, but more about the morphine. New nurses were brought in. Then Mary Lily's sister and brother arrived from Kenansville. On July 27, 1917, Mary Lily Bingham died, suffering terrible convulsions, a possible symptom of morphine withdrawal, though there might have been other causes as well. Ravitch did not sign her certificate of death, as if to detach himself from the event. The official cause of death was an "edema of the brain," according to the death certificate and a secondary cause was "myocarditis."

"It seems to me that my childhood was haunted by the ending of things, and that I never had much faith that the person or place I left would reappear again in the endless vistas of the future," Barry once wrote to Mary. What did Barry know about the death of Mary Lily? About the end of his father's second marriage?

Barry, now eleven years old, was in Asheville with his aunts. What could they have told him? He was old enough to read a newspaper, but he recalls, "I heard about it from my Aunt Sadie, but I was never aware of the fact that this was a national story or anything of that sort. It was just outside the realm of my imagination." Two days after Mary Lily's death, her family took her body home to Wilmington in her private railroad car, despite the Judge's new Cave Hill plots. The Reverend George Ward, who had proved useless as a marriage counselor, performed the service.

Mary Lily's will was filed for probate immediately. Her legacy was more than $100 million. Louise Wise, who had married several months earlier, got the real estate, which included the Flagler hotels, Whitehall and all the pearls, as well as $5 million when she turned forty years of age. Mary Lily's brother and two sisters received the Standard Oil stock. Almost every detail of the bequest was printed in the papers—her personal property, $16 million worth of stock in Standard Oil, and the mansions Satan's Toe, in Mamaroneck, and Whitehall. Her personal property was astonishing: 31 items of jewelry including a necklace with 213 graduated pearls with a round diamond clasp; 51 Oriental rugs at Lincliffe alone. Nineteen states made claims on the Flagler estate.

And then the Judge made his move. In late August he filed his codicil in the Louisville court. Immediately the news swept the country; if this codicil had been hidden, there could well be others.

Louise and Lawrence Lewis had come to Lincliffe immediately after Mary Lily's funeral. The Judge was acting the grieving husband, and Barry was brought back from Asheville to be with his father. *Poor Judge Bingham, left alone again with that lonely motherless child.* Then just before the Judge filed his codicil, the Lewises vanished without saying good-bye.

The story of their sudden departure [the *Courier-Journal* reported] has caused much comment in the city. Judge Bingham left his home one morning to go to his office and when he returned in the evening he found that Mr. and Mrs. Lewis had slipped away from the house and out of the city, without saying good-bye or even mentioning their plans to depart.

Since that time Mrs. Lewis and her husband have been almost continuously at White Sulphur and it is reported that several important family conferences were held at the Greenbriar Hotel and a contest of Judge Bingham's $5 million was decided upon. . . . It appears that some of the relatives of Mrs. Bingham did not expect her to leave her husband anything. This belief was based upon the fact that last December Judge Bingham signed on his own motion a waiver of any dower rights to the estate. The result of this was that Mrs. Bingham was left free to leave her husband as much, or as little, as she thought fit. Some of the relatives of Mrs. Bingham did not believe she would leave him anything. Some people believe that the matter will yet be settled by payment to Bingham of his bequest.

It took the news time to travel, but in the summer, with the gatherings at the spa, the Louisville people began to gossip about the strange circumstances of Mary Lily's demise. The children's dislike of her, the fact that she was marooned at Lincliffe, and then, most damning, that the Judge and his friend Dave Davies presented the handwritten codicil for collection. "So many of our family's fine acquaintances began writing to my cousin Graham Kenan about this sordid business," Thomas Kenan said, "that finally he began to be very suspicious about Mary Lily's death. Nobody in the Kenan family was going to question what had happened after she died. . . . But then this handwritten codicil appeared. The nurses said that she wrote this codicil verbatim, but then they got an expert to question her handwriting, it wasn't the same. They investigated her death because a good many prominent people at the time wrote to my family saying it was very suspicious."

The *New York Times* reported that most of her estate, "with the exception of the handsome country home she bought here [in Louisville] and other minor bequests, go to Mrs. Louise Wise Lewis of Cincinnati." Louise and Lawrence Lewis, a rich society boy, would grow richer investing the Flagler inheritance. Their son, Lawrence Lewis, Jr., now lives in Richmond, Virginia. "There was no question in any of our minds that Mary Lily was murdered," he said. "But the family did not want a scandal, we didn't want to be vilified in Louisville by going after the former mayor. And we certainly today don't blame Barry for his father. Why, some years ago we took our private railroad car hunting in Kentucky and Barry organized for us to be entertained at the Louisville Country Club."

Mary Lily's cousin Graham Kenan was not as generous as Louise's son in forgiving the Judge. It was Graham Kenan who "was the most suspicious about Mary Lily," according to Thomas Kenan, so much so that he hired the William Burns Detective Agency to go to Louisville and look around. The theory is that it was this decision that caused the sudden departure of Lawrence and Louise Wise. The report was "about forty pages long," according to Thomas Kenan, and "mostly the testimony of the nurses." "What the reports seem to indicate is that they stopped giving her morphine and that gave her cardiac arrest."

And so the Kenan family moved, swift and hard, against Robert Bingham. In Louisville with his father, Barry could not have escaped the stories, the fact that his father was accused of serious immorality. For eleven-year-old Barry, this scandal would have had to be far more traumatic than even his mother's death, but Barry's reaction was in character: "At the time I was living at Lincliffe with my father. I didn't know of any such thing, anything of that kind. . . . At that age, I didn't read the newspapers. And it never emerged in later conversation with my father or anybody else in the family."

It is impossible to believe that Barry did not know about the scandal, though he might have repressed it. For Barry's entire life he would never even allow the possibility that his father might have neglected Mary Lily and hastened her death. He denied everything, even that he had read the stories in the newspaper—despite the front-page headlines—that terrible summer and autumn of 1917. Barry was able to discuss the scandal with his oldest sons on only a single occasion when Barry Junior was thirteen. "He said, 'Before you hear this from somebody else, I want you to hear it from me. He didn't do it, but these are the allegations that have been made about him,' " Barry Junior said. "What I remember is not him saying how difficult this was for him, what he was saying to us was, 'You're going to hear this.' You know, 'Somebody is going to say someday in the street or in school, "Your grandfather murdered his wife," and before you hear that, I want you to hear it from me. . . .' And after he told us once about it he never allowed us to bring the subject up again."

A lesser child could have been ruined by this scandal, his trust in human nature gone. For eight months, from August through April, the mysterious death of Mary Lily Bingham was a national news story. Starting with the official probate in late August at the Louisville Courthouse, Barry must have lived through a nightmare of revelations with his father in the headlines. The transcript of the trial was published in the Louisville *Post*. "Now, this may seem incredible, but it's absolutely true. I was blissfully unaware of all of this. I think it was a terribly painful episode in my father's life, no matter how you look at it. And it's not a thing he ever wanted to discuss," Barry said.

Bingham was lucky. In small-town Louisville, no doubt the presiding judge at the probate trial knew him very well. Additionally, the Kenans were naïve enough to have hired Helm Bruce as their lawyer, a prominent Louisville lawyer who had been close to Bob Bingham in their days in the Progressive movement a decade earlier. What could they have been thinking about? The Kenans were Southerners, well versed in the codes of small-town politics. They knew Bob Bingham was "known to the community," as an old Louisvillian remarked. They had been shrewd enough to hire the Burns Detective Agency to investigate the crime, but not smart enough to hire an unbiased lawyer.

On the day of the probate trial Robert Worth Bingham and Michael Ravitch were nowhere to be found. There was no legal reason for Bingham to have been there because the probate was meant only to establish the veracity of the codicil. But Bingham was a former judge, he knew everyone in the courthouse. He stood to receive $5 million. Why wouldn't he have appeared in court? It is easy to imagine that he was trying to stay out of sight, but in fact Bingham had not seen his wife sign the document—only Davies and Ravitch had; moreover, Helm Bruce had neglected to subpoena Ravitch and Bingham, and the probate trial judge, perhaps out of loyalty to Bingham, refused to correct Bruce's mistake. Where were they? Ravitch was "on his vacation in Maine," the Judge said; Bingham was also out of town. That Bingham and Ravitch skipped the court procedure was an exercise in cool nerve. If they could not testify about Mary Lily Bingham, they could never be accused of perjury. In fact Bingham was in Virginia with friends, the newspapers later reported. "If you ask me if the probate hearing was run properly, I would have to tell you that no, it was not well conducted," Gordon

Davidson, the Bingham family lawyer, said. "They should have held up the probate hearing until they got the critical witnesses they wanted. Michael Ravitch is a witness to the deal."

That was an understatement. The *New York Times* reported that W. W. Davies, the only Bingham witness, "under cross-examination denied that he knew that Mrs. Bingham had been given an injection of a drug on the day that the document was signed or that she had ever been given such treatment by her doctor, M. L. Ravitch." No reason was given why Mary Lily was in Ravitch's office signing a codicil to her will using, as legal paper, Ravitch's personal letterhead.

Q. Do you know whether or not any medicine or any drug of any kind had been administered to her on the day of this codicil, either hypodermical or otherwise?

A. I do not know anything about Dr. Ravitch's treatment, but she had nothing in her manner that would indicate any such thing. That is the only way I could judge.

Q. Did you ever hear her speak of receiving hypodermic injections from Dr. Ravitch?

A. I did not.

On the stand, Davies was masterly and a true friend. He said he had no idea why he was called to meet Mary Lily at the doctor's office; this was "a medical matter." Helm Bruce asked him if there was any problem with the stepchildren, any friction in the marriage, but the judge overruled the question. Davies said that he had drawn up three prior drafts of a codicil that Mary Lily had rejected, but he had "destroyed them because she enjoined secrecy about the whole matter."

Helm Bruce, however, had obviously heard that Davies and Bingham had spent the previous night together and must have assumed that they had been plotting about Mary Lily's money. When Davies was on the stand, Bruce attempted to trap Davies into revealing that the codicil had been a plot.

"Mr. Davies," asked Bruce. "Did Judge Bingham and Dr. Ravitch spend the night with you . . . at any time the last two or three months of Mrs. Bingham's life?"

Davies answered, "I was ill one night, quite ill. My family was out of town and I sent for Judge Bingham and he came and spent the night with me. I had a case of indigestion, and was very sick and he came and spent the night with me. That was the only night he spent there I am sure."

Why Davies sent for Judge Bingham and not a doctor to help

him with "indigestion" is another question whose answer is lost to history.

Helm Bruce could not prove that Bingham and Davies had masterminded the codicil. Perhaps if he had been able to show what night Davies and Bingham had spent together, the circumstantial evidence might have pointed to a conspiracy. On the stand, when he was asked the date on which the Judge spent the night with him, Davies's mind went blank. The obvious question remained: Why wasn't Mary Lily's codicil drawn up in a proper legal manner? Davies was even able to suggest an explanation. "She said to me . . . 'I have a will, as you know, in existence and I am going East in the late summer or early fall to make some changes in it—or to make some codicils to my will and I want this codicil so that nothing I do with my will will affect this. I want this to be independent of the will if need be.' "

The implication was that Mary Lily feared that her Standard Oil trustees and the Kenan family would bully her about giving money to her husband. The probate trial became a farce with many unanswered questions and vast holes in the testimony, since Helm Bruce could ask neither Robert Worth Bingham nor Michael Ravitch a single question. And so the judge called a recess. "If I had been the judge, I would have called the hearing off until the witnesses, particularly Ravitch, would have been subpoenaed," Gordon Davidson said.

Two weeks passed. During the recess of the trial, the Kenan family made another blunder: they sent Burns detectives to ransack Dr. Ravitch's office, and the next morning Ravitch arrived at his office to find his wall safe jimmied. Curiously, the only documents that were taken were the drug records, not the medical files. In their haste, the detectives must have overlooked the most crucial documentation—a record of Mary Lily's symptoms. This story made the newspaper as well, but not the front page. "Ravitch's Dope Records Seized," the *Courier-Journal* reported.

Davies and the judge were forced to issue a statement on Judge Bingham's behalf:

It was reported in one of the newspapers some time ago that Dr. Ravitch, who, with Dr. Boggess, attended Mrs. Bingham in her last illness, had received since her death a present or fee of $50,000 and an automobile. Both these statements are entirely incorrect as Dr. Ravitch has at no time received for his services in treating Mrs. Bingham anything other than the ordinary fees charged by physicians.

And yet, at the Filson Club, there is a receipt dated August 23, 1917, for a Packard "roadster" purchased just weeks after Mary

Lily's death. Why would the Judge have bought a Packard when he had use of Mary Lily's cars? "That car belonged to my father," Barry said. "The Packard was his favorite car."

And then, three days later, there were more headlines—BODY SECRETLY EXHUMED AND AUTOPSY HELD LAST TUESDAY, the *Courier-Journal* bannered on September 24, 1917:

> Secretly and in the dead of night, the grave of Mrs. Robert Worth Bingham, at Wilmington, N.C., was opened last Tuesday. The body was exhumed and eviscerated. The vital organs were removed by unidentified physicians, said to be pathologists from Boston and New York, and then taken away to New York. The hurried autopsy was held in the presence of Detective William J. Burns and the body was reburied and a guard placed about the grave.

The grave robbery was hardly a scoop for the *Courier-Journal*. Three days earlier the New York *American,* among a dozen other newspapers, had already headlined: MRS. BINGHAM WAS DRUGGED! The stories reported that the Kenan family wanted to exhume the body. The rumors had been circulating for several days that the Kenans planned to perform an autopsy on Mary Lily. But in Louisville, not surprisingly, the story was still favorable to the Judge: HUSBAND GIVEN NO CHANCE TO HAVE REPRESENTATIVE PRESENT, according to the *Courier-Journal.*

> . . . Clothed in the vesture of mystery and secrecy, an unknown and powerful hand, which is only partly revealed at each legal turn of events, is daily making moves which seem to be aimed to dispossess Judge Bingham of the legacy of $5,000,000 left to him by his wife, who before her second marriage was the widow of Henry Mr. Flagler, multi-millionaire railroad builder and Standard Oil magnate. Startling and ghoulish is the latest move of this sinister hand.

The grave robbery dominated that day's page one even though on that same Monday morning the "flower of Louisville's manhood" had reported for service in the war when 326 young men entered Camp Zachary. But the *Courier-Journal* played the Bingham scandal with three columns on the front page and a jump to another full column inside. "The affair has consisted of rapidly moving events taking in every phase dear to a novelist from high finance, love and romance to death and mystery," the *Courier-Journal* said.

Barry might have spent much of his time that autumn writing poetry for the Aloha Club of the *Courier-Journal,* losing himself in sonnets with a survivor's instinct that was wholly remarkable. Whatever this terrible summer and autumn of 1917 might have meant to him, its memory would vanish from his mind completely. Like many people who suffer childhood traumas, Barry could erase chapters of his life as if they had never occurred. But his reaction was as characteristically Southern as it was idiosyncratic. His inability to recall this scandal or to discuss it with his own children was a reflection of the Southern code he had been reared with, a form of denial that was not dissimilar to the way his grandfather Colonel Bingham had once viewed the Lost Cause. The façade of the beau ideal was all. Barry's perception of his father's past remained so pristine that at age eighty he still seemed as innocent as the six-year-old boy who had once posed with his mother in the Louisville portrait studio in 1912.

10

That autumn in Louisville it would no doubt have been difficult for anyone who observed the Judge to believe that the Kenan family might be contemplating murder charges against him. If there was blood on his hands or if he was consumed with guilt over his neglect of Mary Lily, the Judge was a veritable model of calm, so controlled and graceful that his behavior was surely a future inspiration for his son Barry. He was waiting, and so were the readers of the country's newspapers, to find out what was in the autopsy report. His wife's vital organs were at Bellevue Hospital in New York being examined by the pathologists, yet the Judge was glad-handing and greeting the populace, maintaining a full schedule, as if he didn't have a care. He was involved in his campaign for county commissioner and went all over Jefferson County making speeches, attending lunches and dinners, the very picture of serenity. He adhered to a strict code of courtliness and kept up appearances at all times. He tried to enlist in the military. He helped the doughboys leaving to fight the Kaiser. He organized dinners, lunches and meetings, determined to troop the colors.

September came and went, and no report was released, which was all to the good for the Judge and his political campaign. At Lincliffe, where Barry and the Judge lived, Mary Lily's estate, still in probate, paid the expenses for the houses, Mary Lily's funeral, the servants' salaries, the heating and the telephone bills. The money Mary Lily had once given the Judge financed his run for office. But Bingham, running with the Democratic machine, lost. Although young Barry, at age eleven, had been brought home from Asheville by his father, he "was never even aware that [his] father was running for public office that fall."

In the end, very little came of the probate trial. In early November the judge ruled in favor of Robert Worth Bingham. Two banks wound up fighting with each over over control of the executors' fees and the case went to the Kentucky Court of Appeals. And there it stayed for months, a victory for Bingham. It

was a small-town game, for the lack of evidence and the poorly
run hearing were in fact more proof to the doubters that the
Judge had been wronged by the Kenans and Standard Oil. Meanwhile, as time passed, the Judge's case had become a cause
célèbre in Louisville: big money against an innocent pipsqueak;
Standard Oil moving against a hometown boy. Ida Tarbell's
muckraking study on the misuse of power at Standard Oil had
been published a few years earlier, and editorials pointed to the
Bingham case as a splendid example of Miss Tarbell's thesis.
The *Courier-Journal* and the Louisville *Evening Post* mercilessly
attacked the Kenans in editorials.

A typical article:

> The heirs of the Flagler fortune continue the career of
> lawlessness by which that fortune and the power of the Stan-
> dard Oil Trust were established. They recognize no right of
> individuals or of a State that may put any portion of that
> wealth, however small, beyond their reach. The wild but
> anonymous slanders hatched at White Sulphur and directed
> against Judge Bingham when reported in the Evening Post
> were denied for the purpose of concealing the diabolical
> schemes by which character was to be assassinated. . . .
> Somewhere there is a Mephistopheles, or a gang of them,
> watching over this great fortune to see that none of it es-
> capes the Kenan clutches, as it has escaped the natural heirs
> of Henry M. Flagler.

Much of this rage had to do with the potential deprivation of
the State of Kentucky of $3 million in estate taxes, but whatever
the reason, Bingham benefited enormously from the publicity
campaign. "The whole story of Standard Oil, as written by so
impartial an observer as Miss Tarbell," the *Post* continued, "is
a story of rapine and corruption, a story of a gang of men who
had that brutality always developed by irresponsible power,
whose conscience was the conscience of a Kaiser, and whose
methods were the methods of the savage."

At the same time, the Haldeman family, which owned the
Courier-Journal, was now split apart by a fight over the war.
Henry Watterson wrote strident editorials against the Germans.
The local merchants, many of German descent, canceled advertising. The Haldemans could not agree on what to do about
Watterson or anything else at the newspaper, and their family
fight finally ended in court over the question of who controlled
the newspaper. Paper shortages and loss of manpower brought
on by the war made matters worse. The *Courier-Journal* fal-
tered, and the Haldeman family, plagued with problems and
debts, told Arthur Krock to help them find a buyer.

Like most prominent Louisville men, Krock ate lunch most days at the Pendennis Club, where the black waiters still wear white jackets as if they were serving at a Kentucky colonel's plantation. For years the Pendennis Club, which excluded most Jews and everybody else who wasn't whiskey or tobacco or horse money, was where Louisville cut its deals. Before lunch, Krock, one of the few Jewish members, stepped into the Pendennis Club library. He picked up Somerset Maugham's *Of Human Bondage*. While he was reading another member appeared, but instead of going to the bookshelves to see what was new, "he walked to a window and stood looking out, the droop in his shoulders contrasting totally with the normal military erectness of his posture," Krock wrote in his memoirs.

I saw that my companion was Bingham, and when he turned, the dispirit indicated by his bowed figure at the window was matched by the expression on his face.

"You seem troubled," I said.

"I have been rejected from military service," he replied, "and abstention from it in wartime is alien to the tradition of my family. Also, I don't know of anything useful to my country in its need that is available to me to do."

"Wouldn't you be performing a great public service as the owner and publisher of the *Courier-Journal* and *Times?*" I asked.

Bingham, according to Krock, seemed surprised and took a moment to recover. "'. . . could I buy them?' he asked."

And so, in fine small-town style, the transfer of ownership of the finest newspaper in the South began in a gentlemen's club.

In April of 1918 the Kenans mysteriously dropped their suit against Bingham. The autopsy report was never released. Today Thomas Kenan says that the autopsy report "might be in a vault attached to the detectives' report." The Kenans decided that they would only describe but never "show" the papers. "We all decided we wanted nothing more to do with controversy," Lawrence Lewis, Jr., said. Thomas Kenan explained, "The Kenan family prized its anonymity and nobody wanted to be in the papers in Louisville. The family knew that if they did not pay off the Judge their name would be ruined in the papers. Only my cousin Graham Kenan wanted to pursue this despite the investigation, and he died in the influenza epidemic of 1920." Even with the immense Flagler fortune that the Kenan family inherited, they stayed out of the papers completely for forty-five years. "Until an unrelated court case in 1965, we have been completely anonymous," Thomas Kenan said. "But I have always thought it odd that nobody pursued any of the suspicions in the report.''

By August of 1918 the Judge had collected $5 million, with which he bought the *Courier-Journal* and, later, Melcombe, and presumably paid off Michael Leo Ravitch so handsomely that Ravitch moved from his apartment to a finer one near Cherokee Park. After a decent interval of five years, Ravitch left town for Chicago and then moved to New York. In the 1930's he published a book on Soviet medical practices that lauded Stalin. Shortly thereafter he died. The autopsy report on Mary Lily remained hidden and her medical records vanished.

Certainly, the Judge behaved miserably. He did not call in good doctors or even get Mary Lily to the Johns Hopkins hospital that he himself frequented. He kept the handwritten codicil in his private papers but did not attend the probate trial. His private papers from 1913 to 1919 were obviously culled. Years later, on the eve of the publication of David Chandler's book, the Bingham family lawyers prepared a thick folder of ''answers'' to explain these and other oddities of the Judge's behavior and made it available to all reporters at Bingham's lawyers' office. It included portions of the probate trial transcript, Mary Lily's will and death certificate. There was also a lengthy memorandum defending the Judge written in March of 1933 by his old friend Dr. Hugh Young when Bingham was nominated for ambassador, a favor that the Judge had requested:

> About six months after his marriage, just as I was leaving for the War, Bob telegraphed me that he was in great trouble, and on his way to see me. He explained that his wife was a periodic drunkard. Regularly, once a month, under some strange impulse, she would shut herself up and drink herself into insensibility. . . . On my return after the War, Bob came to me with the terrible story of what had happened. His wife had refused all medical aid and finally died in a drunken orgy. The newspapers carried insinuations that she had met foul play, and even some suggested she had been poisoned.

Young wrote that he had learned from two of the pathologists that ''no evidence of poison had been found; that examination of the tissues showed she had died of alcoholism.'' He said he had telephoned one of the Kenans, who

> absolutely refused to let any statement be given out by the doctors. . . . I begged Bob to allow me to report the facts and advised that he sue the Kenans for $50,000,000, one-

half their ill-gotten gains. With great magnanimity he said, "No, Hugh, that would again drag her name through the mire, bring up her terrible drinking habit and besmirch her character. I'd rather bear the ignominy which some people have cast upon me."

Gordon Davidson, the Bingham family lawyer, presented the Young memo as if it were the unimpeachable testimony to the Judge's integrity. "This statement makes it clear that there was absolutely nothing suspicious involved," Davidson said. Part of the Hugh Young statement was his assertion that in May 1917 he had asked Herbert Hoover, then Food Conservation commissioner in Washington, "to take Judge Bingham on his staff. The Judge was to move with his wife to Washington, where it was hoped she could be persuaded to take a cure for her intermittent habit of drinking and inebriety." In fact Dr. Hugh Young's memo, written sixteen years after the fact, only raised more questions. If the Judge was going to work for Herbert Hoover, why did he declare himself a candidate for Jefferson County commissioner? Why didn't Hugh Young, knowing of Mary Lily's condition, send proper doctors to Louisville to treat her? The overwhelming question remains: Was Hugh Young a reliable witness for his friend Judge Bingham? Absolutely not. In 1919 Young treated Woodrow Wilson at the White House and lied to the press about the President's condition. Wilson had suffered a series of strokes and his reasoning abilities were severely impaired. Young, as the premier urologist in the country, was called in because the President's bladder had ceased to function. Although Dr. Young warned Edith Wilson that the President would die of blood poisoning if he wasn't operated on immediately, he later issued statements that Wilson had improved.

The slight impairment of his left arm and leg have improved more slowly. . . . At no time was his brain power or the extreme vigor of his mental processes in the slightest degree abated. . . . The President walks sturdily now, without assistance and without fatigue. . . . As to his mental vigor, it is simply prodigious. Indeed, I think in many ways the President is in better shape than before the illness came. . . . His frame of mind is bright and tranquil and he worries not at all. . . . You can say that the President is able-minded and able-bodied, and that he is giving splendid attention to the affairs of state.

Hugh Young was at Wilson's bed and knew very well that he had lost his reasoning ability and often spoke in non sequiturs. For lying to the press, the doctors attending Wilson were severely criticized by Josephus Daniels, the secretary of the Navy, a former North Carolina newspaper publisher and later Judge Bingham's close friend.

But Dr. Young had no qualms about lying to protect the powerful. Like Judge Bingham and later his son Barry, he adhered to the gentleman's code. In 1940 Young wrote the Judge's widow, Aleen Bingham, "As requested by you, I have given up any idea of saying anything about Mary Lily in my biography," which he was writing. He told Aleen that he would submit anything he wrote to both Henrietta and Barry so that they could "make changes, suggestions, additions, etc."

By 1945 even Mary Bingham suspected that Hugh Young had lied about Woodrow Wilson to the press. Mary wrote to Barry:

> I had just written [Hugh] a letter last week to ask him about a reference to him that I came across in a book on Woodrow Wilson I am reviewing. The author intimates that Hugh and the other doctors who went to see Wilson after his stroke more or less falsified their public statements as to the seriousness of his condition, in fact, that they dishonestly misled the public into believing that Wilson was not as ill as he actually was. I hoped Hugh would repudiate this story.

Young never repudiated the story. Certainly, if Young could lie about the President, he could lie about Judge Bingham, his closest friend.

For the next seventy years Barry Senior rarely discussed the scandal with anyone close to him and viewed it as "the most sordid, dreadful gossip." But however much he suppressed the horror, an event like this can hardly remain quietly buried. Is it conceivable that the eleven-year-old Barry Bingham went through this nightmare without its affecting his personality? Yet there would not be a single mention of the scandal in the hundreds of intimate letters he would write to Mary. In this voluminous correspondence, which Mary read carefully before she sent it to Radcliffe, the only reference to his father that was not reverential was his comparison of Roosevelt's duplicity with Henry Wallace to "Papa on the defensive."

By the end of his life, when his empire had collapsed and the accusations against the Judge surfaced again, Barry had become so agitated that he could no longer discuss calmly any aspect of his childhood, including his years in Asheville with his aunts. This kind of agitation is a psychological commonplace: blocking out unpleasant memories puts a strain on the personality and distorts one's perspective. During the winter of 1987 his discomfort was obvious to everyone around him. His social grace had vanished and he would complain, "I feel dreadful. I am so upset about these stories about my father," feelings he did not seem to have about his broken relationships with his two oldest children. Although he was lionized as a newspaper publisher, as one devoted to his wife, and rich, he now behaved as if his very life was at stake, such was his inability to cope with his father's controversial history. When his lawyer finally put him on the telephone with Thomas Kenan in North Carolina to ask questions about the mysterious Mary Lily papers in the Kenan vault, Barry Senior reportedly completed his conversation within moments, his illusions presumably intact.

For years Barry has said only one thing about his stepmother's death. "The Kenan brothers were after my father. But they never released the autopsy report, which proves that nothing was in it." And yet, there must be something more, for even now, seventy years after Lincliffe, the mere mention of that horrible time can reduce Mary Bingham to tears. "Barry managed to sublimate what had been in the headlines," Mary Bingham said. "By which I do not mean he cast it aside. . . . These charges were an absolute torment for him. . . . He survived with an enduring love for his father." At that phrase, "enduring love," Mary began to weep.

11

The newly carefree Judge Bingham now had a piece of the Flagler fortune behind him and didn't hesitate to use it. His newspaper became his glorious toy, the instrument that would redeem his reputation and become the power base that would catapult him into the world and away from the provincial judgments of Louisville.

Under Bingham, the *Courier-Journal* was a mediocre newspaper, but so were most other papers of that era; it covered the local news badly but was merchandised with enormous energy and skill. The Judge's editors ran disaster stories on page one. *Courier-Journal* newsboys physically attacked the competition, for this was the era when distributors were independent jobbers who often carried guns and clubs. They set fire to warehouses, knocked over competitors' racks, and threatened store owners. The Judge's principal rival, the new *Herald-Post,* accused the *Courier-Journal* of padding its circulation figures and swindling the distributors, but the charges were never proved.

During the late 1920's the Judge instructed his management to offer pogo sticks, new cars, toasters, even a ten-thousand-dollar model home to the *Courier-Journal* salesman who sold the most subscriptions. But the Judge stayed out of town much of the time, shooting in Georgia and Scotland.

The *Courier-Journal* was run by the Judge's former law partner, Emanuel Levi, an enlightened conservative and a good newspaper man assisted by a former insurance broker, who thought he could help business by featuring freak accidents as front-page news. For years this was the level of the newspaper, although the editorial page was sometimes spirited and liberal, reflecting the Judge's very real sentiments. The Judge, like many other ambitious new publishers, liked to make large statements, such as his famous motto, "I have always regarded the newspapers owned by me as a public trust and have endeavored so to conduct them as to render the greatest public service," a bizarre claim considering the disaster stories that the *Courier-*

118

Journal ran as news. But the Judge took himself seriously, and pretty soon the town took him seriously too. In a few short years the Judge had become a man of "endeavors" instead of back-room deals and vanishing wives.

He had moved quickly to consolidate his position. First, he had to get rid of Arthur Krock and Henry Watterson, who, in his opinion, had long outlived their usefulness. He dispatched Krock to cover the conference at Versailles. When Krock returned, he discovered that he had been demoted, stripped of his position at the *Courier-Journal* and made the editor in chief of the afternoon paper, the *Louisville Times,* a less important paper.

Henry Watterson was not about to take orders from a man whose career he knew all too well. Marse Henry was an Edwardian, a globe-trotter and a friend of prime ministers and presidents, a literate windbag, forceful and didactic, still fighting the Civil War and, as a magazine said about him, "convinced that Negroes were not quite human beings, doubting that laborers and Yankees were meant for the lily-white heaven which he must have pictured as a sort of annex to the Seelbach bar."

Watterson and Bingham fell out over the League of Nations. Marse Henry was an isolationist, although he had warned of the German menace with such ferocity that he won a Pulitzer in 1918. He was seventy-seven years old when he was awarded the Pulitzer, set in his ways, determined not to cave in to a new proprietor who was anxious to gain the White House's favor. And so, for a year, Watterson's anti-League editorials ran on the same page with Bingham's pro-League views. By the winter of 1919 Watterson had had enough. The world had changed, Wilson was incapacitated by strokes, and a controversial former politician was running his beloved *Courier-Journal.* Watterson demanded that his name be taken off the masthead, and Bingham was happy to oblige. Krock always called Bingham's methods "unfair and unsavory," but Bingham was surely determined to bring Louisville into the twentieth century and, by doing so, himself into the citadels of power.

The Judge needed an important issue to champion, and he found a superb one in tobacco, Kentucky's principal crop. Ten years earlier the bottom had fallen out of tobacco and the growers had kept their crops off the market. Violence broke out through central Kentucky; any farmer who did not cooperate was apt to find his warehouse torched by night riders. Gun battles were common. The state, Arthur Krock reported, "fell into the extreme and violent disorder of a limited civil war." Now, in 1919, the newly rich and powerful Bingham was determined to prevent this from happening again. Krock had come to him with an idea: Why not start a cooperative for the tobacco farmers like

one the cotton growers of South Carolina had? Bernard Baruch,
a South Carolina native, had devised this plan and it had worked
beautifully to keep the price of cotton stable.

Bingham liked the idea and sought old allies to help him. But
first he had to get money for the farmers. Bingham asked for it
from a local banker named James Brown, self-made, unedu-
cated, a former cashier who got his first job from Boss Whallen
in 1889, when he was seventeen years old. From there he had
moved quickly through the ranks. By 1906 he had become president of a bank—a smooth operator who had made a killing in
Standard Oil stock. He and Bingham were friends. In his one-
year term as mayor in 1907 Bingham made Brown president of
the city's oil lease concession agency, appropriately named the
Sinking Fund. Bingham and Brown campaigned to improve Louisville. Together they directed the Kentucky Jockey Club, which
ran Churchill Downs, and they were as dogged as the most determined Rotarian to put Louisville in the center of the universe,
each for his own reasons.

Just before the First World War, Brown blocked Bingham's
plans to run for governor, but a few years later, after the Judge
had inherited his $5 million and bought the *Courier-Journal,*
Brown was ready to help. With another local bank, he lent him
$1.5 million for the tobacco farmers until Bingham could get the
cooperative legislation through the federal government. Then,
allies once again, Brown and Bingham arrived in Washington
together to persuade the War Finance Corporation to bail out the
tobacco men.

The War Finance Corporation agreed to guarantee loans of
$10 million in a plan that would become a model for New Deal
reforms. But far more important, the Burley Cooperative and his
interest in agriculture later cemented the Judge's relationship with
a young reform-minded Democrat named Franklin Roosevelt,
who shared Bingham's interest in farm problems and who no
doubt saw in this Louisville publisher a rich man with overwhelming ambition, much like himself.

Bingham was now a hero to the farmers of Kentucky, and he
was a great man in the eyes of his son, away in New England at
Middlesex School, still frail and lonely. Barry would later seize
on the cooperative as another example of his father's sterling
character. ''The [cooperative] he set up for the farmers gave me
one of my first indications of what a person might do, using
their power of the press which they could not do as individuals,''
Barry said. And just as his son would do someday, Bingham
joined every committee, every advisory board that would have
him. The L&N Railroad was now pleased to make him a director, as was the Liberty Bank and Trust. The Judge was a member

of the Associated Press, which was a superb base. Calvin Coolidge consulted with him about agriculture.

However poor the *Courier-Journal*'s reporting, the editorial page was often good. The Judge deplored Kentucky's public education system; he tried to help Negroes and the rural dirt-poor of Appalachia. He was advised by General Percy Haley, whom he frequently consulted and who helped him give the *Courier-Journal* its strong new liberal line. Haley was on the Judge's payroll and an insomniac, who worked only at night from his suite at the Brown Hotel. In her wartime correspondence Mary always called Haley "the dear General" and reminisced how he would take off his glasses and arch his eyebrows when he had a pronouncement to make saying, "My feelings about that are . . ." Haley was passionate about the idea of a New South. He was a subtle thinker, and he helped the Judge and Barry, in particular, to understand the distinction between the deplorable, reactionary South and "the somehow hopeful, somehow worthwhile region that none of us would ever want to desert," as Barry once wrote.

Such views were no doubt hateful to the two hundred old families that ran the town. The Judge denounced the Klan as "unAmerican and unpatriotic" and pushed hard for the League of Nations, warning that the United States would have to accept international responsibility if the world was to be spared another war. Although he was a Democrat, he refused to give the party blanket endorsements, and once even endorsed a Kentucky Republican for a United States Senate race.

In 1924 the Judge married Aleen Hilliard, the window of his stockbroker. Barry and Mary never had much use for her; they felt she was both pretentious and common. "They were extremely plain people—the Muldoons. Her father made tombstones . . . ," said an old Louisvillian. Aleen was the kind of woman who kept scrapbooks of all her husband's activities and wrote home every detail of her adventures, right down to the kind of golden silk frocks her dressmaker concocted for her when she was ushered into "the Presence," as she called royalty. In Louisville she was a member of a ladies' social circle called the Thursday Club, which met weekly on the maid's day off "and slaughtered every young girl's reputation in Louisville," said the old Louisvillian.

The Judge had learned a bit from his previous marriage. In London, two days before he married Aleen Hilliard in Westminster Abbey, he presented her with a handwritten codicil to his will, dated August 18, 1924, and written on Hyde Park Hotel stationery: "In view of my approaching marriage to Aleen M. Hilliard on Wednesday, August twentieth, 1924, I . . . bequeath to her my real estate at Glenview, Kentucky. . . . I further devise

and bequeath . . . the sum of one million dollars to be paid to
her by my executors. . . ." Here was another codicil mystery:
did the Judge will Melcombe to his third wife and not to his son
because he was disappointed in Robert, the heir apparent? In
1924 Barry was only a Harvard freshman and had yet to prove
himself. In any event, this codicil would long be forgotten by
the time the Judge died.

Aleen was always promoting her own son, Byron, Barry's con-
temporary, and everything Barry was not: a sportsman, a great
shot, an equestrian, a perfect example of Southern upper-class
manliness. He became a favorite of the Judge's, although Byron's relationship with Barry was affectionate. Byron bred horses,
and could converse with his stepfather on the fine points of Kentucky mares. "He was kicked out of Princeton," his daughter,
Elsie Hilliard Chambers, said. "He blew up a lab or something. . . . He was very proud of being kicked out." He then
went to Cambridge University, where he lasted a year. Aleen
followed him to England and took a house near the campus, but
could not keep him at his studies. Aleen would encourage Byron's relationship with the Judge, even inviting him to move into
Melcombe for a time.

"When he was involved in a battle, there was never any doubt
as to where he stood," a political opponent once said of the
Judge. "He was most courtly, and unfailingly polite, but he
never hesitated a moment to hit hard." In 1924 James Brown,
Bingham's erstwhile ally, bought the Louisville *Herald* and the
Louisville *Post* and combined them into the *Herald-Post* a year
later, whereupon Bingham began a circulation war that lasted
through the late 1920's. By the time it was over Bingham would
have spent more than a million dollars and, helped by the stock
market crash, driven Brown into bankruptcy.

Bingham was lucky. In 1926, a year in which he was often out
of town, the *Courier-Journal* won another Pulitzer Prize for a
highly popular series about a miner named Floyd Collins, who
was trapped in a cave in southern Kentucky. The *Courier-
Journal* employed a young reporter named "Skeets" Miller, who
was thin enough to be able to crawl through a tunnel in the
collapsed cave to interview Floyd Collins in his deathtrap.
Charles Lindbergh flew pictures from Louisville to New York,
and Miller's bravery captivated America's readers, including the
Judge's younger son, who was then a Harvard sophomore. "Oh
Lord, reading those stories made me a newspaper man!" he
said. Luckily for the *Courier-Journal* and Miller, the unfortunate
Collins lasted nineteen days before he died.

The year that "Skeets" Miller won the Pulitzer, the *Herald-
Post* claimed that the *Courier-Journal* padded its circulation fig-

ures and published photographs that the *Herald-Post* said showed piles of undelivered newspapers—papers that the *Courier-Journal* claimed had been distributed. Charges and counter-charges were traded. But Brown had outsmarted himself. The Kentucky Audit Bureau investigated the charges and found that not only had the *Courier-Journal* not been padding its circulation figures, it had been *underestimating* its sales. The Audit Bureau suspended the *Herald-Post* for a year for bringing false charges against the Judge. By this time the Judge and Brown were political enemies as well. The Judge was now trying to break the power of the Jockey Club, which controlled Kentucky gambling, a fight he would lose when his candidate for governor in the 1927 race lost in the primary.

When the *Herald-Post* resumed publication a year later, it engaged the *Courier-Journal* in yet another battle. In 1929 every Louisville daughter pined for a *Courier-Journal* doll called Flossy Flirt, which had "real hair just like Mamma's." Anyone who sold seven subscriptions could have Flossy Flirt. The *Herald-Post* then offered its own doll for each five subscriptions sold; the *Courier-Journal* dropped to five and then one, adding something called a "real baby doll."

Not to be outdone, the *Courier-Journal* sent to Alaska for reindeer and an Eskimo to set up a winter street scene called Santa Clausland at Fifth and Broadway, a block from the Brown Hotel. Eight reindeer arrived in Louisville from Alaska as well as a trainload of Canadian snow. Thousands gathered to see the *Courier-Journal* tableau. Unfortunately, the Eskimo herder drank heavily, and the local actor who had been hired to play Santa Claus insulted the black children. The *Herald-Post* then responded with "a real Indian chief," Chief Rainwater, but he was exposed as a fake.

More effectively, the *Courier-Journal* started the National Spelling Bee, which it ran until 1941, when the Scripps-Howard chain took over. But far more than dolls and reindeers and spelling bees, the *Herald-Post* would be done in by the Depression. By 1930, when young Barry Bingham had given up his dreams of writing fiction and was home in Louisville to start work at WHAS, there was a run on Jim Brown's bank, the Kentucky National, and Brown was wiped out. Everything was gone—the paper, the real estate, the bank itself. Perhaps as sweet revenge, Robert Bingham announced he would guarantee half of the Christmas accounts. "My father wanted the people of Louisville who had had money at the bank to be able to buy Christmas presents," Barry would explain.

At the beginning of the Depression the old Judge was rich enough to earn the devotion of the Kentucky National Bank depositors, rich enough to help his old friend Franklin Roosevelt

piece together support for his presidential campaign, rich enough
to ride out the circulation wars by spending a total of $1.2 mil-
lion to help put the *Herald-Post* out of business, guaranteeing
that the Bingham newspapers would control Kentucky. The family now had immense power, and by 1936 the newspaper would
be a monopoly. The Judge could leave Louisville behind for
larger worlds with infinite resources to support his ambitions. It
would now be up to his son Barry to run the *Courier-Journal*.

12

Autumn, 1931. No one could have been happier than Mary Caperton Bingham that fine September, when she and her new husband returned to Louisville from their wedding trip. Their summer in Europe had been a triumph. On their last glorious weekend in Paris, Mary had become pregnant, as she discovered a few weeks after she got home. With any luck the baby would be a boy to be named after the Judge, and Mary's status in the family would be assured.

Mary and Barry had traveled all through Scandinavia and France. Henrietta joined them in Antibes. "Barry invited her," Mary said. For Mary, no doubt the relationship with Henrietta was still tricky. Although Henrietta was wildly possessive of Barry, she also provided fun, parties, famous friends. What an unusual summer this was for a honeymoon in Europe. The Depression had driven most of the rich Americans home. There was a feeling of melancholy in the air, even at Antibes. Mary remembered the atmosphere of self-consciousness—the effort to pretend that the 1920's hadn't ended, or that the world wasn't on the point of financial collapse. On their honeymoon Mary and Barry had seen the Nazi Brown Shirts at the train stations, and the news from America was no less grim: the Hoovervilles, the riots, the lack of jobs. But however ominous the atmosphere, Mary and Barry had had three months of good hotel suites, champagne and parties before Barry brought his bride home to the Little House, back to the closed world of Louisville and the still more hermetic life in the Bingham enclave in Glenview.

Mary was twenty-six years old and had not lived in the South since before she attended Radcliffe. Whom could she have talked to in the Louisville of 1931? "I was a lot less Southern than most of my contemporaries," Mary said. "I was really rather a reclusive girl." Mary was not the kind of young woman who needed a circle of women friends. "We were hardly the Sahara of the beaux arts," she said.

As a bride in 1931, Mary Bingham put her large iron key into the keyhole on a pair of carved antique wooden doors. The Little House had a wide foyer with a living room to the right and a guest room to the left. The rooms were beautifully proportioned, with very high ceilings and double windows that looked out to the Glenview lawns. The library, the dining room, the kitchen were all off the passageway, "in the Italian manner," as Mary said. The banisters were wrought iron, and there were fireplaces in almost every room.

In the morning when she awakened, she could look out her windows and see the vast expanse of Bingham property, with its acres of oaks, boxwood, gingko, copper beech trees and red-buds, the lawns that overlooked the river. As she took walks with Barry down their hill toward the Ohio River, past the am-phitheater and the stables, she knew that someday all this land and the grand Georgian manor house would be hers. Years later, when Mary thought about this period in her life, she could hardly remember anything but Melcombe. "I can barely remember get-ting off the train in Louisville," she said. "But I vividly remem-ber the drive up to the Big House."

By 1931, fourteen years had passed since Mary Lily's death. Louisville had seen a world war and Prohibition, and now was stuck in the Depression. The Judge had performed miracles for the tobacco growers and the depositors of the Kentucky National Bank. If the subject of Mary Lily's death ever came up, the Judge had a ready answer. The Kenan brothers had falsely ac-cused him. It had been no more than a family feud. Everyone in the South understood that. Anyone who doubted this version of Bingham history would be reminded of the autopsy report: if the evidence was so damning, why didn't the Kenans release the autopsy report? There was no answer to that mystery. You judged a man by his deeds, and Bob Bingham had done much for Lou-isville. Thus his image changed. "In Louisville, like everywhere else, if you have a lot of money, you're considered a winner," a descendant of his former general manager later said. The Judge had lots of money and a newspaper behind him. His son Barry had gone to Middlesex and Harvard, and the family was rapidly making inroads into the national establishment. In just twenty-five years, the Judge, once a ward heeler, was now the intimate of presidents.

Aleen was now a pillar of Louisville society. She and the Judge moved between the Louisville Country Club, with its vast lawns, tennis courts and swimming pool, to the smaller, more exclusive eating club near Glenview called the River Valley, which overlooked the Ohio River and had a membership of ap-proximately seventy families, as opposed to the Country Club, which had perhaps twice that. When the Judge was in Louisville, he ate lunch at the Pendennis, with its men's-club comforts of deep leather chairs, carved wood furniture, scarlet carpets and white tablecloths. The Judge always had the kindest words for his neighbors, whom he inevitably greeted by name. He dispatched his reporters to write front-page stories about important Louisville weddings, such as that of the daughter of Owsley Brown, the bourbon magnate. The Judge could now dispense favors. He told stories of Scotland or of his friends Lord Airlie and "Barney" Baruch, or what a success the grouse season in Scotland had been that year. In Louisville the Mary Lily scandal was becoming little more than an unpleasant memory, although the Judge was still shunned by a few old families who refused to entertain him because of their friendship with the Kenans.

In Louisville, however, the Judge's borders were narrow, and at first Mary was forced to accept them. Louisville women were wives, mothers and hostesses. "You know what it's like here, you just go from one grand party to another," a Louisville woman said. At Christmas and at Derby time, there were often three or four large parties a day. "You would call dinner for seven-thirty and never sit down until ten," one hostess said. "People just drank and laughed and talked about everyone who wasn't there." Negro waiters in white jackets served. Men wore dinner clothes, women long dresses; the finest silver and crystal were on display. The Judge and Aleen kept three houses, including the castle in Scotland, fully staffed. "Come shoot grouse with us in Scotland," the Judge would say to his cronies at the Pendennis.

The contrast between Mary's life at Glenview and what was going on in the rest of the country was remarkable. Mary was rich at a time when Louisville had been crippled by the Depression. Almost 28 percent of the population was out of work. A billboard at Eighth and Broadway was a constant reminder, if anyone needed a reminder: ENLIST IN THE WAR AGAINST DEPRESSION. Prohibition had long since closed the distilleries, and they would not reopen until 1933. Six banks had shut down completely, including two that served only Negro customers. In 1931, Mary's first Christmas, men were selling apples on the street corners. The *Herald-Post* had gone into receivership just about the time Mary and Barry returned to Louisville, and was being run poorly by a new owner from New York who could barely keep it afloat. Things were so bad that the Louisville Country Club asked Emanuel Levi, the Jewish general manager of the *Courier-Journal*, to join; Mr. Levi turned it down. With all this, the Binghams flourished. The *Courier-Journal* was distributed all over the state; the Judge was able to spend most of the year in Scotland or Georgia, and he donated approximately

thirty thousand dollars to Franklin Roosevelt, who, although
governor of New York, had a keen eye on the White House.

At first Aleen made a supreme effort with Mary. "She gave a
lovely musicale for me in the outdoor theater," Mary said. "And
then that night at dinner I sat next to the dear Judge and what a
charmer he was." Aleen must have thought Mary an odd, snob-
bish girl who didn't understand the pleasures of being, as Mary
said, "girls together. . . . I didn't play bridge or go in for ladies'
lunches." Aleen's Thursday Club would have horrified Mary as
did "her ornate feminine tastes which ran to taffeta and satin
covering everything." In private, Mary and Barry referred to
everything Aleen did as the Muldoonery, an allusion to her simple family of tombstone makers. Soon their relationship with
Aleen became ceremonial. During the war, when Aleen was still
living in the Big House, the Judge's grandchildren would be
brought over only twice a year, and each time, Barry Junior
remembered, "Mother dressed us in coat and tie as if we were
being presented at court." Later, Mary would treat the wives of
her own married sons with comparable formality. Barry dismissed Aleen and worshiped his father, and so Mary did the
same. The Judge adored his new daughter-in-law; he reveled in
her Radcliffe classics degree and could see the positive effect she
would have on his youngest son. He would have seen in Mary a
kindred spirit; she had risen from poverty through ambition and
discipline, and she also had fine liberal notions and a cosmic
world view.

It would have been easier for Mary to settle into this rarefied
life if only her own mother had resisted the urge to use her
Richmond years as material for her journalism. Just before Mary
came to Louisville as the new mistress of Melcombe, her mother
had published a lengthy article in the *Woman's Home Companion*, which stripped young Mary Bingham, despite her imperious
Radcliffe ways, of all mystery. "How We Raised Our Six Daughters" must have been wonderful reading for the ladies of Aleen's
Thursday Club. Helena revealed the entire Caperton family
story—the hand-me-downs, the cunning, the lack of money—all
in four pages of the most ornate prose. Here was Helena Caperton on the subject of discipline: "I had only three laws but
they were as those of the Medes and the Persians; implicit, un-
deviating obedience; nothing but the truth; no matter what you
have done, if you confess it fully and truthfully you will not be
punished." Helena continued:

> Winter coats were more of a problem. Fortunately I had
> been astute enough to supply the eldest with an affluent
> godmother, who made her a present of a coat every winter.
> This privileged young person stepped out new every au-

tumn, while the ex-costume was handed down to the next sister. No one ever complained about this arrangement although it is on record that the youngest never knew what it was to have an entirely new coat until her fourteenth winter.

When Mary was seventeen she announced that she did not care for even the one year of gayety allowed her sisters and that she was going to undertake a college career. "Very well, my dear," said her father. "I expect it's like Chauncey Depew's model farm. He used to say to his guests, 'Will you have milk or champagne? They cost the same!' " She announced to a more or less inattentive family that she would try for a scholarship. She did, and got it, the Distant Work Scholarship, which is open to anyone who cares to try for it all over the country.

These revelations mortified Mary, according to Willie Snow Ethridge, the wife of Mark Ethridge, who became the editor of the *Courier-Journal* in 1936. Helena followed her *Woman's Home Companion* piece with an essay on man-trapping, in which she revealed how she had told her daughters to marry up; how to "implant the seed of fastidious selection from earliest childhood." However innocent and characteristic of the period these articles may now seem, in the closed world of Southern society they were considered to be in dubious taste. Louisville people were not written about in the national press. "One did not get one's name into magazines, that just wasn't nice," a Louisville matron said.

There are those in the Bingham family who believe that Mary's glacial and imperious manner was only intensified by her mother's magazine confessions. Her defense against her family had always been her ability to retreat into her studies. Now, as the young mistress of Little Melcombe, she isolated herself with Barry, retreating from, as she said, "womanly pursuits." A descendant of Emanuel Levi said, "My mother used to say, 'Who are Mary Bingham's best friends? With all those servants and all those children!' "

But nothing could blemish her happiness that autumn. Mary and Barry were sure that the baby they were expecting had been conceived in their small room at the Napoleon Hotel in Paris on their honeymoon. Later, when Barry returned to Paris during the war, he visited the Napoleon.

The red-haired concierge and all the old staff left the Napoleon in 1938, and the place is now full of WACS, but I had a drink in the little bar by the front entrance and thought of all our especially close and intimate connections with

that place. (It has always struck me as the most improbable
spot to have seen the genesis of Worth. . . .)

That spring of 1932 Mary didn't pay too much attention when
Barry began to sneeze and cough continuously because he had
such terrible hay fever. "At first, they thought it was pneumonia," Barry said, "but then, I was diagnosed with scarlet fever." The spring of 1932 became a nightmare for Mary. Barry
was severely ill and in quarantine. They had been married less
than a year. "I can remember that spring with sharp and close
detail," she wrote to Barry during the war. ". . . what a fine
one it was for lilacs, and the pleasure of picking a great bunch
of them to put in your room when you were sick, and how lovely
it was to be with you and take care of you then, before the
exorbitant Dr. Smith declared you had scarlet fever." On another occasion she wrote him, "My anxiety about you sharpened
all my perceptions to such a point that I can remember how
fresh and still the flowers were, and just exactly how you looked,
flushed and feverish in the cool white sheets. . . ."
No doubt she was terrified that she was going to lose him,
which intensified her need for him even more. Barry remained
in quarantine for weeks, although he was soon out of danger of
dying. In the last days before the baby was born Barry was well
enough to have visitors if they stayed out of his room. Mary, in
her ninth month, would stand on a ladder outside Barry's sick-
room in Glenview to talk to him.

I have been thinking back with so much pleasure . . . to all
the circumstances of Worth's arrival, how funny it must have
been when I used to mount the step ladder, in my condition,
to talk to you from the window when you were sick in bed;
of that wonderfully cozy and amusing moment on the lawn
with you and Addie, before I actually had to leave for the
hospital, and the heaven sent joy of the moment when Worth
and I came back from the hospital and you ran down the
path to meet us and see him for the first time.

Robert Worth Bingham arrived on May 7, 1932—"Derby
day," Mary said, pronouncing it "darby" day, in the English
manner.

If any event symbolized the ascent of the Binghams of Louisville into the American power structure, it was the Democratic
convention of 1932. On the opening day, June 27, more than
three thousand delegates and thirty thousand spectators thronged
Chicago's new stadium. Twelve million people were now unemployed. Farmers rioted in the Midwest. Tar-paper slums ap-

peared on the outskirts of such large cities as Philadelphia and
Boston. Each day the newspapers reported more foreclosures,
suicides and bankruptcies. In Chicago, the group of millionaires
who were backing Roosevelt—Judge Bingham, Joseph Kennedy,
Herbert Lehman, among others—were busy working the phones.
The Judge was a powerful figure in the South and stayed close
to Kentucky's Senator Alben Barkley, whom the *Courier-Journal*
had helped to elect and who was so influential in the party that
he would give the keynote address.

In the style of the era, Roosevelt was nowhere around. As
Judge Bingham worked the Southern delegations, no doubt
promising favors and endorsements from the *Courier-Journal*,
Joseph Kennedy was frequently on the telephone to William
Randolph Hearst in San Simeon, trying to swing his support to
FDR. For four days the convention held out against Roosevelt.
Often the delegates didn't leave their chairs until dawn. Through
it all, Mary and Barry sat with the *Courier-Journal* reporters,
while their baby, Worth, was at home "with a very respectable
nurse," as Mary said. This convention was of such symbolic
importance to the Bingham family that when Barry as an old
man thought about the Roosevelt triumph in Chicago, the visual
images stayed with him, the poetic truth of the event, but not
the actual facts. For Barry, for the Judge, for Roosevelt and the
United States, it was a kaleidoscope of dawns, a new day, a new
deal. "I saw Roosevelt come into the convention in the most
dramatic way. Mary and I were sitting in the press box, watching
him. . . . dawn broke, and light began coming through these
skylights into the room. And then, into this pool of light walked
Franklin Roosevelt. On the arm of his son. The most dramatic
entrance I've ever seen in my life. . . ." What was Barry thinking of? When the final ballot was taken and Roosevelt was the
winner, the governor of New York was in Albany, listening to
the radio. A few days later, when he took one of the new commercial airplane flights to Chicago to give his acceptance speech,
it was 6:00 P.M. when he entered the hall.

That autumn the Judge sent Mary, Barry, baby Worth and the
nurse to Washington, where Barry went to work in the *Courier-
Journal* bureau. Mary and Barry set up in an apartment at the
Shoreham Hotel, and Barry worked under the *Courier-Journal*'s
Washington man, Ulric Bell. Bell had immense influence in
Washington and had served as president of the Press Club; he
was a good Southern liberal who was known for his hobby as a
Sunday painter and his vast circle of powerful acquaintances,
many of whom he introduced to Barry.

Incredibly, the Judge believed that his large contribution to
the campaign was going to make him Roosevelt's new secretary
of state. He told acquaintances in Louisville that he and Roo-

sevelt had become extremely close friends, but "there were probably four thousand people in the country at that time who believed that they were on close terms with FDR," the historian Kenneth Davis said. Certainly, in December of 1932, Roosevelt thought no such thing. The Judge had made a close friend, however, of Colonel Edward House, the Texan who for over a decade was considered the premier Washington behind-the-scenes man, and the colonel promoted him for the job. Roosevelt joked what a "stiff dose for the international bankers" Bingham would be. In the end, Cordell Hull was Roosevelt's choice for the position, but, thanks again to the support of Colonel House, and against the advice of Eleanor Roosevelt, the President sent Robert Worth Bingham to the Court of St. James's.

At first this caused a small furor in Washington. Who was this small-town publisher with his affected English manners? Bingham was thought to be too biased in favor of the British to make a proper diplomat. His ridiculous Anglophile manner was almost a joke, even in Louisville, where his nickname was still Lord Bingham. He had many enemies who resented his penchant for political intrigue and back-room deals. During the confessional hearings on the Judge's nomination, the Judge's old enemies started a whispering campaign against him. A Kentucky representative named A. J. May vilified the Judge on the House floor. May's attack sprang from a vendetta; the *Courier-Journal* had written an editorial against one of May's bills, and May despised Bingham. On the floor of the House he called him "a swivel chair Colonel. . . . I imagine when he gets to England he will be an admiral, but I do not know what kind, and he may be what he was during the World War, a cowardly slacker." He went on to call him a "profiteer," a "police court lawyer," who took the "profits from the blood of the men who sang the song of victory at Flanders Field."

May was interrupted several times during his twenty-minute diatribe against the Judge with applause and, presumably, laughter. He called him a "carpetbagger," who

so corrupted the election [of 1905] by conspiracy and corruption that the ballot boxes were disregarded, and the supreme court of the State denounced him and his associates as perpetrators of a fraud and set aside the whole election. . . .

Who is Robert Worthless Bingham? He is the man who is going from the police court of Louisville to the Court of St. James. He is the man who at the sacred altar promised until death do us part when he married the wealthy widow of a southern railroad magnate. He married her, and in a few months after marriage she died under mysterious and suspicious circumstances, and he turned up as the beneficiary of her will to the tune of $5,000,000.

With that, the House burst into applause, but May was only warming to his theme.

Who is Robert Worthless Bingham? He is the man who, with this filthy lucre, acquired the Courier-Journal and the Louisville Times. . . . When this police court lawyer arrives at New York Harbor en route to London, if the crews on the ships know it, the whistles will sound on every vessel, there will be a chorus of triumphant song when he leaves, and the flag on every masthead will go down when he returns.

During these attacks, Barry and Mary must have suffered every bit as much as the Judge, as the Mary Lily scandal again threatened the Binghams' social and political status. "May was out to get my father for political reasons," Barry said. "But Alben Barkley, our senator, defended him." As a reporter, Barry was in the Oval Office frequently during those first hundred days, a fact that could not have hurt his father's chances. There he was, blond, charming, a twenty-seven-year-old Harvard graduate, who could banter with the President. Just as the Kennedy sons would someday bring glory to their father's reputation, Barry's affable intelligence was nothing but a credit to the Judge.

We gathered around the President's desk in the Oval Office, and each reporter was allowed to ask any question he wanted to ask, and would nearly always get a direct response, by name, from the President. And the first time I heard him say, 'Well, Barry, I think I can tell you that . . .' responding to me personally was a great thrill. . . .

Presumably at that desk, in a private conversation, young Barry could tell Roosevelt why Representative May had it in for his father, or how spurious the Mary Lily Flagler gossip was. Certainly, Roosevelt had too much on his mind to give May's partisan attacks much credence. But inevitably the story of Mary Lily's death began to get around. The President's aide Raymond Moley personally went to the confirmation hearings and told the committee there was nothing to the rumor. After that, Bingham's nomination was quickly approved. For the Judge, this appointment was answered prayers, the fulfillment of his own triple crown: to marry rich, to own a newspaper, to become the ambassador to the Court of St. James's.

13

The *New York Times* pronounced the new ambassador "a pleasant conformist." He loved the royal family and was genuinely upset about the Prince of Wales's pro-German politics. In 1937, when the new king abdicated and became the Duke of Windsor, Bingham wrote to Roosevelt,

> The Duke of Windsor was surrounded by a pro-German cabal and many people here suspected that Mrs. Simpson was actually in German pay. . . . However, the whole crowd has been cleared out. The Court has become respectable again. . . . The present King is the most stable and reliable of the four brothers and the young Queen is all they could wish for in character and fitness for position. Her parents were near neighbors of mine . . . in Scotland and we are old friends. Indeed, I have known the whole family well for a long time.

Bingham had a sense of the coming war and the danger of Neville Chamberlain's conservative politics. He wrote to Roosevelt about the "dangerous and menacing possibilities" in Spain. He often met with Fleet Street press lords to try to persuade them to cover American stories other than Hollywood and crime. He had every good intention, but he was frail and was slowly dying of cancer, which no one could diagnose. He took months off to shoot grouse or to go home to Pineland, or to see Dr. Hugh Young at Johns Hopkins Hospital. He took so much time off that Roosevelt once commented on it in a private letter. The British thought he had a condition called "latent fever." In fact no one knew what was wrong with the Judge.

Certainly, as the American ambassador, he was highly conventional and even wore the traditional black satin knee breeches to his induction. He made speeches praising Kipling and restored a tiny church in the Cotswolds. He visited his forebears at the town of Melcombe. The English, with their affinity for

134

Southern squires, especially those who love dogs and shooting, adored Bingham, and his time in London was notable, *Newsweek* remarked sourly, for the number of honorary degrees he was awarded by English universities.

In April of 1933, even before Barry and Mary got to London, the Judge was seriously ill. As always, the ever-loyal Hugh Young was called in for discreet medical advice. Aleen wrote home to her sister from Washington, where Bingham had gone to confer with the State Department:

> Bob has been quite ill with an abscess at what you might call the old 'seat' of trouble which became infected, and he has had a good deal of trouble. . . . Of course, we didn't want the rumor to get out that Bob was very ill, and he thought I ought to accept all the invitations, which I did. . . . If he feels better we may slip over to Baltimore, where he will be nearer Hugh [Young]. . . . I think you better not make too much of his illness because we don't want it started that he is an ill man, which he isn't.

In Washington, while her husband was confined to bed, Aleen kept busy. She went to the White House for dinner, and remarked upon the dinner table in "the shape of a horse shoe" with "all the gold and the china with the American crest on, which I have in London." She visited her dressmaker, who made her "two Court dresses, one a pale yellow heavy silk with bunches of velvet flowers on it. This sounds tacky, but it is really perfectly beautiful. The other is a heavenly shade of blue with silver lace over it. They are both sort of 'robes d'style.' "

A few weeks later the new ambassador felt better, and they were ready to sail. Aleen and the Judge were taking Henrietta with them to London, perhaps hoping to find her a husband or to launch her in British society. On May 10, Henrietta, Aleen and the Judge left in a "battery of cameras," as Aleen wrote home, for the first sailing of a new ship, the *Washington*.

Arriving at Plymouth, they were met by a delegation from the embassy and a cluster of reporters, including the *Daily Mail* photographer. Henrietta, in a wide-brimmed hat, grinned at her father as if he were the only man in the world. "New U.S. Envoy Arrives," the *Mail* headlined, "to Revel in the Countryside." Just above the Binghams' photograph was a darker headline: "Hitler's Speech: Will Disarm If Others Do."

The Binghams of Louisville now occupied the very center of power. The Judge brought his credentials to court and chatted with the King. "Bob looked too sweet for words," Aleen wrote her sister. Aleen taught Southern debutantes their court curtsies and presented a record number of young ladies to the Queen, including Henrietta's companion, Helen Jacobs. She redecorated the residence at Prince's Gate and got rid of the "dirty Aubussons of that hideous red color" that had belonged to the former ambassador Andrew W. Mellon. *Time* viciously criticized Bingham's speeches, and once at dinner Aleen had a fight with George Bernard Shaw. Cables flew back and forth, from the White House to the ambassador's residence. "Dear Mr. President," "Dear Ambassador Bingham." "My Dear Bob." Bingham wrote of his feelings about Anthony Eden, his attempt to deliver special foreign stamps to the King, trade agreements, debts, the coming Spanish Civil War, "the pomposity and vanity" of key Roosevelt advisers who had passed out of favor with the President. He gave speeches all over England, and the news index of the period is filled with his pronouncements: *Bingham Wishes King "Godspeed." Bingham Says Bankers Helped Depress Stocks. Bingham Praises Kipling as One of the Immortals. Bingham is Honored Twice in Britain. Victory in Arms Race Is Seen by Bingham. Roosevelt Calls Bingham Suddenly.*

Barry and Mary did not remain in Washington for long. Their second child, George Barry Bingham Junior, was born September 23, 1933, in Louisville. Barry wrote to Mary:

I remember so vividly the morning when I drove back to Glenview . . . after he was born and I had seen you for a few minutes. It was a particularly brilliant, crisp, cool blue morning, and the sun came up as I drove out the River Road, feeling sleepy and terribly happy and relieved. The condition of the weather seemed to me at the time an augury of the kind of disposition he might have. I love to think of his dear fat little figure and the freckles on his agreeable Irish face. . . .

A few months later Barry and Mary left their apartment in the Shoreham Hotel in Washington and came home to the Little House so Barry could keep an eye on the newspapers. He was now "assistant to the publisher" and filled with plans to turn these mediocre newspaper with their movie-star photographs and circulation gimmicks into something better. But he was annoyed when he came home that Emanuel Levi and Howard Stodghill, the two men running the *Courier-Journal,* dismissed his ideas and would not give him any real responsibility.

"My father discussed the appointment as ambassador with me," Barry said. If Barry had been afraid to supervise the newspaper, his father would have turned down the appointment as ambassador. "He realized that he was throwing me into pretty deep water," Barry said. ". . . I just thought I'd better take my courage in hand and go ahead and do the best I could. . . ." He was only twenty-seven years old, but he knew enough to know he needed, as he would later say, "a complete housecleaning."

"The whole time the Judge was in England we only went twice to visit, and that was only for two weeks each time," Mary said. In the summer of 1934, as much to plan newspaper strategy as to have a holiday, Mary and Barry sailed from New York. That June, in London, Mary remembered, "We were staying with Barry's father and we were driving down somewhere in the embassy car. The chauffeur noticed a car in traffic and turned around and said, 'That is Mrs. Simpson.' " The word quickly got around that Mary and Barry were visiting at the residence. Aleen presented Mary at court and "Wallis asked us to come to a cocktail party in her flat and the Prince of Wales was there. It was the first time I had ever seen Wallis." Soon, however, Mary and the future Duchess of Windsor would become friends.

Barry and his father had business to discuss: Emanuel Levi and Howard Stodghill could never make the *Courier-Journal* the world-class newspaper Barry wanted. That summer, he demanded that his father give him full responsibility at the newspaper. At first his father resisted, but Barry was adamant. He had worked with the police reporters and in Washington, and had a vision of what a newspaper ought to be. If Barry didn't have the power, he did have the salary, for his $1,500-a-month paycheck was equal to that of Emanuel Levi's and more than Howard Stodghill's. Although his salary may have seemed disproportionately high in relation to his actual duties at the time, he had a sense of his real worth and was determined to create a superb paper, and he wanted to begin by bringing in a prestigious editor. Barry's passion was the editorial page, which he intended to supervise. "I think his happiest times were when he could go into a special room he kept at the paper and write a column, which he did almost every day of the week," Barry Junior later said.

To cover the news, Barry needed a new managing editor, and he knew exactly whom he wanted, a man who could restore the *Courier-Journal* to the national position it had had under Henry Watterson. What Barry wanted was a great newspaper man, a liberal; a man who could feel comfortable with the small-town Kentucky publishers, the local rednecks and the advertisers, as well as with Barry's Harvard friends. The new editor would have to be a passionate Southerner and a liberal who was progressive enough to help bring Kentucky into the modern age. He would have to attack the corruption in the legislature in Frankfort, deal with Kentucky's backward education system and fundamentalists, go after the Klan, and push for the rights of the Negro and the labor unions. Barry's father had had General Haley as adviser, but Barry needed something more. Not surprisingly, Mary was powerfully involved in the search. They found the man right in her hometown. "I began to hear a lot about Mark Ethridge, who was at that time with the Richmond newspapers," Barry said. "Fortunately, I had a sister-in-law living in Richmond at that time who had become a great friend of Mark Ethridge and his wife, Willie, and I asked her what her impression had been, and she said, 'Oh, they are just the most wonderful people and you have to come here and meet them. I'll give a little dinner party. . . .'"

Ethridge was a pale Mississippian with a soft speaking voice and, as one of the reporters remembered, "a liberal firebrand" personality. During the 1920's he had worked as a special assistant to Franklin Roosevelt, and he was later passionate about the New Deal. He had even worked in Washington for Eugene Meyer, who owned the *Washington Post*. He was also a heavy drinker who loved to sing at parties. "My father would say to his guests, 'I challenge you to sing!' " David Ethridge said. The reporters responded to Ethridge's vigorous mind and social charm, and marveled at how he could "sit all night with the publisher from the little newspaper in Paducah, Kentucky, just drinking and laughing," said Barry Junior. But Ethridge was hardly provincial. He was idealistic, the best of the South, and Barry adored him on sight. "We kind of took to each other, I think, from the beginning. . . . I decided *this* was the man I wanted," Barry said.

When the Judge heard about Ethridge, he came back from England to meet him. Immediately, he saw that his son had made a superb choice, and the Judge turned the full force of his charm upon Ethridge. "Please come to Louisville to help my boy," he reportedly told him. "Help him turn the Courier-Journal into a great newspaper and I will see to it that you are rewarded." He offered him twenty-five thousand dollars a year, a tremendous salary for that time, and, most important, stock in the newspaper to be left to him in the Judge's will. Even so, it took the Judge a year to get him out of Richmond and settled in Louisville. Mark Ethridge arrived in April 1936, and began work with the title "general manager" at just about the time the *Herald-Post* finally went out of business, leaving the *Courier-Journal* a monopoly. Emanuel Levi was hired as publisher of the Hearst newspaper in Chicago for sixty thousand dollars a year. Later that same month Barry hired a financial man named Lisle Baker from a Frankfort bank. This was, as the newspaper inevitably called it in a promotional supplement, "the beginning of the unique Bingham-Ethridge-Baker team, a three-way association which ushered in the true golden era of The Courier-

Journal." The Judge retained the title "publisher." The "editor" who supervised the editorial page was Harrison Robertson, who dated back to the Marse Henry era.

With Ethridge in place for the *Courier*'s news staff, the Judge and Barry now needed a prestigious voice on their editorial page. Herbert Agar was to be their man. The Judge found him in London, a historian, a novelist and a critic, who had won a Pulitzer Prize in 1934 for a book he wrote on the presidency. He was six feet four inches tall and pompous. Henrietta knew him not only because of her London friends but because she had gone to Smith with Agar's first wife. When the Judge got to London, Agar was editing a literary review as well as contributing to the *Nation* and the *New Statesman*. The Judge loved Agar's elevated manner and immediately hired him to write a column as well as to advise him on "English journalistic practice," according to an internal *Time* memo. Agar was, the *Time* reporter wrote, "newspaper struck" as well as eager to get back to America, so much so that he even liked the idea of the South. Soon after, Agar was persuaded to work in Louisville, and Barry and the Judge could say they had a Pulitzer Prize-winner in the *Courier-Journal* stable.

Agar was tremendously useful in bringing the newspaper the prestige the Judge and Barry wanted. "He was like a kid with a new toy," the *Time* writer said. He had nothing to do with the news staff and dealt only with the editorial page. He immediately created an op-ed page like the one in the New York *World*. He changed the graphics and gave reporters five dollars each for op-ed contributions. He was a pacifist until he realized the danger of Hitler. Then Agar took over interventionist organizations such as Fight for Freedom. He was all over London and New York. Now he called himself "Herbert Agar of the Louisville *Courier-Journal*." The *Courier-Journal* was talked about by the same group who paid attention to the *New York Times*. The fact that the paper came out of Louisville was less important than the notion that it represented the South. "During that period whenever the *Times* or a national magazine wanted a Southern opinion, they would call a *Courier-Journal* reporter," the editorial writer John Ed Pearce later said. Barry, with his genius for public relations and his splendid taste, could not have picked two better representatives.

Agar was passionate about Britain and, before the war, wrote an editorial that caught the attention of *Time:* "We must give more and more aid to the British. We must send them planes, tanks and motor boats as fast as they are produced. . . . We must give them more of our over-aged destroyers. . . . So long as Britain holds out, the German-Italian-Japanese alliance is frustrated." *Time* devoted two columns to the *Courier-Journal* in its press section, more proof that now with Agar and Ethridge the paper was on its way.

The trauma of Barry's childhood was long behind him. Like his father, Barry was devoted to the Roosevelts, eager to assist them in whatever way he could. "The old propaganda story is being passed around in Louisville to the effect that Mrs. Roosevelt has made herself offensive to Southerners by a too great affection for Negroes," he once wrote to a member of her staff. "The tale is that she was visiting in South Carolina recently, and was scheduled to make a speech in one of the larger towns. She is said to have ridden to the auditorium, through the streets of the town, in an open car in which she sat next to a Negro woman, with whom she conversed sociably all the way." He wrote that it would give him "a good deal of satisfaction to know if I am right in saying that not only did such an incident not occur, but that Mrs. Roosevelt has not visited South Carolina in recent months."

Eleanor wrote to Barry directly: ". . . the tale that I was scheduled to speak somewhere and drove through the streets of a town with a Negro woman beside me happens to be untrue but I would, however, not have a single objection to doing so . . . but probably would not do it in North [sic] Carolina." The point of mentioning this exchange is the exchange itself: "Dear Barry," from the First Lady, in one generation.

That summer of 1936 the Judge once again left his post at the embassy for home and his beloved Pineland. Often he would be joined there by Hugh Young, who wrote an entire chapter in his autobiography called "Bob" in which he described Bingham riding in a hunting chariot as "a perfect replica of Julius Caesar." But Bingham wasn't well, and there were rumors in London that he would soon resign. He denied the rumors, but he missed warning the State Department about the abdication of Edward VIII and that mistake was blamed on his poor health. Bingham could sense war was coming and no doubt urged Henrietta to get out of London. To make it easier, the Judge bought his daughter a large farm just outside Louisville. Henrietta must have imagined herself in a Kentucky version of Ham Spray, Lytton Strachey's retreat, surrounded by friends who would come to visit. Henrietta called the farm Harmony Landing, although it would hardly be that.

During the war Henrietta would become very isolated and begin to drink even more. NO FUN ON THE FARM, read a large sign in her kitchen. It was her intention to breed horses, in the manner of her stepbrother Byron Hilliard. The family knew that she was already an alcoholic, and that narrowing her borders would make her drinking worse, but characteristically the Judge's solution was not to force her to seek help but to pretend everything was all right and even to hire a companion to keep an eye on her.

The Judge lavished attention on four-year-old Worth and three-year-old Barry. He gave them a pony called Jubilee, read them Uncle Remus stories, and one Easter filled a wheelbarrow full of rabbits for them and staged a lavish egg hunt in his outdoor theater. The Judge was now sixty-five years old and would soon die of Hodgkin's disease, which in those days was called "abdominal Hodgkins" and no one knew quite what it was. The Judge was forced to spend more and more time in America under the care of Hugh Young at Johns Hopkins.

In the spring of 1937 the Ohio River flooded and 75 percent of Louisville wound up under water. The Judge toured the area with the Kentucky governor, Happy Chandler, and Roosevelt's top man, Harry Hopkins. During the flood the family was praised even more because WHAS remained on the air for twenty-four hours a day with emergency information and the newspaper was printed in nearby Shelbyville. Later Barry would receive a CBS award for his work during the flood.

The Judge would not live another year. The following summer he was at White Sulphur with the family and had just enough strength to get back to London, but in November he cabled Hugh Young that he wanted to come to Johns Hopkins for treatment. He arrived at Thanksgiving and was immediately operated on, but nothing could be done. The Hodgkin's mass had spread all over his body. Hugh Young was in Bermuda, and by the time he returned "poor Bob was unconscious." Henrietta was by his bedside, of course, along with Barry and Mary, Aleen, the ubiquitous Byron and the Judge's sister Sadie. Curiously, there was no sign of his older son, Robert. "In a few hours he was dead," Young wrote. The *New York Times* reported that Dr. Young had escorted Henrietta out of her father's hospital room with his arm around her. The Judge was buried with appropriate ceremony with the British ambassador and the assistant secretary of state in attendance. Even the new king of England sent a short tribute, which the *New York Times* and the *Courier-Journal* noted in their stories.

Besides the newspaper, the Judge left $4,625,000, almost the exact amount he had been willed by Mary Lily. Far more important than the money was his legacy of the Louisville *Courier-Journal* and the *Louisville Times*. In his will the Judge repeated his maxim about the newspaper being "a public trust," and to prove his point, he had arranged for the family business to go to the only member capable of handling it. Barry got complete control of the newspapers and the radio station, although three thousand shares of preferred stock in the Louisville Times Company, valued at one hundred dollars each, were given to Henri-

etta and Robert in trust. As a further sign of his lack of faith in
his two oldest children, he appointed their younger brother as
their trustee. How galling that must have been for them, especially Robert. The Judge had been shrewd when it came to his
will. He made it impossible for anyone to challenge Barry's control of the business. He kept Henrietta and Robert from the
board and didn't leave them any Louisville property, as if he
wanted them out of Barry's way. When his own children were
adults, Barry would not display the same common sense.

"My son, Barry, has been associated with me in the publication of these papers and in thorough accord with my ideas and
purposes. . . . I am desirous of his being able to continue the
publication of these papers after my death, knowing that he will
conduct them along the lines so much desired by both of us,
which he thoroughly understands." Henrietta was given Pineland and Harmony Landing and the income from her preferred
stock. Barry got the Big House, but he allowed Aleen to stay
there. True to his word, his father reportedly had told him privately to give Mark Ethridge some stock in the newspaper, but
for some reason Barry didn't. "We just don't have enough in the
estate to give you stock," Barry Bingham told Ethridge, according to a family friend. "I'll make it up to you when you retire."

14

By 1940 it was clear that there was going to be another war. Everyone at the *Courier-Journal* knew it, wrote about it and agitated to get into it. Herbert Agar was spending more and more time in New York with his committee, Fight for Freedom, to try to enlist support for the Allies. Often Barry was away as well. During the coming years Barry would devote himself to public service and the war effort. However admirable this seemed at the time, his public obligations often took precedence over his family, a pattern he would continue long after the war was over. Years later, when the Bingham children were grown up and settled, they would often think back to the war years in an attempt to discover when the family had gone wrong.

Almost everyone they knew had a father who was away for those years. The fathers came home or they didn't come home and the families seemed to bump along all right. Like many children of this war generation, the young Binghams eventually would have a hard time unraveling exactly who this distant hero in a uniform was. But the war fit their own father like a glove: he was the elusive charmer, the perfect gentleman, admired by the city and the world for his contributions. When he did come home, he rarely scolded or disciplined his children, insisting that Mary take this task, typically avoiding any risk of confrontation. Barry Senior prided himself on being an Anglophile and believed that he was rearing his family in the traditional English aristocratic style, cosseted by servants and boarding schools.

By 1940 Mary and Barry had had their third child, three-year-old Sallie, who had been born in January of 1939, a year before the Judge died. Incredibly, despite the threat of war, Mary was trying to become pregnant again. A year after Sallie was born, Mary had a bad miscarriage and her doctor wasn't sure she should have more children. Her health was not good, she was too thin. Worse, her father had just been killed in Richmond—

a possible suicide, although this was never discussed openly. Perhaps Mary's way of coping with that loss was to want another baby. She was under great strain, but she wanted a dynasty for Barry, not because she was particularly maternal but because, as she wrote him, giving birth to *his* children was a "serious and deep joy." Perhaps with each child she could create another Barry, and she wrote that she had "the hope and belief that they might be as strong, and good, and tender and gay as you are, my dear love."

In Louisville the Binghams had become increasingly isolated because of their interventionist politics, and even eight-year-old Worth noticed how little time his parents spent at home. Mary and Barry had good reason, of course—these war meetings were crucial—but they were away so much that when Worth was a child and first heard the name Walter Mitty, he thought it was Walter "committee" because that was a word he already knew well.

"We were very committed to the idea that Hitler was going to try to take over Europe," Mary said. "And this, of course, was not acceptable . . . and the papers were very outspoken on that issue. We had all sorts of awful discussions and unpleasantness with some of our really good friends. It got so bad that at one point we just decided we could not go out to dinner." The angrier readers would often call in the middle of the night. "I had a regular way of dealing with this. Any call that came in at an unreasonable hour I would insist on taking. An enraged voice would say, 'I want so speak to Mr. Bingham,' and I would say with absolute dulcet tones, 'I am so sorry. I am the housekeeper and I'm afraid I have orders not to disturb him,' and people soon learned that they were not going to get by this housekeeper."

That summer of 1940 Mary and the three children had gone to fashionable Narragansett in Rhode Island to get out of the dreadful heat, leaving Barry to go to meeting after meeting with Herbert Agar in New York. Barry wrote Mary that Herbert "seems to have decided that the only way to speak forcefully is to call everybody a son of a bitch and a God damned louse." But the issue was vital, and the *Courier-Journal* was deeply involved. While Barry met with Agar, Worth and Barry Junior ran up and down the beach taking a straw poll for the coming November presidential election. In the summer of 1940 Narragansett was hardly an oasis of liberalism. Mary remembered looking up from her beach chair and seeing Worth running toward her, tears streaming down his face. "Worth came to me in despair and said, 'Mother, President Roosevelt is not going to be reelected, you know, because there is nobody on

the beach but us and Nursie who wants to vote for him,' "'
Mary said.

Barry was now only thirty-four years old, but he was considered a man of high ideals and good connections. His father had been dead for three years, and he had almost outgrown the famous-father identity. The "son of the ambassador" business rarely came up anymore, and when it did, it was to his advantage. That summer he had gone to Washington to call on Lord Lothian, the British ambassador, to confer with him about British war needs. "He asked me if I was the ambassador's son, and then if I was the son of the present Mrs. Bingham. . . . He burst out laughing and said he had asked Robert the same question and had had an indignant repudiation of Aleen as 'no relation to him, merely his stepmother.' "

Barry, like most other men of the era, was determined to go into the military. He enlisted in the Navy, "before Pearl Harbor," as Mary inevitably pointed out, in March of 1941. His motives were exemplary: "It seemed to me that it was essential that the United States should line up on the side of the Allies against this terrible tyranny that Hitler had organized in Germany. . . . I believed that I myself ought to go ahead and volunteer for military service of some form." There would be no difficulty leaving the newspaper with Mark Ethridge and Lisle Baker, who could easily run things while he was away. Barry even appointed Ethridge publisher, so that it would appear that he had full powers, a decision he would later regret. Barry was sent to Lake Forest, Illinois, to train in public relations work with a commission of lieutenant junior grade. The Navy's idea of training was to have him give speeches to priests and Salvation Army officers. He wrote to Mary that "the whole atmosphere in [Lake Forest] reminds me of the kind of life people lead when they have just gotten out of college and gotten their first jobs. There is a kind of raucous irresponsibility." He was far too busy to be homesick.

In Chicago he went to see *Hellzapoppin,* which he found pedestrian, read the right-wing *Chicago Tribune,* which he despised, and was taken to elaborate houses in Lake Forest where he was "baffled" by Chicago society because it was so "tacky," like a "country club." He regaled Mary with stories. At some of these elaborate houses, as he referred to them, "old trouts" would stagger up to him and say that they had played "a third assistant fairy" in the theater at the time of "the Iroquois Fire in Chicago." On the better nights he saw a lot of Adlai Stevenson, and one night at Stevenson's house there was the first Mrs. Hemingway. "It was fascinating to see the kind of quality in her that must have appealed to Hemingway, and yet to find her almost an old woman in terms of the Hemingway tradition." As

always, he kept his thoughts on the immediate present. Barry
did not allow himself to think too much about Mary and Glenview and, as he wrote to her, "all the lovely life you have built
up for me." He wanted to get out of Lake Forest, and so began
a campaign to get posted to Washington, where the family could
be reunited.

By June 1941 the Binghams had taken a house in Georgetown
at 2812 N Street, and Barry went to work in the public relations
office of the Navy. This was a particularly fine time for the
family. The three children were with them. Since the country
was not yet at war, Barry didn't even have to wear his uniform
when he was off duty. He often entertained such friends as
Archibald MacLeish, the Pulitzer Prize–winning poet. Mary
and Barry also spent a great deal of time with Jonathan Daniels, who worked at the White House and was the son of his
father's friend Josephus Daniels, the ambassador to Mexico.
Daniels would be a source of influence and information during
the war.

At night he and Mary would spend whole evenings lying on
their living room sofas, reading and talking. They took long
blissful walks down the Georgetown towpath with their children. That August they went to Chatham on Cape Cod, and
Henrietta came to visit. Her arrival was a disaster; she was
drinking constantly, and Worth and Barry Junior didn't know
what to make of it. Henrietta was so out of control that, finally,
Mary and Barry had to pack her off to an institution called
Hayfields, presumably the local sanatorium. Having done so,
they were so relieved to have gotten rid of her that they stopped
at a roadside café for a meal, as Barry once reminded Mary in
a letter. In his letters, Barry always referred to this experience
as "the deplorable Chatham episode," and it particularly horrified him because, he wrote to Mary, it reminded him of when,
as a child, he would see his older brother in this condition.

While they were in Chatham their son Jonathan was conceived. "The moment of his making was surrounded by so many
disturbing incidents," Barry once wrote to Mary, perhaps because of Henrietta's breakdown. Barry wasn't sure they should
have had Jonathan, what with Mary's previous miscarriage and
the expectation of the war. He would always feel removed from
this son, as if he didn't really know him. But Mary wanted more
children, and she would feel particularly protective of Jonathan.
He would be, without question, her special baby, and she lavished attention and affection on him in the years that Barry was
away, as if to compensate for her own loss. She carried him
through one of the most frightening and uncertain periods of her
life, but as her own mother once wrote to Barry, "I think he is

the greatest solace and comfort to Mary, a Balm in Gilead if anything can be in your absence.''

December 1941. Mary's youngest sister, Melinda, was to be married in Richmond. The ceremony was held on December 6. The next day was a Sunday, and the family gathered at the Commonwealth Club for lunch. Suddenly, the Negro head-waiter, "a very, very courtly gentleman came into the room and said, 'Ladies and gentlemen, I must inform you that the Japanese have attacked the American fleet at Pearl Harbor,' '' Barry later said.

Barry rushed back to Washington, and a month later he was borrowed from the Navy by the Office of Civilian Defense, headed by Fiorello La Guardia and Eleanor Roosevelt. His re-lationship with the First Lady and Jonathan Daniels, Roose-velt's assistant at the White House, had paid off. Mrs. Roosevelt decided that Barry should analyze British civil defense policies in England, a three-month assignment. La Guardia was con-vinced that soon New York would be under siege. So Barry was dispatched to London. Typically, there was delay after de-lay. The trip would take five days, but he wrote to Mary only the good things. The "embarrassing" Negro orchestra playing at the hotel in Bermuda, the great pheasant dinner he had—dressed crab to start!—the sunshine, the good times. When he got to Ireland and was faced with even more delays, he orga-nized a tour of eighteenth-century houses for the other passen-gers on the plane. In London he checked into Claridge's, then immediately went to a cocktail party at the Savoy and saw "forty other Americans on various newspapers." The next day he "was astonished to find seven invitations at the office." He was taken to the Ministry of Home Security and began touring shelters. He was even made an honorary member of a shelter team. He followed demolition teams and began sending dis-patches back to Washington.

He was a public man, as his father had been before him. In London he often took walks in Hyde Park past his father's old residence at Prince's Gate. At the park he listened to the soap-box orators and wrote to Mary about one wonderful exchange: "A heckler yelled at the speaker, 'Are you circumcized then?' The speaker yelled at the heckler, 'Only God and I know that.' Can you imagine this kind of thing going on? It's the healthiest, best outlet for people's feelings I have ever seen.'' He went to Oxford, where he sat at high table. One of his first weekends he spent at Ronald and Nancy Tree's house at Dytchley, near Oxford, where the sheets were like "whipped cream." Tree was an American who had moved to England; he was an heir to Marshall Field's fortune, and during the war was a member

of Parliament. Dytchley, like Cliveden, was a dream retreat for
prominent Americans in London during the war. Invitations
were prized for those country weekends. William Paley, who
was there often in that period, remembered it with fondness
because of Nancy Tree's taste, which was so exquisite that
"when she finished a room, it wasn't a room that you saw for
the first time. She couldn't make a mistake." Nancy Tree was
a great hostess and made Barry laugh with her superb stories
about life at the Astor ménage at Cliveden and about Nancy
Astor's astringent personality. Barry wrote home every bit of
gossip he heard: Can you imagine, Barry wrote, Dorothy
Thompson, Virginia Cowles and Nancy Astor were all in this
house for dinner one weekend, which had to be, Barry wrote,
"a baboonery beyond compare!"

A week later Barry had his own report from Cliveden after
"the old school friend," as Barry and Mary called Nancy Astor, had been on the telephone "with considerable slinging
around of invitations." He was delighted to accept one invitation and wrote to Mary about the beauty of the Astor "flesh
pots" and the view out the windows down the sweeping lawn
to the river. His feelings about the Astor ménage were complex. Nancy was his mother-in-law's friend, but Helena was
very much in her shadow. Politically, Barry hated Lady Astor's
pro-Nazi "Cliveden set," but would surely have minded if he
had been excluded from the grandeur. His subsequent letters
from Cliveden were often melancholy, as if he was overcome
by homesickness. The spring weather caused him to think of
"the exact yellow of our bedroom in the clear morning light."
At dinner Nancy had held forth about Russia—how dreadful and
hypocritical the Russians were. She reported that Russian ballet
dancers were paid "$300,000 a year" and "had to pay only
$20,000 a year in tax." Lady Astor had given over part of
Cliveden as a hospital, and he toured with her through the wards.
She would open the doors and yell cheerfully, "Has anyone died
in here today?" On another weekend, he wrote to Mary,

Our hostess was unfortunately in one of her most irritating
moods, and she rattled and ranted until it got very obviously
difficult for her husband to stand. He began to look like St.
Sebastian with all the arrows sticking in him, the way Papa
sometimes looked when Aleen got in her altitudes, and he
finally flung out at her with "I will not and cannot argue
with you since you don't know anything of what you are
talking about."

The detailed letters flew across the ocean: a walk he took in
Sunningdale, the students at Oxford, the interior of a Norman

church (a description that ran four pages, single-spaced), Vivien Leigh looking over his shoulder at the Ivy Club to see what famous people were coming into the room. He clearly did not want Mary to miss one incident, large or small, but his prose was often impersonal. At one point, Barry went to Coventry to view the devastation of the bombing and then spoke for fifteen minutes on the BBC about the extraordinary spirit of the people he encountered who have "no tendency to sit among the ruins and bewail their losses." When he gave his radio talk, he cabled home so Mary and Edie and the children could listen on Henrietta's shortwave at the farm.

Barry was thinking about investing in a West End play, having already taken a flier on a play called *The Fledgling*, which had run in New York. He wrote to Mary that he thought *The Morning Star* was superb, but "it is tied up by Robert Montgomery." One night after the theater he was having dinner at the Savoy Grill, and Clare Boothe Luce was at the next table being greeted by everyone who came by. "Everybody called everybody else 'darling' a good deal in these encounters," he wrote. He often wrote to Barry and Worth, but if he ever wrote to Sallie, none of his letters survive. To Worth he wrote that it was good that he had been elected captain of his basketball team by his "own men," as Worth had written him. To Barry he sent a diagram of an English train compartment and a long affectionate description of the passenger who had traveled with a fresh egg in his pocket. His letters to Barry were usually more detailed and loving than his letters to Worth.

Even stranger, in all these letters so filled with accounts of incidents and anecdotes, Barry, who had left for London in January, when Mary was several months pregnant, never once referred to Mary's condition. Could Mary have kept this fact a secret? Mary's letters to Barry are equally detailed and equally opaque, as if she were keeping her pregnancy a secret, perhaps because she knew he was ambivalent about having yet another child in the middle of a war. If Mary had kept her pregnancy a secret, Barry must certainly have been surprised when he came home in April to discover that he and Mary were to have a baby due in June.

Jonathan Bingham, whose godfather would be Jonathan Daniels, was born on the first of June in Louisville. "Thank God, I did not prevent Mary's having this splendid child!" Mary's doctor said as she came out of the delivery room, according to a letter Barry later wrote to her. Barry had to hurry back to Washington from Louisville to his job at the Office of Facts and Figures, which was run by Barry's good friend "Archie" MacLeish. The ninth of June was their eleventh anniversary, and Barry

wired Mary at Louisville: ''Am thinking constantly of the Swannanoa Club and the eleven wonderful years that have followed.''
Mary joined Barry in Washington with the baby, but a few
months later Barry was out of the Office of Facts and Figures
and on his way back to London to work with the Navy. The
summer of 1942 would be the last the Bingham family would
spend together for four long years.

15

"I won't dwell on that . . . blank hour of waiting after we got through [at the airport]," Barry wrote to Mary as he was leaving America, possibly for years. They had closed their house on N Street and said good-bye to a part of their life forever. Mary had moved to Louisville and into the Big House with her four children. "I imagine the children will have an awful case on it," he wrote.

It took days for him to get back to London, but he had a fine time on the trip. His airplane, he reported to Mary, was filled with Hollywood people, such as the producer Alexander Korda and the director John Ford. Korda had been on his flight home the previous spring and he had with him, Barry wrote, "the same copy of War and Peace he had dragged along in the plane last April, though he again found no time to read it." But more important, on this flight he struck up a conversation with a marine named Weldon James. James was young and from South Carolina, and, like Barry, a bit of a dandy. He had already been on the staff of *PM*, the left-wing New York tabloid, and had been a Nieman fellow at Harvard. James's style was very much like Barry's. He was courtly and adored the theater. "If you didn't understand the South, you might have thought Weldon James was effeminate," a friend once said of him. Barry and James immediately became close friends. They had much in common, including a reverence for the Southern liberal tradition and Harvard. From this one plane ride, their lives would be bound together for the next twenty-five years. They would share a flat in London; and after the war, Weldon would come to live in Louisville with his wife, the former Lady North, and work as a *Courier-Journal* editorial writer. While they were in London Barry often talked to Weldon about the importance of Southerners remaining in the South, and about the need for change that could be brought there by the educated classes. James agreed with Barry, and, like many educated Southerners of that time, felt far more comfortable operating from his native region. That

151

relationship would remain close until the war in Vietnam when James would disagree violently with the antiwar position of the paper and would sever the bond that had first begun to form on a Navy plane in 1942.

But that rift was to be in the distant future. On the night that Barry and Weldon James arrived in London the sky was bright with moonlight—what pilots called "a bomber's moon." Barry drove through London that night and could hardly believe the devastation. He checked into the Connaught, ordered grouse for dinner, and the next day reported to the Navy public relations' "crowded but cheerful office." He was sharing his office with an ensign who had been on the staff of *Time*. "The American correspondents mill in and out with no ceremony, and we hear many fine tales of who has the worst hangover, and who wants to cut a piece of shrapnel out of his jaw with a razor blade and save it as a souvenir of Dieppe." The reporters, then as now, met in Fleet Street at El Vino's bar, "like a set for a play by William Saroyan" with its wine casks, cobwebs and Victorian champagne advertisements. Barry was nervous, adjusting to the sirens, the blackness, the dirt, the sound of distant bomb attacks. It was, he wrote, very much like being at "a boarding school in which there is no discipline." The Americans in London moved between Mayfair and the West End, theater and parties—the endless parties.

He would have a terrific time working for the Navy as a public relations officer. He took the reporters around; they interviewed Russian survivors, went to Navy hospitals and air bases, and made inspection tours. Barry drove everybody in a Navy station wagon and wrote home how jolly it was—the drinking, the laughs, the complaining about the bad food. He organized press conferences, gave speeches on the BBC, helped plan press coverage for the Normandy invasion, and spoke on *Brains Trust* programs to answer questions about Roosevelt and America. Everyone who met Barry in London commented on his spirits and grace, and when he was awarded a Bronze Star by the Navy for his skills, the citation commended him particularly for his "cheerful and diplomatic liaison."

In these first few weeks back in London, Barry saw a lot of Douglas Fairbanks, Jr., played tennis often at Queens, the private grass courts club, and arranged inspection tours for Arthur Sulzberger, who was coming over from New York. He took Joe Liebling of *The New Yorker* around and went to see Hermione Gingold on stage in the West End. London was filled with Americans. Grosvenor Square was nicknamed Eisenhowerplatz or Little America. It wasn't so bad at all, he wrote to Mary, except when he thought about the early morning light at Glenview and the first sight "of Jonathan kicking his feet on his canvas bath-table.'' He had a few sad moments like that when he saw other people's children and they made him think of his own, or later when he heard the Derby broadcast on the BBC and heard the strains of "My Old Kentucky Home." Then he would remember the "translucent spring weather" when he and Marry, pregnant with Worth, would get up before dawn to watch the workouts. For that matter, whenever he heard any song that reminded him of Mary, his "heart would be in his mouth," and often his eyes would fill with tears, he wrote to her, if he heard "Dancing in the Dark" or "The Very Thought of You."

He knew he would be happier when he was settled into his own flat with his new friend Weldon James. They were looking for something smart and near the office, but a good flat was impossible to find. The embassy told him that he should get "special treatment" and to use his father's name, but he had no intention of doing that. And, in the end, he didn't have to. One night, at a party, he met a famous actress who had a terrific flat at 49 Hill Street that she was delighted to rent to him and Weldon James. The sitting room was large and bright, with Hogarth prints and chintz curtains framing the windows. There were two large bedrooms, a bath, a kitchen and the use of Lady Jersey's faithful charlady. Barry wrote to Mary about the flat's red-and-white-striped satin upholstery and the pale yellow sitting room.

Mary settled into Louisville, as sad as she had ever been since that gray, cold Paris winter of 1931. She was forced to be both mother and father to her four children, and as the war progressed she would become much harsher from the strain of being without Barry. It is easy to imagine the pressure Mary was under, trying to cope with four children who ranged in age from three months to ten years—the relentless, grinding demands of two active little boys and a four-year-old daughter seeking constant attention, all of which would have been punctuated by an infant's cries. Many women left at home had severe reactions; they found solace in alcohol, had affairs, spent their time doing war work, or simply became helpless. Mary would react to her personal grief over Barry's absence by seemingly becoming tougher toward those around her and more judgmental, a pattern she would seem to repeat decades later when Jonathan and Worth were killed in tragic accidents. As the war dragged on, Mary's letters to Barry became fiercer and filled with opinions.

At the beginning, however, with no sense that the war would go on for years, Mary was grateful that Barry was so well taken care of in London. She wrote that she knew she was a lot luckier than most women, and she took no pride in her feelings of special grief, her inchoate longing for him. She knew he was more or less safe being in London as a Navy public relations officer.

Although Mary hired retired police captains to take care of her children, she had a strict sense of obligation and refused to ask for extra gas rations, even though she qualified for them because of the newspaper. Consequently the family was somewhat isolated in the country and Mary rarely took her children to visit friends in town. The newspaper became her life because it was Barry's life, and she wanted to be his eyes and ears while he was away, but also because she surely must have felt secure around the liberal coterie at the newspaper. She often spent three days each week in the office, traveling by bus into town an hour each way, to write editorials and attend news meetings. Every three days she sat down and wrote her husband a letter, thousands of words, page after page, single-spaced, typed or written in her own delicate hand. Who was saying what at the newspaper, who was thinking about running for office in Kentucky, who had been over, if Henrietta was drinking or not, what gaucheries had been committed by whom, who was an anti-Semite, and what the children were doing. But mostly she wrote of her longing for him: "I take great comfort . . . that the roots of our life together are very strong and very enduring so that our thoughts flow on together in a harmonious and marvelously sympathetic course, even now. To think of that makes me feel less *banished*, as poor Romeo used that word in an anguished moan in Father Lawrence's cell." Years of letters fill crates at the Schlesinger collection for women's studies at Radcliffe. Writing those letters must have been almost a full-time occupation in itself.

Mary never did traditional women's war work and at first was criticized for this in Louisville. By working at the newspaper, she was thought to be doing her "husband's work" instead of contributing by sewing bias hems at Bundles for Britain or serving coffee at the Tenth Street canteen. When Mary heard these accusations, she was outraged. Why would she sew hems or serve coffee? Her mother-in-law, Madam Queen, as she and Barry called her, was the head of Bundles for Britain, and Mary would have viewed working there as a punishment, an extension of the vile Thursday Club. Her work, newspaper work, was the real work, and that was her contribution to the war effort.

Mary took some consolation in knowing that Barry would receive special treatment during the war because of their relationship with the Roosevelts. By this time Mary and Barry had stayed at the White House after a cabinet dinner, and Eleanor Roosevelt had come to Louisville and spent the night in Glenview. "Papa's friend," as Mary and Barry called Roosevelt in code, would keep an eye out for Barry. Even Mark Ethridge had a strong relationship with the President, for Roosevelt had appointed him head of his Fair Employment Practice Committee at the beginning of the war. And so, Ethridge, like Jonathan Daniels, would be a source of more information and influence.

Herbert Agar was working for the American ambassador, John Winant, in the embassy in London, and Barry and Agar were often in the English newspapers and in the local gossip columns, after giving speeches or going to parties. Only rarely did Barry have a difficult relationship with other naval officers, men who resented his prestige and social connections. For a time one of Barry's commanding officers would light fires with his unopened *Courier-Journals*, a practice that enraged Barry. But the officer was finally won over when he happened to see a picture of Barry's children posed outside Melcombe. "Is that your house? Boy, look at those columns!" the commanding officer had remarked, and from that moment on he left Barry alone.

In the meantime Mary wrote Barry so much about life in Glenview, pages and pages of detail, that he never had to worry that he was missing anything, or that later, struck with war fever, he would have to hurry home. She wrote Barry that the servants were cleaning out the "the entire estate" to donate everything metal to the war effort. Out went the Judge's "dog exerciser" from Pineland, the outworn boilers and the mowing machines, eight tons out of Melcombe in all. She sent the Judge's priceless matched set of Purdey shotguns off to the Battle of Britain. To this day, her son Barry Junior will never forgive her for sending the guns to England. But Barry Senior had no sentiment for his father's hunting gear and wrote to Mary how amusing it was to think of "those capitalistic dream clothes of Papa's hunting days" going to the Soviets, and the "incongruous picture presented by some kulak trudging across the steppes in Huntsman's best tweed shooting costume, topped off by a pearl grey fedora from Locke."

Mary maintained proper standards of behavior: at night the children had to dress for dinner and first met in the library for an aperitif of tomato juice. She required Worth and Barry to put on "clean shirts" and Sallie to wear "a long dressing gown." This was, Mary wrote, so they would not all descend to a "perpetual nursery existence."

There was little chance of that. Mary was still the wife of the president of the Louisville *Courier-Journal* and *Louisville Times*. She was a queen bee in a small town. Politicians fawned over her, and she certainly was sought after for favors and influence. Like many newspaper owners, she surrounded herself mostly with admirers. She believed that she had the power to reward and punish through the influence of the newspaper, and developed an increasing sense of her own power. On the train coming back to Louisville, the governor of Kentucky, Happy Chandler, whom she despised, had sat down next to her and attempted "the great-eyed country boy" act to explain how he happened to build a private swimming pool with state funds. "The boys were nearly desperate with boredom," she wrote.

Mary reorganized the *Courier-Journal* book page and assigned reviews to all of her friends. She wrote searing editorials on day care and " 'the latch-key kids' and the children left in automobiles all day." She attacked Clare Boothe Luce's campaign for Congress in the same querulous tone she would later use with her children. "Like . . . the rude girl in the fairy story, when she opens her mouth, lizards and toads begin to fall in profuse abundance. . . . her campaign . . . could hardly be more ignorant, more brattish or irresponsible."

That autumn Roosevelt's vice president, Henry Wallace, came to Louisville to speak at a meeting of a group called Friends of the Land. Although Mary did not know Wallace personally, she was expected to entertain him. She was thrilled to do so not only because Wallace was vice president but because his politics were exactly hers. Mary wrote to Barry:

His tacky host . . . asked if he might play tennis here. . . . There isn't anybody else I can think of that I would go to so much trouble for, but since he is such a crush of mine I have had Loubelle and Captain Bud carrying off the leaves for the last two days, both of them as agitated as the gardeners in Alice who were trying to paint the roses the right color before the queen came along.

It would take years for Mary to understand that Henry Wallace, with his strange mysticism and Communist connections, was hardly a hero, and in fact was the kind of myopic politician whose excesses someday would give liberalism a bad name. During the war Mary marveled at his "pure virtue" and compared him with Abraham Lincoln. Mary honored him with one of her grandest dinner parties. She invited Mark and Willie Ethridge, of course, but had been trapped into having her sister Helena and her archconservative husband, W. L. Lyons, whom Mary disliked.

. . . the children got themselves suitably dressed in order to shake hands with the Vice-President. I'm afraid he was rather a disappointment to them as he is without any small talk, even to children. . . . Barry said afterwards that he seemed to be a very silent man, and he seemed to have nothing to say standing up and nothing to say sitting down.

Mary talked to the Vice President about "Group Medicine," learning languages, and "the vermin press's attack on him" over his position on the rubber shortage. But the evening collapsed after dinner. "I don't believe I have ever had a more simply miserable time," Mary wrote. Helena, who had been "acutely flannel mouthed even before dinner," now cornered the Vice President "with that wild mascara'd eye . . . and, I suppose, reviled the New Deal until the Vice-President was rescued."

After dinner, Mary ventured into the dangerous late-night "bourbon zone" of the country club. For a Bingham, this was hazardous territory. The "bourbons," as the old Kentucky whiskey and tobacco powers were called, were a loud-mouthed, conservative group. Many were white supremacists and anti-Semites, with little use for the *Courier*. Mary gloomily wrote Barry about one of the bourbons who, deep in his cups, told Mary that the *Courier*'s position on "mental hygiene" was absurd and mentally ill people should be killed. A local Republican politician bragged to Mary that he had "massacred" Wallace about the rubber-shortage issue. In a rage Mary wrote, "You see, these people never change. They are pure Fascists, and I believe American Fascism of this type more deadly even than European Fascism. It has the violence of lynching in it, and, with people like these, there is absolutely no historical perspective. They are like greedy children. . . ." She went home from the country club in a foul mood, feeling lonely and isolated, and not consoled at all by her conquest of the Vice President. None of the harsh words had bothered Wallace, however. The next time he came to Louisville, Wallace made sure to alert her to his arrival and arranged to spend the afternoon playing tennis on her court.

Christmastime, 1942, was a terrible holiday for her, the first Christmas without Barry. Even the children were little consolation to her. Now, with Barry in London, Mary was sleepless, worrying about the bombs. She grew panicky if his letters were slow in coming and would often send cables to make sure he was alive. She was too heartbroken that Barry wasn't with her in Glenview to do up the tree, as they had always done on Christmas Eve, her birthday. One particularly bad night Mary had awakened "with the queerest nightmare," she wrote to Barry, ". . . that it was *next* Christmas, 1943, and that things were just exactly as they are now, and that the prospect of your being away was endless. The sense of dread that hung over me made me realize that quite a large part of me is unable to accept the *duration* part of this sentence."

On the first Christmas they were separated, Mary tried to have a holiday heart. She invited Robert and Henrietta to Glenview. The Binghams' nanny, Nursie, and the children arranged a surprise entertainment for her birthday, "with much surreptitious rustling of paper costumes, and hoarse whispers for days in advance." The children had presented their mother with what they knew she would love, a theatrical entertainment in the music room. Mary described it to Barry in detail, noting that "dear Nursie's heavy hand was apparent throughout." The first scene consisted of four-year-old Sallie in a red, white and blue costume, "a toothless and smirking Columbia," while the boys in their Cub Scout uniforms waved American flags. Then there was a tableau in which "Sallie in a blue head veil [held] Jonathan, in swaddling shawls, while the boys, dressed in your Father's red Oxford robes, adequately supported the main actors as Melchior and Balthazar, singing 'Silent Night.' "

Mary wrote to Barry that his birthday cable arrived and was "read to me by the operator at the Courier, whose voice was so sympathetic that she nearly broke me up." Mary thanked Barry for the loving message and "for my real birthday which came when you loved me, and for all our beautiful and happy life together. Nothing can assuage the constant pain of your absence. . . ."

Mary was an independent woman who was deeply in love with her husband, and in 1942 she had four children to supervise without their father to help. As a mother, Mary ruled from the head rather than the heart. She had a huge house, servants and money, which certainly made her job easier, but exacerbated her tendency to pursue her own interests. "I'm afraid I am a very unnatural mama, as I really regret the prospect of long days tending the swimming pool instead of days delving into the Congressional Record and following minutely the curious convolutions of American politics," Mary wrote before one school vacation.

She loved her children, but if they did not live up to her standards, she never blamed herself, she blamed them. "Original sin," she would call these lapses. She seemed to have little guilt and less empathy, even at the end of her life when her two favorite sons were dead and Sallie and Barry Junior would hardly speak to her. She advised her younger daughter, Eleanor, who was born after the war, "Focus on your husband. He is the one who really matters. He is the most important."

And yet, however cold she later appeared, Mary was not an inattentive mother. She read her children stories—endless Dickens, Jane Austen and Jemima Puddle-Duck. She taught them gin rummy, poker, bridge, took them on nature walks, and helped them to memorize passages from Euripides. She ate dinner with them almost every night. Mary was so worried about the lack of male companionship for Worth and Barry Junior that she had three retired police captains working in shifts at Melcombe to assist her with the boys. When it came to her sons, nothing could be left to chance. But Mary was not the kind of mother who would roll on the floor with her children, lavish affection on them, and allow them to think that they possessed her. She was filled with notions about child-rearing, as if she had read too many textbooks, and she berated them on their schooling, manners and friends, and often made them feel they could not measure up. She explained her attitude to Barry once in a letter:

Not that the dear children do not give body and meaning to this time. But one's children, do not seem to me as much a part of one's own inner and personal life as one seems to move on the periphery of theirs. Their very dependence upon you and the whole condition of being a parent makes one into an adjunct, or a secondary kind of creature. . . . I hope I am a conscientious and reasonably adequate mother, but I can't believe I have a real talent for being one.

There was no question but that she was more attentive to her sons than she was to Sallie, whom she called Miss Priss. Having grown up in a houseful of sisters she didn't find "sympathetic," Mary was hardly a girl's girl. Boys were a complete novelty to her, so straightforward and uncomplicated. She loved her daughter but it seemed from her letters that she might have felt more of an affinity to her sons, especially Worth and Jonathan, a bias that was evident in her letters to their father. She wrote to him mostly about the boys. Their character traits were analyzed constantly: Worth was "responsible," "conventional," "popular," "handsome." Barry was "cheerful," "original," although he was also "fat," "lazy," "willful" and "vague." Jonathan was her heart's delight, "the most outgoing and affectionate little creature." Mary mentioned Sallie with more reserve. Sallie was "pizzy," "prissy," "pale," "skinny," "white and stringy." Later, as she got older, her mother began to write about her fine looks, her achievements, her reading skills, her attempts at writing, but never in the detail she used for her boys. Once, in a letter to Barry, Mary described the difference between small boys and girls. "The little girls . . . are *naturally* prissy in the extreme, and are full of easy rather dull conversation. . . . [The boys'] conversation is more broadly based and their exchanges are more humorous than the little girls' are. By the way, darling, did you know that Jim and Jo Henning have at last accomplished a boy baby?" However much Barry Junior and Sallie would later achieve, Mary's attitude toward them during their formative years would have immense repercussions on their personalities. Later Barry Junior and Sallie would say they resented the ineffable "standards" that their mother had reared them with as well as the subtle harshness that would cross her face if they didn't catch a reference or failed to read a classic text. Sallie's rage would be such that years later when she began to publish short stories, she constantly wrote of a cold, neglectful, imperious mother, and her portrait was so one-dimensional that her family would speculate that in fact she was not only angry at Mary but jealous as well, as if she resented her mother's intellect, talent and power. "I will never understand Sallie's writing," Mary would say years later. "Sallie was a beloved child."

During the war the Bingham children appeared to have everything. Their mother and servants smoothed their way, and the family seemed so happy, so rich, so privileged. The older boys had the police captains to entertain them; Jonathan had his mother's complete attention. Sallie was, as her mother said, "the princess of the kitchen." The four servants paid her endless attention. Once she memorized a speech from *Henry VIII* and recited it for the Negro staff to great applause. Sallie loved the white Kentucky farm woman named Lucy Cummings whom the family called Nursie. "I thought of her as my real mother," she said. She was close to her grandmother Caperton, who obviously adored little girls and would write to Mary about Sallie, "I have a weakness in that area." Munda advised Barry, "Her very quickness must be guarded against, and she has the quickest mind of any child I have dealt with. If only we can train this into such concentration as Mary always had she will be a great woman some day. . . ." And once she wrote to Barry, "I hope Sallie will soon grow out of the phase of needing so much attention."

Although she concerned herself with her children's education and manners, Mary seemed less able to understand her children emotionally. Possibly her own feelings had been suppressed by her passion for books and her worry about her family's poverty. It seemed difficult for her to understand that her children might be more lonely for their father and might need him even more than she did, although sometimes she did mention this in her letters. Her own unhappiness appeared overwhelming. One year after Barry left for England Mary wrote to him about her "actual and tangible pain," her "forlornness and bereavement" and "terrible kind of desolation." She seemed less aware of her own children's anguish. "Small children are not capable in my book of maintaining a sense of dissatisfaction and unhappiness," she said, long after her children had grown up and the family had collapsed. And yet she was too intelligent not to realize that Barry's absence would have a profound effect on her children, especially Jonathan. "Your being away from him now is a serious deprivation for him—and one that I can not begin to make amends for, I'm afraid." As the war progressed, Mary saw this loss as "one of the worst of all the wastages and bad things about war, for all children everywhere." But her inclination as a mother would be to fill her children's days with ceaseless activities. "One can certainly not compensate for such a loss by over-indulgence and a breaking down of nursery standards," she wrote.

Mary must have believed that her own life set the standard. She had been unhappy as a child because she was poor and her parents didn't get along, so she could see no reason why her own children shouldn't be less troubled. "Barry and I were so in love with each other, we believed the happier the parents, the happier the children," she once said. "Surely we know that we do mean much more to each other in every part of our lives than most people who are married," Mary wrote to Barry.

Each morning the children walked down the hill to the Ballard school, a small stone building covered with ivy, which was segregated but run on new "progressive" principles, and which eventually Mary grew to despise. She organized all kinds of expeditions for the boys: trips to caves, naval bases, even nearby Fort Knox so they could ride in a tank. She then insisted that they write about the experiences. Their compositions, she wrote to Barry, were characteristic. Barry's was "filled with charm and mistakes"; Worth's was a "drab bit of composition but showing a most well ordered mind." At night she read a war novel, *They Were Expendable*, to Barry and Worth, and she reported, "Worth and I both cried." Her activities with Sallie were somewhat more remote. Sallie needs "a prissy companion," she wrote. She reported that it was charming to see Lizzie reading to Sallie in the kitchen, and she knew that Sallie would be happy with her Christmas present, a large dollhouse "that will delight her for years." Sallie "hoards up everything you send her and all the enclosures are pasted into her scrapbook."

Sallie, Barry and Worth could communicate with their father only through letters that Mary forwarded along with her remarks about their clumsy sentences or increasing vocabularies. Seven-year-old Sallie wrote to her father, whom she called "Darling Daddy." In one letter she thanked him for some small ivory animals, and told him she was reading Kipling and learning the Navy hymn. She also reported that Jonathan had gone to his first birthday party and "behaved very well." She signed her letter somewhat formally: "Your very loving daughter."

"Dear father," wrote thirteen-year-old Worth. "A thousand dollar bond!! and out of your navy pay too, that certainly is a present!" From boarding school, eleven-year-old Barry wrote,

Dear Mother,
Yesterday we had a fine Thanksgiving dinner. We had chicken, turnip, peas, onions, potatoes. After gorging on that there was a touch game of football between the masters and the boys. The masters won 70 to nothing. . . . The days

are getting very dark. At flag this morning we could hardly
see the flag. I hope you can send the newspaper to me.

Another of Worth's letters from boarding school:

Dear Mother,
I have decided to attack the tariff more from the points of
trade agreements and future peace than disagreements of
North and South on the subject. I got your data, it is wonderful. . . . For my birthday I would like the books Frank-
enstein, and Dracula. . . . When are you going to fill the
swimming pool?

And earlier, eleven-year-old Worth had written to London:

Dear Father,
I have had a cold and an ear ake *[sic]*. . . . Mother gave us
a surprise on Easter morning. We got our own personal jars
of pickles. I helped mother de-bulb the peonies. . . .

And from Mary to Barry, on a day she had taken Jonathan
and Sallie on a picnic,

This sort of innocent and childish outing in which the children are at their charming best, so pink and excited, so glad
to be doing just what they are doing at just that moment,
makes me so sad to think that you are not there . . . , and
they are being deprived of sharing such small moments of
oddly significant happiness. . . . I can hardly imagine the
day when you will come home and we can be so spendthrift
with your time, when there will actually be enough of it, to
take the children for a walk in the woods, and be as leisurely
as we please.

Mary adjusted to the loss of Barry by staying close to her friends
at the newspaper, especially Mark and Willie Ethridge, and her
New York and Cambridge acquaintances. She was friendly with
Wilson Wyatt, who had been the lawyer for the newspaper since
1937, and was now the mayor of Louisville. Mary had power
over those closest to her, at least in Louisville. She wrote to
Barry that there was a great deal of plotting and scheming going
on. Should Wilson run for governor? Perhaps it would be considered that the *Courier-Journal* had put Wilson into the state-
house, Mary wrote, with a fine sense of self-importance.
    Early in the war Mary went to Radcliffe to stay with the new
president, Ada Comstock. Mary had a plan. She wanted to get
a special visa so that she could fly over and be with Barry in

London. Her plan was to persuade Miss Comstock to allow her to visit English universities as a Radcliffe representative, reporting back on "what was happening to liberal arts education now." Her heart leaped at the possibility that Miss Comstock, who was vaguely agreeable to this plan, might work it out, and Barry and Mary wrote back and forth about this for months. He imagined all the places he would take her, what country weekend they would accept, and how she would like his friends. But the plan collapsed. Mark Ethridge told Mary that it would look wrong for her to go, and Barry agreed that it might hurt his image at Grosvenor Square. Miss Comstock said that maybe Mary had misunderstood. So Mary decided to go to London for the *Courier.* But Barry did not like that idea, either. "There are a good many newspaper men here who have been trying for months to get their wives over, and the excuse of having them work for their papers has been frequently tried, without success. . . ." Barry told Mary that she could not use "the same kind of pressure and pull which we have always found so deplorable in other people" even though he was desperate to see her.

Mary insisted that her role at the paper was different from that of other "newspaper wives." Certainly, her vision of herself was paramount—her "image" as the wife of the president of the Louisville *Courier-Journal.* As the proprietors of a small Southern newspaper, Mary and Barry took it upon themselves to be factors in national society. Their vision of themselves was so grandiose they never for a moment thought that being publishers in Louisville meant they were out of the mainstream of national life.

The *Courier-Journal* had every feature of a first-class newspaper, right down to its own "Roto" section printed by the family company, Standard Gravure, a vigorous op-ed page and a streamlined page one. The typeface had been changed to a more elegant gray from its harsh and messy black. Possibly no other newspaper owners from a city Louisville's size were as ambitious about national life or as concerned with quality. Mary and Barry were considered, as *PM,* the New York liberal paper, once reported, "bright and wealthy young people" out to shake up a venerable institution. Barry wrote to Mary that the "refaned," as he parodied *PM*'s use of the word "refined," description of them as "bright" and "wealthy" made him "shiver," but the reporter was absolutely right. They were drastically changing the family business Barry had taken over when he was thirty-one years old. Happy Chandler, the governor of Kentucky, used to complain to Aleen during this period that "those children," as he called Mary and the news staff, were "ruining her newspaper and that she had better look into matters before the properties were hopelessly ruined and depreciated."

Meanwhile Mary could laugh about the tacky Kentucky governor with her East Coast friends.

Mary and Barry reveled in the status that the newspaper conferred on them. They wanted to liven up the dull Kentucky nights by importing friends to Louisville, "moving the clientele of 21 to Glenview," Mary wrote. They offered Alexander Woollcott and Arthur Schlesinger, Jr., jobs, and they believed that Woollcott and Schlesinger might consider leaving New York to work for them and were somewhat mystified when they did not. "Clearly Arthur had a larger view of his future," Mary said years later.

When Mary went to New York, she would ask Alice Guinzburg, the wife of the founder of the Viking Press, to invite S. J. Perelman to drinks, or Tallulah Bankhead. She would write to Barry about Alice's "highly congenial and sympathetic atmosphere." One night her friend Dorothy Parker was there, as were the John Steinbecks. Dottie, she reported, was in good spirits, not drinking, with "the viper's sting utterly concealed." Mrs. Steinbeck was pregnant, and all they could talk about, Mary reported, was their visits to "scores of horoscopists." "I always believed my parents were social climbers," Barry Junior would someday say, but Mary and Barry cared less about social grandeur than they did about being with people who were doing things in society. Mary's and Barry's letters to each other were filled with names, and more names, from the social arena they most admired—writers, theater people, social wits—as if they intended that these private letters would someday become public.

Mary wrote to Barry:

Did you ever hear the story of D. Parker's run-in with [Janet] Flanner years ago in Hollywood? Dotty [sic] was just back from Spain, and I believe Janet shared at that time the reflexes of her Fauberg [sic] Paris friends on the subject of the Civil War. After some vinous rudeness from Dotty, and table banging from Flanner, the former swept, rather staggeringly, out of the room, throwing back over her shoulder as she left, the remark: "No one, Janet, has a right to *look* like Voltaire, and not *be* Voltaire!"

Barry responded in kind, but far more impersonally, as if he were writing not a letter but a diary. He had taken Sybil Colefax to the theater and had met up with Noel Coward. "Afterward I took Sybil to the Savoy Grill for supper. . . . The whole place was a buzz of theatrical conversation, and Noel circulated from table to table, looking more than ever like a paper doll, with his high-cut shoulders and that amazing thinness through his body."

He reported he had seen Dorothy Parker's husband, Alan Camp-
bell, at a later party. "He has been with his unit so long that he
is sick of the whole damned thing. . . . All the other people
pass through and out the other end, and there he still is, feeling
older and older while his companions grow so so juvenile that
he feels he should help to seat them on the potty-stool." He
went to Kathleen Kennedy's wedding to the Marquis of Harring-
ton where the guests talked of little but Rose Kennedy's contempt for her daughter's marrying "out of the papacy." She has
been "burning up the cables with dire warnings of hell fire to
come," he wrote. Later, when her brother Joe had been killed
in a plane crash, Kathleen asked Barry to give her some American money quickly so she would be able to get home. Perhaps,
Barry wrote, Joe Kennedy Jr.'s death "may provide an occasion
for a reconciliation with her family."

Names and more names: At a luncheon at Averell Harriman's
house one day, he ran into Lady Randolph Churchill, "a pretty
red-haired, cream-colored girl, who used to hunt with Miss
Natt." John Steinbeck pitched up at Barry's office to cover the
war for the *Herald Tribune*, and Barry was annoyed that Steinbeck pretended not to care that he had a new play opening in
London that very week. "He put me off a little by saying that
he didn't know what night it was to open. . . . That kind of
casual literary pose does not befit him, and I hope it is only an
aberration of a hung-over moment." William Saroyan and Irwin
Shaw showed up at his flat for drinks. Once Hemingway's ex-
wife the journalist Martha Gellhorn stopped at Barry's desk to
complain about Hemingway. Her hair was cut short "a la Maria," and her features reflected "not the horrors of a mass Fa-
langist rape, but the unfairness of Ernest in having sailed right
in and snapped up what she had hoped was going to be the great
assignment of her journalistic career. 'That lug,' she complained, 'not only tried in every way to ruin my life, but now
he is stealing my copy.' " How cozy and small wartime London
was for Barry. He felt it was so much like Louisville, the same
people over and over again, as well as the same "terrible racism
he heard among the social crowd that he saw all through Pic-
cadilly."

In Louisville, Mary defined herself though her newspaper
work. Mary and Barry carried on at length in her elegant letters
about the *Courier-Journal*'s "position" on various political top-
ics. She dissected which editorial writer thought what on Cordell
Hull's every pronouncement, or the Beveridge report on the potential of the British social welfare program, or Churchill's most
recent speech. It is arguable how much the citizens of the Louisville, Kentucky, of 1943 cared about the paper's editorial
page, but what made the *Courier-Journal* both fine and infuri-

ating was the fact that in this period Mary and Mark Ethridge
did care and the newspaper was not pitched to a small-town
audience. There isn't a hint of the fact that their editorial page
was reaching a Kentucky population that was less advanced than
the most rarefied "Cantabrigian," as Mary would say, seminar.

All through Mary's letters to Barry there are detailed descriptions, right down to the exact dialogue, of portentous fights at
the C-J's editorial meetings, of what Mark had said to their editorial writers Tarlton Collier, Molly Clowes, Russell Briney, as
if the very opinion of the *Courier-Journal* would affect the fate
of the nation. "Tarlton said . . ." "Molly believed . . ." Mary
reported their every sigh as if she were writing about Walter
Lippmann, not editorial writers who were working for a newspaper with a circulation of 140,000. Not even the ambitious and
energetic Dorothy Chandler, who was married to Norman Chandler, the publisher of the *Los Angeles Times,* was as involved in
her husband's newspaper's opinion page as Mary Bingham was.

Here, from Mary to Barry, a characteristic observation, one
of hundreds, about the *Courier-Journal:*

> I am sending you in another envelope the first long piece
> Molly Clowes has sent in from Canada. We sent her up
> there to cover the Canadian crisis over conscription, and I
> think she is doing a very good job both of reporting and of
> creating the background of information about Canadian af-
> fairs which is so woefully lacking in this country. As you
> can imagine, the press service coverage of a complicated
> and deep-rooted question of this kind is thoroughly inade-
> quate, and I think the New York Times Service is so also,
> as their man on the spot seems to be a French-Canadian
> who leans so to the Quebec point of view that I cannot feel
> his stuff is even remotely objective. It makes me proud for
> the Courier to be able to do a rather special kind of job of
> this sort, and I do hope after the war we can develop people
> with specialized knowledge and understanding of the mul-
> titudinous problems which arise every day, and send them
> about to cover that sort of news.

With Mary and Mark Ethridge at the *Courier,* Barry could
completely relax in London, knowing that the paper would run
just as he would want it to. But since this was the 1940's and
Mary's place as a woman was truly on the book page or in
society news, she often denied her power in a style that was as
self-deprecating as a belle's. "Here is one of my pathetic little
efforts," she would write to Barry when she sent him a blistering
column she had done for the editorial page. Once she wrote a
lengthy article on education:

It has to do with a recent Gallup Poll which showed that 54 percent of the people believe that treaties ought to be ratified by a majority of both houses of Congress, and only 25% approve the present method. . . . I'm afraid I shall feel quite ill when I see that mass of print . . . and I imagine your sympathetic but astringent eye falling on it too late to correct the excesses.

The feeling that she could influence the *Courier-Journal*'s political opinions would never leave her. Mary would never learn how to bow out, and in the years to come she would write letters to the editor to attack her own son's editorials when he was running the newspaper. Often she would call reporters and say, "I don't want to exercise prior restraint, but . . ." and then she would tell them her view of things. Once in the 1970's, while speaking to a reporter who had published an exposé on the Kentucky prison systems, she said in effect that it was too bad the libel laws were so liberal and it was difficult to sue a newspaper for stories that were revolting.

Just before the 1944 election Mary had to bring Tom Wallace, the editor of the *Louisville Times*, sharply into line. Wallace had come to Mark with a half-page statement designed for an editorial stating that he could not vote for Roosevelt for a fourth term. Mary told Barry Senior in a letter that when she read the statement she "could feel the blood rise to my face and drain altogether away, leaving me . . . very chalky and ghostly." Wallace said he wanted to take a leave, and that he didn't feel right endorsing Dewey either. Mary said that this statement from "one of our papers" would weaken the Roosevelt campaign because the national press would pick it up. It would be a terrible thing if a Bingham paper was seen to pull away from FDR. Still, Wallace was the editor of her afternoon paper and, as the editor, had the power to decide what the newspaper's opinion would be. Mary wrote to Barry that she and Mark had worked on him and he had finally relinquished the editorial. "I have no bad conscience at all about having pulled out all the feminine stops in my possession." And so, the *Louisville Times* stayed on course.

Barry had the wisdom to recognize his own newspaper's occasional pretentiousness and wrote to Mary that at times "I do wish the C-J didn't give its support with the sublime condescension of a White Sulphur belle accepting her eightieth proposal of the season." He was happy when Mary turned in a strong editorial, particularly about anti-Semitism. He would write to her that he was "terribly pleased."

I have always wanted the Courier to have that touch of really dynamic liberalism, expressed literately and with distinction. It is wonderful that you should be doing it, my darling, and I am so glad we can always know that there will be some readers of the Courier who will appreciate it properly. I feel all the more strongly than ever that we must keep the editorial columns of the paper aggressively and effectively devoted to the liberal cause after the war.

During the war he was horrified by the conversations he would hear, especially in splendid drawing rooms.

One of the few things that is getting progressively harder for me to bear is the constant harping by many of the people I see on the faults of one or another group—the Jews, the Catholics, the French, the Russians, or somebody else, depending on the dominant prejudice of the speakers. It horrifies me to find such growing devotion to the belief that blocks of human beings are different and inferior by nature, here in the midst of a war which was started by the votaries of that same anti-religion. . . . I have to keep reminding myself that I am seeing only a tiny section of West End London and the British, American and special foreigners who inhabit it. . . . I think it is almost tragic that the American newspaper correspondents limit themselves so much to the same stultifying environment I have been complaining of.

Mary resented giving Mark Ethridge the title of publisher, not because she didn't like Mark but because his title seemed to take credit away from Barry. She was insistent in her letters that Ethridge should not get the title of ''editor'' because at the C-J the editor supervised the opinion page:

My own opinion is that the very best thing that could happen from every point of view would be for you to become editor and publisher yourself. It seems to me a sinful waste for you not to be writing all the time, and laborious as the daily stint is sometimes, the necessity for doing it is very fructifying, I think. It always seemed to me wasteful and unintelligent for you to have spent so much time on administrative work at the paper. . . .

So it was particularly galling to Mary, when Mark Ethridge would get most of the credit for the vigor of the newspapers. When *PM* published a two-part series on the *Courier-Journal* that was filled with praise for the Binghams and their product, Mary and Barry demonstrated the paradoxical oversensitivity of newspaper people when they themselves are written about. *PM* reported that the *Courier-Journal* was now "the South's Guardian" and Mary and Barry were ideal newspaper owners. But, it added, in a note that *The New Yorker* picked up, that Mrs. Bingham looked like Clare Boothe Luce, which for Mary was a nightmare, and that Barry seemed shy and tugged nervously at his tie. They hated these characterizations. They were unable to see the irony in their reaction to these innocuous remarks amid a sea of praise for their newspaper. Hundreds of words back and forth in letters were devoted to their reactions to being written about in such a national forum. A national reporter buzzing around the *Courier-Journal* was big news in 1945 and a sign that the paper was becoming as prestigious as it had been during the Watterson days. Mary and Barry's reaction to all this attention was characteristic of owners who see that their best people, however much they respect them and need them, are receiving a little too much glory. ". . . the tag line at the end I found hard to take because, as Mark himself is the first to say, the character of the Courier-Journal today is not simply 'the character of Mark Ethridge,' " said Mary, who was angry at the *PM* writer and told Barry that she had "gooseflesh" at the "underlying innuendo . . . that we are both sort of rich, fortunate, and inevitably from the PM point of view, light-minded people and that the serious and socially-minded Courier must therefore be a creation of someone else's—Mark's." Barry was particularly annoyed at the term "wealthy" to describe him: ". . . what a stinking tacky refinement that is for the word rich, which has a kind of vulgar gusto about it," he wrote. Their excessive reaction to the *PM* story was also a symptom of another aspect of Mary's and Barry's characters: however much they complained, they obviously adored the attention, as they would forty years later when they granted interviews to reporters about why their own family and their empire had fallen apart.

In their hundreds of letters there are surprisingly few references to the actual problems of running a newspaper—the advertisers, the circulation, the overhead—as if those concerns were beneath them. Mary wrote to Barry about "the advisability of giving up . . . the patent medicine advertisements," because, however profitable they were, they "lower the tone" of the *Courier-Journal*. During the war Mary and Barry refused $1.2 million worth of advertising because of the paper shortages, which they did not want to affect their news coverage. In July of 1944 they wrote a letter to all their advertisers, which then ran as an announcement in the C-J, that they where cutting their ad space, cutting 20 percent from what had already been a reduction of 25 percent. "With the greatest war in history and one of the most important presidential elections in our history under way this year, we do not feel that any further reduction in news content can possibly be made,'' the letter said. Other newspapers had a news content of 30 percent, the *Courier* letter said, but ''the average news and feature content of The Courier-Journal and The Times in 1944 has been 51.5%.'' As a result, for some years after the war, the Bingham family lived on what they modestly called ''our austerity plan.'' But the important thing was maintaining the quality of the *Courier-Journal*. The newspaper had committed to a $5 million new building at Sixth and Broadway with the most modern equipment. In order to be able to build it, Barry had to sell some of his stock. ''I imagine there is already a good deal of gossip in connection with the disposal of the $750,000 of preferred stock to the Jefferson Standard [Bank],'' Barry wrote to Mary near the end of the war. When he finally came home he would decide ''on what scale we should organize our lives, and what sacrifices may be necessary in order for us to maintain the really important things in connection with . . . the children's lives.'' He did not need to explain ''the really important things,'' for Mary understood that the most important thing of all was grooming her sons for ''the sacred tradition'' of running the Louisville *Courier-Journal*.

16

At times Barry was understandably worried about what effect his absence would have on the children. "I get a nightmarish feeling sometimes that the children will be so far along in adolescence and so absorbed in their own interests by the time I see them again that I will feel strange with them," Barry wrote to Mary while he was away, "but I know there isn't any real foundation for such a tormenting thought." He was right, however, to be concerned: Mary ruled Melcombe as if she were running a corporation. She had routines, schedules, drills, discipline, and specific times for their every activity, right down to the hour they took their cod liver oil and did foot exercises with rubber balls to prevent fallen arches.

Mary's day was also tightly charted. She wrote to Barry that she "awakened at 7:45 a.m. when Curtis brings me my breakfast on a tray and I lie in bed in sybaritic ease until at least 9:30 reading the newspapers, and answering mail. I don't even have breakfast with the children." Three days a week Mary would be on the River Road bus after breakfast, heading for the Courier building at Third and Liberty Street, where she would remain till late afternoon in conference with Mark Ethridge or Russell Briney on the day's editorial pages. In the afternoon she would scoop up Jonathan and head for the play area at the tip of their property called the Duck Yard because it had real ducks behind a fence, sandboxes, swings, carts and lots of old toys. Mary usually spent her evenings with the children, supervising homework or putting Jonathan and Sallie to bed. After dinner she would listen to a Beethoven symphony on the radio in the library.

As the war progressed Mary seemed to show a preference for Worth and Jonathan. Mary was passionate about Worth and was grooming him to take over the newspaper. As the oldest son of a Southern family, Worth was treated like the heir to a title, and Mary's bias was apparent in her letters. She described how popular he was in school, the captain of his basketball team, hand-

171

some and "oddly religious." She believed her oldest son was
"one of the very nicest little boys imaginable, and there is something so solid and good about him, such a sense of absolute
integrity that I believe the miseries of adolescence . . . will
hardly be able to change him very much." He was indeed very
good-looking with astonishing blue eyes that could fix a companion with the look of utmost sincerity and would later break
female hearts. Worth was the kind of boy who would come back
from town and remark about the poverty he had seen, or wonder
why Negroes couldn't go to the Fourth Street theaters and had
to drive to Cincinnati to see *Gone with the Wind.* When he was
a teenager, a girlfriend of Worth's remembered driving with him
in a car and his pulling over to the side of the road. "I thought
he was going to kiss me," she said, "but instead he turned to
me with those piercing eyes of his and said, 'Helen, what do
you think of anti-Semitism?' "

Worth and Mary would often take long walks by themselves,
and his mother always talked to him about his obligations as the
first Bingham son. He wanted to impress his mother with his
abilities and loved to talk with her about politics. At age eleven
he was only one inch shorter than his mother, and she wrote to
Barry Senior that he was "very erect and handsome, and with
that quality of physical effulgence . . . that the Greeks used, in
adoration, to call the 'bloom' of their youth." He asked "voluntarily" to be allowed to be confirmed, Mary reported, and
although Mary despised their minister, she was allowing Worth
to go to religious training twice a week until he was prepared
"to put on the whole armor of God." Despite his seriousness,
he was intensely boyish, and was the ringleader of the Glenview
gang. Inevitably, the boys congregated in the summers around
the Binghams' swimming pool and tennis court. Mary wrote to
Barry, "Streams of little boys have been surging back and forth
over the lawn and the tennis court all afternoon—as usual, the
whole neighborhood is gathered here, and their happy, or indignant, or argumentative cries have been floating in through the
windows with the curious nostalgic meaning that those particular
noises always have."

Barry Junior was very much in Worth's shadow, and his personality was markedly different. He was more like his father,
gentle and mannerly, eager to please. But he was a poor student
and fat and called "Belly" because of his size. "The poor darling child is certainly heavy in the haunch," Barry Senior once
wrote to Mary about his son. He was horrified to see that his
namesake had "almost a Fatty Arbuckle quality." Obesity was
particularly worrisome to both Mary and Barry because it symbolized for them sloth and a lack of pride. Mary seemed to

believe that fat was one of the cardinal sins of the human condition.

But Barry had other severe problems; he could not read properly, nor did he have the least grasp of phonetics. His parents became convinced that their second son was a problem child, a notion that would never seem to leave them, even after he had slimmed down and had successfully graduated from Harvard. All their lives, Mary and Barry's bias would appear fixed in their minds and no doubt affected the negative way they viewed Barry Junior's later management of the family empire. Even when Barry Junior was over fifty years old, Mary and Barry freely discussed the reading problems he had had as a young boy.

Mary was baffled by her son's performance in his childhood. At the Ballard school, where his classmates were the sons of the Ohio River worm fishermen, Barry received failing grades, although his IQ tested at 128. But she was convinced that her son was still "the best adjusted, most serene, and most stable emotionally of all the children." The teachers told her that he was the "best informed child in the class, and the best speaker," but he could hardly read. Mary wrote about ten-year-old Barry:

. . . the real truth is that he has no conception, even yet, of the multiplication tables, and so of course cannot do anything at all in division. I have had a basal metabolism test made to see if it was possible that he had a thyroid deficiency which might been making him unambitious and lazy and vague. He has got quite a lot fatter this winter. . . . I am sorry to say that his thyroid is quite normal, and I'm afraid his frivolity and laziness at school are just original sin, and much harder to eradicate than a glandular disturbance.

Mary tried everything. She subjected him to pituitary shots because she felt they might accelerate his development. She hired remedial reading teachers and required him at age nine to take buses and streetcars by himself for hours each way into town on hot summer days to work with these well-meaning Louisville ladies. She even thought of sending Barry to their friend Spaff Ackerly, the psychiatrist, but she decided against it because of the possible "ego-enlarging effect of the psycho-analytic method" on Barry's character. Mary knew she would have to send both boys away from home to a good boarding school if for no other reason than to help Barry over his difficulties. She wanted the absolute best for her sons, and she knew that they would need to be highly educated to maintain the standards of the newspaper. She could not help comparing them constantly, and she knew that Barry "suffers by contrast with Worth's un-

usual doggedness and application in everything. . . . Worth has
spent an hour each day working in the garden, but Barry will
begin with very grandiose ideas, and never finish. . . .'' She
contrasted their looks and reported that Henrietta favored Worth.
''I'm afraid he puts our dear tubby little Barry at a disadvantage
by comparison. . . .''

Mary could not tolerate these imperfections. She investigated
the Harvard Reading Clinic. She queried her friend Alice Guinzburg about her son Tom's boarding school and wrote away for
private school brochures. One day Worth and Barry saw a letter
that Mary had brought home. It was a brochure for children with
''nervous and behavior problems.'' However poor his mother
believed Barry's reading skills to be, he had no trouble reading
this missive. Mary tore up the letter and quickly assured him
that ''of course such a place was out of the question.'' She was
so upset by the encounter that she wrote to Barry Senior in
London about this terrible gaffe. Later she wrote of Barry's in-
adequacy and about his ''fear of not being able to read,'' but
she never blamed herself for his malaise, calling it, as always,
''original sin.'' At times, however, she connected Barry's reading
problems to his father's absence.

Barry became passionate about radio serials and comic books.
He began to cut up in class. His father wrote from London that
Barry was getting to be the kind of ''boy who doesn't really
learn anything and covers up his deficiencies by all the time-
worn devices, even down to the contention that he will be a
mechanic and therefore needs no knowledge of the simplest subjects. His native charm is such and my predilection for him is
so strong, that I can hardly keep from being amused by his
representing himself as a 'killer and a card.' '' It would take
until he was almost twelve years old for a reading expert to
diagnose Barry Junior's real problem, which had nothing to
do with laziness, dyslexia or psychology. He had been taught
to read improperly at the Ballard school and had fallen further
and further behind. For years Barry spent most vacations and
his hours after school with reading tutors trying to overcome this
weakness. Finally, he did. Barry's problems were entirely rem-
edied by a series of special drills, which he did so dutifully that
his mother noticed as he got older that he was much graver and
was no longer ''the merry little boy'' he had once been at the
Ballard school. But all his life Barry could not escape the impression that he was the slow one in the family. When later his
parents tested his reading ability, he scored well—he could comprehend easily one hundred fifty words a minute.

Even as a child, Sallie could not help noticing her mother's
attitude toward her older brother. ''He was such a pathetic
thing,'' Sallie would later say, and her attitude toward her

brother, like her parents', would never change. She felt superior
as a child and would seem to feel that same superiority when,
as a member of the *Courier-Journal* board of directors, she
questioned his every move. She resented the lavish attention
Barry received when they were young, even though it was often
negative attention. Sallie could memorize anything and read
beautifully by the time she was six years old. Once Mary came
upon Sallie and Barry Junior pitted against each other in a reading contest, which was orchestrated by Worth. "Sallie had, of
course read off her bit with great ease and expression. The humiliating evidence of Barry's inferior ability embarrassed him
very much, and I've never seen the poor darling look so flushed
and miserable or read worse," Mary wrote to Barry.

Sallie quickly learned that the way to her mother's heart was
through doing well at school, and her mother was astonished at
Sallie's abilities. She often invented plays with herself as the star
to amuse Nursie, Cordie, Ollie and Lizzie in the kitchen. Once
she came home from school to find her mother sorting through
books. Sallie began flipping through the children's pile. "She
. . . became so engrossed in 'The Pied Piper of Hamlin' that
she crouched on a packing box and read the whole thing through
before she could remember to take off her hat and coat, or go
to the pantry for her bread and milk," Mary wrote to Barry.
Sallie was "a really bookish little creature."

"I think the thing that must be avoided in her case is the
development of a princess fixation—an idea that Lizzie, Ollie,
and Cordie assiduously build up, and one which she is only too
willing to entertain about herself," Mary wrote. "They were
like a family to me," Sallie said later of the kitchen staff. But
she would never be able to understand that her mother had studied her closely as well: "I believe blue stockingness in otherwise
normal and comely women is easier to curb than light minded-
ness, and I think Sallie is probably going to be quite pretty
enough to be able to afford some intellectual life."

Sallie was often sick and absent from school. "The only time
Mother really paid attention to me is when I wasn't well," Sallie
said. Like her father after his mother's death, she developed lung
problems and twice contracted severe pneumonia. Barry Junior
remembered creeping down the drafty, cavernous hall, with the
ivy-patterned red wallpaper and the family portraits, toward his
sister's room, where she was lying, pale and frail, under an
oxygen tent. "It was terrifying, all those tubes and canisters,
and that hissing noise, my mother telling us to be quiet or we'd
wake Sallie," he later said. When Sallie recovered she began to
dictate strange poems to her mother about death and God, all of
which Mary sent to Barry, although she did not inform him until
much later that Sallie had almost died. "Her verse about God

has astounded me,'' Barry wrote about a verse that five-year-old
Sallie had dictated to her mother. ''The whole thing has a slightly
ominous atmosphere that is like a child's dream expressed by a
mature poet. Do you think it is possible that we are nurturing
an Emily Dickinson?'' Sallie did not rebel against her mother
but, instead, seemed to imitate her. When Sallie was seven,
Mary read her a Bible story one day and Sallie responded as
imperiously as her mother might have: ''. . . when I read, 'She
called his name Dan,' she said in a dismayed sort of voice, 'But,
Mother, isn't that a rather *common* name?' '' Even Barry, in
London, knew something wasn't quite right about Sallie and
Mary's relationship. Worth had written to his father that Sallie
had said to him ''a stranger who came to the door of the house
would surely think that Ollie was her mother.'' Ollie, of course,
was one of the Binghams' maids.

As the youngest child, Jonathan was spared most of his mother's opinions. By the time he came along Mary was relaxed
enough not to worry so much about his every developmental tic,
but just enjoyed his ''agreeable Irish face'' without plaguing him
the way she had the older boys. Nursie spoiled him terribly,
Mary would write to Barry, who often expressed concern that
Jonathan seemed willful or ''imperious'' when he was two years
old. The Binghams despised middlebrow child-rearing theories
and would never rationalize misbehavior with terms like ''the
terrible twos'' or ''It's a phase.'' ''I'm sorry to say . . . his
manners are not what they should be and he has a way of saying,
'Go way!' . . . and wishes only to point in a lordly fashion to
whatever he wants and say 'Read!' or 'Build blocks!' or 'Tricycle!' '' Mary would write to Barry that she was taking this
toddler in hand, and was going to be quite tough on him, as she
had been with the other children, but she would add how ''he
was still the most lively and amusing companion.'' She had endless patience with his ''interminable'' tea parties in the Duck
Yard, and she wrote to Barry about how he would come to her
and say, '' 'Eat this, maw-maw.' . . . And then I have to make
noisy drinking sounds and exclaim mightily at the good hot
tea. . . . This game will go on for half an hour and is one of the
pleasantest ways to spend a beautiful autumn afternoon in the
world.'' She reported how Jonathan, at twenty-one months,
would put his arms around her neck and say, ''Dear, dear,
Mama.'' She adored this little blond boy and described his
''warming his charming little behind'' in front of the fire or how
wonderful it was to see him collapsed on top of their poodle,
Popo. When he was two and a half, Mary reported proudly that
Jonathan came into her bedroom and wanted her to put her
breakfast tray away, to get up to play with him: ''I didn't rise as
quickly as he wanted me to, so he rushed into the bathroom,

seized my girdle from the chair, and dragged it to me saying
'Here is your corset, have you got a petticoat?' . . . He is as
sharp as he can be.''

But Jonathan too would later have severe problems, which first
appeared when he was a toddler. Mary wrote:

> He is much more of a mother's boy than either Worth or
> Barry ever was. His pitiful scene when I did go to town
> after Nursie's return, in which he clung to my skirts and
> cried and said 'Don't go to the Courier-Journal,' was so
> unlike the older boys' behavior at his age. . . . I wonder
> uneasily if your absence and the sharp break in the tranquil
> and happy security in which the older children basked has
> imbued him with the ordinary infant terrors.

Mary made a decision. Worth and Barry would have to go away
for school. The only good private school in Louisville was miles
from Glenview, and Mary believed that the gas shortage would
make it impossible for the boys to be driven there, even though
she could have qualified for the gas ration. The Ballard school,
which had been a noble liberal experiment of the Glenview
mothers, was a dismal failure. The mothers had had the best
intentions; they were sure that if they subsidized the local three-
room public school they could improve the curriculum, which
was ''hag-ridden . . . by the pedagogical ideas of the Teachers'
Colleges.'' But Mary was soon furious with the Ballard school
for the very egalitarian quality she had once found attractive.
When Sallie was in the second grade, Mary wrote to Barry Senior,

> I do wish primary school curriculum authorities were not so
> obsessed with the subject of the American Indian. Of all
> peoples in the history of the world this character seems to
> me the most threadbare of interest, his life the most narrow
> and brutish. . . . A childish study of the life of the Virginia
> or New England colonies, or of the Beowulf Britains . . .
> would seem to me far more remunerative than this laborious
> probing into Indian affairs, dull as they are, and, fortu-
> nately, quite vanished.

She believed that Ballard had wrecked Barry Junior's intellectual promise, and in the spring of 1944 she took the boys to New
England to visit schools. They all later agreed that Eaglebrook
was the best school for both children, despite the ''glandular
exuberances'' and overwhelming personality of the headmaster's
wife. After about a week of travel, Mary wrote, ''Worth, in one

of his rare moments of perception, suddenly said, 'I wish Daddy was here. Everything is so much more fun with him.' ''

As the day came for Barry and Worth to go off to Eaglebrook, Mary was depressed that Barry had missed his sons' childhood. The night before, Cordie had prepared their favorite meal. The boys didn't notice, so Mary pointed out to Worth what she had done. ''Mother,'' he said. ''Please don't be so sentimental.'' When they got to New York, she took them to the St. Regis roof for dinner, and she was overcome when Worth, at age twelve, asked her to dance.

Her last view of the boys that autumn was at the train station, when ''there was a sudden swish through the gates'' and the little boys were swept away. ''I thought I detected a faint look of sudden panic and fear upon Worth's face. . . . Barry, though I believe greatly more harassed by uncertainties, kept up a brave and cheerful countenance to the last.'' From England, their father remembered his own misery going off to boarding school at Middlesex. ''Oh Lord I do feel so sorry for both of them in what they are about to face, and I only hope it will be easier for them to take this in their stride when they are so young, as the British so devoutly believe.''

17

It is, of course, impossible to know how Barry's years away from
his children during the war truly affected them. Certainly, common sense would suggest an emotional truism: an extended lack
of parental attention can often lead a child to confusion about
his or her place in the world, as well as confusion about his or
her relationship with the absent parent. The psychological literature of the war period is filled with case studies of the various
ill effects—ego problems, an undeveloped superego, excessive
narcissim—suffered by young children whose fathers were gone
for years during the war. Frequently the perception of war children was that they had been abandoned.

The Bingham children specifically received a double message
from their father. Barry was by nature physically affectionate
with his children yet emotionally remote, an odd combination
that must have been mystifying to them. At Easter he later would
dress up as the Easter bunny and stage glorious egg hunts. When
he was at home, he always seemed to have a child or a baby
crawling on his lap, but he found it difficult to have intimate
talks with his children, especially his sons. But, like Mary, he
read to his children constantly and often took them horseback
riding on the Glenview trails. This physical affection masked his
later inability to confront unpleasantness in his family. And now
with the war raging, he was even physically removed.

Certainly, Worth, Barry Junior and Sallie came out of the war
with a distorted image of their father. Worth, who was ten years
old when his father left for England, probably suffered the most
from his father's absence, coming as it did when he most needed
male guidance. Much later, Worth, by then an ambitious young
man, tried to explain his father to a friend: "My father loves
humanity in general and no one in particular." The look on
Worth's face when he made that remark was so heartbreaking
that the friend could still remember Worth's pain after thirty
years. Worth was wrong, of course; Barry Senior loved his children a great deal, but as the war progressed he was becoming

more and more of a public man, burdened with obligations that
even when he was finally home often took precedence over ordinary family life.

The war began his real absences; Barry was gone for almost
four years. He missed his children's Halloweens, their costume
parties, their commencements, their sleep-over dates, their multiplication tables. He was away from his own sons almost exactly
as long as he had been left by his father in Asheville with his
aunts. His sons had the same reaction to their father's absence
as he had had to his. "We thought Father was a total hero,"
Barry Junior said. "He was like a god, an important man, and
we viewed him as completely brave and powerful." Sallie
mourned her father's absence as well. She was his only daughter
then, four years old when he left for England, a charming blond
child who later agreed that her father was "almost [her] alter
ego." At the age of four, a girl often goes through a natural
phase of pulling away from her mother and being closer to the
father—the so-called Oedipal stage—but her father simply was
not there to help her make the proper emotional transition. Sallie, like her brother Barry Junior, had a hard time seeing her
relationship with her father realistically. "I think he felt I represented his suppressed creative side," she said, perhaps indulging in the wishful thinking that comes from the idealization
of an absent father.

Now, at the height of the war, Barry was an important man
in London, responsible for naval press relations, and although
he was given the opportunity, he made no attempt to abbreviate
his service and come home to his children. He was so highly
esteemed by the Navy and so well connected to the White House
that he could have come back to a good job in Washington in
1944. But he refused. He said that he wanted to serve in the
Pacific theater. He wanted to be taken seriously. He had already
excelled in Europe, now it was time for him to go to the other
theater of war. He wrote to Mary, "How could I understand the
demands of the post-war world without rounding out my experience in the war?"

Mary was beside herself that Barry would not put her and the
children before the demands of his wartime conscience. She must
have had the same kind of terror that she had felt when she fled
years before to Paris, the fear that she would lose him again to
the outside world. But Barry had grown secure in the war. His
life had become the world of Bronze Stars, combat duty, the war
effort.

At first he had complained in his letters about public relations
officers "not being taken seriously," but since then he had been
promoted several times, and details that bothered him when he
first arrived in London, such as the presence of his stepmother,

had ceased to be important. Barry loathed Aleen, and always had. Mary and Barry felt that she was too provincial for the Binghams of Louisville. Even worse, Aleen did not fade into benign widowhood after the Judge died. Far from it. She was now the widow of the former American ambassador to England and she was going to make the most of that fact—as the head of Bundles for Britain, a vast national organization for English war relief. When Aleen was in London, which was often, Barry was inevitably viewed as her stepson. Newspaper photographers would take pictures of Barry escorting his stepmother. He was always waspish about Madam Queen in his letters home.

What was worse for Barry was that he was inevitably asked, as her stepson, to organize her London tours. Once, he described meeting her at the train station in the "hustle and bustle" of the London blackout and how Aleen "flushed with excitement and pleasure" when she saw the reporters. But "her face fell several yards" when she discovered that they had come to meet the First Lady, who was arriving at the same time. Upon getting back to the hotel, he noticed that a "grand floral tribute, replete with green orchids, soon arrived from the Churchills," and when he took her down to dinner, "she squeezed out those two mechanical tears she can always produce at will when she tried to tell me how it felt to be back in London without Papa."

He was so caught up in his own activities that at times he was mysteriously detached from what was happening to his family. He wrote bland and impersonal letters to his children. When Worth was confirmed, he wrote about the "parable of the talents in the New Testament" and told his oldest son that "talents" mean "a much broader thing—advantages, natural gifts, opportunities—and the whole point . . . is . . . to use them for a worthy purpose. . . . You and Barry have a fair share of talents in that way, and there is nothing I hope for so much as to use them to good effect in your lives. I have no doubt about your being happy people always if you will determine to make yourself useful people." To his son Barry he sent letters that described "Toughie," the cockney newsboy who delivered the papers at Navy headquarters. Sometimes his father would send Barry Junior twenty riddles, carefully written out, then sign his letter, "Your affectionate Father."

When six-year-old Sallie contracted severe pneumonia, his response was peculiar. He wrote home a lengthy letter, to be sure, but the first three pages were typed, single-spaced and devoted to his own dinner preparations, the view from his flat in London and a country weekend he had spent with the Sackville family:

I have just come back from spending the afternoon at Knole, and have established myself at the flat for a welcome

bit of peace and privacy. . . . I have fixed myself a mighty
good Sunday evening repast, starting with some good
canned vegetable soup into which I have put a dash of
sherry, two hard boiled eggs . . . and a wonderful great
plate of sardines from one of your parcels. . . . I shall end
up with one or two modjeskas. . . .

As he sat with his soup in his Mayfair kitchen, he looked out

over a very pleasant expanse of Mayfair, with the trees in
full leaf, the endless chimney pots stretching away into the
distance, and all those little whirligig ventilators on top of
flues on people's roofs spinning cheerfully in the breeze. In
the far distance the sky is dotted with barrage balloons,
floating lazily and peacefully on their wires like great fish
idling in the Gulf Stream.

Three pages later Barry inquired about Sallie's pneumonia.
He was worried, he wrote, that Sallie had been so ill, an understatement, since his daughter had almost died of pneumonia.

My own darling, I have said nothing so far about Sallie's
second illness, but it has worried and grieved me since I
got your letter a few days ago, I can't bear to think of her
being ill, and I am haunted by that curious sense of guilt
about her at such times as you say has been in your mind.
I pray most earnestly that I will be given a chance to get on
a closer and more satisfactory footing with her before she
grows up, as it is clear to me that she needs some special
form of attention from us which we, and I especially, have
never quite succeeded in giving her.

Another father might have inquired at the beginning of a long
letter about his seriously ill daughter, but Barry's emphasis was
not necessarily a sign of coldness. After all, what could he have
done? He was in London, with no chance of coming home.
Mary had been discreet, she had decided not to tell Barry about
Sallie's illness until the crisis had passed. She wanted to shield
him from bad news. Mary would never tell Barry about anything
unpleasant, except matters concerning Henrietta or Barry Junior,
even though he asked Mary many times in his letters not to
shield him from "worrisome events" in Glenview. He wrote to
her that it would upset him if he thought she was hiding news
of the family from him, yet how impressed he was with the
splendid way she was handling everything at home.

18

June 1944. It seemed the war would go on for years, and although Mary was increasingly miserable without Barry, she was extremely busy at the newspaper and more and more in the public eye. Sometimes it appeared that Mary and Barry were moving further away from each other, as each became more and more caught up with the obligations of what had become their separate public lives, but these were perilous times and the distancing was unavoidable. In London, Barry was planning how the press would get into France during the Normandy invasion. At about the time Barry was on the *Tuscaloosa* watching the shells fall on Cherbourg, Mary was taking the train to Chicago for the Democratic convention. The 1944 convention would be a heartbreaker for Mary. She was there as an editorial writer for the *Courier-Journal*, not just as a spectator or a newspaper wife. But Mary would hate the convention. Those few days in Chicago disillusioned her for months about FDR. Her idol had ensured his nomination for a fourth term by throwing Henry Wallace off the ticket as his running mate in favor of Harry Truman. Mary felt personally betrayed that he had done this to her new good friend.

Mary was tense when she got to the convention because Barry had written her that under no conditions were the other *Courier-Journal* wives to go to Chicago, not after the spectacle of the 1940 convention, when Henrietta had brought a friend and the *Courier* reporters couldn't be seated because Willie Ethridge and the wives in their hats and jewels were taking all the seats. That kind of embarrassing scene was everything Barry Senior hated, for it made the *Courier-Journal* look like a small-town newspaper. "It makes me blush and wriggle with embarrassment to think of any other feminine contingent from Louisville trooping into the convention hall, as the 1940 sideshow undoubtedly made a laughing stock of the papers with all the other representatives." So Mary had direct orders: No women.

Mary and the *Courier-Journal* had no less than a political

mission at the convention: they had to be the best of the South, there to somehow oppose the reactionaries who were moving against Roosevelt and Wallace. Just before Mary left for Chicago, she had turned in a blistering editorial on the dreadful archconservative South and Mark Ethridge played it for three columns. She wrote to Barry that she couldn't help her angry tone; she had spent the winter poring through the *Congressional Record*, reading the remarks of the old guard leadership who still spoke on the floor about "kinky-headed niggers," as well as indulging in "Jew-baiting so open and unashamed that it shocked me to the marrow of my bones." She wrote to Barry, "To me, there is little doubt that the South is really a dangerous breeding ground now for Fascism." The editorial was so tough for a Southern paper that the AP put it on the wires. Mary later had doubts about the harshness of her tone, especially when the AP put it out, and she wondered if she had gone too far.

Had she gone too far? There it was: Mary and Barry's perpetual conflict. They were liberal Southerners, but not radicals, and they traced their beliefs all the way back to great-grandfather William Bingham and his antislave societies. But they were still proud Southerners. Barry once commented on the sad fact that "the educated class in the South has produced absolutely no leadership since the first days of the Republic." "I hardly thought anybody could make my hackles rise about the Fascist-minded small town deep South," Barry wrote to Mary after reading an anti-South diatribe in *Harper's*. "I suppose . . . liberal people in America have reason to fear the growth of a Fascist movement from these regions. We have said much the same thing ourselves. But it is curious what an emotional reaction one gets to criticism of this kind from a really alien and unfriendly source." And yet Barry wanted his boys to know something besides "the hideous trivialities of the average River Valley mind."

For Louisvillians like the Binghams the race matter was tricky, especially for Mary. She was in a perpetual uproar on the subject and was horrified by a current popular novel *Strange Fruit*, about "miscegenation," to use her term. In 1944 there were so many other fights liberals had to wage that race was not of the utmost importance to Mary. Indeed she was often annoyed by the attitude of the Louisville Negroes who had pestered her until she had gone on the board of the Urban League. She had agreed to go on the board, she wrote to Barry, "simply because it is so hard to turn down nigs when they ask for your support for things of this kind. . . ."

But none of this affected her passion for Roosevelt and Wallace. Wallace had given the speech seconding Roosevelt's nomination. Whatever Mary's ambivalent feelings on the subject of the Negro, when Henry Wallace stood up, Mary wrote to Barry,

"I have never in my life been more moved. . . ." In the very face of the "white-supremacy revolt" and "the pussy-footing that had been done on the negro plank in the platform," Wallace stood up and said, "The poll tax must go." She wrote,

> The reception of him in that really great moment was the kind of experience that one can rarely hope to be a part of in politics. All the diffidence and uncertainty, the surface irresolution which has always marked Wallace in personal contacts was gone, and he simply stood up and said what he stood for with an air of freedom and happiness and complete conviction.

As an insider and wife of a newspaper owner, Mary knew every sordid detail of Roosevelt's duplicity. "The President seems convicted of having perpetrated one of the most brutal double crosses that expediency has devised." She was so upset that after Wallace's defeat she went to his suite at the Sherman Hotel and found him "in his queer dark and lonely-seeming . . . room." He was sitting "in his shirt sleeves . . . the floor pretty littered." Like a good party loyalist, he told her, "Don't listen to the gossip you hear around here," but she couldn't help herself. "The last thrust of maladroitness and duplicity was . . . a telegram he [Wallace] got from the person most concerned in the affair, on the morning after his defeat," Mary wrote to Barry. "It said, 'Congratulations on your magnificent fight.' " Mary found this last evidence of Roosevelt's hypocrisy "monstrous."

And so, back in Glenview, she sat down and wrote a searing letter to Eleanor Roosevelt:

> Dear Mrs. Roosevelt: I am moved to write to you out of a deep sense of bewilderment and sadness. . . . Like many, many other devoted friends of the President's and Henry Wallace's, I came away from Chicago sick at heart over the methods which were employed there to assure the nomination of Senator Truman and to defeat the Vice-President. . . . I found it hard to believe that any man who had so fired the imagination of the country, who has spoken out so courageously for the things nearest to the hearts of so many people, who had shown overwhelming strength in public opinion polls was not entitled to a fair chance to win the nomination in a convention as free as those occasions can ever be. . . .

For two pages, Mary ranted.

At the *Courier-Journal*, Mark Ethridge wrote three pages of single-spaced heartbreak to Roosevelt. Ethridge's letter was masterly:

> As a native Mississippian, I know that the Southern revolt was not a revolt against Wallace, but against you; it was the revolt of the Ku Klux-minded and the tight-minded bourbons against a New Deal they have never liked and were determined to knife whenever they got the chance. They had to accept you this time because they felt you were the only one who could win. They couldn't get at Mrs. Roosevelt, the other object of their bitter hatred, because she was not running for anything. But . . . Wallace bore the scars of many a dagger aimed at you.
>
> As a Southerner, as a liberal, I have never felt it either necessary or honorable to compromise with the Ku Kluxers or the bourbons. . . . I have alienated kin and kith to fight the fight with you. . . . I have taken two nasty jobs because you have asked me to take them. I feel, therefore, that I have got the absolute right and, moreover, the duty to tell you that I am sick and bewildered by your attitude toward Wallace, but beyond that, by your own position in all the maneuverings in Chicago.

Could any major newspaper editor and owner have been so naïve about the workings of the American political process? And yet, Mary and Mark Ethridge were so passionate about Roosevelt that it was impossible for them to think of him as fallible. *If only he had announced he didn't want Wallace, everything would have been forgiven.* It was the hypocrisy they hated as much as the actual decision. The *Courier-Journal* had been Roosevelt's most ardent Southern support, and now these letters, of maudlin ''heartbreak,'' came from his friend Ethridge, who had known Roosevelt since 1925 and witnessed all his schemes and flimflamming, and from Mary Bingham, who had been around the Judge long enough to have known about political expediencies. Roosevelt's response was immediate. However annoyed he was at these hothouse flowers who were taking him to task, he still had to mollify the *Courier-Journal* in an election year. And so he wired them to come to the White House so he could tell his side of the story. Even Eleanor Roosevelt wrote to Mary, ''Since you undoubtedly have watched the political scene within the Democratic Party in the past few years, I can not understand why you should have been surprised.''

The moment the President's wire arrived, Mary's rage subsided, as Roosevelt no doubt knew that it would. The President and the First Lady, in the middle of the war, had taken them seriously. ''I never in the world imagined that my somewhat

emotional letter to Mrs. R. would secure this sort of attention,"
Mary wrote to Barry, "and I must say I think the gesture is very
magnanimous as there could, of course, never be any question
of what the Courier's position would be in the fall, no matter
what happened at the Convention. . . . I suppose it will be all
right for me to go? I am devoured with curiosity as to what will
be said."

This meeting would be a peak moment in Mary's life. She
talked about it for years, for she believed she was taken seriously
on her own, not just as Mrs. Barry Bingham. She was no longer
the penniless little girl from Richmond but a representative of
the *Courier-Journal* as an editorial writer and a vice president
of the corporation, and she was on her way to see the President
of the United States. She was so taken with actually going that
when she got into the Oval Office, she became all "mazy" and
her heart turned over in the presence of "That Man." Anything
he said would have been all right. "Being in the same room with
him gives me such a hard pain in my throat that I find it impossible to function except on a hazy, doting sort of level. I love
him to distraction." Mary wrote Barry a six-page memo about
the meeting. The President looked better than she had expected
he would, although his hand was trembling when he lit his cig-
arette. Roosevelt had asked all about Barry, of course, whom he
had known since Barry was twenty-six years old.

> We then all sat down on chairs ranged in front of his desk,
> and, giving one of those head-thrown-back glances all
> round, he said, "I didn't get you up here to hold a post-
> mortem—that is, unless you want one." There was an un-
> comfortable silence which he took to mean that we did *not*
> want one, and then he went on to say that until he read the
> Eastern papers he had known nothing about the activities at
> Chicago attributed to him. We said nothing to this, so there
> was a rather miserable pause, and I suppose my grief at
> hearing him utter such a fib was plain to be seen on my
> unsubtle face.

Finally, he said that Wallace just did not have the votes, which
wasn't true either. He laughed and said he was going to give
Henry the secretary of commerce position, and in an eerie repetition of what he had once said about appointing Mary's father-
in-law secretary of state, he said, "Wouldn't that give business
fits!" He was toying with Mary and Mark, "fobbing off a little
home cooking" on them, as Mary would later say, but it didn't
matter because at the end of the session he talked to her about
Barry. "There have been many times when I have wished he
were here, but I put myself in his place and I did not think it

would be fair for him to pull out under the circumstances. He has done a grand job. Perhaps he can come home soon,'' Roosevelt told Mary, who was so affected by this that she forgot her ire about Wallace and all she could do was respond with "a huge dry grin." She left the office with her heart pounding and made an "inane" comment about Barry having been on the *Tuscaloosa* and how she knew that was one of the President's favorite ships. Only later did she think how foolish and clumsy that must have sounded to the President of the United States.

But Barry had no intention of coming home, despite Roosevelt's offer, and later Worth would wonder if his extended absence was due to an affair he was having during the war. Whatever he was doing, he was certainly having too fabulous a time to consider coming back. In September of 1944 Barry went to Paris and, like everyone else in Paris that glorious invasion autumn, he was overwhelmed by the experience. He saw Mistinguett, the great cabaret singer of his youth, doing the Lindy with a GI in a nightclub, unrecognized. He revisited the Parc Monceau, Mary's favorite; spent two dollars per champagne cocktail at the Ritz Bar, where Frank the bartender remembered him immediately; thrilled at the swarms of children who marveled over his white naval cap. He even stopped into the Hotel Napoleon, where Worth had been conceived. From Paris he wrote home, "Getting into bed without you is a bitter and unceasing privation every night that passes, but when the night is cool and there is moonlight through the windows, as there will be tonight, my loneliness for you is worse than usual. . . ."

And yet, like every man caught up in war, he didn't spend all his time thinking about home. Everything fascinated him too much. The prices, the glut of newly minted money: twelve dollars for a pair of nylons or twenty dollars for a pack of cigarettes. Barry was taken with the "old, festive air about the place," and the fact that the French were filled with their "old self-esteem," accusing everybody else of being collaborators. The entire experience would have been just perfect, he wrote to Mary, "if you and I could walk down to the Ritz together this afternoon, and come back to my room here . . . how I have adored being with you here and all the other places in our blessed years together."

But with all that, he had no desire to come back. Although he wrote Mary that he was going stale in his job and all of his friends were going home, he didn't think he himself should leave. He didn't want to be judged poorly, as if he had bailed out of the war too soon. Mary was sensitive to his mood: "I seem to detect from your letters now a definite feeling of letdownness, and post-crise depression—or not depression, really, but something as near to that as your wonderful and God-given disposition can allow you to come.'' Mary believed the ''demands of the great hour'' had been so ''stimulating'' that Barry was frustrated by the daily routine of his London life. She may have felt that after D-Day Barry would come back to her, but she was wrong.

Everyone Barry knew was carrying on with someone. Herbert Agar would leave his wife for a woman he met in London. Weldon James would marry Margaret North. But Barry's letters, with their pages of impersonal detail, occasionally ended with a loving yet defensive remark to Mary that stressed how different their marriage was from others'. He felt that the war would only bring them closer together.

> We will have . . . to fall back on the one great fundamental comfort of our lives, our complete love and devotion for each other and our faith in each other. It is more, as you said in your last letter, than most people have, though in the more immediate sense it only makes our separation more painful. I find so many people who are haunted by a fear of change, of some unknown shock of misunderstanding and maladjustment in their most intimate personal lives, after the war is over. That is a thing I am completely spared. The thought of you is all that is certain and constant and satisfying in the world to me, as steadfast as the bright star Keats wrote about, and if these months of separation can compel any change in our relationship it can only be to make me value you and all your lovely qualities more vividly and with more maturity than I was capable of before.

Whether or not he was having a love affair would not have made the slightest difference.

For Worth the fact that his father had chosen his public pleasures over any private obligations, including his revered wife and children, must have been hard for him to accept.

Barry made a hard choice: he was going to the Pacific. Mary was distraught—who cared about the Pacific press coverage, when Barry could come back to work at the White House and be with his family. She wrote to Barry, in surprisingly strong terms, how she felt. None other than the President had told Mark Ethridge that Barry could have a superior job in Washington.

> I can hardly express to you, my darling, with what absolute dread and misery I regard your being sent off for such a ghastly interminable period of duty. . . . You have been away for such a very long time and . . . the caste system of

types of duty and theaters of operations is not going to mean very much more this time than it did after the last war. . . .

I am trying not to think too much of my perfectly overwhelming stake in this question. You know all about that. But I do think that we both ought to remember that two or three more years of separation from you for the children would amount to the most serious deprivation for them, and for you, that I can possibly imagine.

Like a lot of other men, Barry now seemed war-crazed. It appeared as if it was impossible for him to come home, and his letters expressed contradictory feelings. After D-Day, he wrote to Mary, "I suppose it is fundamentally wrong to view a great event in history with so personal and selfish an eye . . . the really strong and sustained emotion for me has stemmed from the thought that this vast action brings me closer to the day when I can come back to you. . . ." A few months later he seemed less determined to come home so quickly. "Our happiness together may have all been too personal and exclusive in the past. . . . I think in time we may be able to spread the influence of such perfect joy."

He was home for six weeks at the beginning of 1945, filled with plans for Navy press coverage in the Pacific. He and Mary took the children on a ski holiday to North Conway. At the end of this holiday Mary and Barry took the train together to San Francisco, where he got on the ship that would take him to Guam. On her way back on the train she stared at the "sage brush and mountains" she had first seen on her trip West with Barry; she relived every moment of their time together, especially the misery of their last hour: "The only real thing is our last moment in the taxi cab with your hand in mine. . . ." On the train, she knew as she stared numbly into her Greek history text that "of all our good-byes this one was the worst. . . . I suppose these raw and bleeding amputations, the severing of our perfect oneness will not be important from the long view—whenever we may be together again. . . ."

Now desperately unhappy, Mary wrote letters that turned increasingly sharper. She had no interest in the Pacific and was as tough about the island mentality as she had been about Sallie's study of the Pueblo Indians. Mary wrote to Barry how "tiresome" she found tropical settings, "the whole gaudy melon flower backdrop." And: "I imagine the great displays of flowers are essentially tacky and frightening." Perhaps she was angry that Barry was there, and she was taking it out on those who were near to her. Her judgments became more and more severe. During spring vacation, when Barry Junior brought a South American boy home from Eaglebrook, Mary at first was merciless about the child. He was "too sharp at cards." He had committed the unpardonable sin and remarked on their "mansion." He read comic books after dinner, and Mary was struck by how even Barry Junior was ignoring his friend, which reminded her of the times when his uncle Robert would invite guests to Glenview and then ignore them.

But Mary's anger was understandable. Barry had now been away from America for more than three years. Like every father who was away during the war, he had missed so much. Mary wrote to Barry once that she was struck when she saw the boys in "their new DePinna pajamas. . . . I sometimes feel Nursie and I make pretty grim companions for them and I cannot get over this overwhelming feeling of sadness when I see Worth with his narrow hips in his PJ's and Barry with his shirt out to hide his girth as if he were wearing a zoot suit." At times, like every mother, Mary would indulge in wishful thinking about her children's mental state. "I have sometimes wondered if the undertones . . . of our happy and fortunate life with these two has made as deep an impression upon them as I hope they have. . . ."

Mary, however, believed, perhaps mistakenly, that Sallie was flourishing without her brothers around. Mary reported that she was shocked at how fiercely Sallie yelled "No!" if anyone asked her if she was missing them. Her mother was surprised at how well she was doing in dancing school. "I would not call Sallie a Mata Hari myself," but Mary was delighted to see that Sallie "carries the conversational burden untiringly." She wrote that "it is very queer suddenly to have the household back on the footing it used to be five years ago with the oldest child around only seven years old. I must say that I feel that this situation will be good for Sallie. I had hardly realized what a predominant part of my time and interest was devoted to the boys, and how much she played an also-ran part until they went away."

Mary reported that Sallie had calmed down, her manners had improved without the "teasing and by-play." After a holiday at the beach, Mary wrote, "I cannot tell you how very charming she looks now with her brown face and her white hair. . . ." Perhaps Sallie was too sensitive to be teased. Later in her life she would tell stories of sadistic crimes her brothers had supposedly subjected her to. Once, when Worth's daughter, Clara, was eleven years old, her aunt Sallie took her into the spooky basement of the Big House. "Your father was so horrible to me that when I was your age he took my cat and strangled it right here in the basement," she said to Clara about the father she had hardly known.

With Barry in the Pacific, having defied her wishes, Mary's mood grew increasingly dark, and then, in April of 1945, Franklin Roosevelt died. Mary spent hours by her radio weeping and weeping. She was inconsolable. Sallie later remembered those awful days: "It was the first time I ever saw Mother cry." Mary listened to every word of the eulogies and would not leave the radio for even a second. As if to assuage her own grief, she wrote to Barry every detail of the death, and how it had affected the *Courier-Journal* staff:

> I have just heard, with Edie, the Guam broadcast on the President's death, and that eerie connection at this moment with the place where you are made me feel even more desolate. Like everybody else in the whole wide world, I suppose, I feel quite numb with the shock of this news and incredibly distressed. . . . I've never seen so many stricken faces as there were around the Courier building.

One of the reporters "broke down" completely and had to be excused from the news meeting for the extra edition they were putting out on Roosevelt. Mary wanted Barry to know every detail of the death from her, in case there might have been "a hiatus" in his getting a newspaper, but mainly as a way to have the illusion that they were experiencing the terrible event together. Roosevelt, she informed him briskly, had been at Warm Springs and looked better than he had at Yalta. He was sitting for a portrait when he announced, "I have a terrible headache." At 1:15 P.M. he "fainted and never recovered consciousness." Mary reported Eleanor Roosevelt's magnificent comment, "I feel sorrier for the people of the country, and of this world, in his death than I do for us," and added, "Every time I take Jonathan up at night, I think quite irrelevantly, of the curious pathos of the President's colored valet when he carried the President to his room after his stroke, and the compassion and grief of that gesture."

She suffered doubly because she was deprived of experiencing this crisis with Barry, and wrote,

> This tragic thing gives me a sense of the end of an era as nothing else ever has, and since that era has been one of such intense personal interest and personal involvement with our life, I feel lost and sad not only because of the big public implications, but because of all the years of deep personal fascination and participation from a distance in the President's political career.

There wasn't a Bingham who wasn't affected by the death of his president. Even Worth wrote home from Eaglebrook, "I could hardly believe it when I heard about the President's death. I was almost sure he would live through this term.'' Fourteen years of Mary's marriage had been wrapped up with Papa's friend. ''I believe you and I have discussed Franklin Roosevelt for more hours on end even than we have talked about Natt or Aleen,'' she wrote to Barry in the most mournful tone.

After Roosevelt's death, Mary and Mark Ethridge moved against Roosevelt's enemies, such as the columnist Westbrook Pegler, and dropped him completely from the *Louisville Times*. In a small Editor's Note, the paper announced it had killed the column:

During the lifetime of President Roosevelt, The Louisville Times allowed Westbrook Pegler to make any criticism that Pegler wanted to make. We considered a great deal of it vicious, below the belt and far beyond the privilege accorded by decency or the libel laws. Pegler's column today has been killed because we don't intend to carry Pegler in the role of carrion.

19

When Mary felt her most vulnerable, she retreated within herself and hardened her attitudes toward everyone around her. Now, in April of 1945, with Roosevelt dead, Barry in the Pacific and no sign that he was coming home, Mary turned her anger toward Henrietta in particular, who had had several breakdowns during the war and whose lack of self-discipline Mary abhorred. Mary and Barry, however, believed they were partially to blame for Henrietta's problems and wrote that their ''deep intimacy'' must have affected her negatively.

During the spring of 1945 Mary was surprised and worried that she did not hear a word from Henrietta when Roosevelt died. She wrote to Barry how inconceivable it was for Henrietta to disappear at the time of the President's death. Even Robert had sent a wire to Mary from New York, to mark the very personal nature of the family's grief. Barry had sent cables and written endless pages from the Pacific about his ''stunned, lost, and empty feeling.'' He raced to the airfield to meet his friend ''Jimmie'' Roosevelt as he was stopping in Guam on his way back to Hyde Park. Barry wanted ''to keep the correspondents off his neck,'' and wrote Mary that he looked ''tired and shaken'' and was ''very plainly moved when he tried to talk about what had happened.''

But there was still no word from Miss Natt, so Mary knew that something was wrong. With Natt, it could mean only one thing: she was having yet another breakdown brought on by drinking and the loss of will. She had had a series of what the family called ''episodes,'' drunken collapses, really, when Natt would fall into a stupor. She was isolated on her farm, an hour's drive from Glenview, with only her nurse for company. Sometimes she would go to New York and stay with Robert in his depressing suite of rooms at the Roosevelt Hotel, or, later, in the small apartment he and his wife, Felice, took on East Sixty-eighth Street in Averell Harriman's building. After these visits, Natt would come back to Louisville and what Mary called ''the narrowing of Natt's life and interests" in Goshen, Kentucky, and she would begin to drink. Barry Junior remembered one of Henrietta's later breakdowns at the Big House. "We thought she was dead," he said. "And an ambulance had to come from the Norton Infirmary." All through the war Mary wrote to Barry about his sister. The family counselor, Dr. Spaff Ackerly, was constantly consulted about Henrietta's problem and often had to send nurses out to the farm with sedatives. Mary was furious about this: how dare Natt be so profligate during a war to waste Spaff's gas supply that way! Mary's very discipline and character were a taunt to Natt, and often made her worse, Spaff Ackerly told Mary. "I sometimes think I only succeed, in my efforts with her, in accelerating the destructive nihilistic impulse that brings on these crises." Although she was not "a clinical depressive," and not suicidal, according to Spaff, Barry Senior advised Mary to pack off Natt to "Dr. Sprague's," the local asylum, the next time Henrietta broke down.

When Natt was not drinking, Mary would often send the boys to Harmony Landing to ride her horses or to help her pick apples at the farm. Barry Junior would always find it odd that his mother just dropped them at Henrietta's gate, as if she wanted to keep her distance. Worth, with his rather stiff personality, was confused by Henrietta's sense of humor. She literally lived in a different time zone as a joke, pretending to be on Eastern War Time rather than Western War Time, so that it was always an hour later at Harmony Landing than in Glenview. Mary wrote that Worth seemed "simply baffled" by this behavior. "Aunt Henrietta was a three-dollar bill," Barry Junior said.

Henrietta lived in a different time zone in her own head as well. She imagined she was still young and "Papa's princess" living at the American embassy, having flings with John Houseman and dancing with the Prince of Wales. "I suppose, poor dear, she may think of . . . the fine years here when we all had parties and guests and everything seemed very exciting and glamorous," Mary wrote. Henrietta's father had given her everything to make up for her shattered childhood, but no one could blot out the image of her mother's death or the reality of the Mary Lily scandal. And now the war was too much for Henrietta because, as Mary wrote to Barry, she still believed it was 1934 at the Polo dinners. But now she was forty-three years old, without an occupation, parents, a husband or children to give her perspective. Barry wrote:

In the unreal world in which she exists, I don't believe it has ever really occurred to her that (after the war) England will be changed, that nobody can hunt anymore . . . that there is still only a minute basic gasoline ration, that she would have a hell of a time finding a habitable house in either London or the country. . . . It would be a shocking change from the old days, when Natt could make demands on people's time to suit her whims.

Natt had long periods when she seemed just about normal, or even exhilarated, and during those times she would put on her fanciest clothes and go to Lexington for a horse sale. Then, especially if she got a good price for a Harmony Landing filly, she would return from the parties and the attention to the "solitude and heat and boredom of the Farm," when "the next stage of her mood pattern began to appear," Mary wrote to Barry. She would start drinking beer after beer, five or six in rapid succession, "with an almost desperate concentration," Mary wrote, which was always the danger sign that a breakdown was on the way.

Early in the war, Mary devised a plan for Henrietta. She was convinced that Henrietta should take electric shock treatments. Electric shock was the fad for upper-class alcoholics in this period, and was given at all the best institutions. Mary and Barry were surrounded by drinkers, which seemed part of the genetic structure of fine Southern families, and there was an entire vocabulary of euphemisms to describe family alcoholics. They had "bouts," "spells," and "moods," and institutions were all over the South where these genteel drinkers could go to find help. But Mary and Barry seemed to have more than their fair share. Mary had two sisters who were alcoholics. Barry's brother, Robert, was, of course, hopeless, and used to keep his "bottles safely-hidden in the back of the water closet," as Barry wrote to Mary. Even Aunt Zaddie in Asheville was a closet tippler. Mary worried that no one in her family was capable of taking care of her children if anything should ever happen to her and Barry. The children would be in an "extremely hazardous situation," she wrote, "the two people who would naturally inherit that role are, I'm afraid, almost equally disqualified for it by alcoholism. . . . We must both be very careful now and run as little risk as possible of being blotted out."

Mary saw many of these family drinking problems in larger social terms, as a disastrous debt left over from the Prohibition era, what she called "the inability to admit that one ought not to drink at all. All of us who grew up then are inclined to feel that to refuse a drink or to admit publicly that we can't drink is some sign of moral decrepitude." Mary's point was that since Prohibition was a government act, staying drunk in the 1920's was a way of maintaining one's political freedom. This had been a fashionable notion when she was at Radcliffe. Barry liked to take a social drink, as did Mary, but as Mary once wrote to him, "Isn't it nice not to feel the need to drink but to be able to be together not feeling happy or sad brought on by alcohol?"

By insisting that Henrietta take electric shock treatments, Mary might have felt that she was trying to control Miss Natt and her "willfulness" in the same way she controlled her children. For Mary, this was a form of "improvement," such as seeing to it that Barry Junior had pituitary shots for his weight and development. Although Mary did not trust psychological theory, which she called "murky Freudian assumptions," she wrote to Barry that she believed Henrietta was "psychotic," "a narcissist," and had a "deep maladjustment." When Mary read *The Lost Weekend,* the new best-seller of the period, she was impressed by its realism, and immediately sent a copy to Barry in London. Barry was struck by how well the author depicted the alcoholic's tendency to evade small matters. The refusal to take responsibility, Barry wrote, "had a hauntingly Natt-like ring for me." Barry suggested that Mary take the book out to Natt's farm, not in any way that would upset her, but just to say, "I found this book interesting." Mary did just that, according to her letters, only to have Natt say, "It was so boring and disgusting. I couldn't read past the first chapter."

But Miss Natt knew Mary was after her, and however much she feigned a febrile lack of will, she often had her housekeeper answer the phone to say she wasn't there when she knew Mary was calling. Mary wrote to Barry that Natt was avoiding her. Henrietta wrote to Barry in surprisingly strong terms:

> I have given the electric therapy treatment deep consideration even before your letter arrived, and I have thought a great deal about it since. It might help, and God knows I would do anything to avoid these cycles of depression and their serious consequences to my personal relationships. . . . However it doesn't seem sensible to take the treatments for a condition at a time when it doesn't exist. Unfortunately it doesn't act as an insulator against future troubles.

Natt's breakdown when Roosevelt died brought a characteristic response from all those involved with her. Mary reported every detail, in diary form, to Barry: "I shall not send this letter until I can assure you that Natt's current breakdown is well in hand and over with, as I believe it shortly will be. . . . she is almost hysterically opposed to my knowing about her present difficulties for fear I may write you about them." Although Natt was hiding, Mary knew something was wrong. Finally, Natt's companion, Jeanette, called and said *Natt wasn't feeling well.* What this meant in fact, Mary reported to Barry, was that Natt was in "a rather advanced stupor" and was so "unintelligible as to be delirious." Furthermore, she wrote, Henrietta's increasing "lack of candor and love of intrigue" seemed to her "downright psychotic."

"This is just the minute when Spaff told me he wished she would consent to try the shock therapy—that is when her depression is beginning to beset her and which the sort of nervous tension which heretofore has been released by drinking is mounting," Mary once said. Spaff later wanted to treat her for "manic-depression" when she was in one of her more euphoric states, but Natt inevitably refused. "She never would know anything unless her own psychiatrist, Ernest Jones in London, sanctioned it," Mary said years later. Jones was, Mary said, "Freud's disciple . . . and so the master did not approve of our Louisville methods."

That April Mary sent Spaff to the farm. He reported that Natt was better. "In general narcissists have amazing recuperative power because the area of their emotional interests and worries is so much smaller than that of average people." It was Dr. Ackerly's belief, Mary wrote to Barry, that nothing short of a "Gates of Tarsus awakening" or spiritual rejuvenation could have an effect on Barry's sister. Dr. Ackerly wrote to Barry that Natt had told him that she sank into deep depressions "every five months after she has been on a high and feeling finely. . . . I told her it was not unusual for people to request electric shock treatments . . . during a 'spell'. . . . She said . . . she wanted to have a show-down with me about it. She also wanted me to write you what I said to her."

As the war progressed Mary increasingly hardened toward Natt, as if having power over her sister-in-law would make her feel more in control of her own situation. Barry wrote to her from Guam, counseling her, in his own way, to ease up on his sister. But besides trying to help his sister, Barry often had to reassure Mary that Henrietta could never affect his feelings for her, as if Mary believed Natt was still her adversary.

. . . the chance that she might ever damage in the slightest degree the relationship between you and me is utterly nonexistent. Our complete affection and identification with each other is proof against any such outer forces. . . . I sometimes think it is the very imperviousness of our love for each other which unwittingly taunts Natt, and there is no doubt that our life together sets us apart from the whole world in which she lives. Whether we are partly to blame for seeming smug and secret in our deep intimacy is beside the question, for I believe it is the fact of that intimacy rather than the outward manifestations which may prove psychologically tantalizing to Natt.

Mary wrote that "good works" alone could not serve for Natt's "regeneration." At the very least, Natt would have to become a "practicing Roman Catholic" to escape from "the slavery of her ego." Mary explained,

> In the Second Part of Faust, Goethe resolved Faust's spiritual defeat by making him set about building dams or draining marshes. It always seemed a phony denouement to me. Because I do not think one's inner house can be set in order without a more personal coming to terms with oneself than Goethe's expedient encompassed. The ego is very subject to cancerous reduplication and expansion. I think it can only be kept in check by Christian humility or classical proportionateness. Natt cannot call either one of these traditional sources of virtue and self discipline to her aid in her present unanchored and self-centered life.

What could Barry have thought in the heat of the tropics reading this diatribe against Goethe as his wife defended her dislike of his sister? Was it possible that he blamed himself, as he realized his being away from home had caused Mary to harden toward the rest of the family? Mary wrote that she knew her feelings toward Natt were "hard and prideful." In a supreme understatement, she added, "My judgment is very harsh." But perhaps she was still fighting, even in May of 1945, with Natt over her brother.

Mary might have recognized something powerful and disturbing in Natt, for she had the same affliction—an overwhelming need to possess Barry, often to the exclusion of her children and family. She seemed to be as territorial toward Barry as a mother lion toward her cub, and so subtle and discreet that she appeared to have never discussed her feelings about Henrietta with anyone in the family, except her own husband and Edie Callahan. No one in the family seemed to know that she wanted Natt to be given shock therapy. Often she would go to the Norton Infirmary just to talk to Dr. Ackerly about her plans for Natt, or so she wrote to Barry. Ackerly would then write to Barry long complicated letters of psychiatric jargon about *his* attempts to persuade Henrietta to take shock treatments.

Natt's problems were another family secret. The children only knew that she would get drunk and throw scenes, particularly at Derby time. Mary never allowed herself to discuss the possible childhood roots of Natt's problems, perhaps for fear of implying that Barry shared the same devils. "She was always very affectionate with me," Mary said publicly. "She was a most subtle and complicated person." A fine line of tension appeared on her brow as she spoke. "My sister had the life she wanted," Barry said, then changed the subject.

And yet Mary gave to Radcliffe all her letters in which she laid out her entire case against Henrietta. She even included Spaff Ackerly's letters to Barry Senior, written on his medical letterhead. What was she thinking about when she did that? Barry Junior remembered his mother rereading her letters very carefully before she donated them to the library in 1981, so she was well aware of their content. Perhaps she wanted the world to know what *she* had had to put up with from Henrietta Bingham and that the evidence in the letters would support her case.

Mary's relationship with Henrietta was hardly one-dimensional, however. Although Mary hounded Natt about electric shock, she was also her affectionate sister-in-law. Like Natt, she had good days and bad days, and on her good days she was perfectly capable of writing Barry that she was filled with "remorse" about her years of outbursts and "uneasy fear" about Henrietta. "The very fact of bringing it out in the open has altogether done away with it," she wrote him, although that wasn't true. In those moods she and Henrietta would spend hours together, laughing and talking, as they did when they were young in Paris in the 1920's and Natt was still the sexual vamp, with the blue bows in her hair, that Noel Coward adored. They were "family," after all; though perhaps intolerant of each other, even jealous and furious at times, they were linked by marriage, if not by blood. Natt relied on Barry for money as well as family ties, as did her brother, Robert.

Natt and Robert were close, but Robert's new wife, Felice Desmit, was a safe subject for Mary and Henrietta because neither woman liked her. Robert called himself "an investment banker," but in fact he simply lived off his *Courier-Journal* dividends. Sallie later believed her uncle had syphilis, but there is no evidence of this. "He was a burnt-out case," Barry Senior said—a not untypical product of a gothic Southern upbringing. What Barry didn't mention is that Robert had been old enough to grasp his father's unorthodox behavior. Worth and Barry Junior used to stay with Robert and Felice in New York on their way to boarding school, and Barry remembered how strange it was at bedtime because "Uncle Robert would get down on the floor and tell us that Lizzie or Cordie was hiding under the bed, like he either believed it or thought we were three years old."

Robert and Felice had married suddenly, and Mary was convinced that Felice was a fortune hunter. Mary was the one who informed Aleen of the news. She wrote to Barry that Aleen "is convinced that Felice D. is an adventuress who has snagged off

Robert for his money, and she dreads the thought of possible children. I'm afraid Robert is much too distracted to be able to engage in any such concentrated activity. . . ." Mary described how Felice had done their New York apartment in shades of beige, "very dun." Felice was acting like Robert's "governess," Mary would report, which was probably for the best, since Robert desperately needed someone to deal with the "neurotic indecision and the utter drift of his life." But Mary also said, "I believe her elbows, knees and nose could sharply bruise any bed companion. . . ." In fact they had separate bedrooms on East Sixty-eighth Street, which was a sure sign, Mary said, that there were no "midnight feasts."

Just after they married, Robert brought Felice to Glenview as a way of including her in the family. Mary could not get over feeling that "her eye is very green and her interest in everything about our menages is very sharp and prying. . . . I still feel a little concerned as to just what her influence upon Robert might be now that she has seen life at Harmony Landing and at Glenview." Mary had offered Robert "some of the silver which had been reposing in the vault downstairs for so long." Mary pulled out Barry's mother's tea service, a few silver platters, a vegetable dish and an urn. "I told them I would have Ollie polish them and send them on to them next week. At that point there was a hasty whispered consultation between them, and upon which I am certain was Felice's motion, Robert said that they thought they might as well take the silver along with them on the train. I thought this exhibited a kind of avidity that was far from attractive." Until he died more than twenty years later, Robert and Felice would live in a small house in Nevada, far from Glenview and the judgments of the family.

Mary went to Eaglebrook in the summer of 1945 for Worth's commencement. She was as proud of her oldest son as any mother could be, and was thrilled when in a swim meet she heard the "fine cries of 'Bingham!' as he ploughed ahead of the other boys." Worth entered a speech contest and Mary wrote, "I don't know why mere youth should be so appealing, but I found a great lump rising in my throat as he advanced to the edge of the platform, looking very tall . . . with that thin high-shouldered air that is so moving." She was almost sure she would send Worth on to Exeter that fall, but not Barry because he would need "a smaller school where he could get special attention." She had decided against St. Paul's because the headmaster had informed her proudly that there were "few New Dealers in the school." Mary reported this shocking remark at Harvard to Arthur Schlesinger, Sr., who said, "Obviously, they thought they were speaking to a Long Island mama." Barry came home that summer playing a mellophone, which was, one of her friends remembered, "considered a nerdy thing to do" even then. Dutifully, he had agreed to continue his exhausting daily trips into town for reading lessons with a middle-aged woman who, as a child, had been a friend of his father's, in the children's literary group, the Aloha Club.

It was very hot that July in Louisville, and one afternoon Worth, Barry Junior and two friends were splashing around in the Bingham's huge swimming pool. Worth looked over and saw George Retter, the seventeen-year-old son of the Binghams' Negro gardener, Loubelle. George was working hard and perspiring in the heat, so Worth called out to him to jump in the pool. *Hey, George, come have a swim.* In strict defiance of all Southern conventions, the grateful George stripped and went into the Bingham pool. That night at the vast dining room table, Barry told his mother what had happened. "Mother screamed at us," Barry Junior remembered. "She began to go on and on about polio and syphilis and the germs that colored people have. . . . Then, she drained the pool. This was the first sense Worth and I ever had that our parents were really hypocrites. The newspapers could stand for one thing in public, but in private, it was a different story entirely."

Mary suffered miserably over this incident and knew that she had shown herself to be a phony to her most cherished son. "This was a most extraordinarily painful dilemma," she said, using an expression she would use repeatedly in the years to come. Just after dinner she sat down and wrote Barry a long letter describing every word of what had gone on between her and Worth, for somewhere in her maternal heart she must have known that this was one of those incidents that children never forget, the moment when they realize that a parent is an imperfect being. She had to share this dreadful experience with Barry, and needed, as a mother, to feel less alone.

My own darling:
To-night at supper, I was frozen to my seat when the boys told me that George (Loubelle's son) had been in swimming with them in the pool. I prodded around until I discovered that Worth had invited, even urged him to come in. . . . I said flatly that he was not to go in anymore, and when Worth said, "I thought all men were born free and equal," I was left without any answer except to say that I would discuss the whole thing with them later. I did not think a thorough discussion of such a subtle and explosive question would be good to carry on before Sallie.

But as the evening wore on, Mary was struck by Worth's "depression and mulish resentment," not understanding why he was so silent and angry.

It amazes me that any child brought up in this part of the world would not have taken in through his pores a sense of the mores which forbid inviting nigs to swim in the pool.

I was afflicted with the strong desire both to laugh and to cry at the bewilderment and the belligerence Worth showed.

She tried clumsily to unravel for Worth the intricacies of how she and his father, as Binghams and liberals, viewed the race question, although she did not admit to Worth the "repugnance" she felt about George. "I can hardly think of a more unfortunate choice than George for Worth's experiment in literal Christianity," she wrote to Barry in Guam. He was "a rather surly one, lazy and spoiled, and an incipient bad egg. . . . It is surely wrong to pervert the native and uncomplicated lack of prejudice that Worth so plainly has by planting in his mind the pernicious doctrine of racial superiority." Mary was worried about George's health habits and the idea of his being in the pool with Sallie, since she was sure he was "precocious" as well.

Sallie quite often goes down to the pool alone now, as she can swim quite well to take care of herself, and it makes real Carry Me Back to ole Virginia goose pimples break out on me to think of George's falling into the habit of swimming whenever he takes the notion.

I wish I could convey to you the tormented and near-tears atmosphere about the child when we were talking. For the first time I felt almost out of my depth in a matter of advice and counsel to the children, and I'm not at all sure that he doesn't think that I am a female Simon Legree. . . . He asked me how I would like it if he should refuse to play football for Eaglebrook because there was a negro boy on the opposing public school team, if he should say, "I won't play because there is a nigger on the team," and, of course, I said, I would be very shocked indeed. What, then, he asked was the difference between that and asking George to swim, or to play tennis on our court? Did you ever hear of such a booger in your life?

Her sons knew that their mother was floundering amid intellectual rationalizations, and in that relentless way of smart teenagers, even twelve-year-old Barry was moved to take on his mother. "Barry piped up then to ask who would be the first to dine and to swim with negroes when they reached that point, and how would we ever know whether they had or not, unless we associated with them in those ways.'' Mary insisted that Worth call George and tell him that he wasn't going to go back into the pool. Barry wrote from the Pacific that he saw nothing wrong with swimming with Negroes if they were clean, just as he would hate going swimming with a seventeen-year-old white boy ''of dubious habits.''

> . . . I would not hesitate myself to go in swimming at the beach here with the two Negro correspondents at this head-quarters, both of whom are Harvard graduates and as clean and healthy in appearance as any other correspondent in the place. Further, I would not mind going in even a small swimming pool, I believe, with a Negro child Worth or Barry's age who might be the son of any one of these correspondents. . . .
>   It is probably preposterous to speak of our dear Worth in terms of Mr. R[oosevelt]'s personal struggle for liberal ideals, but I cannot help but feel that his motives are strikingly parallel to those which inspired the President to turn away from the Groton-Harvard tradition and set his course in the direction of what Maury Maverick used to term, ''the God-damned raggedy-assed liberals.''

None of this made Mary's conflict any easier, and years later, as an old woman, Mary described the incident at the swimming pool with total recall. ''I had to go to Loubelle with tears streaming down my face,'' she said, ''And I had to say, 'Loubelle, George can just not go swim in our pool and you know, that is just the way it is.'' Loubelle said, ''Yes, m'am, I know.''
   All that summer, ''the negro question,'' as Mary called it, preyed on her mind. Richard Wright had written *Black Boy*, and the notion of race and segregation was being written about more and more as the black troops began to come home from the war. In August, Benny Goodman came to Louisville to give a pops concert at Churchill Downs. He had a letter of introduction to the Binghams, and Mary invited him to lunch ''with his clari-net'' and whipped up some mint juleps and daiquiris on the west porch. The Ethridges and Edie came to lunch to meet the visiting celebrity, and Cordie outdid herself with ''vichyssoise, very cold and very full of parsley; a moulded chicken salad faintly impregnated with curry, mayonnaise; old ham; cucumbers in sour cream, and a beautiful salad of tomatoes, watercress and Bibb lettuce; beaten biscuits; and peach ice cream made with Natt's stand-alone cream.'' Goodman ate himself into ''a perfect stupor,'' she reported, and Mary was delighted to point out to Barry the refreshing way that he disregarded the staff ''with that

HOUSE
OF
DREAMS

Louisville heiress Eleanor Miller,
the future mother
of Barry Bingham, Sr.

Robert Worth Bingham,
1933.

Mary Lily Flagler,
the future
Mrs. Robert Worth Bingham.

Dr. M. L. Ravitch.

Louisville, Ky., June 19, 1917.

I make this a codicil to my last will and it shall be a valid devise as such codicil and if at my death I have no will or have a will or wills made subsequently to this instrument it shall nevertheless be an independent devise at all times and under all circumstances of change, modification or revocation of my present will or any will or wills. I give and bequeath to my husband, R. W. Bingham, five million ($5,000,000) Dollars to be absolutely his, and he shall have the option at my death of taking this from my estate in money or in such securities as he and the administering authorities of my estate may agree upon with respect to market values.

Witness my hand on the date above shown.

Witnesses;   Mary Lily Bingham.
  W. W. Davies.
  M. L. Ravitch.

Lincliff, where Mary Lily Flagler lived and died
before celebrating her first anniversary.

Ambassador Robert Worth Bingham and his third wife, Aleen,
at the coronation of George VI, London, 1936.

Henrietta Bingham: The Bloomsbury artist and writer Doric Carrington
called her "a Giotto Madonna."

Made for each other: Barry Bingham with his bride, Mary Caperton, in Richmond, Virginia, July 1931.

Barry Bingham *(left)* on the campaign trail with Adlai Stevenson
and Mrs. Edson Dick, co-chairman of Volunteers for Stevenson, 1955.

Great ladies clasp hands:
Mrs. Jacqueline Kennedy and Mary Bingham at the White House, 1961.

Jonathan at his christening
shortly before his father was to leave
for the war, summer, 1942.
"I think he is the greatest solace
and comfort to Mary,
a balm in Gilead if anything can be
in your absence,"
Mary's mother would write to Barry.

Jonathan Bingham, 1962.

Father and sons,
Barry Jr. *(left)* and Worth,
wartime, 1942.
"He was like a hero to us, a god."
—Barry Jr.

A family portrait of American success,
Paris, 1950.

Worth at prep school.

Father and son: Barry Sr. and Barry Jr.

Melcombe, the Big House, Glenview, Kentucky.

Home for Christmas, 1959.
The Binghams at a peak moment of their happiness and prestige.
From left to right: Worth, Joan, Whitney, Sallie, Jonathan, Barry Sr., Barry Jr., Mary, Eleanor.

Worth Bingham: heir apparent, 1966.

Worth and baby Clara, 1964.

Joan Bingham at home in
Washington, 1986.

Barry and Edith
on their wedding day, 1963.

Good times in Chatham, 1982.

Edie Bingham at home in the Big House, 1986.

The bride-to-be: Sallie, 1958.

Tim Peters,
Sallie's third husband, 1986.

Sallie Bingham, 1986.

Coming out in Louisville:
Eleanor Bingham with her parents.

Eleanor Bingham Miller, 1986.

Rowland Miller, 1986.

Eleanor *(left)* with
Mary and Barry at the
Kentucky Derby, 1987.

Mother and daughter at the
Kentucky Derby, 1987.
"She is such a considerate girl
with such flair,"
Mary would say about Eleanor.

Barry Jr. *(left)* and Allen Neuharth, the chairman of Gannett,
on one of the final days
of the Bingham ownership of the *Courier-Journal.*

Mary and Barry Bingham at home in the Little House, March 1986.

Mary and Barry Bingham
as their dynasty collapses.

utter imperviousness to Ollie and Frances moving round the table that is so agonizing in visitors from other parts.'' Goodman had just read *Black Boy,* ''and gave it as his opinion that he was sick and tired of negroes who made a profession of being members of a badly treated minority group. 'They are negroes. Well, so what? Let them go on from there. I'm a Jew, but I don't cry in public about it all the time.' His hard-boiled and humorous approach was rather refreshing, I think.'' Mary was delighted that at least someone who had passed through Melcombe that long, hot summer could make her laugh.

August 1945. When President Truman dropped the atom bomb on Hiroshima, Barry was fast asleep on Guam. He awakened hearing all the ''outcry from the neighboring officers' quarters'' and learned what had happened. Then, he wrote, the news arrived about the Russian move, ''and that was the day on which I went around with a grin on my face from ear to ear. I felt suddenly smug and certain about the outcome, and up to that point it was all comprehensible, all within the bounds of ordinary human emotion.'' Barry had been miserable in the Pacific, stuck on Guam with little to do but shuttle correspondents' dispatches on to the proper airplane. Now it was clear he would soon be home and he was overjoyed, although years later he would gloss over this unpleasant Pacific duty as if it had been as thrilling as his time in Europe.

When Hirohito surrendered, Barry and the rest of the Americans in Guam went wild. He wrote:

It has been almost impossible to sit still for a moment and try to think of all the implications of these world-shattering events. ''At all hours of the day and night I keep coming back to the only completely real and utterly significant thought for me, which is that I will soon be back again with you to spend the rest of my life in the unspeakable happiness of our love for each other.

On V-J Day, Harold and Alice Guinzburg's son, Tom, appeared at Barry's cubicle and said, ''I've paid $20 for a bottle of vodka!'' Later, Barry had to prevent Guinzburg from being arrested when he tried to congratulate Admiral Nimitz by crashing an officers' party. ''I know this young man,'' Barry told Admiral Nimitz. ''His family is very fine and they are dear friends of mine.'' And with that he escorted the drunk twenty-one-year-old back to camp.

Barry wrote to Mary that however miserable he was in the Pacific with the mundane job he had been given, he did not want to put his papers through too early because of the way it might

appear. He was sorry he was going to have to miss "the dear
boys" before they left for school. Besides, he was going on a
Navy attack transport to Tokyo with eighty-nine reporters. He
had an entire battalion of press to shepherd around, and he
couldn't miss Tokyo, not after all he had been through.

Yet that too would be disappointing for him: trapped on the
ship, hating the hot weather and the crowds, he seemed to be in
the worst mood he had been in for the entire war. He was tired
and he wanted to come home. The Pacific was alien to him.
When he arrived in Japan, he was revolted by the "tawdry,
cheap, and tasteless" modernization of the old, quaint ways. He
felt none of the exhilaration he had when he went into Normandy. His spirits were so low that he waited four or five days
to write to Mary about his experience of even being on the *Missouri* for the Japanese surrender, although being on the ship was
all that he had hoped for when he had come to the Pacific. When
he did write to her, he wrote less than a page about the signing
of the treaty on the *Missouri*.

> I will not try to write much . . . as you must have read
> thousands of words on the subject. . . . I had a place at the
> rail on one of the decks directly above the table where the
> surrender document was signed, so that I could see each
> representative approach and watch their expressions as they
> wrestled with the manifold pens provided for the purpose.
> The Japanese were surly, stiff, and ridiculous in their ill-
> fitting European diplomat's clothes. Their top hats would
> not have graced one of the cab drivers outside the Plaza in
> New York.

He was rushing to finish this letter for the Guam mail pouch,
which might be why there is a lack of detail about the ceremony,
for he left out the overwhelming moments that everyone had
remarked upon. He did not comment on the tension, or the fact
that there was no applause or throwing of caps in the air once
the Japanese delegates signed. A formation of planes went over
the ship, and the Americans were not sure whether or not it was
a kamikaze raid until they saw the stars and stripes. Barry, who
never missed a detail, did not tell Mary how the sun burst
through the clouds exactly as the planes passed over the *Missouri*. None of that was written to Mary, although he spoke
about it later, as if his subsequent pleasure at being a witness to
history had taken the place of his actual emotions when he was
there.

From Louisville, Mary wrote to Barry that she had been at a
julep party when the news of the surrender had come through
on the radio, and the next morning "Worth and Barry woke me

up to hear the seven o'clock broadcast Friday morning when the news of the Japanese overture was first announced. . . . The news has even penetrated into Jonathan's busy and independent world, and it is his opinion that, now that the bad Japanese have been beaten, you may descend at any moment from the skies in a silver airplane.''

For weeks she wondered whether they should go on holiday to Pinehurst or to Southern Pines.

I want to be somewhere with you where we can walk and where the climate is good for that, and good for going to bed together (as if any climate could diminish the joy of that) and where we can sleep late and get up when we choose and have our breakfast together, and talk and talk and talk. And I want to be with you every minute of the day and night, without even the dear children for a while, so that I can really begin to believe that that icy and terrible morning will not arrive when I shall have to say, ''This is the end,'' and go about putting things in your bag, while the misery and terror of your going away makes me as dumb and despairful as some poor animal left behind.

Mary wrote that she was determined not to ''get caught up in the sort of squirrel cage that threatens every person of good will in a community like Louisville,'' but she would not be able to help herself. Mary wanted Barry to take the title of editor and resume command of the editorial page. ''The page badly needs the writing distinction that you would bring to it, and it badly needs your editing both on the large matters of policy and on hair line decisions of taste, judgement and finesse.'' And she was adamant that he should spend more time with their children, and his former routine of remaining ''in town every day and rarely even coming home on Saturday afternoons'' was going to have to change: ''I think we have a great deal to make up to Jonathan and Sallie for these half-orphan years.''

One day that summer before Barry finally did come home, Mary was having lunch with her children when Barry Junior turned to her and said, according to a letter,

''You know, I can hardly imagine what it will be like when the war is really over. Do you think Daddy and all of us could maybe go to Chatham next summer?'' . . . From this he launched into one of his deeply savored and stored up reminiscences . . . and ended with a wondering and wistful remark. Did I realize that Sallie could hardly remember when the war was not going on, and that Jonathan did not know what it was like for Daddy to be at home? The child

is . . . almost overwhelmed by the sense of the rushing
away of all that time . . . and earnestly aware of the vastly
impoverished quality of our life at home without you for so
many years. . . . My mind turns, like his, more and more
to the almost unbelievable thought that next summer we
may all be at Chatham together again, and that we shall
never never be parted again.

20

At last they were together again. When Barry finally returned to Louisville, he and Mary did everything they had planned to do in their hundreds of letters. At first the *Courier-Journal* reporters joked, "Mark Ethridge will never give the paper back to Mr. Bingham," but Barry took the title of editor. Although he knew his children had been "half-orphans," as Mary had written him at the end of the war, Barry traveled extensively through the late 1940's, even going to Berlin twice to study reconstruction. If during the war he had been geographically inaccessible, after the war he was so caught up in his new public life that however fine his intentions he simply no longer had the time to lavish on his children.

The Bingham children had predictable reactions to their father's return. Suddenly, Mary's focus was not on them but on her beloved Barry. She often traveled with him and, as a family member said, "would not miss a committee meeting if Barry wanted her there." She had been devastated by his absence and no doubt felt the need to make up for lost time. Thirteen-year-old Worth, no longer the gentle boy that Mary had once so appreciated, was beginning to show signs of serious wildness, as if he were desperate for attention. Finally, Exeter would expel him. In contrast, Barry Junior had become a boy who tried hard to please his parents, especially his father, and was excessively polite, as if he were trying to imitate his courtly manners. When Mary and Barry went out walking with their sons, Barry Junior naturally fell in step with his father, and Worth with his mother, which might have reflected each parent's subtle preference. Although Sallie was a fine high school student, she would also become unruly and fight bitterly with her mother. If Worth's and Sallie's reactions were this severe, the other Bingham children must also have been painfully affected, especially three-year-old Jonathan, who had had his mother's complete attention and now no doubt perceived that his father, a stranger, had taken his mother away. In any event, just back from the war, the sheer excitement of the events of Barry's life quickly overcame him; he was consumed by his desire to serve the public, as his own father had been.

Barry, a distinguished publisher of a prestigious newspaper, would soon occupy himself with foreign affairs. Sallie later said, "Mother's role was very much the role of 'Don't upset your father. He is so important. He is so busy and if you say that he might be upset. He is a very important man.' " That he was: Barry's status had been greatly enhanced by the war, and he was now on close terms with State Department leaders and the Truman White House.

The *Courier-Journal* had become so powerful that after the war, not only Barry but Mark Ethridge and James Pope, the managing editor, frequently went on foreign diplomatic missions. Even better, as Louisville prospered, so did the *Courier,* and advertising revenues began to make up for the war losses. A *Time* reporter called it the "most sincerely liberal newspaper in the South." The *Courier-Journal* printed six editions a day that went to all 120 counties in the state. "Our top writers were like movie stars," a *Courier* public relations man said. The food editor, Cissy Gregg, known for her genius with Jell-O mold salad, was often mobbed in the small towns. Her cookbook sold for twenty-five cents and was a Kentucky best-seller.

Later even Barry Senior himself would write a column of personal musings called "Editorial Notebook," which ran on the editorial page. He wrote hundreds of columns about his travels, his passions, his famous friends, teenage mores, his passion for leeks ("a minor sort of onion"), the pleasures of Devon. "What Kind of Job Is the Newspaper Game?"; "Only Memories Remain of the Richmond School"; "Consider Now the Beagles of the Field"; "Oh, How I Hate to Get Up in the Morning!"; "Dickens Set to Music and Dance." Some reporters began to make fun of this column, but the readers liked the owner's poetic style. It was a perfect forum for a newspaper owner to exercise the power of opinion, as William Randolph Hearst had often done on the front page of his papers, but Barry's columns were mostly charming and not controversial. Five years after a trip to Oxford to attend a seminar, Barry wrote about the view from his favorite inn, likening it to a scene in a poem by Matthew Arnold, the stream curving through "wide grass-meadows which the sunshine fills." In fact, the style of his column was so detached, that in the end, when the family collapsed, his angry children would call his tone of perpetual cheer "the Editorial Notebook voice."

Even in the daily editorial meetings, which were held at 10:00 A.M., Barry rarely became ruffled by the inevitable arguments. Five writers conferred every day: Weldon James, Molly Clowes,

John Ed Pearce, Russell Briney and Tarlton Collier, who was the expert on the South. They often disagreed, and would argue violently. "When Mark Ethridge ran the meetings, they were vigorous intellectual exercises. Sometimes he would call names and say, 'You smart aleck son of a bitch,' " John Ed Pearce said. "But when Barry Senior took over, he would go around the table once and say, 'What do you think?' and that would be that." The moment the conversation became too spirited for Barry, Pearce remembered, he would just shut the whole thing off by saying, "I must make a note of that."

What was astonishing was that Mary and Barry seemed more in love, if that was possible, than before. Within months of Barry's return from Guam, Mary was pregnant again, although Barry was never "quite sure we should have had another child." He would say this with a smile, of course. His second daughter, Eleanor, was born in July of 1946, "a sunny and cheerful" child, although her mother would tell family members that Eleanor was "certainly not as pretty as Sallie had been." Later Sallie took over Eleanor's care, and spent hours with her. In Glenview they had adjoining rooms and shared a bathroom, and Sallie, Eleanor said, "was really the person who was more like a mother to me than my own mother, who was always so busy and preoccupied." She was always in Sallie's room, and Sallie later said that she was glad "for someone to take care of." She invented games for Eleanor, and even constructed an elaborate "job jar," which was filled with instructions on small sheets of paper, such as "Go count your marbles," or "Go look at a picture book." As if they had to protect each other, Eleanor and Sallie would became staunch allies and would remain so until after their family empire was dismantled.

But mostly, Eleanor later would remember her childhood as a time when her parents "were forever busy." Mary maintained her morning ritual of staying in bed with her breakfast, the *Courier-Journal* and her correspondence until her children left for school. Jonathan, Sallie and Eleanor were often left with Nursie, who was on the verge of retirement, and Eleanor's French "mamselle." Now that she was in her forties, Mary did not have the physical stamina or patience required to give the two youngest children the hours she had devoted to Worth, Sallie and Barry Junior. "It was logical," said Barry Junior. "She was just tired of raising children by the time Jonathan and Eleanor were small." Barry Senior wanted her time, and Mary wanted to do what she wanted, which was clearly to be involved with Barry in public life. Eleanor, as the sunniest of the five children, didn't seem to resent this, but Sallie did.

In Sallie's play, the autobiographical *Milk of Paradise*, Missy, the daughter of the family, is left on her fourteenth birthday. The

parents, "Mr. Robby" and "Miss Alice," are crossing the Atlantic, standing on ship deck in the final scene.

MISS ALICE: . . . You know, I believe you've forgotten.
Today was Missy's birthday.

MR. ROBBY: I didn't forget. I just didn't want to cloud the
day.

MISS ALICE: Cloud the day! You think we were wrong to
leave her alone?

MR. ROBBY: She won't be alone.

MISS ALICE: Well, no . . . You know, I can't imagine what
they all do when we're not there.

MR. ROBBY: You mean the children?

MISS ALICE: The children. And the others.

MR. ROBBY: Why, they keep things going. We have to let
them spread their wings, Darling. They can manage without
us—but you and I—we can't live without this. (He begins
to dance with MISS ALICE as the music grows louder and
then abruptly ends.)

In 1949 President Truman appointed Barry Bingham to be
head of the Marshall Plan for France. At first Mary stayed in
Glenview to pack. The family was set to arrive a month after
Barry got to Paris, crossing on the *Mauretania*, the very ship
Barry had taken to Europe when he had left with the Judge,
Aleen and Henrietta in 1930. Barry wrote from the boat about
"a bad sinking spell" he was having without Mary, his "des-
peration" that she would not be with him until July. "I miss
you with even greater intensity than I did during our long sepa-
rations during the war," he wrote. The letters were just as they
had been during the war, as passionate and filled with detail.
Social "tripes" on board, glimpses of Noel Coward, who was
crossing with Robert Sherwood's wife, Madeline; bridge games.
When Barry arrived in Paris and set up in the Hotel Lancaster,
he wasn't the only *Courier-Journal* man in town. Mark Ethridge
was on his way back to America after the Palestinian negotiations to which he had been sent as a United Nations observer,
and Barry reported how "very tired and strung up" Ethridge
seemed. "His eyebrows have gone entirely grey under the strain
of the Palestine negotiations, which gives him a curiously griz-
zled appearance," Barry wrote. As always, Barry concerned
himself with Mark's drinking, and reported to Mary that he and
Mark had had lunch at Le Doyen with the secretary of state.
Acheson, Barry wrote, "is the first person I have ever seen who
would tell Mark to go on and eat his lunch, when the intake had
been confined to martinis and wine." In those few weeks before
Mary arrived, he dined with the Duke and Duchess of Windsor,

and reported that the Duke seemed to him as "nervous and brittle as Robert." He gave parties for both the French and American press corps and dazzled his new staff of ninety-four to such a degree that in a newsletter a secretary was quoted as saying, "Are All Mission Chiefs Handsome?"

That summer, when fifteen-year-old Barry Junior got off the *Mauretania* in France, he was terrified. He had finally adjusted to private school, and was now doing well at Brooks, where his mother had sent him instead of the larger, more competitive Exeter. He was thinner now, and a bit of a dandy like his father. Barry Junior wasn't sure how he felt about being uprooted to spend a year in France, especially after his first view from the ship. The harbor was "a disaster"; the bomb damage had yet to be cleared out, and he said, "I'd never been in a country where people spoke a foreign language before." He had become a rigid boy who liked structure, and was often forced to be the one to bring his wild older brother in line: "I was often with Worth when he got drunk. . . . I was the pain-in-the-ass kid brother who was to try to help him out saying, 'Worth, it is time to go to bed.' "

Ever since his father had come home from the war, Worth had been increasingly difficult to handle. Barry Senior later said, "He resented my return because he was no longer his mother's focus, or so his psychiatrist said." But like all teenagers, Worth would often blurt out anything to get his parents' attention. Once at the dinner table, Barry Junior remembered, Worth told his mother, "If you're coming home from a party at three A.M. from the country club, it is better to drive a hundred miles per hour because you meet fewer cars. Most accidents are head-on collisions, so you would meet fewer cars than you would if you were driving fifty miles per hour." Although even his brother knew that it was "ninety-nine percent put-on," Barry remembered his mother going pale and saying, "Oh, well, oh . . ." and his father not responding at all, as if he didn't know what to say. "My father always thought Worth was like Uncle Robert," Barry Junior said. "He never knew how to handle him."

The year before the Binghams left for France, Worth was expelled from Exeter for drinking. Worth's sins were the usual boarding-school show-off behavior: "barfing contests"; "dropping trou," the current prep school term for what would later be called "mooning." When Worth was a junior, he got in with a fast crowd; one of his friends was a descendant of a president, as Mary remarked in a letter. They would get drunk frequently, and finally, the school had had enough. Worth landed at Lawrenceville. There he confided to the school psychologist, according to a friend, that "the whole time my father has been home he never once has written me a letter." He complained that his father was too busy for him, that he spent all his time with the newspaper or racing around the world, and with the sullen outrage of the wronged adolescent, he said, "My father never once has come to one of my swim meets."

The psychologist told Barry Senior that Worth was obviously reacting to the loss of attention he had suffered when his father came home. Additionally, the psychologist reportedly told Barry Senior that he was identifying his son's wildness with that of his own brother, Robert—a negative and wrong association. It is conceivable that even if Barry Senior had written Worth dozens of letters—and there is no evidence to prove Worth right—the response would have been the same. Nevertheless Barry Senior's reaction was hardly to get on the train for the next Lawrenceville swim meet or to take Worth off on a long trip by himself. He simply couldn't: Barry Senior was on his way to France. He wrote Mary, "I can't help but hold my breath he'll get into Le Rosey" for his senior year in high school. He sent both older boys to Lausanne for summer school. "I hope that Worth will stick to his resolution on drinking. . . . I can already see [a friend's] demonic shadow falling over our lives in Paris," he wrote.

The boys were supposed to be in summer school to perfect their French. Barry Junior remembered that a quasi-religious movement called Moral Rearmament had swept Lausanne that year, and Worth was recruited by some Americans he had met on the street. Moral Rearmament was a forerunner of the self-help confessional groups of the 1970's. It was anti-Communist, probably a touch fascist, and certainly zealous, a forum where members could "confess" their blackest thoughts. "This is a whole lot more fun than going to summer school," Worth told his brother. Dutifully Barry tagged along with Worth to a few meetings, and at one of them, "A guy from Detroit got up and started talking about how he used to deflower virgins," Barry Junior said. "I said to myself, 'This place is weird,' and I told Worth I wanted nothing to do with it."

That summer Barry roomed with a Turk who "did not have one word of a mutual language," and at school his companions spent their time downing bottles of cognac. For Barry, at age fifteen, the summer would be the end of innocence. Now he was in school with military brats, who had seen it all and were used to running wild. "There was a girl . . . who used to distribute her picture in a bubble bath and whose claim to fame was that she had slept with every marine guard at the American embassy," Barry said. Mostly, he tried to keep Worth in line, but it wasn't easy. Worth told his parents that he had no intention of going to Harvard, but instead intended to travel the world with Moral Rearmament.

During the summer Worth got drunk often, and despite the ministrations of Moral Rearmament, he stole a car and wound up in a Lausanne jail. "My father had to come from Paris to bail him out," Barry said. However detached Barry Senior could be, when Worth got into real trouble, he certainly was there. The car incident seemed to end Worth's infatuation with Moral Rearmament, and he wound up in a school called Lycée Jaccard, not at the exclusive Le Rosey. Mary had disliked the headmaster's name-dropping at Le Rosey as she once had at St. Paul's in New Hampshire and "marched Worth down the road to Lycée Jaccard when she heard this man talk about the princes and counts who were his students," Joan, Worth's widow, said. By the end of the summer, Barry Junior decided he had had enough of boarding school, and went to Paris to live with his family and attend the American School. Worth followed that February after he took his Harvard boards.

A family story has it that Worth's headmaster at Lycée Jaccard appeared in Paris that winter and said "Worth had written dirty words on the walls," so the school could not recommend him for Harvard. Worth, however, was first in his class at Lycée Jaccard and had done well on his college boards, so Barry Senior was able to tell him, as Joan Bingham said, to "get lost." The complaint by the headmaster was obviously a subtle request for a large donation to the school to compensate for Worth's defacing the walls. Like many powerful men, Barry Senior always believed that people wanted from him either money or some special favor. He was increasingly obsessed with money, perhaps because his assets were tied up in the business. His sense of financial persecution was intensified by Worth's reports from school.

For the first few months in Paris the family lived in the St James and Albany, and Jonathan, at age seven, used to play elevator operator for the building. Sallie and Barry attended the American School, but typically Sallie came to her mother and said, "I'm not learning anything," and asked to go to a school where no one spoke any English. "For her birthday that year Sallie demanded a new desk and she and I went up and down the Avenue Foch until we found the right one," Mary said. Each day Barry Junior took his homework down to the lobby, where a harpist played. Often he went with his mother to the designer fashion salons—Piguet was a special favorite—so he could "watch as the models all swished these big skirts around." His good friend at school was a boy named Nick Daniloff, whose father ran the Packard agency in Europe and who later would gain wide attention when, as a *U.S. News & World Report* correspondent, he was detained by the Soviets. Years later Barry marveled at the Daniloff household in Paris with a Russian

grandmother and an English one, and how the two women disliked each other so much that Nick had to be the go-between;
"Tell your grandmother to pass the salt," one grandmother
would say. Barry remembered the contrast: the Daniloffs expressed every emotion, while in his own family everyone was
so genteel and detached.

Some months later the Binghams moved to a grand house in
Paris at 17 Rue Alfred-Dehodencq, where Mary and Barry en-
tertained frequently or "were out every night of the week,"
Eleanor remembered. Diplomatic receptions, grand parties,
conferences with ministers and politicians. "I don't think I saw
Mother once for a year," she said.

That winter a *Life* photographer came to Rue Alfred-
Dehodencq to photograph the Binghams of Louisville. They
posed on their eighteenth-century marble staircase and smiled,
but not too broadly. Barry and Mary stood at the bottom of the
staircase. Barry looked no more than thirty years old in the
picture, although he was forty-three. His hair was slicked back,
his lips full. Mary was the very picture of fine breeding: blond
hair neatly coiffed, her mouth set in a pert and tiny line. She
was gloriously dressed in black with a wide belt that showed her
thinness to advantage. Next to her was chubby Eleanor, almost
four years old, in plaid and wearing bangs. Then, standing on
the staircase, in order of ascending ages, were the other children: Jonathan, in knee pants; Sallie, with long blond hair
touching her shoulders, a dreamy-eyed twelve-year-old "Alice";
Worth and Barry, with their great strapping teenage American
looks. What was remarkable about the picture was the way the
children were spaced, apart from their parents, apart from each
other, with no hands held, no leaning toward a favorite brother
or sister, no laughter. The children looked like models who had
wandered into a family portrait of American success. Mary
looked straight ahead into the *Life* camera with a triumphant and
regal stare.

21

The Binghams came home from Paris in the summer of 1950. Through the next decade their five children would come to realize their extraordinary place in the community and their family's immense power in Kentucky and the South. The Bingham children could watch politicians fawning over their parents; they could see the green-and-white *Courier-Journal* trucks circling their neighborhoods and listen to their parents discussing how world events should be covered in their family's newspaper. While their parents traveled extensively in these years the children were surrounded by servants, and the necessities of everyday life were taken care of "as if by magic," Sallie later said, so much so that when she was learning to type, each time her typewriter needed a new ribbon her father would take the machine into town and have a *Courier-Journal* secretary change it. "Compared to the Binghams we lived like paupers," said a daughter of the family that controlled the *Atlanta Constitution* and its communications empire.

The Bingham children were becoming used to their parents' grandeur and their own public exposure, and had often been teased by their parents that if they misbehaved, "We'll run it on page one." The message was tacit and never needed to be said: *We make the news, and this gives us the power to reward and punish.* The Bingham children knew the vocabulary of the newspaper world. News could and would be perceived differently "inside the building" and "outside the building." At school the *Courier-Journal* stories were studied often, and it was their newspaper that had begun the National Spelling Bee.

How powerful the family must have been from the Bingham children's point of view. The new buildings were up in downtown Louisville, and if the children walked from Sixth and Broadway toward the local courthouse, they passed two large Bingham monuments: the limestone newspaper headquarters and the Standard Gravure printing plant. Barry would sometimes take Eleanor, Sallie and Jonathan to the paper to watch the Sunday

comics being printed. "It was psychedelic!" Eleanor said.
"There was this incredible noise and odor and vision and the
family joke was that nobody could go into the business unless
they liked the smell of printer's ink." On those days they would
wear their best clothes, "like little English kids," Eleanor said,
and shake hands with the old employees, as if they were royals.
Their status was such that later, when the Bingham children were
grown up, life away from Louisville could never compare to
their childhoods, and not one of the five children would be able
to resist coming home.

On Derby day Mary and Barry would give the famous "Bingham breakfast" and open Melcombe to hundreds of Kentucky's
finest, who would flock to Glenview to eat turkey hash, fresh
corn cakes and the same brand of Trigg County ham that Mary
used to send Barry during the war. The tulips and dogwood
bloomed all over Melcombe, and, inevitably, national celebrities
such as Adlai Stevenson would be staying in the house for the
parties. In 1951, the first spring after Mary and Barry returned
from Paris, the Duke and Duchess of Windsor came to Louisville for the Kentucky Derby, and the Binghams gave a party in
their honor. Yet another canard circulated in Louisville: it was
commonly believed that the Windsors had sent the Binghams a
bill for one thousand dollars for their mere appearance at Melcombe, a story that was later published in a biography of the
Windsors. But that absurd story was probably another example
of how old Louisville still attempted to cut the Binghams down
to size. "They were the king and queen of Louisville. No one
in Louisville behaved as grandly as they did," said a childhood
friend of Sallie and Jonathan.

Mary and Barry Bingham were now magisterial, part of the
rarefied world that included Adlai Stevenson and traced back
through Harvard, the Marshall Plan and the former Roosevelt
Democrats who belonged to Americans for Democratic Action,
which the Binghams' lawyer and close friend Wilson Wyatt
helped to launch. Barry Senior was so close to Stevenson that
before the Illinois Democrat agreed to run for president in the
1952 election, he stopped in Louisville to consult with Barry.
"I only pleaded that he should leave himself uncommitted, so
that a genuine draft could have an opportunity to develop. . . ."
Barry Senior told a Stevenson biographer. In the spring of 1953,
after he had been defeated in the race for president, Barry and
Stevenson traveled for months together through the Far East—a
trip that had been suggested by Wilson Wyatt "to get Stevenson
out of Eisenhower's hair so Ike could run the country without
Stevenson's remarks in the press." This trip through the Orient
solidified Barry's relationship with Stevenson to such a degree

that in 1956, during the second Stevenson campaign, Barry was
the head of the citizens' group Stevenson for President.

Barry Senior never felt there was anything unethical about
being so cozy with a political candidate, but later his son Barry
Junior would feel differently. When he became publisher in 1971,
Barry Junior's stringent sense of journalistic proprieties would
cause increasing conflict in the family. But in the 1950's, Barry
Senior was often aggressive, in his elegant way, pushing his
candidate and his theories. For example, when Adlai Stevenson
was defeated in 1952, he called for Sigma Delta Chi, the journalism society, to make an "exhaustive study" to see if news
coverage had been biased in favor of Eisenhower. Barry Senior,
in the kingmaking newspaper publisher's style of the era, spoke
out on every major issue; he traveled the world and conferred
with heads of state. He was now a perfect son of his father, a
factor in American liberal social and political life. His name
appeared frequently in the fine print of committee listings in the
New York Times. He was on censorship committees for the International Press Institute; he was chosen by Prince Bernhard of
the Netherlands to attend an economics conference with David
Rockefeller and Paul Nitze. He served on Pulitzer boards and
presidential commissions. He was a Harvard overseer, a frequent speaker at the American Society of Newspaper Editors.
He appeared on *Meet the Press*, published speeches in the
Atlantic Monthly, endowed colleges in Kentucky.

His sons later believed that their father had "an awards complex," that he needed the committee meetings and the certifi-
cation of Pulitzers or honorary degrees and would do anything
possible to please, and in so pleasing, he became the man who
bestowed prizes. In 1949 his listing in *Current Biography* went
on for a page and a half.

Louisville would change tremendously during the 1950's, and
however liberal the Binghams appeared, what with their support
of Stevenson, the Marshall Plan and the Americans for Democratic Action, their principles would be sorely tested during the
McCarthy period and the civil rights years.

As always, the Binghams had the best intentions. Their liberalism was safe, respectable, conventional, typical of their New
Deal friends. But for Louisville during the McCarthy years of
the early 1950's with its segregated backward schools, hospitals
that would not admit Negroes, department stores that would not
allow Negro women to try on clothes or use the bathroom, and
archconservative local prosecutors searching for local "Communists," even their tepid liberalism was extreme. To their
credit, the Binghams were trying through the influence of the
newspapers and their own power to make huge changes in the
state, but their method was of the Southern "gradualist" vari-

ety—"all in good time." For example, the newspaper would
repeatedly run stories about schools that had been peacefully
integrated.

Mary was as involved in the community as Barry was during
the 1950's. She was the book editor of the *Courier-Journal* and
had brought bookmobiles into the state. She ran councils on
education to try to better the conditions she had railed against
so ferociously at the Ballard school. She even helped to integrate
Louisville's restaurants. "We went to every restaurant and they
all said no," Mary remembered. "And there was one dear gentleman who had a fish restaurant called Rio Hideaway on Market
Street and he said, 'Allright, Mrs. Bingham, I'll serve Negroes.' " And so Mary found four "very well-dressed rectors"
and sent them into the Rio Hideaway for lunch. "They sat down
and ordered their lunch and a bottle of champagne. . . . And
then a man came up to the Jewish owner of the restaurant and
said, 'I'm never coming back in here with these nigrahs in here,'
and the Jewish owner said, "They are not Negroes, they are
rectors."

The newspaper had been pushing for the rights of the Negro,
but so discreetly that the more radical members of the community felt the *Courier-Journal* was not doing enough. One of those
radicals, Carl Braden, worked on the *Louisville Times* as a copy
editor, and he and his wife, Anne, provoked a crisis that nearly
"wrecked all the progress we ever made in the community,"
the editorial writer John Ed Pearce said.

In May 1954, four days before the Supreme Court ruled on
Brown v. *Board of Education*, the Bradens made a dummy purchase of a house in a Ku Klux Klan section of West Louisville
where signs still read, ALL NIGGERS OUT BY SUNSET. The Bradens then sold the house to a Negro family named Wade, which
set off a furor in the segregated neighborhood.

Andrew Wade had come from a prosperous local family and
was an electrician, a war veteran, who had been unable to buy
a decent house in Louisville. He had been reared in a Louisville
world of "forbidden parks, forbidden buildings, forbidden restaurants . . . a hemmed-in world." By the early 1950's he was
active in civil rights work and had met the Bradens at local
meetings. Wade knew there might be a few problems when he
moved into this neighborhood, but he had no idea what he would
soon be forcing. The night he moved in, shots were fired at the
house, and the next month the house was bombed. The Bradens
were arrested under the state "sedition" laws, accused of "block
busting," and their own house was raided. The local prosecutor,
trying to make points with the blue-collar voters, had a field day
with the Bradens' library. "If it sounded Russian they took it,"
Anne Braden said. "Tolstoy, Marx, Lenin, Dostoevski." The

community "erupted into hysteria." The *Brown* v. *Board of Education* decision exacerbated Louisville's reaction. "We were the lightning rod for the changes that were coming. . . . It was as if Louisville society took out their anger on us. We heard remarks like 'You should be lynched,' " Anne Braden said.

"The newspaper was in disgrace," Pearce said. The Binghams were forced to ride out some rough times. There was talk about the "Communist cell" operating from the *Courier.* Richard Harwood, now the deputy managing editor of the *Washington Post,* was then a young reporter from the *Louisville Times* who was covering the story. He was subpoenaed by the grand jury.

When the subpoena was delivered to the newspaper, Ethridge called Harwood and said, "I'm going to tell them to go to hell." Then Ethridge instructed his reporter, "Don't take the Fifth Amendment," with its echoes of the McCarthy hearings. Harwood took Ethridge's advice and was cited for contempt for refusing to testify before the grand jury. In front of the judge, however, the prosecutor flared at Harwood, "If you want to protect Communists, that's your business. Now get the hell out of here." The contempt charge was withdrawn.

During Braden's trial Mark Ethridge was constantly asked, "Why don't you fire that Communist?" His answer was firm: "Hell, even Commies have to eat." But Bingham was not nearly as aggressive in his copy editor's defense. "He was under huge social pressure from the country club set," Anne Braden said. "But he was always personally charming to us." Bingham defended Braden while his trial was in progress, but took him off the paper, as the Braden case became a cause célèbre among national radicals. Braden was convicted of advocating sedition—and blamed for the bombing—and sentenced to fifteen years in prison and given a five-thousand-dollar fine. "Sedition is Communism and Communism is sedition," the prosecutor said. Bingham fired Braden, and ran a box on the front page announcing that he was now severed from the newspaper.

Bingham's statement appeared in the *New York Times:*

Carl Braden's employment by The Courier-Journal has come to an end with his conviction. This newspaper has gone on the time-honored principles, rooted in our American Constitution, that a man is innocent until proved guilty. . . . His conviction now puts a permanent end to his connection with the Courier-Journal.

His appeal bond was set for forty thousand dollars, the highest amount ever set by the state at that time. Anne Braden traveled the country to try to raise money, but it was clear that the newspaper was not about to crusade for her radical husband, nor would Barry Bingham help Carl Braden appeal the conviction. And so Braden served eight months in jail. After he was released on appeal, the Supreme Court ruled that state sedition laws were unconstitutional, and the Kentucky Appeals Court overturned Braden's original conviction.

Mary and Barry had been vastly relieved when Harvard admitted Worth to the class of 1954. Although Worth was wild and would become wilder through the 1950's, he was the firstborn. However rebellious he could be, he was also a natural leader with fine instincts, and the Binghams were trying to groom him for leadership, as Otis Chandler had been groomed by his parents, the owners of the *Los Angeles Times*. The sons of newspaper owners often accompanied their fathers to the yearly national editors' conventions where a separate hotel suite would be kept for the children so they would all get to know each other. "I can remember the card games we used to play at the St. Regis," said Stewart Bryan, who later became publisher of the *Richmond Times-Dispatch*. "Worth always won."

Worth had been erratic at Harvard. He could study for three days and then stay drunk for the next five. He gambled a great deal and later had to be straightened out by Norman Isaacs, who was then the editor of the *Louisville Times*, the Binghams' afternoon paper. Isaacs was fierce but loving, and became Worth's mentor. "I taught him lessons that his father couldn't. I could discipline him, yell at him, and read him the riot act. Worth could confide in me. He was like my son." Worth adored Norman Isaacs and often felt more relaxed with him than he did with his own father. Isaacs was so loyal to the paper and the family that he had taken a large cut in pay to come to Louisville from the Des Moines *Register* because Barry and Ethridge had offered him the opportunity to work in what they called "a vacuum of freedom." Isaacs had taken to Louisville; he was on every cultural board, and he made it a personal project to try to straighten out the heir apparent.

But it would take Norman Isaacs some years to settle Worth down. During the summers when he was at Harvard, Worth would work on the newspaper. The first day he reported to work he was wearing, Isaacs remembered, "filthy gray dungarees and old tennis shoes. . . . I said to him, 'It better be a quick trip for you to drive home, change and get back here because nobody works for me who looks like this.'"

Worth already had a reputation as a fast driver. The newspaper, in fine paternal style, dealt harshly with family members who were arrested for speeding. Ethridge had once been picked up for drunk driving; Isaacs had played it on page one. Mary had been arrested on the River Road for running a red light, and Isaacs had run that story in the first section. "I said to Worth, 'You had better not get arrested for anything, not driving or drinking, you have one of the great misfortunes of having the last name that everybody in Kentucky knows. You have got to live with it.''

That summer Worth worked as a police reporter, as his father had in 1930. He also spent a lot of time gambling. "It was of great concern to everyone," Isaacs said. "We were always worried that in one of his high-stakes games with other young Southern publishers' sons, he would gamble away the newspaper. . . . They were all too wild, too rich, and too young." At Harvard he was "drunk and crazy" all the time, his friend Jay Iselin remembered. Once in a card game he lost his new Chevrolet convertible and became enraged when the winner refused to take his car. "A bet is a bet," he said. He was half a bully, half a life force, who wore his mantle as a Bingham son "as a kind of tophat," the novelist Ward Just later said. "There was no question he was my favorite friend." Another friend said, "Worth was always doing something to improve himself." On his shelf he had several books on how to improve your memory.

David Halberstam was at Harvard at the same time and remembers a swim meet where the spectators erupted with cries of "Worthless! Worthless" Halberstam was a part of the other Harvard, serious boys who hardly left the *Crimson* and who were, as he says, "obsessed with Joe McCarthy and what to do about him." Halberstam said, "Our lives were the *Crimson*, we talked and lived and breathed journalism. And here was the heir who was just pissing the whole thing away." Halberstam resented this young Southerner who would get everything that Halberstam and his friend Jay Iselin were "just killing ourselves for."

When Worth went home to Glenview during vacations, he was very much the outsider at the country club dances, "an almost bumbling guest" and out of step. Rumors floated around the country club: he was dating "Negroes" at Harvard; he had run up thousands of dollars in gambling debts. The Louisville boys drank as much as Worth did, his former girlfriend Helen Jones remembered. They were Southern, their parents drank, had little ambition, and they were content to live and die in the small-town comforts of the Louisville bourbon zone. But not Worth Bingham. "They [the Bingham children] were all very sophisticated but not suave," Helen Jones said. "Well, let's leave it at Worth." Once Worth was naïve enough to announce to his parents that he had decided to marry Helen and "there was some sort of exchange with his parents," who said, "Her family is not good enough." And yet Helen was always struck by how gracious to her both the Binghams inevitably were. "All of that articulate, beautifully phrased sophistication kept under wraps this black dragon,'' she said. ''It was really a way to gloss over feelings . . . to hide them.''

Someday Worth and Barry Junior would tell their future wives about the tortures their parents had always put their girlfriends through. ''It was unbelievable,'' Barry Junior said. ''If Worth or I fell in love with . . . an inappropriate woman, they would invite her over again and again until we were so thoroughly embarrassed by her behavior.'' Mary would lay out three forks at dinner and fingerbowls and soon ''we would see that these girls did not fit into the family's life.'' It is easy to imagine how terrifying a dinner at the Binghams' must have been for these Louisville girls, for thirty years later Mary would intimidate financial planners who had come to advise the Binghams about the sale of the empire in the same regal manner. Mary was known for her style as much as her rigor and often wore long white gloves, even in the summer, as well as dresses created by such French designers as Patou. But Mary and Barry knew what they wanted for their sons, ''women who had poise, sophistication, intelligence, beauty and who could carry the family forward,'' Barry Junior said. There was no need to make the inevitable comparison. Anyone with less panache than their mother would not do.

Worth's antics, his drinking and gambling were probably a way of carving out a separate identity from the rigid standards of the family. Even dutiful Barry once tried to escape the mantle of being a Bingham son; after starting at Harvard, he left for a summer in Africa, and while he was there with a group from Louisville, he spotted a tea plantation on Mount Kilimanjaro that was inexpensive and ''absolutely fabulous,'' he said. He wrote his parents, ''This is a wonderful opportunity for me.'' His parents' response was immediate. ''They had one of the men from Louisville I was traveling with spirit me out of Africa on the next plane.'' Most parents would not welcome a son's exile to a tea plantation, but in the case of both Worth and Barry their parents so clearly had other plans for them that no such diversion could so much as be contemplated. The Bingham children would all eventually suffer this same affliction, that they had a shared dream to fulfill. For Worth and Barry, nothing was to be considered more important than the family communications company. All differences, all distractions, had to be put aside, and it was made clear to both of the older boys, Barry remembered, ''that Worth was to run the newspapers and I was to run the television station.''

Worth and Barry were both settled at Harvard during the spring of 1953 as their father traveled for three months through the Far East with Stevenson, leaving sixteen-year-old Sallie, ten-year-

old Jonathan and seven-year-old Eleanor in Glenview. Barry
Senior wrote home dozens of letters, as always, filled with accounts of his activities: lengthy descriptions of Malaysian colo-
nials, a meeting with Nehru, a lunch with Generalissimo Chiang
Kai-shek on Taiwan, a twelve-course banquet with aging Viet-
namese diplomats whose ancient syntax made French "sound
. . . like Chinese." However close he was to Stevenson, he did
not spare Mary any of his negative opinions concerning his
friend. "I fear he is a gourmand," he wrote, and reported that
Stevenson on the ship going to Japan had locked himself in his
stateroom and eaten candy all afternoon from the boxes "cruel
admirers had sent him. . . . His stomach and his behind are
much too big and it makes his legs seem shorter than they are."
Adlai had become "in large degree a Public Figure rather than
a human being," he wrote. "My impression is confirmed that
he is interested in ideas but hardly at all in people."

Just as in his earlier letters from the war and from France,
Barry's letters from the Orient were filled with his hectic and
all-consuming public life. His children's development came second, but read decades later, these dozens of letters contain fascinating clues to how the Bingham children were developing.
Barry wrote to Mary that he was annoyed that Sallie, at home
in Louisville for her junior year in high school, had not written
him a single letter. Sallie had not gone to boarding school, and
Barry wrote how sorry he was to have to miss her college tour.
It didn't occur to him that Sallie might be angry with him for
leaving again, this time for three entire months. For some reason
the letters Mary sent to Barry in the Orient were not donated to
Radcliffe, but it is evident from Barry's letters home that Mary
did not write to him about the difficulties she was beginning to
have with Sallie.

From the Orient that spring of 1953, Barry wrote Mary that
he was glad Barry Junior would not follow Worth into his Harvard club, the Gas House. He didn't want his namesake, who
tried so hard to please him, under Worth's spell. Barry Senior
knew that Worth was drinking his way through Harvard and that
the "Gas House fleshpots," as he called them, weren't helping
his oldest son. What he might not have known was that Barry
Junior had wanted desperately to get into Worth's club, "but on
the one night of his life he got drunk he pulled out the Gas
House telephone," Joan Bingham said, and for this he was
blackballed and, despite Worth's efforts, did not get a bid. Barry
Junior wrote his father that he was happy being in Adams House,
and Barry Senior, busy with Stevenson in the Orient, did not
seem to notice the possibility of his son's having been rejected.
"The four years of Harvard are . . . a kind of bonus that has
come to him for the hellish hard work," he wrote.

At the end of the trip, exhausted by the heat and the hectic pace of his travels, he wrote to Mary that he wouldn't have missed the experience for anything but was desperate to come home to Louisville in time for Jonathan's eleventh birthday on June 1. It was unfortunate that he would have to leave again in a few days for his twenty-fifth reunion at Harvard, where he was to be a featured speaker. He knew he was doing too much—the traveling, the speaking—and so he had "dodged an invitation" from class marshal Bill Saltonstall to moderate a panel on the Far East.

Mary could never understand when and why Sallie had begun to change. "She was particularly sympathetic to us because she had early on a wonderful receptive mind," she later said. Once when Sallie was a teenager, she had come home from a youth group at church, baffled and upset. "Mother, they wanted us to talk about why I hate my mother and they came to me and I couldn't think of anything to say."

Later at her girls' school, Sallie was, as a classmate remembered, "determined to be the oddball." She staged *Hamlet* in her amphitheater at Melcombe. She refused to have a deb party or to wear braces on her teeth, which she badly needed. "She wasn't pretty at all, not compared to those gorgeous Southern girls," her younger classmate Louise Duncan said, "and in Louisville that was a curse." According to Sallie: "I didn't go out on a date until I was sixteen years old. I was ugly and so gawky. I was a wreck." She lacked confidence and certainly had no accurate sense of herself. If Sallie wasn't a beauty, she did, however, have striking blond hair, good skin and a lovely slim figure.

As a teenager, Sallie observed her parents' romantic life and later would sound bitter and even jealous when she described their intimacy. "Every day before Daddy came home from the paper, Mother would bathe and change into a tea gown and there would be that dramatic moment when they would kiss at the foot of the stairs," she said. Sallie adored her father. "Daddy was so glamorous, he was so interesting. I've never seen anyone enjoy life more. The weather, the flowers in the spring. . . ." Later it would seem to family members that Sallie was obsessed with her father and resented her mother's hold on him.

Sallie's feelings about her mother were less positive. "Mother was one of six sisters and she had a way of dealing with women relatives, so I often felt that I was as much a sister to her as a daughter," Sallie said. "The only time I spent with my mother was when I came home from school and she would be gardening and she would let me work in the garden with her." "They were more interested in each other than in some nasty three-year-old.

And of course that was what was expected of that class in that era. . . . Everything was beautifully planned, but there was a lack of intimacy. . . . There has always been a lack of intimacy in our family,'' she said. As she moved from childhood to adolescence, she railed against her mother, as many teenage daughters do. But Sallie believed her rebellion was special, and as a middle-aged woman she still seized on minor incidents to prove how she had been so mistreated. She could remember her mother's most minute infractions. Mary ordered Sallie's clothes from the Best's catalog, the only ''suitable'' store for children's clothes. Sallie, in an early fit of independence, took it on herself to order ''a black rayon blouse that had polka dots, and when my mother saw it in the closet, she said, 'What is this? I never ordered this!' '' Sallie interpreted these normal moments as symbols of a larger truth. She dwelled on these incidents as more examples of her mother's coldness to her and her need for iron-clad control.

Later, Sallie would say about her mother that her temper was so terrible that she ''has a tongue that just will take your skin off,'' and certainly, Mary was often angry at Sallie when she was a teenager. Once during this period, Mark Ethridge's son, David, took Sallie to a dance and Sallie was out a bit past her curfew. When she came home, her mother, waiting in the driveway, yelled at her, ''You get out of that car, you little whore!'' Another time, Sallie went downtown in what her mother considered inappropriate clothes. Mary reportedly yelled at her, ''How dare you walk down Fourth Street in slacks!'' Later, Sallie would remark wistfully that all through her childhood she could never remember her beloved father ever saying a single harsh word to her.

22

Five years later, Sallie would be graduated from Radcliffe and be married. Worth too would have settled down considerably. He was engaged to a beautiful, very young Pittsburgh girl, and was working as a reporter for the *San Francisco Chronicle*. This Christmas of 1959 Worth and Sallie were coming home to Louisville, where the entire family was gathering, as always, at the Big House. With Sallie's recent marriage to Whitney Ellsworth and Worth's upcoming marriage, it seemed a perfect time for Barry and Mary to ask a *Courier-Journal* photographer to take a picture of the family for the newspaper activities. And so, this splendid Christmas, the family gathered in the living room of the Big House and posed for what would become the symbolic portrait of the Binghams of Louisville at the peak moment of their happiness and prestige. It was so striking a picture that almost thirty years later when the family had collapsed, the *New York Times* would run it across three columns of the Sunday business section. The surviving children would later wonder if their parents had had a sense of foreboding that caused them to record this glorious family at this particular holiday, and they would point to that Christmas picture of 1959 as one of the last records of the good times.

Mary and Barry are smiling in the picture, there is nothing forced or strained in their expressions; they are happy with each other, their family, and their place in the world. The fire blazes in the fireplace, and the mirrors and sconces are swagged with garlands. On a brocade sofa to the left of the portrait sit the new family members. First, Worth's fiancée, pretty Joan Stevens, the picture of innocence, dressed in a cable-knit sweater with a Peter Pan collar, a collegiate wool skirt and penny loafers. She is leaning forward as if eager to make a good impression. Next to her is Sallie's new husband, Whitney Ellsworth, wearing glasses, with his arms folded, smiling pleasantly at Mary across the room in an armchair. Twenty-two-year-old Sallie is on the other side of Whitney looking radiantly happy. Standing behind Joan, his hands on the back of the sofa, stands twenty-seven-year-old Worth, leaning forward as eagerly as Joan. Next to Worth is seventeen-year-old Jonathan, who resembles him, the same open face and warm grin. Barry Senior is in the center of the portrait, standing by the mantel, his head turned toward Mary. Next to him is twenty-six-year-old Barry Junior, is subdued as his father, looking away from his mother, toward Joan and Worth. Thirteen-year-old Eleanor is by Barry's side, an overweight teenager with her mother's profile and a spirited smile.

The Binghams' world was so smooth now and so gilded that their daughter Sallie would later remark, "When we went anywhere we were like a flock of very special birds." This Christmas of 1959, particularly, it was wonderful to have everyone gathered in the living room by the fireplace with the blazing sconces and the garlands swagged around the mantelpiece. Worth, Barry Junior and Sallie had all graduated from Harvard and were well launched on promising lives. Worth's drunkenness and Sallie's teenage anger toward her mother seemed a memory. Jonathan and Eleanor appeared no less trouble-free. The Binghams had much to celebrate. Even Adlai Stevenson was staying with them that Christmas, no doubt discussing with Barry Senior whether or not he should run for president yet again.

That Christmas, Sallie and Whitney had come home from Boston, where they lived. Whitney, whom Sallie had met at Harvard, was "a bit stuffy," a friend said, but he had a social conscience. Mary and Barry both considered him "very suitable," although they weren't sure he was strong enough to handle Sallie. Whitney had worked as an editor on the *Atlantic* and, like Barry Senior, was bookish, somewhat delicate, and had a baby face. He and Sallie had married in triumph in Louisville a year earlier. Sallie had worn her mother's heirloom Irish lace veil. Her gown was elaborately beaded, but at the wedding, a guest remembered, it was Mary who was dressed to kill, in flowing pastel chiffon, as if to outdo the bride. Adlai Stevenson came for the festivities, as did Henrietta, who got so drunk that she invited one of Whitney's friends into her bedroom, threw herself down on the bed and began to talk about London and her glorious past and then told a vulgar story about Noel Coward and Tallulah Bankhead, which the friend never forgot. "I had never seen so much drinking at a wedding," he later said.

From San Francisco, Worth had brought home his fiancée, Joan Stevens, an exuberant Miss Porter's School graduate he had met when she attended Harvard summer school. Joan was "more of a Bingham in terms of her poise and good looks than the sisters of the family," a friend said. Joan had certainly helped calm Worth down since his wild college days, but while her family was from the "right" part of Pittsburgh, she was not quite as suitable as Ellsworth because her family was not in the social register. "My family was very Republican, conventional, hardly grand. We were right out of Sinclair Lewis," Joan said. Like Worth, she would be up at dawn every day, and she shared his voracious curiosity and loved journalism. Her friends called her "Joansie," and marveled at the sexual electricity that always sparked between Worth and Joan. "They were madly in love with each other," Ward Just later said. "It was so obvious to all of us."

Worth had at last come into his own and was acting the part of the responsible heir apparent. After Harvard, he had spent two years as a Navy gunnery officer, but even that experience did not totally straighten him out. Nevertheless, when he got out of the Navy, Norman Isaacs called his friend Bob Smith, who ran the *Minneapolis Tribune* and told him to hire Barry Bingham's oldest son as a general-assignment reporter, which Smith was delighted to do. But when he got to Minneapolis in 1956, Worth still could not settle down. Smith told a reporter that Worth was a willful, spoiled brat, who "wasn't worth a good goddamn." His copy was filled with mistakes, his spelling was terrible, his attitude was bad. Smith called Isaacs to complain and Isaacs sent Worth a letter "which read him the riot act." Isaacs said, "He had his feet up on the desk, he was working crossword puzzles, he wasn't answering phones. I wrote him every single person was watching him, from the assistant night man to the managing editor, and told him that this was his last chance." And then he sent a copy of his letter to Mary Bingham. Isaacs told him, " 'Get off your ass, check your spellings and get to work!' "

Miraculously, Worth paid attention. He begged Smith for another chance. "Smith threw his stories back at him, hounded him unmercifully, demanded more and more," a *Time* reporter once remarked. Finally, he got lucky. A murderer went on a rampage in Wisconsin, and Worth was sent to help the local correspondent cover the story. Although there were dozens of reporters on the scene, Worth found the murderer's girlfriend and got his story. Then he was sent to a Minneapolis hospital to get a deathbed confession from another killer. From then on, Worth was fine. "It was amazing," David Halberstam said. "When I saw Worth five years after he graduated, he had become serious, imbued with a sense of responsibility of what life could bring to him and the family, and he had a sense of what he could be. It was a complete transmogrification."

Twenty-six-year-old Barry Junior, a Harvard graduate, had come home for Christmas from Washington, where he had a research job with the news division of NBC-TV. At Harvard, his friends remembered, he was riveted by the news programs on TV and read everything he could about the medium. Barry Junior had done well at Harvard; he was now disciplined. He had been on the Harvard crew and been through the marines. "I loved what I was doing," he said of his NBC job and wasn't sure that he ever wanted to come back to Louisville to live.

Sallie followed Worth and Barry to Cambridge and was admitted to the Radcliffe class of 1958. Although later she complained that Worth and Barry ignored her in Boston, she had loads of beaux at Radcliffe and was considered a glamorous bohemian. She "dressed beautifully and had that marvelous hair," a friend remembered, and was considered "highly attractive," just as her mother had been. But at Radcliffe, Sallie had rebelled against the parietal rules, against the so-called "apathy" of the silent generation, as if she were a child of the 1960's who found herself at Radcliffe ten years too soon. David Halberstam remembered she was considered "fast" and she once broke parietals by staying out till dawn after a Bill Haley & the Comets concert, "as if she were trying to make a political statement. . . . Sallie did not come to Radcliffe to leave it as she found it." Like her mother before her, Sallie had very few women friends—an odd fact, considering that she would later become a passionate feminist.

At Radcliffe, Sallie won an honorable mention from *Mademoiselle* for her first short story, "Winter Term," a risqué piece for the time. Its main character was someone whom Sallie would write about again and again, a woman who was unsure of herself but craved the attention that had been denied her. "The Radcliffe dean called me in and said, 'The alumni will give no more money if they read this,' " Sallie said. Sallie loved her first real attention as a writer. "It was the first time I realized how much trouble my writing could cause," she said. However upset her mother was or wasn't about this story, Sallie thought it weird that "Mother never mentioned it to me once." Yet another canard went around Louisville, this one started by the book columnist of the *Courier*, that Barry and Mary had bought up all the copies of *Mademoiselle* in which Sallie's story appeared.

Sallie took to the limelight as she later would when she spoke out against her family. In college she was considered "the premier writer in the class," a college friend said. Like her father, she graduated magna cum laude and Barry gave that year's commencement address. The summer after she graduated, she worked at *Mademoiselle*. Just a year later she was married and would soon publish her first novel.

In Boston, Whitney and Sallie lived in a wonderful town house on Charles Street, complete with servants and a monkey. "It was elaborate for her age," a friend said. "They would give dinner parties with place cards when Sallie was about twenty-one." Sallie wrote her mother that the Radcliffe *Quarterly* had asked her to write an article about women, a subject that she viewed with distaste, she said. "I am asked to write a piece about women. What am I ever going to say?" Typically of that era, Sallie had passed from childhood into adulthood the moment she married, and surrounded herself with fine silver, porcelains, fingerbowls. When she and Whitney married, she received over two thousand wedding presents. Sallie's novel *After Such Knowledge,* published seven months after the wedding, was about a well-bred woman who finally breaks away from her "proper" marriage with a dull, sexless, oppressive man—an odd theme for a young, supposedly happy bride. Her friends were mystified. Soon Sallie began to complain about the provincialism of Boston and, as a friend later said, "Unhappiness pervaded the house. Whitney did not know what to do about Sallie's turbulence."

This Christmas of 1959, Jonathan, home from the Brooks School, was waiting to hear if he had been accepted by Harvard to follow the tradition his parents had set and all three of his older siblings had maintained. "Jonathan was the brightest boy in the family," Barry said. He had a gentle vulnerable air, what his childhood friend Diane Sawyer called "a wounded-animal quality." At times he seemed as tied to his mother and home as he had been as a toddler during the war. His Louisville friends later remarked upon his detachment. "He seemed to always be dressed in a coat and tie, and he rarely talked about his family. Although he could be reserved, he had a wonderful laugh that was joyous and just burbled up from inside," a childhood friend of Jonathan's said. Once Mary remarked to a friend how astonished she was after Jonathan had come home from a trip to Europe. "Europe is very nice, Mother," he reportedly told her, "but real beauty is the view of our state capital at Frankfort." Like Worth, he could be full of mischief. That year he had wired his dorm at Brooks with an electrical circuit that buzzed each time a housemaster came near.

Eleanor was thirteen years old that Christmas, still not as pretty as Sallie had been, her mother would say, but a gregarious child. She had a weight problem, which bothered her father so much he once wrote a postcard to a cousin saying that Eleanor is now "fat" and a teenager. As a child she had been left on her own a great deal and often hovered in the kitchen near the servants. But Eleanor's weight was hardly a serious matter; she was filled with laughter and pranks. Mary and Barry were planning to send her away to Concord Academy, which would mean that soon there would be no children left at home.

And so as 1959 came to an end, and they gathered, as always, to celebrate Mary's birthday on Christmas Eve, the family

seemed blessed, launched on the path of specialness in which
Barry and Mary had so believed. Barry wanted the family portrait to be taken in their vast drawing room with the arched
windows and the sconces the Judge had brought back from
France. It was especially important to have a decent rendering
of the family placed in the photo files of the *Courier-Journal*,
just in case the family should find itself thrust into even greater
political prominence. With Adlai Stevenson talking about making yet a third run for the presidency of the United States, anything seemed possible for the Binghams of Louisville. Eleanor
Roosevelt was encouraging him to declare himself and uphold
the principles he had once espoused; but Stevenson was more
than ever ambivalent. No doubt Barry knew that if Stevenson
won, he could name his job. And, of course, there was a job it
was talked about that he was interested in having, a job his father
once had: the ambassadorship to the Court of St. James's.

For days during that Christmas holiday of 1959 Joan Stevens
of Pittsburgh hadn't slept at all. She was on edge, nervous, and
overwhelmed by the surroundings. She was deeply in love with
Worth Bingham, and this holiday he had taken her home to Louisville for the very first time. Joan believed that everything she
did on that visit was wrong—her clothes, her conversation. She
wanted to make a good impression on Mary and Barry, her
future in-laws, but she felt, she remembered, "totally out of my
depth." When she walked into that immense house with its
ballroom-sized foyer, her stomach turned over. She knew rich
people, but she had never before seen this style of high-English
"bohemian Brahmin life," as she called it. It was their grandeur
and power that terrified her, the same grandeur and power that
had set Mary and Barry apart from their own children. "The
stuffing was coming out of the gold brocade sofas," she remembered, "and the fires were lit in every room, there were flowers
everywhere, and the conversations were so intellectual I
was overwhelmed." Adlai Stevenson's presence in the house only
added to her nervousness. "I had never even met a famous person before, much less Stevenson, who was like a god to us,"
she said. "What was I going to say to him?"
     The first night at dinner, Mary and Sallie both swept down
the stairs in tea gowns. Joan was mortified by her own "wool
dresses, cable-knit sweaters, and penny loafers. I was Miss
Campus," she said. Her perception was that Mary and Sallie
hardly said a word to her for two weeks, except that "we would
say that we wanted to look for china and silver and Sallie would
turn up her nose and say, 'This is hardly the place!' " Sallie,
Joan remembered, "was trying to imitate her mother, so every
outfit was just so fantastic. . . . The clothes were so beautiful,

velvets, brocades. It was awesome," she said. It was Stevenson
who realized she was nervous and "made an enormous effort
with me," she said. As did Sallie's husband, Whitney, who had
been the first to marry into the family, and who had presumably
undergone the same initial coolness. "I don't know how I would
have survived without Stevenson and Whitney," she said.

The Worth Bingham she knew was a free spirit, unpredictable,
liked filthy khakis and tennis shoes. Long after San Francisco,
he would drive around in a battered old station wagon, and when
he was teased about his wreck of a car, he would laugh and say,
"You have to be really rich to have the confidence to drive it."
They were both away from their conservative families, spending
their time, Joan remembered, listening to Allen Ginsberg reading his poetry. Earlier, Mary and Barry had already come to San
Francisco to meet Joan, to make sure she was appropriate for
their son to marry. Worth had warned Joan, "My father is so
courtly that you won't believe it." But Joan had liked his parents
in San Francisco, and was impressed by Barry Senior's charm.

They had met a few years after Worth graduated from Harvard
and just after Joan graduated from Connecticut College. It was
at Harvard summer school that Joan first met this "handsome,
incredibly wild and smart Worth Bingham," whom she had heard
described by a girl in her dorm who would sneak out to meet
Worth, then report it all to Joan. Thereafter, in Chatham they
had a few dates, but then Worth left for a six-month trip to
Africa with his brother, and Joan was sure she would never see
him again. Joan moved to New York, and began dating another
man. It was 1958, and nice girls got married.

On the trip to Africa, Barry and Worth toured Kenya, Tan-
ganyika and the Congo. Barry Junior still had dreams of living
in Africa as he did five years earlier when he had wanted to buy
his tea plantation, but his father had told Worth in private that it
was his job on this long safari to dissuade him. Barry Senior
himself, however, never told Barry Junior he disapproved of his
son's African ambitions. "It was a great opportunity for two
guys who were going to work together in these two companies
to get to know each other even better," Barry Junior said years
later, still believing this myth. On the trip, Barry remembered
Worth talking endlessly about newspapers and his desire to be
publisher. It was the sheer force of Worth's vision that diverted
Barry from his white-hunter plans, and by the end of the trip he
was talking about running the broadcasting end of the business.
Barry Junior never lost his passion for Africa, however, and later
he would decorate his Louisville office with an animal skin and
beads taken from the stomach of a crocodile he once shot.

In Africa the brothers learned that Sallie and Whitney Ellsworth were to be married in October. They drew straws to see

who would have to go home to attend the wedding. Worth lost, and somewhat irritably left for Louisville. When he got home, his mother took him aside and said, "Send a telegram to Sallie." So Worth did. "Congratulations to you and Shitney," it said. Worth swore that this wasn't a prank but an error in transmission. Sallie and Whitney did not think the message was a bit funny and never believed that the operator had made the error. After that, Worth liked Whitney even less and complained that Whitney was such a New York snob that when he saw the wedding china and silver he said, "This isn't good enough."

Now that Worth was back from Africa, he called Joan Stevens. "Hey, he said, 'You want to go skiing with me over New Year's?' " Joan was engaged to another man. "I'll have to see," she said. "I hung up the telephone and I thought to myself, I want to go skiing with Worth Bingham."

Now Worth had new plans: he was moving to San Francisco, where he would start work. A few days later Joan called him back: "I'd love to go skiing with you." Then she called her mother in Sewickley and announced to her, "I have just broken my engagement and I am moving to San Francisco to go to art school. When my mother heard that, she went into a complete decline," Joan said.

If Joan had acted on impulse, she had no need to worry. Worth was crazy about her, and the two became inseparable. It was a love match to rival that of his parents. Even Joan's mother adored Worth. "When I took him home I had to prepare him. I had to say, 'They are Republicans. They play golf at the country club,' " but then Worth walked into her mother's house, "he had such presence, those blue eyes that were so much like Mary's, she was wild for him." And what was more astonishing was that Worth "adored going to the country club and playing golf with these people. He couldn't have cared less. He just was so human. And he used to think I was crazy that I didn't like going home to Pittsburgh." He proposed to her in Pittsburgh. When Mrs. Stevens heard the news, Joan said, "It was the happiest day of her life."

Sallie, on the other hand, did not find Worth charming. She was fascinated by his charisma, she would later say, but repelled by his temper. "He was profane and a bully," she said. She told friends that he was self-destructive and too wild for his own good. She began to embroider on stories about the boys as children. She later told a reporter that Barry felt so outclassed by Worth that he had once said to him, "You can have the moon and all the stars, just give me the evening star." Barry was furious when this statement was published. "This was ridiculous," Barry said. "Teenage boys don't talk like that." Sallie cited "Nursie" as her source. Sallie's lively imagination may have invented her source as well as her story. Worth was "so highly favored," she said, there was hardly room for her. "I was afraid of Worth," she said. "He was fascinating, but he was out of control. He would scream at the dinner table and fly into terrible rages for no reason at all."

Certainly, Sallie might have been jealous of Worth's closeness to her mother, but whatever her reasons, Worth never understood why Sallie was always so tense around him. "He liked her, but he didn't pay any attention to her because she was not a factor in his life," Joan later said. At Harvard, Worth and Barry had been given a special allowance to take their sister to dinner, but as Sallie remembered, "It didn't go too well because we didn't want to be together. Why should we be together?" Joan met Sallie at a clambake at the Cape after she had known Worth for only a few weeks. Sallie appeared, Joan remembered, wearing "a dress and a picture hat to the beach, so elegant, when all the rest of us were in jeans and sneakers." That evening stayed in Joan's mind because Worth mentioned Sallie's story "Winter Term" in the most innocuous way. "He said to her something like, 'That was some piece of work,' and Sallie turned on him absolutely viciously. 'What do you mean?' she said. And then she stalked away."

This Christmas, Joan couldn't see that Sallie's imperious treatment of her was nothing personal, that she was simply unable to transcend her mixed feelings about her older brother and be gracious to his fiancée. "She treated me like dirt," Joan later said. At night, Joan would complain to Worth about the family. Worth said, "This is just the way they are. Don't pay any attention to it." Joan knew that life as the oldest Bingham child wasn't easy for Worth; there was so much pressure on him to perform. "Sometimes he would just cry to me at night," she said, "and he would say, 'I will never be able to live up to all that is expected of me.' " In San Francisco he would "scream to the rafters" about how tough his parents were on him. Although they would become much closer later, Worth did not understand his father's coolness and did not know how to communicate with him.

At this point Worth's relationship with Barry Senior was so correct that he called him Father and rarely challenged him, as if their relationship could not sustain the normal give-and-take. "They were such different personalities. Barry was meticulous, and Worth was the kind of person who would drink coffee out of the same cup for days without washing it," Isaacs said. "That was the kind of thing that would make his father shudder." Worth relied more and more on Norman Isaacs and would tell his friends that Isaacs was sometimes more of a father to him than his own father. But whatever the complications of their relation-

ship, Worth's longing for closeness and his father's detachment
were "put aside for the sake of the newspaper," Jay Iselin said.
"All that mattered to both of them was furthering the *Courier-
Journal.*"

Joan and Worth were married in February of 1960 in San
Francisco at Grace Cathedral. Their wedding picture caught
their joyous mood. They seem to be running down the steps.
Joan's face is tilted up, looking at Worth with the most adoring
smile. Their wedding party was at the fashionable restaurant
Ondine on the bay, and after the reception a speedboat pulled
up to the club's dock to spirit them away. Both families came
for the wedding, of course, and Joan's family minister even
flew out from Sewickley to perform the rites. "I didn't want
to get married in Pittsburgh," Joan said, "because I did not
want to expose the Binghams to those know-nothing fools at
the country club."

That summer of 1960 Mary and Barry were at the Democratic
convention in Los Angeles. Stevenson was ambivalent about
running; his candidacy fizzled out in the wake of Jack Kennedy's
popularity and the power structure of the Democratic party
moved from Barry's generation closer to Worth's.

The Louisville newspapers backed Kennedy, of course,
and Barry's powerful friends reportedly jockeyed with the new
president-elect to ensure Bingham the ambassadorial appointment he so desired. Adlai Stevenson went to Jack Kennedy and
"personally asked as a payoff favor to give the appointment to
Barry." This was the family version of the story, in any event.
Barry told his children that Kennedy had offered him St. James's,
but that he had turned it down. He told the president of the
United States, "I can't afford to go," and told the family that
he believed that Worth was not yet old enough to take over the
newspapers, as he himself had once been able to do, and that
Mark Ethridge was too near retirement to effectively run things
if Barry was away.

But the real reason, he told his children, was money, showing
again the concern he had displayed in France. He said he was
just not rich enough. Barry suggested to the president-elect that
he appoint David Bruce. Kennedy did. And in early January of
1960 the official announcement was made: the distinguished David Bruce, the former ambassador to France, would become
Kennedy's envoy to the Court of St. James's. When the story
was published in the *New York Times*, James Reston reported a
different version of events. Kennedy's advisers had pushed for
Bingham, Reston said, except for the secretary of state, Dean
Rusk, who wanted Bruce. Rusk prevailed. The family version

included a postscript; Bingham, Stevenson and Kennedy had
made a gentleman's agreement. The president-elect, Bingham
told his family, had promised him another chance at the Court
of St. James's in 1964.

23

Now that he was married and home in Louisville, twenty-eight-year-old Worth was showing a real talent for every aspect of newspaper publishing. Worth's egalitarian manner and passion for reporting was markedly different from his father's aloofness. Worth's earlier wildness and bully-boy quality was almost gone, and in their place was a young man who despised pretension and hypocrisy, just as he had when he had challenged his mother's view of blacks during the war. Worth took every job he could; often he would ride with the circulation trucks all over the state, always incognito, and he loved it when subscribers or advertisers yelled about the "god damn Binghams." Inevitably, he would agree and come home to regale the family with the incident. His mother, in particular, would laugh. "He loved to thumb his nose at the establishment," Ward Just later said, so much so that when the black reporter Carl Rowan showed up in Louisville, he arranged for him to play golf at a local segregated country club, just to annoy the bourbon powers.

Still, despite Joan and his new maturity, Worth retained a touch of his former wildness. Often Worth would go out drinking with Mark Ethridge or gamble thousands of dollars away on football games. Once when Barry Junior was home, Joan called him crying, "You've got to bring Worth home. Worth went to lunch with Mark Ethridge . . . they are stone drunk. He can't drive home," Barry Junior said.

When Joan and Worth returned to Louisville in the spring of 1960, the Little House was rented. So they settled into a retreat in the country miles beyond Glenview, in a house overlooking a bend in the Ohio River. While Worth worked at the newspaper every day Joan would stay at home writing "literally thousands of thank-you notes." She didn't know how to cook, and "the nearest grocery store was an hour's drive," she said.

As a bride, Joan never understood why her mother-in-law treated her so formally. She was afraid of her new in-laws and still called them "Mr. and Mrs. Bingham." That spring, Mary's mother, Munda, came to town from Richmond. "Joan, it just will not do for you to call Mary 'Mrs. Bingham,' " Munda told her in front of Mary and Barry, who remained silent.

That summer Worth was covering the 1960 presidential campaign for the *Courier-Journal*. Joan was home alone and hadn't realized that their house was near the LaGrange prison. Now and then she would read in the *Courier-Journal* about prisoners who had escaped down the Ohio River. "I was terrified," she said. "I was alone on this farm, no one was around for miles." She did not go to stay at the Big House with Mary and Barry, but she did have a neighbor who lived a mile or two down the road, and often she would stay with her. One night, a barn on Joan's property caught fire and once again she fled to her neighbor's. "The prisoners were coming down the river, the buildings on the property were firetraps and I did not feel comfortable enough with the Binghams to be able to say, 'May I come to stay with you?' " Joan said.

Just after Kennedy was elected, Barry Senior made a decision. "I wanted Worth to go to Washington to be around Kennedy as I had been around Roosevelt." Barry Senior knew that the Kennedy administration would be as much of a clean sweep as the New Deal had once been. It would be important for Worth to associate with the highest levels of government if the family was to move forward.

It was in Washington with the Kennedys and their coterie that Worth Bingham truly showed what a maverick he was, to his father's dismay. Worth took his reporting seriously and needled the administration. He saw Kennedy's flaws because he had come out of the same privileged world. "He had a great eye for a con," Ward Just said, who collaborated with Worth on articles for *The Reporter* magazine. Their first effort was called "The President and the Press," which was highly critical of the new president's manipulation of journalists. But Worth complained to his friends that his father did not like him to criticize the administration—an example, Worth said, of their unsolvable differences.

Once Worth wrote a lengthy series for the *Courier-Journal* called "Our Costly Congress," which attacked the franking privilege and the perks of congressional life. The series caused a minor sensation and fifty newspapers picked it up, often praising it in editorials. But not the editorial page of the *Courier-Journal*. It was astonishing to Worth that his own father would not endorse his work. "Every other newspaper ran these statements but not the *Courier-Journal*," a friend said. "It was too muckracking, too much against the Democratic party establishment. Worth's father did not know how to react. He hated the controversy."

The series won awards and was later reprinted in the *Reader's Digest,* but Worth never confronted his father about his reaction. He groused to his friends, especially Ward Just, who came from a newspaper family and was also trying to break away. Worth and his friends had a nickname for his father, Wealthy Barry, because that was inevitably how he was described in *Time* with its love of adjectives: "Wealthy Barry Bingham."

Worth and Joan stayed in Washington for only two years. In the summer of 1962 they returned to Louisville, where Worth at thirty was more than ready for a management position on the newspaper. Besides, all their friends were scattering. Ward Just had been hired at the *Washington Post* and was trying to get his new boss, Ben Bradlee, to send him to Vietnam. Another Washington friend, Jay Iselin, would soon be going to work for *Newsweek* in New York. It was time for Worth to return to the South.

That summer "Worth demanded his birthright and told his mother to kick the tenants out of the Little House so we could move in," Joan said. The house was a mess, as run-down as the Big House had been when Mary got it away from Aleen in 1942. For months that autumn Joan painted and papered and planted four hundred boxwoods to spruce up the amphitheater. Worth now had a title: assistant managing editor. One of his jobs was to make up page one of the *Courier-Journal.* "I knew he was fine when I asked him one day, 'Where is that page one?' " Isaacs said. "And Worth looked up at me and said, 'There's only one man who can do this job at a time. Now, will you take care of your work and let me do mine?' . . . I told Barry and Mark Ethridge what had happened and I said 'Looks like our boy is just about ready to take over. He's talking back.' "

Winter, 1962. Barry Junior was now back at home too, but he had fallen in love with a Washington girl named Edie Franchini, a beautiful divorcée with two young sons. Soon, he, too, would be married. Because of Edie and his promising career at NBC, Barry had not been enthusiastic about returning to Louisville. But his father had insisted, calling him in the autumn of 1962 and saying, "Isn't it about time you came back and started to work with the family?" He was too dutiful to refuse. And so by Christmas Barry was back and living in the Big House with his parents. He redecorated a few rooms and lived at home for almost a year, but he took frequent trips to Washington to see Edie. "Louisville was a desert after Washington," he said.

Edie Stenhouse Franchini, with her high cheekbones, pale eyes and skin, and chestnut hair, was, like Barry Junior, reserved, disciplined, controlled and filled with rectitude. "I like to do the correct thing," she said. Like Mary Caperton, Edie came from a distinguished family without money, but Mary would not be as fond of Edie as she was of Joan because of Edie's "stiff-necked" quality, as Mary would later say.

Edie had been warned about life at the Big House and the frosty reception she could expect—from Mary Bingham, in particular. But she didn't have as rough a time as Joan did the Christmas of 1959. "I knew Mary was watching my every move," Edie said. "But what could one expect? They had an immense communications company and they could not permit their son to marry just anyone."

Mary did not like Edie's family, the Stenhouses, and complained when she had to see them, "Oh God, they are such bores." What was most annoying about Edie, from Mary's point of view, was her style. She was too correct, and didn't know how to strike that light, amusing Noel Coward social note the senior Binghams adored. Joan could make Mary laugh with her gossip and her passions, but not Edie. Worse, her very correctness struck Mary as "dreary." Edie had a fetish about staying thin, and Mary and Eleanor, with their love of rich food, butter and sauces, began to criticize Edie's Spartan ways, a campaign that would later overwhelm Edie when Barry Junior became publisher of the newspaper.

That January of 1963 Worth's first child, Clara, was born. Even as a baby she had the same steady gaze that Worth had. Worth was passionate about her. He would get up in the morning to change her diapers, and his mother remarked how "curious" it was that Worth was so involved with this baby girl. "He dressed her every day," she said. "Wasn't that a remarkable thing to do?"

24

Jonathan Bingham started Harvard in the autumn of 1960, a dangerous time to be in Cambridge for a boy like Jonathan, who was inventive but weak-willed, and seemed to have dangerous fantasies that he possessed superior powers. At this time at Harvard, Timothy Leary and Richard Alpert were still conducting their LSD experiments and had yet to be discredited, although they would be during Jonathan's junior year. Tragically, however, by the time Harvard fired Richard Alpert for exposing undergraduates to the hallucinogen, Jonathan had sought him out and taken LSD with him. Alpert still believes that Jonathan had a delusional reaction. Soon after, Jonathan dropped out of Harvard and came home to Louisville. But with or without LSD, his delusions grew to such an extent that he believed he could find a cure for cancer. He was also convinced that he could work with electricity without training or expert help.

Before Jonathan dropped out of Harvard, Sallie and Whitney often saw Jonathan in Boston. "I thought he was in terrible trouble," she said. "He seemed to get more and more remote . . . he would come home because the outside world was so rough. . . ." He had always been a dreamy boy, remote and vague. "The family used to laugh because he was so preoccupied that sometimes when you spoke to him he wouldn't even answer and everyone joked about it." His nickname was Toad, and Sallie said, "We would all say, 'Isn't it funny? Toad's mind is elsewhere.' "

However vague he seemed to Sallie, Jonathan had been accepted at Harvard without difficulty. Perhaps in reaction to his two older brothers, his interests were totally different from theirs. He was a decent student; interested in science, he was neither as exuberant as Worth nor as mannerly and dutiful as Barry Junior. "Jonathan did not know where he fit into the power structure; he was the lost boy," a childhood friend said. "I always thought he was a little depressed." Like his parents, he was passionate about the theater. He took over the staging of the

243

Bingham children's Christmas pageant and would call his girl-friend in a panic at the last minute, "Do you have a large topaz I could borrow?"

Mary had especially protected and cherished Jonathan all through the war, but when Barry came home Mary's attention naturally was diverted. When Jonathan was a teenager, Mary was not nearly as strict with him as she had been with her three older children. She never woke Jonathan up to smell his breath for signs of liquor, as she had with Worth, nor did she rail against him if he stayed out too long, as she had with Sallie. Barry and Mary were often gone while Jonathan was growing up, and he was left, along with Eleanor and Sallie, in the care of the black servants and the governesses that replaced Nursie in the Big House. "We knew everyone else's parents but never Jonathan's. And we would not have dreamed of asking him about them. As we all talked about our parents Jonathan would be silent," a friend said.

Jonathan, like his childhood friends Louise Duncan and Suzanne Browder Hamlin, had fallen under the spell of a brilliant Louisville boy named Peter Ardery, tall, good-looking, wild and brittle, especially by the standards of the sheltered Glenview teenagers. He was not part of the hidebound Louisville social world, but an outsider whose family had moved to Louisville in the 1950's from England, where his father had been in the military. Peter had been immediately accepted by his peers. "He was like Montgomery Clift. He was star-crossed, filled with humor, self-destructive." Jonathan was totally devoted to Peter, as if he needed a strong force to influence him. "Looking back, you knew at age sixteen that Peter would be dead by thirty-five," a friend said. Years later, while he was in medical school, Ardery would take a trip to India with a girlfriend and die of a drug overdose. "It was a terrible tragedy because it was as if Peter, who had become so purposeful, felt compelled to return to the dark side of his youth," said George Plimpton, for whom Ardery had once worked at the *Paris Review*. But as a high school boy in Louisville in the late 1950's, he was good-looking and tall, with "opalescent eyes," his friend Louise Duncan said. "He was one of the sexiest boys I ever met." Jonathan was fascinated by him, and Ardery adored the Big House and the Binghams' world. When Jonathan and Peter Ardery learned they had both gotten into Harvard, they made plans to room together in the dorms.

At Harvard in the early 1960's, signs of the coming ferment were evident. It was the era of the Kingston Trio and Joan Baez, folk songs at the Club 47 on Mount Auburn Street. The fast preppies were already smoking marijuana, although the use of the drug was yet to be pervasive. Timothy Leary was reigning as a "scientist," doing LSD and psilocybin tests in the Harvard labs, experiments that had been going on for years. Many Harvard graduate students had signed up to be volunteers for this starry-eyed Irish charmer who truly believed he could change the world with acid dreams. He shared his lab with Richard Alpert, an assistant psychology professor, who later gained fame as Ram Dass, a guru who led his followers through the mystical shoals of the 1960's.

In the early 1960's, when Jonathan and Peter Ardery got to Harvard, Leary and Alpert were still considered benign prophets of the new age. *Look* had done a long article about the Leary-Alpert experiments. Few were aware of the dangers: that LSD could give the user the delusion that he could walk out a window or colonize outer space. Even Worth Bingham had taken LSD with Leary, Barry Junior said, under the auspices of the school. But by the time Jonathan got to Harvard, Leary and Alpert were getting out of hand. They were less careful of who took the drug, even giving it to "extraenthusiastic undergraduates," Alpert said.

At that time Jonathan was a junior and fascinated by Alpert's lab. He wrote to his girlfriend Louise Duncan that "he had been involved with Leary and Alpert and how fascinating all the experiments were they were doing with LSD," she said. "In those days nobody knew anything about LSD and they thought it was an amazing truth drug with properties that were going to help people. Leary was persuasive and so was Peter Ardery, and those were the kind of people Jonathan looked up to." Alpert ran one session for Jonathan, and "maybe two or three other boys who were around the *Crimson.*" In the session, Alpert later remembered that Jonathan "at one point was paranoid and delusional." He calmed down, Alpert said, "until the chemical ran its course." Later, Alpert was contacted by Dana Farnsworth, the head of Harvard University Health Services. Farnsworth, along with Alpert, did psychiatric counseling for the health service. "Farnsworth told me that Jonathan had checked into Mount Auburn hospital. . . . And he wondered if I thought the drug experience might have made his emotional problems even worse," Alpert said. Alpert remembered Jonathan as "emotionally disturbed. I thought of him as a very tortured Southern boy. He was very intelligent, but he seemed like he was hiding his intellect, as if he had severe emotional problems. I think he felt crippled as a person. He was brusque sometimes, to make up for it, and he never talked about his family, as if he had some kind of a block about them. . . . I think his problem was that he was very, very frightened of emotional closeness. He wouldn't have been able to handle the pressure of Harvard, he was too tangled up in his emotions."

Sallie was unaware of Jonathan's experiments with LSD. "Something terrible went on at Harvard," she said. "And I think it had to do with the fact that he was so protected at home. I think he was very deluded. And I think there was something in his relationship to Peter Ardery that didn't work. Peter was a natural scholar, a very bright guy, and Jonathan had a terrible struggle keeping up with him." Louise Duncan said, "Jonathan followed Peter Ardery around like a bird dog."

Louise Duncan's diary from January of 1963 described her sitting next to Ardery on an airplane going back to school from Louisville: "Peter wants me to come to Harvard to stay at his apartment. He has a devilish personality. I told him I would not sleep with him, but he is insistent. He said that he is a Nietzschean and believes that looks are the basis of all morality." At the time Louise Duncan was at Vassar and in love with Jonathan Bingham. Through Jonathan's brother-in-law, Whitney Ellsworth, Ardery met George Plimpton, who was impressed with his abilities and offered him an internship on the *Paris Review*. "It was always Peter who was seizing the opportunities that Jonathan opened for him," Louise Duncan said. "It was so terribly sad."

During the spring of his junior year Jonathan told his parents he wanted to "drop out of Harvard" to pursue "medical courses at the University of Kentucky near Louisville." Mary and Barry did not flinch when they announced to their friends that Jonathan was coming home. They acted with their accustomed calm, as if this were the most normal thing in the world. "Jonathan wants to pursue research with schizophrenics at the University of Louisville," his father explained.

His family and friends have speculated for years about why Jonathan quit Harvard just before the end. Louise Duncan felt that he had been "asked to leave by Harvard because of his association with Alpert. . . . In those years Harvard was very much the kind of place where a person was asked to take charge of his own life," she said. "It is possible that his parents never knew and that he made up excuses about it. . . . But he was clearly biding his time to go back." Sallie's explanation was bleaker: "Maybe he was schizophrenic. I think he was very deluded. He kept telling me that he had found some kind of cure for cancer, and he simply wasn't making any sense to me at all. I could not get through to him. I thought he had gone completely off the deep end." Sallie told a friend that Jonathan had a white doctor's coat, which he often wore. Once there had been a car accident in Glenview and Jonathan had gone down the road pretending to be the doctor and actually worked on an accident victim. Sallie was understandably worried about her younger brother's state of mind.

Mary and Barry always said, of course, that they saw no problem. Mary told the family that she was proud that Jonathan was headed for a career in medicine. Doctors were beginning to experiment with biochemical treatments for schizophrenics, and Jonathan "was deeply involved in research with this group," Barry Senior said, with his chilling and pleasant smile. Jonathan was filled with ideas for the future—his science experiments with the schizophrenics at the local state hospital and his desire for a career in medicine. If the parents knew about his experiences with Richard Alpert, they never discussed it with their other children. It is possible, however, that the head of the Harvard health service, who had discussed Jonathan with Richard Alpert, had contacted his parents as well. Nevertheless, Barry Senior maintained, "It was simply a question that Jonathan wanted to pursue research with schizophrenics on his own. . . . You know, he was doing some fascinating work when he came back here to take those science courses at the University of Louisville."

Certainly, Jonathan seemed to flourish back in Louisville. He was always happy at home and grew even closer to his mother, and he told her that he wanted to live at Melcombe until he went back to Harvard. There was a barn on the property he wanted to renovate, and he asked his mother if she minded if he wired the former groom's quarters for electricity.

Often now in the spring, when they retired to the library for tea in the late afternoon, Mary and Barry looked out the windows at the glorious Melcombe grounds. They had always liked cool weather the best, and this afternoon, the seventh of March of 1964, it was particularly chilly in Glenview, as if rain was on the way. Mary and Barry knew where their two youngest children were, which was unusual. Eleanor was home from Concord Academy because, annoyingly, she had been suspended for a week for the most idiotic prank: "We let out some mice in the biology lab to annoy a fat professor. . . . They got under her robe. You should have seen her scream when this rodent went running out," Eleanor said. The school had not been amused and had called Mary and Barry to tell them that Eleanor was on her way back to Louisville. She was home, but this afternoon she had gone out shopping.

Jonathan was at his groom's cottage in the barn, wiring it with a group of friends. Jonathan had always been mechanically inclined and had badgered his mother until she agreed that he could wire it without the help of an electrician. Now his wiring job was done. He had called the Louisville power company to ask them to come out and hook up the power lines to see if his work had been successful.

In the library where they sat this March afternoon, Mary and

Barry had placed a most enchanting picture of Sallie taken on the beach at Chatham, playing with her new baby, Barry. Sallie's long blond hair formed a corona around the child. Barry and Mary doted on Barry Ellsworth, their first male grandchild. Sallie's life seemed tranquil. Whitney and Sallie had moved to New York, and Whitney was now the publisher of the *New York Review of Books,* which had just begun to appear. Sallie had now created the life she had always wanted: dinner parties, bookish friends. She spent her mornings writing short stories. The picture of Sallie on the mantel would remain prominently displayed at the end, a powerful reminder of a time when Sallie's life seemed blessedly free of anger or tragedy, as did their own.

In the late afternoon, Mary and Barry decided to take a walk. They strolled down the hill on the south side of their property, as they had done so many times before. As Mary and Barry walked under the bare branches of the redbuds and elms, they saw far in the distance a man up on the power pole. They had no idea who it was, and assumed it was someone from the Louisville power company, although they thought it odd that they hadn't seen a truck. "Who could be up there?" Mary remembered saying to Barry that afternoon. Suddenly the man went flying through the air. "I had better go back to the house and get some blankets for that poor man, whoever he is," Mary said to her husband as Barry raced down the hill to investigate. It was only when she walked back and saw Jonathan's friends leaning over a body on the grass that Mary began to feel that something was terribly wrong.

Eleanor was driving on the freeway listening to rock music on the car radio when she heard a news bulletin: *There has been an accident at the Bingham house in Glenview. An unidentified man has been injured. Details will follow. . . .* Immediately she got off the highway and turned toward home. As she drove up the driveway she saw several police cars and an ambulance. When Eleanor saw the stricken faces of Jonathan's friends sobbing in the driveway she began to realize something unimaginably dreadful had happened. As she approached her house Eleanor learned, to her horror, that her favorite brother had been electrocuted. As if this wasn't hideous enough, Mary and Barry had been forced to watch Jonathan die as they waited forty-five minutes for the ambulance to get to the house. No one in the family knew how to revive him, and so they stood by helplessly and watched as the life ran out of this kindly, fragile boy. By the time the ambulance arrived Jonathan was long dead.

His friends were at the house weeping, Eleanor remembered, and as more and more friends heard the news over the radio the cars began pulling up the driveway to the Big House. "My mother simply fell apart," Eleanor said. She collapsed and had to be taken to her bed. That afternoon the family learned the details of what had gone on. Jonathan had been frustrated waiting for the power company truck to arrive. Like Worth, he was impatient, and believed he could do anything himself. Although a light rain was falling, he was sure he would have no problem finding the proper wires to tie together to hook up the power to the barn. "How hard can it be?" he said. His friends told him he was crazy to shin up a power pole, but Jonathan wouldn't listen. And so he climbed up the pole, pulled a wire, the wrong wire, and screamed as the massive voltage traveled through his body. A friend was behind him on the pole and reportedly heard his last words: "I'm in trouble. Help me down."

For days it rained in Louisville. The Ohio River crested. Mary would not leave her room. "You have never seen grief like this," Joan Bingham said. Mary blamed herself, completely and absolutely. Jonathan was the one child she had tried desperately to protect all through the war, but she could not protect him from his own impatience. He had not yet experienced life; he was so sheltered, such an innocent. She believed that of all her children he was the kindest. She called him "the healer" because he could bring his brothers and sisters together when they quarreled. She wept that he had never known true love, nor the joy of being a father. He was, she would say, "cut off from having had a proper life." She asked herself over and over again, why had she ever allowed him to wire the barn? What had she been thinking of? Mary's guilt was so overwhelming that she told a family cousin that she "would never be able to read again." Barry Senior, however, was as usual a "pillar of strength," Eleanor remembered. One night he remarked to his family, "I don't believe I ever really knew Jonathan very well."

Barry Junior went with his father to Pearson's, the local funeral home, to pick out a casket. "It was grotesque," Barry Junior said, "Mr. Pearson pointed to a casket that was very elaborate and said to my father, 'This is the model that your father, Judge Bingham, was buried in. You certainly wouldn't want to do anything less for your son.' I felt like slugging Pearson, but my father just passed it over with some pleasant remark."

Jonathan's closed coffin remained in the living room for two days. Candles burned all day and all night. Hundreds of the Binghams' friends made the drive up the flooded River Road to pay their last respects. The friends who knew the family well would go up to Mary's bedroom to try to comfort her. Once Mary came down from her room and saw Mr. Pearson trying to open the casket to display the body. She pulled the family minister aside and said, "For God's sake, get that man out of here."

Jonathan's friends arrived from their various colleges. At the funeral the organist played *Finlandia,* and the music was so sad and haunting that to this day Louise Duncan is unable to stop herself from crying every time she hears a note of Sibelius. Louise and Jonathan had had plans to spend their spring vacation together when Louise came home from college. "We were going to hide in the third floor of the Big House, and then sneak off on a trip," she said. She was not comforted when Peter Ardery told her at the funeral that he had believed that Jonathan was going to ask Louise to marry him. The day Jonathan was killed was her twenty-first birthday.

The rain never stopped. After the funeral, when the family got to Cave Hill Cemetery the earth was so muddy that Jonathan's casket would not go into the ground. Sallie came down from New York for the funeral and, as she said, "to put away Jonathan's things." Her behavior was strange, the first real sign of trouble to come. She stayed for only one day and then returned to New York because, as she said, she was too enraged with her parents, who could not discuss Jonathan's death realistically with her. She was unable to be empathic with them, as if her reaction was all that mattered. "I only came for the funeral," Sallie said. "And it was so hard on me, I only stayed twenty-four hours and I was gone. I just didn't know what to do. I was so unable to cope with that kind of emotional devastation. It seemed to me there were so many unanswered questions. . . . Jonathan had come home because the outside world was so rough and then he couldn't survive at home either."

Sallie was angry that her parents could not recognize that Jonathan's "thinking was off," she said. She believed that her parents were encouraging Jonathan to believe that he in fact had discovered a cure for cancer. "He was being encouraged, I felt, in this delusion," she said. "The last time I saw him I argued with him because he had set up some kind of laboratory in the basement and he was making claims about what he was achieving down there, and I said something to him like, 'This is ridiculous, you have no background in chemistry, how can you claim this?' He was upset with me. That to me was part of how he died because there are few people that age who would take it upon themselves to climb a pole with enormous high voltage wires on it and cut one of the wires. . . ."

Later Sallie was guilty about her behavior at the funeral. In New York, she rationalized, perhaps with the help of a psychiatrist she had begun to see: "It was clear to me that I wasn't doing anything for anybody. I was bewildered about what happened. It was all so strange. . . . There were so many people rushing around, there were so many unanswered questions in our family."

Sallie told her friends that she thought Jonathan might have committed suicide. Later, she wrote a short story called "Mourning," which was published in *Mademoiselle*, a startling piece of work in which Ellen, the daughter of a privileged family, returns home when her sister commits suicide. Ellen's intention is to help her parents, but she is incapable of empathy because she resents their denial that the dead sister has committed suicide. Ellen is angered by their orderly customs, the rituals of death, their perfect manners, the telephone calls with her brother's pleasant voice intoning, "We all appreciate . . ." She cannot stand seeing her mother in her white embroidered bed jacket making a list of all the telephone calls, notes and flowers for her thank-you notes. Why did the sister drown? No one can give her an answer. The father is in control, with all "the thrills and frills pressed out" of his voice, however. "It was not the voice of grief . . . but a dull mechanical patter. Suddenly it occurred to her that he was always holding down sobs."

"Is nobody ever going to know anymore about her?" Ellen asks her mother. The mother ignores her question, as if it were an unpleasant vapor, and tells her daughter to help her brother answer the door. "Thirty-two years old and still acting like an adolescent . . ." the mother snaps. Standing at the mother's bedroom, the daughter listens to her brother answer the telephone: ". . . so very kind." And then she looks down the staircase. "The descent to the hall below seemed suddenly very long, and she imagined rolling . . . into the grinding waves, which must have seemed to her as soft as velvet."

If Sallie believed that publishing "Mourning" in *Mademoiselle* would elicit a tender response from her parents, or even a candid emotional dialogue, she was wrong. "Sallie's writing has been a source of considerable pain to me very often," her mother said.

Much later, Sallie would detach herself from the horror of Jonathan's death to such a degree that she could hardly recall her relationship with him, as if she had learned to cope with grief in the same manner as her father. "Was I close to Jonathan?" she asked me in response to a question. "Did someone else in the family tell you that? Going over these old diaries I had forgotten how close I was to him. . . . But you know, he's been dead so long my memory has shifted slightly."

25

For the first months after Jonathan's death Mary was overwhelmed by grief, lost within herself, unable to reach out to anyone in the family except Barry, unable to do much besides acting out the necessary gestures of the living. She had always been an intensely private person; now, in grief, she turned inward even more. Her children did not know how to talk to her. She would break down and weep at the very mention of Jonathan's name, then be mortified by her lack of self-control. Mary's dignity and reserve were not an effective antidote for a loss as agonizing as the death of a beloved and troubled child.

Thus Mary was seemingly unable to reach out to her other children to help them over their separate grief. Eleanor and Sallie in particular had severe reactions. Sallie raged at her parents, immersed herself in psychotherapy, and her rage would intensify as the years passed. Eleanor, who was just starting college, went from one school to another and became "the family hippie," as her father later affectionately called her. Long after Jonathan's death, as the surviving children attempted to figure out how their family had come apart, they would seize upon the loss of Jonathan as another possible cause. He had been "the healer," Mary said. That was the image they had of him—Jonathan the healer—and nothing was going to blemish that notion. In hindsight the Binghams believed that from Jonathan's tragic death could have come an increased closeness. If the family had been able to grieve openly together, perhaps they could have understood what had driven Jonathan to climb a power pole in the rain. For the Binghams, it was easier not to talk openly with one another—not an uncommon reaction after the death of a child.

Years later, after the family had collapsed and the newspaper empire was sold, Eleanor remembered a time after Jonathan was killed when she once attempted to have an intimate discussion with her parents.

I asked them about their relationship and the fact that their marriage was so strong that none of us could penetrate it. . . . Mother and Daddy started screaming at me, and that was the end of my relationship with my parents for about ten years. . . . But that was in the past. What is the point of talking about all these things now? Then we would have to analyze how everybody got so wild and rebellious, and that would lead directly to Worth and Jonathan being so experimental for attention, which would lead to my parents perhaps believing that they were responsible for my brothers' deaths and think of that guilt. . . . There is simply no purpose in it.

Mary withdrew from those around her, buried herself in religion, spent hours in her garden and wrote lengthy heartbreaking letters to Jonathan's friends about his death. She began to have angina pains. For years after Jonathan's death, she carried nitroglycerine in her purse because, as Barry Junior said, "My father literally said, 'Her heart is broken.' " It distressed Barry to witness Mary's anguish. He had taken her on a holiday just after Jonathan was killed, but when they got home, Mary was just as heartsick. Barry told his family that he knew Mary was overcome with guilt, although when someone suggested that she see a psychiatrist, she told Barry, "What do I need with a psychiatrist? I'm no different than anyone else who needs to grieve. It's a natural grief." Years later when the son of a good friend was killed, Mary appeared at her friend's door, her arms filled with flowers from the Melcombe gardens, tears streaming down her face. She would never recover from the loss of her son.

In this family crisis no one knew exactly how to act. However miserable Mary was privately, the elder Binghams' pattern had always been to camouflage their feelings with their exquisite manners. At a dance, Barry Senior told one of Jonathan's friends, "One must always be cheerful in life." Years later, their friend Wilson Wyatt said, "Their stoicism after Jonathan's death was remarkable. They met the tragedy with a composure which was so admirable." Even more tragically, no one in the family, except Sallie, ever questioned this notion of perpetual good spirits and perfect manners.

Mary seized on scholarship to keep her mind occupied, as she had when she was mired in the poverty of her Richmond childhood. As if to find a target for her anger at Jonathan's death, she raged at the Episcopal Church for its modernization of the centuries-old Book of Common Prayer. Mary became avid on this subject and corresponded with Church authorities demanding that they leave the sacred text alone. She berated the minister of St. Francis in the Fields, her local parish. "If you ever talk

to her about the new prayer book . . . she gets so, so worked
up. She looks like she is going to have a stroke,'' said Barry
Junior, who felt that the Church was bearing the brunt of his
mother's pain. ''Mary had a certain darkening of the spirit,''
Barry Senior later said. ''But she found immense solace in the
Church.''

Some months later Mary slowly began to resume ordinary
life. That summer, Mary and Barry went with Worth and Joan
to Atlantic City for the 1964 Democratic convention. Once again,
there was much at stake for the family because now it would be
up to Lyndon Johnson to make good Kennedy's promise to Bingham concerning ambassadorship to Great Britain. London might
have been a tonic and given Mary and Barry a new routine, a
revival of a past and splendid life. Old friends, royals, high
diplomacy, cables from the State Department, country weekends.

But the appointment was not to be. Johnson reportedly owed
a political favor to Earle Clements, a former Kentucky governor
and senator, who despised the *Courier-Journal.* A Bingham family story is that Clements had complained to his old friend Lyndon Johnson about the Binghams. ''We heard that Johnson was
mad at the papers because the newspaper had written an exposé
on Earle Clements, who was a crony of Johnson's,'' Joan said.
Whatever happened, Barry Bingham, characteristically, always
denied publicly that there was any move to make him ambassador, although the story was all over Washington and Louisville.

After Jonathan's death, Mary and Barry took comfort in their
relationship with Worth. Their oldest son had proved himself in
Washington and had turned out splendidly; he was zealous about
the *Courier-Journal* and, like his parents, deeply involved in
Louisville life. Home from Washington, Worth was closer to his
father than he had ever been, as if they had transcended their
earlier personality differences. He was, at age thirty-two, a perfect Bingham son. His sheer physical energy was astonishing.
''Worth would get up at five in the morning, do his exercises,
read the newspapers, then write an editorial,'' Joan said. ''He
would then get Clara out of her crib, change her diapers, make
breakfast and walk into the bedroom with the baby and the
breakfast tray at eight A.M. on his way to the office.''

When Mark Ethridge retired in 1963, Worth took over his
office. Before Ethridge left, Worth had been worried about his
drinking, for he had loved him ever since he was a boy, and he
believed, as Norman Isaacs said, ''that Mark was killing himself
with the damn bottle.'' Ethridge was spending more and more
time in the late afternoon at Teek's, the local reporters' bar a
few doors from the paper. In the late afternoons the reporters
and the copy desk people would meet at this gloomy hole and

talk about everybody else at the paper or sit around and listen to Ethridge, who now looked like a classic white-haired Kentucky colonel, tell stories about the old days. When Worth first got back to Louisville, he would sometimes go into Teek's, but soon he outgrew it. He would often complain to Norman Isaacs and his father, "Why does Mark have to drink so much?"

Mark's friends insisted that his work at the newspaper was unaffected, although he drank mythic quantities of scotch. His reporters and editors dreaded sitting with Ethridge when he said, "Let's just have one more round." According to Norman Isaacs, "He could drink all night and then be clear-eyed at eight A.M. the next morning." But as he got older he would slur his words and appear disoriented. "Still he would have total recall the next day of whatever had been said to him," Isaacs said. The Binghams, however, were worried. What if Mark crashed a car? His wife, Willie, was often away on the lecture circuit, promoting her books or giving speeches about the South. The Ethridges' house was way out on the road to Cincinnati and it was dangerous for Mark to drive by himself.

On the surface, as Joan remembered, "The Binghams and the Ethridges were the closest of friends." But Barry was emphatic that Mark retire at age sixty-five. This, of course, was much sooner than Ethridge believed he should be forced to leave. At dinners, Willie would complain: Why should Mark have to leave? Mark Ethridge had created the newspaper after all and had agreed to turn it around as a favor to the old Judge. Now he was recognized all over the state and the country as the voice of the *Courier-Journal*, as Henry Watterson had once been.

There was also the matter of the newspaper stock. Barry Senior reportedly had decided not to give Mark Ethridge *Courier-Journal* stock, but his friends later said that he refused to tell him directly. Ethridge had always believed that when he retired, Barry would make good on the Judge's promise. Barry Senior had given all his executives stock in a printing company called Fotan, but Fotan was hardly as valuable as the *Courier-Journal*. When Ethridge realized that Fotan was all Barry would give him, that he would have nothing to pass along to his children, he was bitter and saw it as a form of betrayal. Ethridge's stunned reaction to Barry Senior's inability to confront him directly would mirror how Barry Junior would feel years later when his father would never honestly tell him why he was unhappy with the way he was running the newspaper. Both Ethridge and Barry Junior would be left to wonder about Barry Senior's motives. Ethridge was a proud Southern gentleman, too proud to confront Barry Senior. In 1963 Ethridge had left Louisville and took a job at *Newsday* in New York. But years after he retired, Willie and

Mark Ethridge were still bitter and talked freely about this astonishing fact to Bingham friends they met.

Worth's official title was assistant to the publisher. He was
deeply involved in the business side of running the newspaper
and visited paper plants in Canada and Maine. At the same time,
although he was writing columns for the "Editorial Notebook,"
as his father still did, he was far more involved in the newsroom
and often had dinner with the reporters, editors and even the
men on the copy desk. His parents had inspired him to do community work, and he was active with the Louisville Fund, an
organization to improve the city, as well as the United Appeal,
the local art museum, the mental hospital and the Southern
Newspaper Publishers Association. Worth had even invested ten
thousand dollars in a syndicate that was backing a local black
boxer named Cassius Clay—an investment that would someday
be worth close to $750,000.

The more Worth did, the more he was called upon to do. "It
was as if Worth was frantic to get these community obligations
out of the way so he could go back to doing what he really loved,
which was being in the newsroom," Joan said.

Worth had become very friendly with a new doctor in town,
a Yale graduate named Harvey Sloane who would later open a
clinic in West Louisville. Sloane was a bachelor, clean-cut, liberal, and very much in the Bingham mold. He had worked in
Appalachia and had come to Louisville with a letter of introduction to the Binghams. Sloane's alliance with the Bingham family
would change his life. Over the next years, he would mostly give
up medicine, become a politician with the support of the Bingham newspapers, and would eventually marry an ambitious and
tough-minded young woman who would encourage his political
career. In the early 1960's Sloane was obviously a man of principle, and Barry Senior had taken to him immediately, as had
the entire family. Barry Senior in particular liked serving as
mentor to a bright and willing young man. Although Worth was
fond of Sloane, he confided to Joan that he slightly resented the
attention his father was now paying him. But Harvey Sloane's
relationship with Barry Senior was uncomplicated by familial
bonds. Clearly, Sloane simply admired Barry Senior unreserv-
edly. In 1965 it would have been impossible for Worth Bingham
to conceive that in twenty years his father would have a more
intimate relationship with this young idealistic and ambitious
doctor—who would by then become the mayor of Louisville with
Barry Senior's help—than with his own son Barry Junior, who
would grow to distrust Harvey Sloane and his future wife.

While Worth involved himself in every aspect of the community Edie and Barry kept busy with their children. Barry's activ-

ities caused no resentment in the family because the two brothers did not compete. Their personalities were too different; they complemented each other. Barry was immersed in WHAS and his own family. He and Edie were passionate about the arts, not politics, and were on the board of the new Louisville Actors Theatre.

What could Mary and Barry have thought about Sallie and Eleanor at this point in their lives? Sallie and Eleanor were both beginning to have serious problems. Sallie's marriage was in trouble. Eleanor was "very much at loose ends," Sallie later said. Yet Mary and Barry, perhaps paralyzed by their own grief over Jonathan, seemed as disinclined and powerless to reach out to their daughters as they had been to cope with Worth when he had gotten into trouble at boarding school. It is easy to imagine Mary using her phrase "original sin" to describe her children's problems, as if to detach herself from them, for much later she still responded to any question about the causes of Sallie's anger, in particular, with that explanation: "original sin." All her life, whatever her private torment, Mary would seem incapable of asking her own children the standard mother's question: *What did I do wrong?*

After Jonathan's death, Eleanor started college not at Harvard but at the University of North Carolina at Greensboro. Eleanor seemed to be floundering. Jonathan and Eleanor had been close all through childhood, but years later, just as Sallie would, Eleanor detached herself from the horror of the event and would only say about it, "It was terrible for my mother. Can you imagine how sad it was for her?"

Eleanor lasted two semesters in North Carolina, then dropped out, came home to Louisville, and took up with a local boy whom the family did not approve of. During that year's racing season she would take this boyfriend to sit in the Bingham box at Churchill Downs, and the family believed impressionable Eleanor was acting self-destructively. She then moved from boyfriend to boyfriend, from college to college, winding up at a "pink brick" university in England, a school she would later explain was for those who could not qualify for Oxford or Cambridge.

Worth was convinced that Eleanor had been "out of control" since she was a young teenager, as he used to tell a family cousin, and to illustrate, he told of once watching Eleanor arriving home in the early morning after being out all night with a date just as his father was leaving for the newspaper. "Good morning, Father," Eleanor said briskly as she walked into the Big House. "Good morning, Eleanor," Barry Senior replied, without missing a step. "Worth later said that if his daughter,

Clara, ever tried that, he would tan her hide,'' Worth's cousin James Callahan said.

Eleanor would become a sixties girl. ''Eleanor was certainly the family hippie,'' her father said. ''But at least she never got out of touch with us because she would often write to us asking for money,'' her mother said. She would go everywhere in faded jeans with embroidered flowers all over them, a rich, fun-loving, troubled kid with a trust fund, roaming the world on her credit card. She invested in boutiques in Ibiza and in London, where she sold pants to Mick Jagger. ''We invited him back again and again for fittings,'' she once said. ''She would come here with a series of improbable beaux,'' Barry Junior said. ''One was Spanish, who wore his shirts open to the waist and beads.'' Eleanor told her brother that she might drop out of college to become ''a barmaid,'' he said. ''I said, 'For God's sake, Eleanor, get your education, then you can be a barmaid if you want or you can be a bank president.' '' Her mother later said, ''Eleanor has seen sordid areas of life that I can hardly dare imagine. But it might have given her wisdom.''

In New York, there was now trouble in Sallie and Whitney's marriage, trouble that had been evident to their friends since Boston. For Sallie, having grown up in her parents' house of dreams, imitated them in her style and her choice of a husband. She had, in effect, re-created her mother's life and had set up a miniature Melcombe, surrounding herself with fine porcelains, linens and silver. In those days especially, even among the rich young marrieds of the Harvard set, no one lived like Whitney and Sallie. ''You would always see something like a few Indian bedspreads or a Museum of Modern Art print on the walls in a newly married household, but never at Sallie's,'' a friend said.

Sallie appeared to be the very image of young success, and invitations to her dinners were as prized as her mother's bids to Melcombe. Sallie was very blond and fey, and as Mary Caperton had once done, she seemed to set herself apart. The fact that she had been published early gave her luster, and by the time she was twenty-three she seemed to have sprung into full maturity. Later she would say she had been playacting, trying to live a dream of ideal family life.

Sallie confided to friends that she felt intimidated by Whitney's colleagues at the *New York Review of Books*. The magazine had begun on a shoestring out of one editor's apartment, and Whitney had offered to serve as publisher without pay. Sallie later told friends that the original founders were ''so brilliant and accomplished'' that she felt nervous and insecure in their presence. ''They needed somebody to type some envelopes, and so they asked me to do it and I went in and did it for a day or something. I didn't want to do it . . . and I was intimidated by those people. . . . They were very big literary lions, you know, and I was very small." Mary Bingham seemed unaware of Sallie's feelings and thought the *New York Review* was such a splendid idea that she invested ten thousand dollars in it.

Sallie and Whitney were now living in a grand apartment on the Upper East Side, but it remained cavernous in feeling, a friend remembered, as if it were not a real home. "Sallie just seemed miserable," a friend said. In New York, the marriage unraveled quickly. "When I married Whitney I thought you lived happily ever after as my own parents did," she said. "I had so many false hopes and expectations because of what I had seen of the fairy tale of my parents' life." The promise of re-creating a miniature Melcombe soon vanished as Sallie discovered she was unprepared for domestic life. Her short stories grew even bleaker. She wrote about women in proper marriages who were trapped and suffocated by the expectations of their class.

Worth and Joan suspected that something terrible was happening to Sallie, although she never discussed her problems with them. She was in this respect like her parents. It was not her style to explain. In any event, she was now far too immersed in psychoanalysis. As it happened, Worth and Joan were in New York during that period, and they made a dinner date with the Ellsworths. "Worth and Whitney were finally beginning to get along together after their initial problems. That night, Whitney came by himself, and we had a very good time," Joan remembered. Sallie was too nervous and upset to have dinner, although she was still pretending that everything was fine. Joan looked into the bedroom at their apartment and saw "two single beds," and she said, "I knew there was trouble."

Sallie recalls this period of her life with anger. She used the same vocabulary to describe Whitney's colleagues at the *New York Review of Books* that she might have used for her mother: "judgmental," "rigorous," "harsh." Although she had published a novel and several good short stories, Sallie would later believe that they did not take her seriously. She believed that she was not living up to the standards that had been set for her. Of course, those standards were impossible because of Sallie's high expectations. But her parents applauded most of her writing efforts and perhaps did too much for Sallie, attempting to help her in the unrealistic and ultimately destructive manner they had when she was a child and didn't teach her even how to change her own typewriter ribbons. When it came to Sallie's writing efforts, Mary and Barry perhaps tried to protect Sallie from failure and, in so doing, might have kept her from feeling independent. When Sallie published her novel, *After Such Knowledge,* Mary even asked the poet Fred Seidel, Whitney's Harvard classmate, to review it for the *Courier-Journal.* "I didn't know what to do," he said. "So I wound up writing five thousand words when I should have written five hundred." Even at the end, when the family was warring, Barry Senior would attend Sallie's plays, as if her work was their common ground.

Sallie was talented and perfectly capable of running a complicated household with a child and servants, and organizing dinner parties where friends would remark on her graciousness. "She would look at you and ask you if you needed anything, if you wanted more, and she was so Southern and winning," a friend said. But she seemed to make no deep emotional connections with anyone around her. She had few close women friends. "Sallie's entire problem has been brought on by her years on the couch," her mother later said.

Mary always believed that Sallie was ferociously competitive. If that was true, then she had placed herself in an arduous environment. In New York, Sallie was known as a rich girl, but there were many rich girls, as always, on the fringes of the literary set. Unlike her aunt Henrietta, who was happy just to be a party girl in London, Sallie wanted to be celebrated for her accomplishments. There were few people in New York who cared who the Binghams were, and hardly anyone had been to Louisville. "I'm Sallie Bingham" did not cause the same tremor at a Park Avenue dinner party as it did in Louisville. She saw slights everywhere, and complained that her husband's colleagues never asked her to review a book in the publication that he himself worked for. She began to get rejection letters for her short stories from *The New Yorker*, and this hurt. She was published in the *Atlantic, McCall's*, and the *Ladies' Home Journal*, but it wasn't enough for Sallie Bingham, who had been reared with such grandiose notions.

Sallie later told her family that she felt unsure of herself in front of truly distinguished writers, such as the critic Elizabeth Hardwick, who was an advisory editor at the *New York Review*, as if she thought she should be equally distinguished. Her sense of her place in the world was so warped that she had no idea that she was in fact thought of highly by her husband's colleagues, or that her stories were admired, or that she was considered to be talented by almost everyone who met her. "She was a lovely, arresting young girl who we all thought was charming," Barbara Epstein, one of the founders of the *New York Review,* said. But Sallie's stories were filled with women who were miserable, unsure of themselves, on the verge of nervous breakdowns, and surrounded by lawyers, married boyfriends, possessive nannies, and detached, unfeeling parents. She began to write more and more on the autobiographical theme that would take over her work: the plight of the needy heiress. Eventually Sallie's career would falter. But in 1986 Sallie would again begin to write bitterly of her Louisville childhood in national magazines, not as fiction but as fact. By then, of course, her relationship with her parents was in ruins and Sallie had no qualms about attacking them publicly.

Whitney and Sallie separated after Jonathan's death. Sallie was so distraught that she became obsessive about her baby son, Barry. "She would never leave this baby until he went to sleep," Joan remembered. "It was as if at that point being a mother was the only element that was giving her a sense of self."

In a short story of Sallie's called "The Visit," two rich and detached parents come to New York to see their daughter. Their communication has been sporadic, and the mother, Mrs. Clifton, is convinced that something is wrong. Mr. Clifton wants no unpleasantness, however. "We are going to take little Johnny to the park, and that is all," he says. At their daughter's apartment, they are shocked by the domestic neglect: the dying plants and the crushed sofa pillows, the grandchild attended only by the maid. The daughter tells her parents that she and her husband have been apart for a month. "In the beginning, it was O.K. At least we could spend the night together. . . . We haven't had much fun together since Johnny was born. . . ." The daughter asks her father for an increase in her allowance. Otherwise she will have to let her maid go, and then who will take care of little Johnny? Mr. Clifton quickly agrees to pay but wants to leave immediately. "You want to shrug this off, don't you?" Mrs. Clifton asks him. "You've always been like that. When she was little, you never wanted any trouble. 'Call the nurse,' you'd say when she acted up. You've always been glad to spend money sending her places where other people could deal with her—boarding school, camp, college. Plenty of money! But when it came down to something about her yourself—oh no! That's too much, that's too demanding."

Much later, Sallie would say, "You know who that skinny young girl [in my short stories] is as well as I do. . . ."

In Louisville, Mary never understood why Sallie and Whitney had divorced and could not, as she said, "bring myself to ask Sallie about it. I wouldn't have dreamed of asking her. And I never knew how to get Sallie to talk to me," her mother said, but when Sallie saw old friends she would inevitably complain about marriage to "conventional, dreary, rigid upper-class men." She was living completely on dividend income, and once complained about the economies she had to suffer because her income from the newspaper was only $120,000 a year. Until she was forty-five years old, she later said, "It never occurred to me that I might consider taking an actual paying job."

Her days as a single mother were not to last long. A few months after Sallie and Whitney separated she met a lawyer named Michael Iovenko. He was good-looking and attentive to her son, Barry, and extremely solicitous of Sallie. Soon they were dating seriously and Sallie began to call him "my new hope." Her friends felt Michael was "nice enough" but doubted if he had the strength to cope with Sallie and her moods. Like Whitney, he was mild with "no willingness to spar," as her mother later said, although later he would be tough enough to sue Sallie for custody of his children.

26

July 1966. However unsettled Eleanor's and Sallie's lives had been, thirty-four-year-old Worth Bingham had never been happier than he was this fine summer. He was doing wonderfully at the family newspaper, and was devoted to Joan and his three-year-old daughter, Clara. And just three months earlier, Joan had given birth to their first son, Robert Worth Bingham, Junior, whom Worth had nicknamed Robbie. This July, Worth had planned to take his family for a month's vacation to the island of Nantucket, and was delighted when he and Joan were able to rent a sprawling turn-of-the-century Cape Cod house on a bluff. The house belonged to the mother of his old friend John Wagley, a Harvard classmate.

On Friday, the eighth of July, Worth left to join Joan and the children on Nantucket. On the way, Worth stopped in Washington to see his old friend Dick Harwood, who had taken a job at the *Washington Post*. "He told me he wanted to come back to the paper and take a job as the Washington bureau chief," Harwood later recalled. On Monday, Worth called Norman Isaacs on a business matter. "The weather here is gorgeous," he said.

The twelfth of July dawned bright and hot, a perfect beach day, and that Tuesday morning when Joan and Worth awakened, they decided to spend the day at the ocean with Clara and her pails and shovels. Early that morning Joan called friends who had rented a house nearby to tell them she was making a picnic. The beach was all of half an hour away, and Worth with his new passion for surfing loved the breakers. This summer, he had even devised a clever way to transport his board.

Joan and Worth had rented a Dodge hardtop convertible for the summer that had no centerposts between the front- and rear-door windows, which meant that Worth could rest the board sideways on top of all their beach things in the backseat. The board stuck out only seven or eight inches on either side of the car, and because Clara was still so small that her head was lower than the top of the seat, the board could not bounce forward and

263

hurt her. But Worth was not happy with the arrangement and
had asked Wagley if he could use his station wagon to carry his
board to the beach. "It was an old wood station wagon like the
surfers all used," Joan said. Wagley said no, because in case of
an accident it would be difficult to find spare parts. His decision
not to lend Worth his vintage station wagon would haunt Wagley
the rest of his life.

On Tuesday morning they were late—they were always late—
and at about eleven Joan and Worth realized that their friends
had already long been at the beach. They bundled Clara, the
picnic basket, the towels, the plastic shovels and pails into the
Dodge. The board was already there, resting in place. Worth
wasn't driving fast, maybe ten or fifteen miles an hour, on the
country road. He turned a corner and was going up a hill when
he noticed that some people had gathered by a tennis court and
had parked a car illegally by the roadside—typical summer behavior. Worth swerved to the left to avoid this car, but as he did
one end of the board caught on the fender. The impact sheared
off the end of the board while the rest of the board snapped
forward, smashing into the back of Worth Bingham's neck. The
car went out of control as Worth slumped in his seat. Clara
screamed as Joan reached over and stopped the car. In a panic
she grabbed Clara and ran to a nearby house. "We called the
ambulance," she said. "And these people called the Beckers
took Clara in and tried to calm her, as I waited outside with
Worth. He was just slumped on the seat and I held him and it
seemed like the ambulance took hours to arrive."

A doctor drove by on his way to the beach and stopped. Joan
was sobbing in the front seat with her arms around Worth, a
friend remembered, and did not want to let go of him. The
doctor looked at Worth, checked his pulse and then told Joan
Bingham her husband had died of a broken neck.

In Louisville, Barry Senior was in a meeting with Norman
Isaacs when his secretary put through an urgent call from his
daughter-in-law. "The phone buzzed, so Barry picked it up. . . .
All the blood ran out of his face and he said, 'Oh my God.' "
Isaacs stared at his old friend and could not imagine what had
happened. His heart began to pound. Even talking about this
dreadful day twenty-two years later, Norman Isaacs, long retired, long out of Louisville, wept. "It was so terrible, just hearing it. . . . Barry said, 'Of course, we'll be up as fast as we
can. . . .' And it went on, then he tried what few reassuring
words he could say to Joan. 'Try to keep hold of yourself.' That
kind of thing. 'We'll be there within a few hours.' Then he asked
about Robbie, he wanted to know if he was all right." When he
hung up the telephone he said, 'You've got to get us an airplane

to get us up to Nantucket. . . .' '' Norman Isaacs looked at Barry, still not comprehending what had happened. "Barry took a deep breath and said, 'Worth has been killed in some kind of weird accident. . . .' '' Then he stood up and said, "I have to go home right away. Oh my God . . . how am I ever going to tell Mary?''

At that moment Barry Junior was at a local theater at an NBC correspondents meeting. NBC often sent its international reporters around the country to talk to the affiliates, and some of the reporters from Barry's Washington days had come down to Louisville. Barry was having a marvelous time seeing friends he hadn't seen in years. Suddenly, an usher came to tell him to return to his office immediately.

At Melcombe the moment Edie Callahan heard the news she rushed over from her house on the property. Barry met her in the driveway and she put her arms around her dear friend of forty years. For the first time since she had known him, Barry Bingham began to cry. "Oh my God, Edie," he said. "Why couldn't it have been me that was killed and not Worth? My life has been so full, so blessed, why couldn't it have been me?''

The airline mechanics were on strike and there were no commercial flights from Louisville for Boston or New York. Isaacs called everyone he knew—the bourbon powers, the tobacco magnates, Reynolds Metals executives—until he was able to get a private plane. Late that afternoon, Barry Junior, Edie, Mary and Barry Senior got on the Brown-Forman plane at Standiford Field. "The plane was a DC-3," Barry Junior said, "and it took us almost seven hours to get to Nantucket. It was excruciating. We just sat in that airplane and sat and sat and never seemed to arrive.''

In Nantucket, Joan was trying to hold herself together. She had loved Worth passionately. Now he was gone and her two tiny children would never know their father. John Wagley got to Nantucket just after Barry and Mary arrived and helped make the arrangements to bring Worth's body home. He joined the family on the return flight to Louisville on the Brown-Forman plane and was struck by the calm and stoicism of Mary and Barry, as well as Joan. The news of Worth's death made the papers all over the country. He was already, at age thirty-four, a commanding figure at the American Society of Newspaper Editors' meetings, and the list of his clubs and activities took up seven paragraphs in the news story in the *Courier-Journal*. Norman Isaacs, who had cherished Worth since he was a rowdy college boy, wrote a memoir of him for the newspaper: "He was a big ruggedly handsome man, who had a little of many things mixed up in him—aggressiveness and shyness, pride and humility, reticence and forthrightness. He had great poise, and the indefinable gift of charm.''

Ward Just was home in Washington when the telephone rang. He answered it and heard his ex-wife's voice: ''Worth has been killed. . . . I was on the ragged edge, and had lost a lot of blood when the hand grenade hit me in Vietnam. I was in a terrible state of shock, but somehow I left for Louisville immediately, and when I drove up to that enormous house for the funeral, I was stunned when I saw Barry Senior. His face was so grave it was almost out of El Greco, everything had gone vertical, and I could hardly approach him, he was so overcome by grief.''

In that one terrible moment in Nantucket the dreams truly began to vanish for the Bingham family. Worth's death, coming only two years after the horrible accident that killed Jonathan, no doubt caused the Binghams to turn even further inward, perhaps to retreat so far into their own private grief that they would become even more remote and inaccessible to their children. Jonathan's death was agonizing, but Worth's death would eventually destroy the family.

The ''if only's'' that followed Worth's death must have been torment. If only Worth had not taken up surfing, if only he had had Wagley's car, if only that car hadn't been double-parked, if only he had swerved six more inches. Richard Harwood, Jay Iselin, Ward Just, John Wagley and Worth's lawyer, Gordon Davidson, were asked to be pallbearers at the funeral, and Worth remained in state in the Little House. Mary said about the loss of her second son, ''His death is a terrible tragedy for Barry and me, but it is far worse for the city of Louisville,'' unintentionally echoing Eleanor Roosevelt's words when the President died. Mary invited her sister Harriette to the funeral, Joan remembered, because ''Harriette was very talkative and Mary thought it would keep our minds occupied.'' Henrietta, however, was too distraught to come to Louisville. Worth had been her favorite nephew, the boy who used to seek refuge at her apartment when he was a freewheeling prep school boy. Ailing in New York, Henrietta would not live another two years.

Barry Junior was somber at the funeral. He was thinking not about his own future, he remembered, but about the loss of the brother who ''was the closest person in the world to me.'' He kept thinking, Who am I going to go on safari with? Who can I call on the telephone to talk about the family? Who can I laugh with? Edie worried because her husband, so bound up with grief, was unable to break down and cry.

It was, Wagley remembered, ''a beastly hot day'' in Louisville. A private reception was held before the funeral in the Little House with only about thirty people present. Just before Worth was to be taken to the cemetery, Mr. Pearson opened the casket.

Worth seemed so alive; his skin was still honey-colored from the sun. Seeing him lying in his coffin was too much for Joan. As the casket closed she collapsed, and had to be taken from the room. Mary followed her into her bedroom and put her arms around her. "I know how devastated you are and how much you were committed to Worth," she said. "And I want you to know how I appreciate that your commitment to Worth was as great as my own commitment to Barry." And with that, the two Bingham women sat in the bedroom and cried unashamedly together.

Worth was buried at Cave Hill Cemetery next to his brother Jonathan, six days after he had left Glenview for Nantucket. After the funeral there was a wake at the Big House, which Dick Harwood remembered "as a brawl without any tears, very much in the Kennedy style." Sallie and Michael were there, and when she got back to New York she told her friends that she was sure the family was cursed and that Worth "committed suicide." Years later she would tell a reporter how tragic Worth's funeral had been for Barry Junior: "He sobbed and cried at Worth's funeral; it was absolutely heartbreaking," she said, again speaking a poetic, if not actual, truth.

Just after the funeral Barry Senior approached his second son: "What would you like to do?" He asked Barry, who had always been so dutiful, if he would take over Worth's position at the newspaper, to carry on what he called "our shared dream." Barry Junior remembered being startled. The thought of his taking Worth's position had occurred to him, he said, but it wasn't something he had ever really considered. "He could have told me anything and I would have listened," Barry Junior said. "I think it was a great blow to Barry," his father said. "In addition to losing his older brother, he had lost the one who he had thought was going to carry on the family tradition. I remember going to him after Worth's funeral and sitting down and saying, 'Now listen, our lives have changed . . . I said to him, 'What do you want to do?' and he assured me that he wanted to move over to the newspaper."

"When Barry told me what his father said, I said to him, 'I never wanted to live in that big house,' " Edie said. They had been planning a trip to France for the last part of July. "We didn't know what to do," Barry Junior said. "Do we go? Do we not go?" And so they asked Mary what was the proper thing to do. Her answer was right to the point: Go, she told them, because it will be the last trip you will have together for a very, very long time.

Mary and Barry insisted that Joan and the children come to Chatham with them for August. She was numb with grief, of course, and needed the comfort of her in-laws. But when they got to Chatham, Joan felt out of place and very lonely. She could hardly talk about Worth if his father was in the room because Barry would immediately change the subject. Mary, on the other hand, did talk to her, and the two women would sit by the ocean for hours discussing every aspect of Worth's character. But Barry, bound up with his own anguish, remained distant from Joan, convivial and forbidding all at once. As he had so often done in the past, he tried to put the tragedy out of his mind completely. Barry's detachment was the first sign that life as a Bingham without Worth might be difficult. But as a mother, she also understood that the death of two children was an overwhelming horror from which no parent can ever truly recover.

27

Autumn, 1971. After Worth was killed, it took Barry Junior several years to feel comfortable in the newspaper business, but now he was running the newspaper empire and was working ten and twelve hours a day because he was beset with business problems. Although his style was far more subdued than Worth's had been, his reporters admired him tremendously. Like Worth, he took reporting seriously and sent his staff all over the world. Additionally, Barry Junior had begun a strict ethics policy at the newspaper, which would be nationally praised.

But the *Courier-Journal*, like many other newspapers in the country, was losing circulation. The cost of distributing it to all 120 counties in Kentucky had become astronomical, and Barry was trying to install rigid budgets for the news department, which alienated many of the *Courier-Journal*'s longtime executives, who had been used to running the newspaper with a free hand. Some of Barry's critics pointed to his passion for television and electronic news and quoted an unfortunate remark Barry had once made years before, "Television will replace newspapers." Barry's adversaries would always say about him: *Barry Junior does not understand newspapers.*

Nevertheless, the family seemed relatively peaceful. Sallie and Michael Iovenko now had two sons, Christopher and William. Edie and Barry had two daughters, Emily and Molly. Eleanor was finding success in a new career making video documentary films in California and New York. Joan's life had changed too. A few years earlier she had left Louisville to live in New York, where she was not known as Worth Bingham's widow. Her children, Robbie and Clara, were attending private school, and Joan worked as a professional photographer. Joan and Eleanor had become close friends and saw each other frequently.

But the peace was not to last. Soon the family was to live through another nightmare when the last surviving son, Barry Junior, was diagnosed as having Hodgkin's disease, the abdominal cancer that had killed the Judge. It was only a month before

this diagnosis that Barry's own doctor had examined him and
said he was in such splendid shape he could go back into the
marines. "We simply did not know what we had done to bring
on another tragedy," Barry Senior said.

Barry Junior's cancer stunned the family, for he seemed the
picture of good health. Each morning he was up by five and off
on a two-mile run. He would often be at his desk at the *Courier-
Journal* by 7:00 A.M. His father had even taken the title of chairman of the board a few months earlier at age sixty-five and made
his son editor and publisher, a fact that was noted in the *New
York Times*.

Barry's stepsons, Charles and Philip Franchini Bingham,
whom Barry had adopted, told their mother they believed that
the pressure Barry Junior was under had given him cancer. He
was running three companies without adequate help. Barry Junior had no strong editor, such as Mark Ethridge and Norman
Isaacs, to help him shape the *Courier-Journal*. The family had
tried to hire both Eugene Patterson, now of the *St. Petersburg
Times*, and Claude Sitton, a former *New York Times* reporter
and editor, but had been unsuccessful.

Barry Junior now spent his weekends working at home, for
he was overseeing not only the newspapers but also WHAS-TV
and Standard Gravure. The Bingham printing company, which
specialized in printing Sunday newspaper magazines, such as
Parade, was losing business as new offset printing techniques
made Gravure's presses obsolete. Barry later would decide to
invest millions of dollars to modernize Standard Gravure and to
boost its sagging income, but he also decided not to expand his
empire beyond Louisville, which would turn out to be a grave
mistake. This was the era when many other newspaper owners,
such as the Cox family in Atlanta who owned the *Constitution*,
were expanding out of their market into cable TV or buying
other newspapers or paper plants. But Barry Junior, perhaps
unsure of himself in his new job, was very cautious. "We knew
Louisville. We were a regional company," Barry Junior said.
"And my father always believed in staying local."

More ominously for the papers, television had changed the
nature of the business, especially for afternoon newspapers,
which were folding all over America. The *Louisville Times* was
not yet suffering as many newspapers were because it and the
Courier-Journal were a monopoly, but Louisville's local economy was troubled, and few companies wanted to expand in a
city where the unions were so strong. The L&N Railroad, which
had shored up the local economy since 1850, was about to be
sold. More and more businesses were closing. International Harvester would eventually close, and although General Electric was
still strong, it was not going to expand its local plant.

Fourth Street, which had always been the downtown shopping center, was now a depressing pedestrian mall, which had a Walgreen's, a wig shop and, later, a blood bank filled with welfare cases. At one end of this gloomy thoroughfare the Brown hotel had closed, and on the other the Seelbach Hotel had foundered—not enough tourists came to Louisville anymore to keep them flourishing. The *Courier-Journal* and the *Louisville Times* were constantly reporting this decline, which irritated the Chamber of Commerce because it was trying to lure business back.

The Bingham newspapers were making a small profit and paying a low dividend to the stockholders. Twice a year there were family meetings, for which Barry prepared a slide presentation showing the progress of the companies. "They were ridiculous," Sallie would later say. Joan came down from New York, but Sallie and Eleanor rarely appeared. With two more boys, Sallie was now busy with her family. Sallie usually arrived in Louisville at Easter for two or three days, bringing all three of her sons. "I can remember thinking that I am never going to get to know Barry's sisters because they were hardly over here," Edie said. "Sallie wanted nothing to do with the companies," Barry Junior said. "She thought journalism was second-class and beneath her." Sallie sent her husband, Michael Iovenko, to the board meetings as her representative. As a lawyer, Michael was a valuable participant, Barry Junior remembered, and his contributions made a lot of sense.

Now that Barry Junior had the title of publisher, it was time for him to take over the Big House, if only for the inevitable entertaining Edie and Barry would have to do, Edie said. "I took one look at the size of that kitchen and I said to Mary, 'Gosh, how did you ever run it?' and she said, 'I tried to go in there as little as possible.' " In 1971 five perfect Negro servants were not easy to find in Louisville. "No one wanted to do that work anymore," Edie said.

At the newspapers there were many new systems in place. Barry was experimenting with computers, state-of-the-art electronic equipment, and offset printing for Standard Gravure. Although his top executives, such as Leon Tallichet and later George Gill, advised him frequently to expand outside Louisville, he consistently refused. He did, however, agree that as editor and publisher he should be covered by a million-dollar "key man" insurance policy. He was told he would need another medical examination. "Why can't we use the one I just had?" Barry Junior said. Annoyed, Barry took a day off from work and went in for another complete workup, including chest X rays. "A few days later the company called and said, 'We are not going to insure this guy. He has a bad mass in his chest of some kind.' " Thus in the autumn of 1971 Mary and Barry faced the possibility of another overwhelming tragedy, that their last remaining son might die.

Barry Junior was only thirty-seven years old. He had two tiny daughters and two teenage stepsons. His Louisville doctors were convinced that Barry had an aneurysm and that he needed chest surgery. Barry wanted another opinion, so he left for Massachusetts General in Boston, which was said to have the finest chest surgeons in the country. "Before they cracked me open to see what it was," Barry Junior said, "they did an exploratory surgery and took out a lymph node." Before Barry came out of the anesthesia, his parents were told that their only surviving son had Hodgkin's disease.

"I thought I was at the end of the road," Barry Junior said. But the treatment for Hodgkin's disease had vastly improved since the Judge had died of it decades earlier. "The first thing the doctor said to me was that there were many people who could survive Hodgkin's disease, but the primary side effect of this disease was divorce," Barry Junior said. Barry would have to subject himself to grueling radiation and surgery, and there was no guarantee that he would survive. He was lucky in that his tumor was still small enough so that his chance of being cured might be as high as 70 percent if he could get through the radiation without too many problems.

Suddenly an immense burden was thrust upon Edie Bingham, who had four children to supervise, no adequate help and a move to Melcombe to orchestrate. The small details of life seemed insurmountable. Her house had been sold; Mary and Barry were set to move down the hill. The day before Barry was operated on in Boston, Edie left her sixteen-year-old son in charge of the move and took off for Mass. General.

Back in Louisville after surgery, "my weight dropped to one hundred forty pounds and most of my hair came out," Barry Junior said. "I was vomiting. It was not a happy time in my life. . . . I used to come into the paper more than I should have. . . . It was better for me to walk in so they would not think I had been taken to Pearson's." He insisted that his father take back the title of editor and publisher. He put out memos to the staff on his medical progress, and his staff gave him an acrylic blond wig as a joke. "This looks horrible," Barry said when he tried it on. "Not as horrible as you look without it," his friends said.

His stepsons reacted violently to Barry's cancer. "They couldn't have been at a worse period of their life," Edie said. By the winter of 1972, as Barry was undergoing radiation therapy, both boys had announced they wanted to come home from prep school. "I couldn't say no to them," Edie said. They were sullen teenagers, who had picked up the anti-establishment jargon of the era, and, insensitive to their stepfather's condition, blasted rock music from the Big House. Edie could not control Philip and Charles, who grew wilder as they received less attention. ''They would say to Barry, 'You have cancer because of the stress you have been under, you shouldn't have worked so hard,' '' Edie said.

When Mary complained to Edie about her sons, Edie felt ''torn in two.'' ''Our little girls were the joys of our life,'' she said. ''And now Barry couldn't be with them and he was too sick to deal with Charles and Philip, who saw him as some sort of establishment figure to rebel against.'' In the midst of all this, Barry and Mary wanted to take Edie and Barry Junior on a trip. They wanted to take Barry's mind off his health, and so they settled on a holiday in Antigua between his two courses of radiation. Barry was ill from the radiation treatments, and when he got to Antigua, he could not go outside without feeling worse. ''The last thing I needed was sun,'' he said.

Edie was surprised in that horrible spring of 1972 that Sallie rarely called to ask about her brother. ''Once in a while there would be notes or phone calls, but it was hardly a weekly occasion,'' she said. Even Eleanor had been on the telephone to suggest that her brother seek laetrile treatments in Mexico. Edie knew Sallie was busy with Michael and her young boys, but, still, her only brother had cancer. Edie could not get over how selfish Sallie was. But Sallie was involved in her own life. She and Michael had a country house in Rhinebeck, New York, and Sallie had a new collection of short stories coming out, her first book in four years. From its bright early start, Sallie's writing career had slowed down, and she mentioned to her friends that she felt burdened by her children and had no time to write. Whatever pain she was in she did not allow her friends to see. ''Sallie was very brave. She rarely complained and was very stoical. She would get up at five A.M. to write, and would not moan and groan when her stories were not frequently published,'' her editor said. When *The Way It Is Now* was published the *Times* reviewer commented on how well Sallie's stories were constructed but was harsh about Sallie's characters.

''. . . Her remarkable virtuosity only heightens the fact that nearly all her heroines are look-alikes and feel-alikes who are hopelessly constricted, hopelessly narrow, hopelessly unable to escape the dead center of themselves. ''The Way It Is Now'' is really a statement of how it is for one kind of woman, and a pretty dull kind at that.

The radiation treatment would prove effective, and eventually Barry Junior would be able to survive his cancer. Slowly, he began to recover, although his personality showed a marked change. He was grateful to be alive but less willing to suffer fools or waste his time. Like his father before him, Barry had a clear vision of the *Courier-Journal* and wanted to put his plans in effect. He wanted to be with his children and with Edie, and he had fixed notions of the proper way to run a newspaper. Barry had always detested Louisville social life—the falseness, the politics. Of all the Binghams, Barry was the most principled. If he seemed austere, he was never a hypocrite. His father had changed the *Courier-Journal* in 1936 when he found the crusading liberal Mark Ethridge to run the newspapers, but under Barry Junior the *Courier-Journal* would be known for its ethics. No longer would political candidates feel they could cozy up to the Binghams for endorsements.

Barry and Edie would set the tone by their own stringent behavior where politics were concerned. Memos were issued; systems were put in place. He forbade staff members to get involved in politics, and at first proposed that his rules cover husbands and wives—a ban that was never actually issued—but the guidelines about the actual staff were distributed to everyone at the newspaper.

It was the era of Watergate, and journalists were on a crusade for ethics in government. The *Courier-Journal* was out in front in this effort and had hired one of the first ombudsmen in the country. John Ed Pearce was bumped from the editorial page and moved to the magazine to reflect this new policy. To this day he believes the move was meant to punish him for his friendship with a former governor and mayor. "The news staff was delighted when I issued these guidelines," Barry said, "because now they had a reason to stand up to the community."

Barry Senior and Worth had seen nothing wrong with socializing with Kentucky politicians, but Barry and Edie would have none of it. "We wanted to be with other kinds of people," Edie said. More and more the newspaper was going on social and moral crusades. Barry would turn the reporters loose on strip mining, horse racing and black lung disease.

To his credit, Barry Senior allowed his son to find his own way and never disputed his plans. When Barry Senior talked about the new *Courier-Journal* policy, he radiated enthusiasm. "I wanted him to do things without interference," he said. "When Barry took over from me, I advised him, 'People are going to try to make divisions between you and me.' That had happened between my father and me. People came to me after I inherited the paper from my father and said, 'You just must not do that. You mustn't take that editorial position. That isn't what your father would have done.' My answer to that was always, 'I think I know better than you what my father would have done, and he always said to me, a newspaper has to move along with the times.' I convinced Barry that that would be my position. 'Don't ever let people tell you what your father would have done or would have thought. And look out for people who would tell you that I said something about you or you said something about me.' "

He did not, however, give his son financial control of the newspaper. Ominously, Barry Junior received a double message: You are free, but I still control things. Barry Junior took his father at his word. Foolishly, he believed that he had autonomy. It never occurred to him that his parents might come to dislike the way he was running their newspaper.

The new bright young man in Louisville, Dr. Harvey Sloane, who had become so close to the Binghams, was now married. Since Sloane ran a public health clinic partially funded by the government, he had to spend considerable time in Washington. A few years earlier he had met a pretty, young brunette named Kathy McNally at a wedding. At Wheaton College, her nickname was Smack, and as the other girls dragged themselves into class in sweatshirts and jeans, Kathy McNally was known for her meticulous grooming, her perfect manicure, jewelry, make-up and clothes. She was filled with ambition, even at the height of the 1960's, as if she were from a different era. But her friends at Wheaton knew how determined Kathy McNally was to go beyond her Pittsburgh family. Early on, Sloane brought her to Louisville to lunch at the Big House, where she had been "dazzled by the Binghams, their grace, the way they lived."

Soon after Harvey and Kathy married, their daughter, Abigail, was born, and they asked Barry Bingham to be her godfather. "We thought it was odd," Edie said. "The age difference was so amazing," but Edie and Barry left it at that and saw a great deal of the Sloanes. While Barry was taking his radiation treatments the Sloanes often dropped by. "Barry was just stoic," Kathy Sloane said. "It was so much like him. . . . He can wear a hair shirt better than anyone else in Louisville."

Harvey Sloane was tired of running a government medical clinic. He was idealistic, energetic and potentially a good candidate. Barry Senior began to talk to him about running for mayor of Louisville. Sloane was now active on a local air pollution control board and speaking out more and more on environmental issues. "If you had to think of a perfect candidate," Edie said, "Harvey was it. He was young, attractive, energetic, smart and liberal." Everyone in the family got behind the campaign. When Harvey Sloane announced for the 1973 mayor's race, Joan gave a fund-raiser for him in New York. Barry Junior thought Harvey was a terrific candidate and the newspaper en-

dorsed him strongly, but Barry worried about their friendship.
"I said to everyone, 'I am sorry that Harvey is running because
that is the end of our friendship. It just does not look right for
the publisher of the paper to be close friends with the mayor.' "
During the campaign Kathy Sloane went to two hundred and
fifty meetings with her husband and walked over two hundred
miles. "I loved every minute of it," she said. "I think I was
born for the job."

With the help of the Bingham family, Harvey Sloane was
elected handily, but soon Barry Junior would come to regret his
endorsement of Sloane for mayor and realize he had helped to
create a potentially powerful adversary. "In his acceptance
speech . . . Harvey said, 'The automobile is public enemy number one.' I said, 'Boy, we've really got a mayor now!' " Barry
Junior said. "Well, Harvey's record on air pollution has just
been pathetic. . . . And Harvey just dropped the ball on a lot of
issues." True to his policies, Edie and Barry stopped having
private dinners with the Sloanes, a fact that seemed to have
bothered Mary and Barry Bingham tremendously, although they
never once mentioned it to their son.

Slowly, a very subtle but potentially devastating conflict was
emerging between Barry Junior and Barry Senior over Barry
Junior's stringent ethical standards. Barry Junior was so literal-
minded and so caught up with the newspaper that he remained
unaware in his ethical zeal that he was in violation of the hidden
rules of Louisville life. Barry seemed to be rebelling against his
family and its façade of public virtue. He was also trying to
carve out his separateness in a potentially dangerous manner. In
effect, he was saying to his father, *The old ways weren't good
enough and now they are finished.*

It was his father's style to stand outside St. Francis in the
Fields every Sunday as if he were a second minister, for however
aloof he was, he understood the need to glad-hand. He had the
same style at the ASNE meetings. "He was such a social publisher, so old school tie. I always felt he loved the trappings of
being a publisher," Ben Bradlee, of the *Washington Post,* said.
Barry Senior once asked his friend Wilson Wyatt about Barry
Junior. "Do you think Barry is too rigid to run the *Courier-
Journal?*" Wyatt replied, "Barry, what choice do you have?"

In 1974 the *Wall Street Journal* published a front-page story
about the newspapers headlined "Louisville Newspapers Cherish Independence, Guard It Zealously," praising Barry Junior's
strict ethics policy. The article had an ominous subhead—"A
Trifle Sanctimonious?"—which many reporters believed later
reflected Mary and Barry's and the Sloanes' shared feelings about
the newspaper and Barry Junior. Barry was compared favorably
with traditional and less stringent publishers, such as his own

father, who had turned up in tuxedo "attending fancy parties." Every one of the new publisher's transgressions are noted in the newspaper, the *Journal* reported, his ten-dollar fine for running a red light, his fifty-dollar fine "for hunting doves in a baited field."

The *Wall Street Journal* called the Bingham newspapers "the acknowledged Messrs. Clean of the newspaper industry," and even poked a bit of fun at the lengths taken to appear ethical. All books received from publishers were either returned or paid for. This irritated the New York publishers, since they had no bookkeeping procedure to cope with such unusual negotiations. One reporter complained about fighting with people over five-dollar checks. The newspapers had dropped mail-order health insurance ads, which cost the company a hundred thousand dollars in revenue. The news desk even renamed the Buick Open golf tournament the Flint Open, because they did not want to be accused of promoting Buicks. Barry hired a columnist to write a twice-weekly feature called "In All Fairness," which took the newspaper to task when it made mistakes.

But Barry and Edie remained unaware that they had dangerously isolated themselves by their stringent policies. Louisville was very much a town where the mayor was called by his first name and everyone saw everyone else at the dinners and the country club. In the past, his own father had often instructed editors and reporters to write stories in praise of his civic projects. When Mary had been the book editor, she told a columnist, "If there is a book published by Farrar, Straus and Giroux, do mention it first in your column because Barry is a director of the company." Barry Junior had inherited a plantation that had become so lax that, he said, "even the farm editor owned a tractor company that he was often touting in the newspaper."

Now Barry had changed the newspaper, and he made it clear to the new mayor, Harvey Sloane, that he could no longer entertain him. Still, Edie saw nothing wrong with playing tennis with her old friend Kathy Sloane, or inviting Kathy's daughter, Abigail, to the Big House to learn horseback riding from her daughter Emily. For several years, the Sloanes would be invited to Edie and Barry's annual square dance, and Barry and Edie attended the Sloanes' Christmas caroling party. "I thought Kathy would understand not to drop our name all over town," Edie said.

But Kathy Sloane, a fine political wife, had mastered the social arts of Louisville. "She would tell people, 'Oh, I was out at Edie's playing tennis,' or 'Abigail went riding with Emily,' and in such subtle ways she gave everyone in town the impression that we were still close. She would say, 'The Binghams this' and 'the Binghams that,' and of course Mary and Barry never stopped seeing the Sloanes.'' For her part, Mary Bingham thought that Barry Junior was carrying his ethics too far. "We were a small city," she said. "That was not how things worked.''

Besides, Mary personally liked Kathy and Harvey, and Barry Senior was Abigail's godfather. Kathy was attractive, had an ingratiating manner, enjoyed gossip, and was often in New York with famous friends. She loved to give dinners, which she did frequently. Kathy was involved in dozens of committees in Louisville. "There was so much to be done," she said. "I liked to be involved.'' And she was not shy about complaining frequently to her friend Mary about Barry and Edie's behavior. "Mrs. Bingham was perplexed by Edie and Barry's coolness to us," she said. "But perhaps Barry and Edie avoided us because they resented our closeness to their family." The Sloanes and the senior Binghams took trips together, and as Edie said later, "Many people in town thought that Kathy was the daughter that Mary wished she had had.'' Edie, of course, never told Mary that she didn't trust Kathy Sloane or that she might have been jealous of her intimate relationship with Mary and Barry.

By 1975 the *Courier-Journal* was in severe trouble. The profit margins dropped as the newspaper business slumped all over the country. The oil embargo was devastating for the *Courier-Journal*, which needed "a million gallons of gas each year" to deliver the newspaper. "Gas went from thirty-five cents to a dollar a gallon," Barry Junior said. The cost of newsprint skyrocketed—from $150 to $500 a ton—as did the cost of distributing the *Courier-Journal*, "two hundred fifty miles to the north, two hundred miles to the south, one hundred miles to the east and one hundred fifty miles to the west," the newspaper's public affairs man said. There were "no new advertising dollars to wring out," Barry Junior said. The paper's circulation had dipped, but Barry Junior had no intention of reducing the huge news staff. The *Louisville Times* would soon be faltering. Now more and more, television news was taking over the role of the afternoon newspapers. In Louisville the final edition of the *Times* was dropped. The deadline for the last edition of the day was now 2:30 P.M. "What could you do if there was a story that broke between two-thirty and five P.M.? The TV people would be all over it and the newspaper would look idiotic," Barry Junior said. More and more, Barry Junior stayed out of the newsroom and isolated himself with financial people. The editors remarked on how weary he seemed. "We thought it was the Hodgkin's disease. He seemed to run out of steam," one editor said.

Meanwhile, Barry and the newspapers now faced another crisis. In the summer of 1975 James Gordon, a local federal judge, said that the Louisville schools were not integrated and that busing would have to begin the following September in Louisville. "The newspapers were the only institution in town which supported this," Barry said. "No one else, not doctors, lawyers, the Rotary Club, the Chamber of Commerce. We said it was the right thing to do." The school busing issue was explosive all over the country, and in Louisville the newspaper people knew there was going to be trouble. The year before Gordon's decision Barry took a group of editors, advertisers and circulation people to Boston to talk to the publisher of the *Boston Globe*. Boston had already had riots over busing, and the *Globe*'s reporters were constantly threatened. "This was the era when the crowds pushed the *Boston Globe* circulation trucks in the Charles River," Barry said. He was apprehensive about what would happen in Louisville that September, and he was worried, as a newsman, about how he was going to be able to beat the TV cameras to cover the story for the *Louisville Times*. "What do you do when they turn a bus over at three-thirty P.M. after school and your final edition has closed for the day?" Barry said.

Judge Gordon had decreed that no more than three people could gather anywhere in town except at a local fairgrounds. Although his intention was to avoid riots in Louisville, the *Courier-Journal* fought that part of his order. "At an editorial conference meeting, I said, 'This is unconstitutional. The First Amendment provides for the right to assemble,' " Barry said. At that point one of the editors looked up and said, "Barry, you are crazy." "Well, this looks like an editorial I am going to have to write," Barry said. The order was lifted the day after Barry's editorial ran in the newspaper.

That Saturday, ten thousand people massed downtown. "It was frightening to be there. They broke out three thousand dollars' worth of our windows by using spark plugs that you shot from a slingshot and rocks. . . . The police were there but they just could not control the crowd," Barry said. He was burned in effigy and thousands of people milled around the newspaper building. "A woman put a dime in the newspaper machine and took out every newspaper in it," Barry said. "I asked, 'Madam, did you pay for those?' and she just looked at me and threw the newspapers in the gutter."

The tougher the paper's editorials became, the more the telephone rang at the Big House with people telling whoever answered, "Go to hell." Thousands of readers canceled their subscriptions. The *Courier-Journal* truckers feared for their lives, and to avoid being stoned, many of the *Courier*'s drivers placed signs in their windshields: WE DO NOT SUPPORT BUSING. But the court decree and the presence of the National Guard prevented other violence.

The ice age had begun. The schools remained dreadful, the state government riddled with corruption. As the Sunbelt boomed, Louisville's statistics were grim, especially if you owned the newspaper and needed the ad revenues. In 1940 Louisville and Atlanta were nearly the same size. By the 1970's Atlanta was thriving and Louisville was not. Far worse, the profit margin of the *Courier-Journal* had dropped to 2 percent.

The one encouraging business development for Louisville was the success of the Humana hospital corporation, which had been started in the early 1960's by two local businessmen, Wendell Cherry and David Jones. They were brash, young, and out to make a name with old-money Louisville, as tough and as ambitious as the Judge had once been. Over the next few years Cherry in particular would become close to Mary and Barry Bingham. Like Harvey Sloane, he would come to dislike the way Barry Junior was running the *Courier-Journal*, a fact he would not keep to himself. By 1973 Humana had forty-seven hospitals and an annual income of $107 million. But besides Humana, Cherry was the co-owner of the Kentucky Colonels basketball team. "Somewhere along the line, this city lost pride in itself. And the effort now must be to *reestablish* pride," Cherry once told a reporter.

Soon enough, Wendell Cherry would be one of the leading citizens in Louisville. Humana was donating millions of dollars to local causes, and Cherry and Jones were considered heroes in town. The Binghams would welcome Humana's help in funding their own charity projects, and they were delighted that "the Humana boys," as they called Cherry and Jones, believed in "public service" and were going to pledge millions to Actors Theatre and the other arts. When Cherry later criticized Barry Junior to Mary and Barry, they never told their son.

28

By the late 1970's the Bingham family was already showing signs of the tension and rage that would finally destroy forever the newspaper empire and the family members' relationships with one another. A disaster was in the making, but no one in the family could have predicted as much. Two overwhelming situations unquestionably hastened the catastrophe. First, Sallie's second marriage fell apart, and Sallie, furious and vulnerable, decided to come home to Louisville, desperate for attention and love from her parents. Second, Mary and Barry's relationship with Barry Junior and Edie was slowly eroding as the senior Binghams became more and more displeased with the way Barry Junior ran the family newspaper and the "permissive" way Edie Bingham brought up her children. In 1977, when Sallie finally did come home, Mary and Barry had no qualms about bitterly complaining to Sallie about Barry Junior, whom Sallie had always dismissed as her intellectual inferior. "Confiding in Sallie was like handing a terrorist a grenade," a family member said.

Since the death of Jonathan and Worth, Mary seemed harsher to Edie. "Her knowledge of everything became supreme," Edie said. Although they lived fifty yards apart, Mary and Edie rarely visited each other. Edie's daughters, Emily and Molly, told their mother they felt intimidated by their grandmother, who often criticized their choice of books. Edie felt that she had to make all the effort with Mary and had a difficult time understanding Mary's sense of humor, which could be cruel and cutting, even about their closest friends. "I always felt I had to watch my step because of the way they talked about other people. They would mimic and demean anyone. No one was spared, not even a dear friend such as Wilson Wyatt, whose child they were merciless about," Edie said.

Yet Mary and Edie seemed to have a great deal in common. Edie's family, the Stenhouses, like the Capertons, was well connected but not rich and worried about keeping up appearances. When Edie's own mother died, Edie went to Mary and asked

281

her to "be like a mother to me," Edie said. Mary was correct
with Edie, but never intimate, and this upset Edie so much that
she consulted with a close friend of the family who was a psychiatrist. "I said to him, 'I don't know what is going on here. I
can't seem to have a happy relationship with my mother-in-law.
What is the matter with me? What should I do?' And he just
patted me on the head and said, 'Oh, just be patient with her.
She just has terrible grief.' "

Edie tried to sympathize with Mary, but it was increasingly
difficult because of Mary's formality and harshness. Once Edie
and Barry Junior had a nanny who left to get married. When
Mary learned the girl was pregnant, she asked Barry, "Are you
the father?" A more easygoing person might have laughed, but
Barry was deeply offended. "It was so crude a remark that I
was appalled," he said.

Mary was suffering terribly, however, and no doubt was unaware of the effect her brittle remarks were having on Barry
Junior and Edie. Her grief was such, even by 1977, that "you
could not even mention the boys without Mary weeping," Edie
said. On Worth's birthday each year Barry Senior tried to plan
a trip to take Mary's mind off the date. Sallie was convinced
that her mother's anguish had given her severe arthritis, and tried
to find a therapist who could treat the depression that Sallie was
sure was the cause.

Mary's arthritis was so bad that when Jimmy Carter was
elected president and Barry was approached about possible consideration for becoming the ambassador to France, he had to say
no. "Mary isn't well enough," he told the family. And publicly
he denied that he had been considered for the job.

Mary became even harsher about the prospective changes in
the traditional Episcopalian prayer book and continued to carry
on a lengthy correspondence with Church authorities on the matter. She was equally relentless on the subject of education. Once,
Mary and Edie were discussing schools for her sons, Philip and
Charles. Mary appeared to barely tolerate Edie's sons, and often
froze them out at family dinners and could hardly bring herself
to address the question of their education. Mary erupted and
turned on Edie: "You don't know anything about education. I
am not going to discuss this topic with you ever."

One incident led to another as the anger between Mary and
Edie built. Edie worried constantly about the amount of pressure
Barry was under, and begged Mary and Barry to find a strong
editor to assist him after Claude Sitton and Eugene Patterson did
not take the job. "I went to Mary and Barry and said, 'Please,
can't you find someone to help him?' And she said, 'There is
no one.' " Barry Senior was displeased that Barry Junior was
not more active in national life. "Finally Barry was offered a

position on the Harvard Board of Overseers and Father was so elated," Sallie said. Barry was once mentioned in an article on "young American leaders" in *Time*, which thrilled his father.

There were, however, smooth times. Sometimes Mary would bring Edie flowers from the garden. Barry Senior admired Edie's dedication to Louisville community work. Inevitably, the family would get together during the holidays. One Christmas during the mid-1970's Mary organized a recitation contest for her grandchildren. Joan adored this idea because she was as competitive as Worth had been. Away from Louisville, she was eager to please Mary and Barry, and wanted them to be proud of Worth's children. But Edie hated contests and didn't want cousins pitted against cousins. But Mary was determined that her grandchildren should memorize passages from Shakespeare and Corinthians after she heard seven-year-old Robbie Bingham recite "Casey at Bat" one Christmas in New York. "Why did he memorize that junk?" Mary asked Joan later. For the first contest, Mary sent a sheaf of acceptable recitations, including a passage from *Henry V*. "They were not to memorize anything as mundane as 'The Night Before Christmas,' " Joan said.

That Christmas, Robbie won $350 when he recited "Once more into the breach." Joan was delighted, but Edie was angry that her daughters were being subjected to these competitions. The following year the children were sent selections from *Alice in Wonderland,* and that Christmas, Clara Bingham beat her cousins. "Here was Molly, who was brilliant, and she didn't win. Edie began to blame Mary in an unreasonable way for doing this to her children," Joan said. Joan was convinced that the time of these recitations was "when the souring process in the family really began."

Soon, Sallie's presence in Louisville would make the tensions in the family unbearable. For years Sallie and Michael had lived in a large house on East Ninety-fifth Street filled with old furniture and slipcovered sofas that had tattered with age. Each morning Sallie would write, but she was finding it hard to sell her stories. By now many of her contemporaries were passing her by, writing successful books and winning awards. "My agent dumped me," she said. "And you have to wake up when that happens." She began to feel more and more burdened by her children, her husband, and the demands she felt as a hostess, a wife, a mother and a writer. "Sallie was slowly becoming a malcontent. On her bad days she would blame everyone else for her problems and lash out. On her good days she could sink into a terrible depression. She felt she had to do everything beautifully while contributing to the commonweal. She could not shake those standards she had grown up with," a friend later said.

By Sallie's fortieth birthday she was bitter about her marriage, and told her friends that Michael, like Whitney, was too soft for her. "She could put up with anything from her children and nothing from Michael," a friend said of her in this period. Although Joan was living in New York, Sallie rarely saw her, but Michael had made an immense effort with Joan's children, inviting them to their country house. After they separated in 1976, such was Sallie's anger that if Joan and her children mentioned Michael's name, "she would get in a rage about Michael, who was so sweet, and was irrational about us seeing him at all," Joan said. One day Sallie took her twelve-year-old niece, Clara, to lunch. "Marriage is a dreadful institution invented in the sixteenth century for the purpose of childbirth," she told her. "Take my advice. Never get married. It will ruin your life."

Eleanor's life was not settled either. In New York she had taken a job with a cable television company called Global Village. One night she invited Joan and Sallie to her Soho loft to see her new film. "She was showing some grainy video she had made that was a porno film," Joan's date that evening later said. At this time Eleanor was at the height of her flower-child period and her parents made no attempt to bring her in line. "She had her own money. And the Binghams just acted like she had the vapors and couldn't deal with it at all," a friend said. Eleanor was often at Joan's apartment because "it was a familial atmosphere, the children were glorious, people were in and out all the time, and Joan wasn't a critical human being."

By the winter of 1976 Sallie and Michael had divorced. When Barry Ellsworth learned that Michael was leaving, he announced that he wanted to live with his father, and soon after, he too moved out. Michael, however, was not as weak as Sallie believed; he later sued for custody of the children on three different occasions. Sallie left for Louisville in the spring of 1977 for what she hoped would be a peaceful visit home. In the past Sallie had dreaded these trips and complained to her friends that when she got back from Louisville she had to take to her bed for days. Often she would visit her former nurse, who was still alive, and talk to her about her childhood, asking question after question, and later Nursie would call Mary Bingham. "What is it that Sallie is saying?" Nursie would say, according to Mary, not understanding Sallie's artistic tendency to reconstruct the past. "These are Sallie's phantasms," Barry Senior would say.

But this visit was different. "The spring in Louisville is so beautiful. The grass was being cut out at the Big House," she said. Her youngest son, William, whom Sallie called Willy, struck up a friendship with the handyman at the Big House. "I was concerned with those boys not having any relationship with an adult male," Sallie said. As they were leaving Louisville, Willy began to cry. "It just touched me so, and I thought, they would

be better off being here." Sallie reasoned that her sons would
benefit more from being close to her family than they would by
remaining in New York near their father, who was, as Mary said,
"a perfectly reasonable and loving man." But Sallie was angry
that he was suing for custody. She was ambivalent about coming
home and said, "I thought it would be good for them to be in
the country living surrounded by relatives, although something
told me that this was unwise. Our family had never worked that
way." Her son Chris was very upset about leaving New York,
and it was perfectly obvious to everyone in the family that Sallie
was using her boys as camouflage to hide her own desire to come
home.

Sallie later said it was her father who wanted her to come back
to Louisville. "He thought it would be better for the boys. He
thought it would be good for me to work with Actors Theatre.
And he kept saying something about the book page, which he
kept dangling in front of me." Sallie was delighted with the
attention from her father and thought she had nothing to lose.
She rented her house on East Ninety-fifth Street to friends with
the proviso that she could come stay there anytime she wanted.
In the summer of 1977 she left for Louisville for what she thought
would be just a year or so.

Sallie rented a modern ranch house in a subdivision near
Glenview. Often Eleanor called her: "How is it at home?" she
would say. "At that point it didn't seem too bad," Sallie said.
"It's easier than New York. It's an easier way of life." Soon
after she arrived she sat down and wrote her mother a letter,
saying she believed she had no talent for marriage. Again, her
mother did not seize this opportunity for an intimate talk. "I
believe it must be a very devastating and disillusioning thing to
be divorced," Mary later said. "I didn't know what to say to
Sallie."

When Sallie got to Louisville, Barry and Edie gave a party
for her, and Sallie was angry that they invited "single men."
But she was startled, if not entirely displeased, by how the relationship between her parents and Barry and Edie had deteriorated. "There were endless complaints," Sallie said. "About
Edie, my mother would say, 'Why is she so dull?' 'She is so
dreary.' 'Everything she says is a complete cliché.' 'The parties
they give are so dismal. The food is awful. The people don't
have a good time.' " Although Mary and Barry had never said a
negative word directly to Barry and Edie, they complained at
length to Sallie from the moment she got back. "It was as if
they were eager for me to hear it," Sallie said.

Like any sibling with complex feelings about a brother, Sallie
was delighted to listen, and even felt guilty by how pleased she
was to be taken into her parents' confidence about Barry, whom

she had always found slow and dull. After her years of psychoanalysis, Sallie speculated about her parents' motives in psychiatric jargon. She believed her parents were "playing" to her
because "I was the most interesting of the three surviving children," she said. "It was very preconscious. I became the ver-
balization of their unspoken criticism. . . . If they had these
criticisms to make, they should have made them to Barry Junior.
It was as if our parents wanted to use Eleanor and me to do
this." Sallie later said that she could have told her parents not
to say these awful things about Barry Junior and Edie to her,
but she was enjoying their remarks far too much to tell them to
stop.

29

At first, when Sallie came back to Louisville in 1977, she did not understand why her father was adamant that she become an active board member and later named Eleanor to the board as well. As young women, Sallie and Eleanor had had little interest in the newspaper, no business training, no corporate experience. But Barry and Mary were desperate now, perhaps uncertain whether Barry Junior would survive his cancer, and wanted their daughters in the company. Later each family member would speculate about what had really driven Barry Senior to insist that his daughters become directors, since common sense surely told him that nothing but trouble could come from it. "It was almost as if he wanted to bring the company down," a family member later said. His own father had kept Henrietta and Robert out of the business entirely, and even Mary said, "Only one person can run a newspaper."

Barry Senior must have believed that he could kindle in his adult daughters the kind of passion for the *Courier-Journal* and the newspaper empire he had instilled in Worth and Barry Junior from the time they were children. Perhaps he reasoned that the shared responsibility would bring his three surviving children closer together. "Mother and Daddy really wanted us to get along," Eleanor later said. Mary had always marveled at the Sulzberger family and the way they had been able to inspire a fierce loyalty in their army of relatives. She would often question *New York Times* executives about the role of Iphigene Sulzberger, the grand matriarch of the clan. How had she been able to ensure such devotion to the newspaper in her children?

The Binghams and the Sulzbergers had very different styles. For one, the Sulzbergers were less involved in public life. Punch Sulzberger, the family member who serves as publisher, occasionally overruled his editors on the editorial page, but his influence was subtle and the editors knew how to "read the family tea leaves," as one reporter phrased it. The family retreated to the country on the weekends. But many of their relatives had jobs at the paper. From the copy desk to the business offices, there were Sulzberger relations, cousins whose last names were Adler, Dryfoos, Ochs and Golden. Gay Talese called it "nepotism in the best possible way." Once, Barry asked a *Times* executive, "How does Punch stay on such close terms with his sisters, Marian and Ruth?" The *Times* man replied, "They have always been involved in the newspaper." More significantly, the Sulzbergers, like the Graham family of the *Washington Post,* had taken their companies public while retaining control of the vote, and expanded their holdings so there would be room for everybody.

Mary and Barry had not had their children working at the newspaper from the time they were young. Nine-year-old Binghams were considered too grand to be running errands through the halls. Mary and Barry's devotion to each other and their newspaper was often exclusionary. Mary and Barry concentrated their efforts for involvement with the newspaper on Worth and Barry Junior. Barry Senior retained control of the company, although each heir, through a series of trusts, had a percentage of stock. They had no interest in going public and had remained a local company. When the children were young, the parents didn't mix them up with the help. Later Eleanor had spent one summer as an intern, and Barry once worked in the photo department and toured the state with Joe Creason, the paper's folklore expert. And once, when Worth was still at Exeter, he wrote a book review for his mother's book page on *The Stork Didn't Bring You,* a new 1948 teenage guidebook to the facts of life. When Worth was in college, he worked summers at the newspaper. But when Eleanor's photograph was published in the newspaper, a reporter said, "So that is what she looks like."

Even so, by the late 1970's, Barry Senior felt that it wasn't too late to enlist his daughters in the newspaper, the Binghams' "shared dream," Barry Junior liked to say. To underscore the point, Barry Junior's office had large portraits of all the Bingham grandchildren on the walls, pictures that he had taken himself. There were Joan's teenagers, Clara and Robbie; Sallie's children, Barry Ellsworth, Chris and Willy Iovenko; and Barry's two exquisite-looking daughters, Emily and Molly. Anyone who came into Barry Bingham Junior's office would be told earnestly, "This newspaper is for them."

For all his talk of "the shared dream," Barry Junior was not sure he liked the idea of Sallie being on the board. He felt his father was using the companies as therapy for Sallie and that her presence on the board was unnecessary and unprofessional. "I said to my father, 'This is typical of this family. Sallie has failed as a writer and she has failed in her marriages and now you are trying to wave a magic wand to make it all right. You are using this newspaper company as a vehicle instead of showing her any other kind of love.' '' At lunch one day, he said, ''Why can't you show Sallie love by talking to her rather than trying to put her in a business situation she knows nothing about?'' Barry said his father was stunned to hear this direct talk from his son and refused to discuss the subject. ''I want Sallie on the board,'' he said. Barry Junior had a sense of foreboding about his sister, who he knew had had no respect for him from the time he was a child. ''I have never understood Sallie,'' he said.

But Barry Senior told his son that he wanted to do something to help Sallie mend her life, especially since she held him responsible for what she perceived as her miserable childhood. ''On those rare occasions when my father would actually confide in me,'' Barry Junior said, ''he would say, 'I cannot imagine what I have done to Sallie to make her berate me this way.' '' Sallie had made her father feel responsible for her life failures, and she blamed many of her problems on his years of absence during the war. Barry Senior told his son he was baffled by this because when he came home, he said, ''I spent so much time with her. I read her Dickens and Thackeray.'' Even when Mary and Barry were going out, they would stop in the nursery and read to their children. ''I will never be able to compensate her adequately for what she thinks my failings were,'' Barry Senior told his son. Mary defended Barry Senior as well. ''After the war Sallie and Barry developed the most wonderful relationship. . . . It seemed to me that those years were more pivotal than when Sallie was from four to eight.''

But he was determined to try, and now that Sallie was home Barry Senior believed he might be able to persuade Eleanor to come back to Louisville too. ''It was a natural instinct,'' Eleanor said. ''Daddy wanted to gather his chicks around him in old age.'' Each Bingham daughter had approximately 4 percent of the vote in the company with 11 percent more to come when their parents died. Even with that small a share, Barry Senior saw every reason to try to get them involved in the family business before it was too late. No doubt he reasoned: his daughters were already stockholders in the company; if he put them on the board how much harm could they do? He knew his daughters knew little about business, but the company was so large the Binghams had professional managers who took care of everything. As Barry Senior had gotten older the vagaries of the newspaper business seemed to matter even less to him. He had been a traditional publisher, one of his financial executives explained, and, like other traditional publishers, was ''an expert on . . . foreign relations and everything else, but he paid no attention to his business. Our management techniques compared to other industries were very, very weak.''

Often at the meetings "the hired hands," as the Binghams called their managers, noticed that Barry Senior was less interested in the figures and cared mostly about the paper's editorials—*What was the Courier-Journal's stand?* The company had elaborate insurance policies, day care and a house publication called *Intercom*. Lawyers buzzed around the Binghams advising them constantly on planning and strategy. The company had chains of command, managers who talked about "systems." The board meetings were nicknamed Show and Tell by these managers, who would present to the owners what each division was doing. Barry Junior presided over the meetings. Often the chairman and the publisher would remain silent as the presentations were made to the board. "I knew everything they were saying, since I was running the company," Barry Junior said.

Soon, to please her father, Sallie began to attend the board meetings, but she found them dull. She occupied herself by taking copious notes, as if she were back at Radcliffe, writing down every word that anyone said. "Sallie made us all nervous, she was taking so many notes," her mother said. "She was like Madame Defarge."

One day George Gill, general manager of the company, saw John Ed Pearce in the parking lot of the newspaper. "John Ed, I know I will be the general manager who will preside over the demise of the companies," Gill said. "Why is that?" Pearce asked. "The hatred between them. You cannot believe the hate," Gill said.

It was time to convince Eleanor she should come home. She had moved to Los Angeles to make documentary films with a boyfriend, but they had broken up. Inevitably, Eleanor with her sunny personality and her generous ways was, as her father said, "preyed upon by friends." She would buy them airplane tickets, loan them money and give them expensive clothes. But now thirty-two-year-old Eleanor wanted a real job. She had finished a documentary, *The New Klan: Heritage of Hate,* which was good enough to have been shown at Cannes, and would be shown at the New York Film Festival, as well as aired on PBS. Her father had done the narration. Eleanor now hoped that PBS in New York would hire her as a field producer. That summer of 1978, she sent off her film and her résumé, and went home to Louisville to wait to hear from PBS. Mary and Barry disappeared to Chatham, and Eleanor stayed at the Little House. Sallie was home; Barry and Edie were around, as well as many of her old friends.

Many of Eleanor's contemporaries were in town: the daughters of the distillery owners, the tobacco magnates and the Louisville Country Club crowd. Before long Eleanor met an architect named Rowland Miller, five years younger than herself and from

a Republican family that had little use for the *Courier-Journal.*
He was dark and well built, and had been considered a hippie
in prep school. Although he seemed gentle, family members
thought he liked intrigue. He had a tendency to see conspiracies
where none existed, even going so far as to question motivation
when a reporter asked him for his birth date. "Rowland kept
everyone in the family stirred up all the time," a family member
said.

Rowland's own family had seen a bit of trouble. His great-
grandfather had begun the Four Roses whiskey company and
invented an automatic bottling machine, which, unfortunately,
he hadn't patented. The fortune dwindled, but Rowland's father
made the money back with a chain of food stores. Perhaps because of his own family history he seemed determined that Eleanor should not be shortchanged. After years of picking
inappropriate boyfriends, Eleanor was delighted to find her future husband in her very own hometown.

At first Barry and Edie largely ignored Rowland. They had no
idea, for example, that his great-grandfather had started Four
Roses. Nevertheless they "were delighted when Eleanor began
to go out with Rowland," Barry Junior said. "Because after all
the weirdos she had been with, Rowland was such a step up."
He was after all an architect, and the Millers belonged to the
Louisville Country Club.

A few months after Eleanor returned to Louisville her father
named her to the board of directors. At first she was as silent as
Sallie at the meetings. But soon she began to send her brother
lengthy, earnest memos asking for a "definition" of her role on
the board. "I wanted to know what my goals were as a director," she said. Eleanor and Barry were opposites: she was vol-
uble; he measured each word. Like the rest of her family
however, she often wrote down her thoughts and presented them
in memo and letter form. But Barry and Eleanor's relationship
had been affectionate. Barry often wrote Eleanor when she was
in Los Angeles. He sent her advice on which Super-8 cameras
to buy, and wrote to her when his tractor turned over on the
Goose Creek trails "where we used to ride many years ago."
He told her that his younger daughter, Molly, adored her summer
camp and had come home with a macramé bracelet and was the
"camp mascot." He thanked her for sending a film, *The Lord
of the Universe.* He sent her clips for her film on the Klan. "I
was happy when Eleanor decided to come home," Barry said.
And he wanted to help her, so much so that he encouraged Bob
Morse who ran WHAS to give her a job.

Eleanor refused the management training position that Morse
offered her, and a new job was created for her: "director of
special projects." "It was my job to be a liaison with the com-

munity,'' Eleanor said, a form of public relations. Morse would
often complain to Barry that she would breeze in late or not at
all, and at a time when the company was trying to strip down,
Eleanor had ordered her office to be redecorated. ''Bob Morse
hated me and wanted me out,'' she said. ''Eleanor loved it,''
Sallie said. ''She got the women of WHAS together for the first
time.''

Soon enough, stories began to circulate around the station
about her work habits: that she insisted Bob Morse drive to her
house for meetings; that she was giving orders to the staff. Barry
sent her careful and tedious memos about ''channels'' and ''lines
of communication,'' but Eleanor was not a woman who responded to business jargon. Later she took the *Courier-Journal*'s
editor, Paul Janensch, to lunch and told him the family was
convinced that Barry was working much too hard and she would
like to help him lighten the load. ''I could serve as a link between Barry and WHAS,'' Eleanor told Janensch, who went
back and wrote a two-page memo to his boss about the encounter. Eleanor complained to Janensch that she found her job demanding and often worked ten hours a day. She asked him if the
family should consider selling WHAS, the first time that one of
the ''hired hands'' began to feel apprehensive about the future
of the Bingham management. Janensch was as sensitive as Barry
Junior about his independence as an editor—perhaps overly sensitive—and he began to feel, he later said, that his autonomy
was being threatened.

Rowland and Eleanor married in September of 1979. The
family remarked on the irony of her married name, Eleanor
Miller, because it was the same as her father's mother's name,
the dreamy girl who had met young Bob Bingham in Asheville
in 1894. Eleanor, who had never been closer to her parents,
now visited them almost every day, often saw them at night,
and seemed, Sallie said, ''to be doing some kind of penance
for her hippie years.'' For their last child to marry, Mary and
Barry were determined to have a proper celebration for the
future Mrs. Eleanor Miller. They put up a tent outside the
Little House, and Eleanor wore a beautiful white dress when
she walked down the aisle with her father at St. Francis in the
Fields.

For one brief moment on that late September day the Bingham
family seemed united. Their rolling-stone daughter was settling
down to married life. Her new husband had a profession and a
decent Southern lineage, and was, as Barry Junior said, ''even
conventional.'' Her father would later say, ''Eleanor really was
the child of our old age.'' At the wedding, Sallie wore a pale
peach dress and her hair in a topknot. Mary's sisters Helena and

Harriette were there, as was Edie Callahan, and on the wedding day Barry and Edie gave a lavish lunch at the Big House and later marveled at how well everyone in the family appeared to get along.

30

But family tranquillity was not to last. Soon after Eleanor married, Edie and Mary quarreled violently, but it was expressed, as usual, in the coldest and most civilized way. The two Bingham women were polarized, on the surface, by an issue of architectural preservation, but the real problem between them was the Binghams' inability to speak frankly to one another. This particular argument was made more complicated by the fact that Edie and Barry Junior were beginning to realize exactly how intimate Mary and Barry had become with Harvey and Kathy Sloane. Later, when Barry Junior and Edie thought back on this fight, they saw it as part of a larger pattern in which public issues camouflaged private tensions. The family members often failed to deal with one another properly, they said, and this time they were certainly right.

October 1979. In the beginning, it really did seem that Mary and Edie were fighting about a public policy matter. A few years earlier Barry Senior had called Edie and asked her to get involved with a local group called the Preservation Alliance, which was going to try to save some charming old buildings in downtown Louisville. Edie, the daughter of an architect, had been an architectural historian and loved old buildings. "This was right up my alley," Edie said. She became chairman of the board of the organization, which Kathy Sloane had helped to start.

Downtown Louisville was a disaster, and a group of developers had plans to build a three-story glass shopping mall across from the Seelbach Hotel to try to attract business back to town. Edie thought this idea was fine, but there was one major problem: to build the Galleria, as it would be called, two blocks would have to be leveled, and on one of those blocks stood the old Courier-Journal building at Fourth and Liberty, which had been taken over by a jewelry company called Will Sales.

This was the building that Walter Haldeman had first wired for electricity in 1886, now a Victorian wreck but filled with history for the Bingham family. However, Mary and Barry were not nostalgic about the "Will Sales building," as they called it. They wanted it destroyed for the sake of restoring downtown, but never told Edie and Barry Junior, who were passionate about saving it. "Mary and Barry never once disagreed with anything I was doing or expressed any criticism at all," Edie said. "I thought they were on my side."

The debate over the Will Sales building had dragged on for years. Kathy Sloane was the go-between, shuttling between the preservationists and the city's business interests, who were desperate for the Galleria. "She would tell the developer and the Chamber of Commerce people, 'The preservationists think this' or 'They will do that,' " Edie said. By this time Kathy Sloane had a real estate license and was selling properties all over town, including the Brown hotel, and no doubt did not want to offend potential clients.

To make matters more complicated, Harvey Sloane was squeezed between the preservationists and the business interests. After losing a bid to be the governor of Kentucky, Sloane had made it clear that he was going to run for mayor again in the next race, and the last thing a sensible politician would do would be to risk losing big-business support. "The Chamber of Commerce people would tell everyone that Edie was holding up progress in Louisville," Barry Junior said. "And that if she didn't back down the downtown would collapse."

Edie had requested that the National Park Service, which controlled possible historical landmark designation, come to Louisville to hold a hearing about giving the building landmark status. As the date neared she received a call from Barry Senior, one of the first indications he was opposed to what she was doing. "Call the Park Service and tell them not to come down. Call the hearing off," he said as high-handedly as he had once decreed who would become the governor of Kentucky. "You can do it. You are chairman of the Preservation Alliance." Edie said, "I can't do that, Barry. This is a legal procedure." It was Kathy Sloane's opinion that "Edie was always so stiff-necked. Our downtown was in peril." Barry and Edie later viewed Barry Senior's autocratic behavior as another example of his hypocrisy and collusion with the Sloanes.

But however Barry Senior was maneuvering behind the scenes, he said nothing directly to criticize Barry Junior or Edie. Each week Barry Senior would have lunch with his son, but never implied in any way that he did not approve of the newspaper's editorials that were supporting the preservation of the Will Sales building. "He never once said a critical word to me," Barry Junior said. But Edie could not help noticing Kathy Sloane's car frequently parked in the driveway outside the Little House, for Kathy often came to Glenview to have tea with her dear friend

Mary Bingham. "We have always been close," Kathy Sloane said.

Two weeks after Eleanor and Rowland were married, Barry Junior came home looking grim. He was holding a proof copy of the next day's *Courier-Journal*'s "Letters to the Editor" page. "This is going to be in the morning paper," he said as he handed the sheet to his wife. Edie took the page and was horrified to read a public attack on her from her own mother-in-law:

> To the Editor of the Courier-Journal
> . . . I wish publicly to disassociate myself from the position taken in the matter of the preservation of the Will Sales building by . . . Mrs. Barry Bingham Jr. . . . the denouement of the scenario being written by the preservationists would have all the elements of a farce if it were not for the fact that it would be a tragedy: the Will Sales building bulldozed, replaced, in all probability, by a parking lot at Fourth and Liberty, an empty Atherton building, an empty Kaufman Straus building, and desuetude and decay of Fourth Street permanently insured.

Edie was astonished when she read Mary's letter. "I thought, All right, if this is how she is going to be . . ." The letter had been sent directly to the newspaper as a public rebuke; Mary had said not one word to Edie. "This was an organization that Barry Senior had asked me to get involved in," Edie said. Mary later said, "I had every right to exercise my opinion as a private citizen." But what could she have been thinking of when she moved against Edie with the force she had once reserved for Clare Boothe Luce? "It is pretty horrible when your mother attacks your wife in your own newspaper," Barry Junior said. In response, Edie was as icy as Mary. Instead of calling her mother-in-law and taking her to task, she behaved exactly as Mary did and stayed on the public issue: the Will Sales building. She wrote Mary a timid and ladylike note, typed neatly and single-spaced.

> Dear Mary,
> . . . I realize also that much of the present misunderstanding might have been avoided if I had not thoughtlessly overlooked sharing position statements with you. . . . I would have appreciated being given the opportunity to defend it to you. Possibly out of all this we can learn to be more direct with each other in sharing our differences, concerns and certain need for mutual support and understanding. Our upbringing discourages unpleasant (or potentially unpleasant) encounters. . . .

A few days later, Edie called Mary and invited her to lunch at the Big House. Mary accepted. "I said to her, 'I would like to be able to review this issue with you,' " Edie said. She remembered that Mary said, "Everyone tells me your proposals are unworkable." Edie spoke earnestly about the building, and then the conversation eventually moved along to family matters. Mary complained that her granddaughters did not come to visit her as much as she would like. "They don't visit because they think you are critical of what they are reading in school," Edie said. "They think you are negative about everything they do. They would come more often if you would stop throwing so many rocks at them." Edie remembered Mary's shock. "Well, I haven't thrown stones at the children," she recalled Mary's saying, and Edie was sure that Mary had no idea what Edie was talking about.

31

By 1981 Barry had gotten the profits of the *Courier-Journal* back up to 7 percent, but that was still below the industry standard. The decades when Barry Senior allowed the newspaper to be run haphazardly were now taking their toll on profits. The Standard Gravure plant had union problems, and Barry was constantly negotiating to bring labor costs down. Finally, Barry decided to build a new nonunion plant with offset presses in Morristown, Tennessee. "Sallie was always saying how terrible this was that we were not using union labor," Barry said. All over the country newspapers were trying to cut their expenses and getting rid of their Sunday magazines. "If Standard Gravure was going to stay in the market, we had to print offset," Barry added. "We went from something like eighteen magazines we were printing to eight or nine," he said. At the board meetings George Gill would present the figures and say, "We are headed for trouble." And Barry Senior would say, according to his son, "I guess we are."

Barry Junior had cracked down on the budgets even more. "How could we replace our equipment eventually without the profits up?" he said. He studied all kinds of methods of getting the profits higher—electronic information to send the *Courier-Journal* to home computers in the far reaches of the state, for example. But Barry Junior, like his father, did not want to cut the vast news staff, the benefits, day care, health clubs. Sallie, too, at the meetings now focused on the company's finances. Why had so much money been committed to Standard Gravure? The printing of Sunday magazines was no longer profitable, Sallie said. And yet Barry kept committing millions to this printing company. In private, she began to harp on Barry's business skills and told her friends, "My brother is an idiot."

In fact Barry was a reasonably good businessman who had made a mistake committing so much money to Standard Gravure, but the division was a relatively minor part, less than 15 percent, of the Bingham empire. His mistake was hardly catastrophic. Barry's management systems had in fact cut the newspaper's expenses with no loss of the three-hundred-person news staff. The real mistake had been made a decade earlier when the Binghams refused to expand outside Louisville.

Now Barry Junior was fighting the general problems in the newspaper industry as well as Louisville's decline. The ad base had always been circulation—the advertisers wanted a vast reach—and now that circulation costs were so high the *Courier-Journal* was being squeezed. Barry had 150 counties to cover— 120 in Kentucky and 30 out of state. In Jackson County in eastern Kentucky, for example, the *Courier* rarely sold more than twenty papers a day, but the trucks still had to make the deliveries. "He was really doing nothing to stem the tide," a newspaper executive said. Barry Junior was running the *Courier-Journal* as he believed his father wanted it to be run, with the wide distribution that had given it its reputation in the state. "His father was allowing Barry Junior to make his own mistakes by not interfering," the newspaper executive said, although he wasn't helping him with any guidance either.

To his credit, Barry Junior was trying to cut the circulation costs, but the family board members fought him constantly. Barry wanted to install more electronic equipment to enable him to trim his costs. According to family members, Sallie was adamant against this expenditure. "Computers are the handiwork of the devil," she said. Her mother was equally resistant: "You can't learn anything without paper in your hands." Even an expenditure as basic as computer terminals for reporters caused immense dissension in the family. Nevertheless, with Barry's budgets and space-allotment requirements, he had managed each year to get the profits up, however insignificantly.

For a long while, Barry tried to be patient with his sisters. He was trying to run a professional company, but Eleanor and Sallie kept criticizing most things he did. At cocktail parties the reporters talked about "the sister problem" at the newspaper. As that term, "the sister problem," floated back to Eleanor and Sallie, their anger grew. "People would say, 'Which one are you?' 'Are you Edie?' 'Are you Eleanor?' It used to infuriate me because, of course, I hadn't lived here for twenty-five years and I had a career as a writer," Sallie said. In June 1979 Eleanor and Sallie gave a long interview to a local magazine. The piece was called "The Bingham Black Sheep," and the sisters made it clear what they thought about the family newspaper. They criticized the minority-hiring practices. Sallie spoke of the "repressive gentility" of her childhood and of being reared by servants. The family was displeased by this—a small hint of the public acrimony to come.

For his part, Barry was annoyed that his sisters were "directly interfering in the news operation.'' In 1980 Eleanor and Sallie were upset when an architectural columnist named William Morgan was let go to save money. Morgan was a friend of Sallie and Eleanor's, and their response was immediate. Eleanor sent a tough memo to David Hawpe, the managing editor, and told him that as a shareholder and a reader she was incensed. ''Your moves are gutting this newspaper of its heart and soul,'' she wrote. She said she was looking forward to his explanation at the next board meeting. Hawpe told Joe Ward, the newspaper's business reporter, that his state of mind was not unaffected by this criticism. Sallie wrote Hawpe as well: ''Surely we do not intend to produce a newspaper as bland as this one sometimes appears to be.''

Eleanor's husband, Rowland Miller, was now attending all family meetings and made frequent suggestions that infuriated Barry Junior. Once he declared, according to Barry Junior, that ''since the dividends of the company were relatively low, the family should be able to have more voice on the editorial side of the newspaper.'' Barry flared at him: ''What happens if next year we double the dividends? Then do you have half as much say? And if we pay no dividends, do you become the publisher?'' The newspaper planned to build a new office building for Standard Gravure at the Louisville Riverport. Eleanor asked her mother if Rowland could design it. Barry Junior said, ''Absolutely not.'' The bids had already been accepted; the building was to be filled with complex electronic equipment. ''I am not running a charity for unemployed architects,'' Barry Junior said.

Barry was irritated with Sallie too. He felt she questioned his every decision. ''Barry was paranoid about me. He thought I was looking over his shoulder. The poor thing,'' Sallie said. No issue was too minor for Sallie's attention. Several times at board meetings Sallie brought up the Equal Opportunity form the company filed with the government on which it listed the minorities—blacks, Hispanics, women—in its employ. The form was widely recognized as a nuisance, and, typical of government documents, complicated and incomplete. There were no crossover categories, for black women, for example. ''We had listed one woman under the black category and under 'female,' '' Barry said. ''Sallie kept bringing this up, debating the point, saying, 'How could we list one person two ways?' '' She would talk about it at length and prevent the board from going on to its other business, and then, he said, ''demand that we do the report her way, redesign it and send it off to the government.''

Another time the *Courier-Journal* was considering an investment in the new field of cellular telephones. ''We had a thousand pages of filings and data,'' Barry Junior said. ''Sallie demanded a copy, which meant someone from the company had to stand by the Xerox machine for hours to make it for her. She never mentioned it again and I am sure she never read it.'' If a cafeteria worker was fired, Sallie would insist that ''a hardship fund'' be started for her welfare. She questioned headlines and handling of news stories, according to Barry Junior. Sallie's behavior was not unusual for anyone who knew nothing about business and was trying to be involved in a company. But one board member said, ''Sallie took up everybody's time in the most irritating way.'' However, Barry Senior never said a harsh word to his daughters, and never suggested that they leave their brother alone. But, according to Sallie, ''Mother would always say, 'Don't upset your brother.' She treated him like an invalid. . . . She was angry with me.''

In the summer of 1980 the newspapers were filled with stories of mergers and unfriendly takeover attempts. No company felt safe from the raiders—not even the Louisville *Courier-Journal*. The Binghams' ubiquitous family counselors, Wilson Wyatt and Gordon Davidson, partners in the prestigious local firm Wyatt, Tarrant & Combs, were consumed with the fear of a possible takeover. That summer Davidson came to Barry Junior. ''We need some kind of an agreement to protect the stock in the company,'' Davidson said. The lawyers came up with a simple letter stating that if a stockholder wanted to sell his or her holdings, the family would be given sixty days to match the bid. In that way a raider could not entice individual shareholders with a huge offer to gain a position in the company. Mary and Barry held the majority of the stock. Outsiders were not welcomed. ''When I had Hodgkin's disease my father had all kinds of nibbles about the company. The buy-back wasn't my idea,'' Barry Junior said. ''But when Gordon talked to us we said, 'That sounds like a reasonable thing to do.' ''

A family session was scheduled for June 13, 1980, after the board meeting attended by the managers, and the lawyers advised the family on such personal matters as trusts, stocks and inheritance taxes. The entire family, including Rowland, had assembled on the west porch of the Big House, where Mary had once served curried chicken salad to Benny Goodman. The lawyers brought the buy-back agreement they had drafted as well as a folder called ''the gold book,'' which listed how much stock each shareholder had and what the value potentially was. ''This was the first time it was all laid out so the family could see it,'' Barry said.

Each shareholder could see exactly what his or her stock might be worth. The companies were worth at least $100 million, but the value of stock was not equal. Barry Junior had less than Eleanor and Sallie because he had a great deal of voting preferred stock, which was less valuable than his sisters' nonvoting

common shares—although they were equal when given. ''The
original concept was to strive for equality. If the company was
profitable, which it was, the common stock was more valuable
than my voting preferred stock, although ultimately the control
of the company would be in my hands. So I didn't mind,'' Barry
Junior said. Joan's children had less than their cousins because
65 percent of their stock had been sold for estate taxes when
their father was killed. Still, everyone had plenty, at least $10
million each. ''You cannot fault [my parents] for not being generous,'' Barry Junior said. Typically of the family, lawyers were
there to explain what it meant, as if neither Barry was capable
of the feat.

''What is this?'' Sallie said. ''I don't want to sign this until I
know what it is.'' She said she wanted to show it to a lawyer,
and her mother said to her, ''The room is filled with lawyers.''
But Sallie felt she was being railroaded by her mother, as always,
and chose the issue of the buy-back agreement to make a stand.
''It was clearly a sign of some kind of distrust,'' Sallie said.
Months passed, and still Sallie would not sign the form. ''It was
sheer perversity,'' Edie Bingham said. ''It was Sallie being an
enfant terrible, saying, 'Look at me.' ''

One day at lunch, Barry Junior said to his father, ''What would
you advise me to do about Sallie?'' His father replied, ''I would
just ignore her.''

Barry Junior knew that he could not cope with Sallie. ''I wasn't
political,'' Barry Junior said, ''I could not ignore Sallie. Worth
was far more volatile. He had a different way of dealing with
our sisters. He would have said 'Off with their heads' pretty quickly.'' But Barry Junior was mannerly like Sallie's ex-
husbands, and he attempted, as Michael Iovenko once did, to
reason with her calmly. The more reasonable he thought he was,
the more letters she sent.

In one month he sent her three lengthy letters to answer her
memos. Each was one or two pages, single-spaced. He wrote to
her about headlines she perceived as ''misleading'' and about
the role of the newspaper's ombudsman. He sent her a packet of
the Indiana edition of the *Courier-Journal* to justify the versions
he had sent out of state. Another sister and brother might have
been able to pick up the telephone and say, ''Hey, what is going
on?'' But Barry Junior and Sallie had no other way to communicate. Their behavior was a mirror of their parents' formal
ways.

Barry was tired of Sallie's letters, but he always answered
them dutifully:

Dear Sallie:
I am in the midst of my week at the Data Courier/Dissly

Research Corporation so I am not spending much time in the office. However, I did want to answer your letter regarding the corrections we run in The Courier-Journal and Times. Some of them do, indeed, seem trivial. . . . If we did not publish corrections, the next time we were writing a story on the subject the reporter might well review the clip file and pick up the error again. . . ."

That August in Chatham, Mary and Barry invited all their children to the Cape. Everyone was coming for the long weekend. From Washington, where she now lived, Joan was bringing Clara and Rob. Barry Junior and Edie were flying on the same plane with Eleanor and her husband, Rowland. Sallie would follow with her children. Perhaps, the parents might have reasoned, a festive atmosphere might ease the strain. The cousins were good friends from the times that Mary and Barry had taken them to Europe and on cruises to Greece, where the young Binghams marveled at Mary's style. "One summer in Patmos Granny used to talk to the cook in ancient Greek," Worth's daughter, Clara, recalled.

At the airport in Louisville, as Barry and Rowland waited for the flight a man named David Grissom approached Barry Junior. Grissom was the president of a local bank and was involved in a move to merge the county and city governments. "Barry, could we have some of our committee members come into the newspaper and tell the staff what this movement is about?" he asked. Barry Junior responded, "I am sorry. There's only one type of solicitation that we let in the door and that's the United Way. I can't make an exception. You'll have to do it outside on the street." In Grissom's presence, Rowland said to Barry Junior, "Oh, come on, Barry, you can make an exception one time. . . . You could change that policy."

A more tolerant man might have been able to ignore a brother-in-law's unfortunate remark. But Barry Junior was angry about it, although he conveyed none of this to Rowland. "The last thing I needed was to have David Grissom going around town saying my brother-in-law thought I was rigid." Rowland's gaffe made Barry Junior like Rowland even less. "Rowland would always say, 'I hate reporters,'" Barry said. Everything about Rowland seemed to irritate him—what he felt was false intimacy, the lack of motivation, and mostly the way Eleanor clung to him as if she were incapable of making a decision on her own. However, as a Bingham son, Barry Junior never said an untoward word to Rowland; he simply shut him out. Rowland said, "If I said, 'I like to hunt ducks,' he would say, 'Oh, ducks.' . . . Instead of just talking about hunting we would get bogged down."

Mary was upset because she was determined that Eleanor's marriage should work. "I don't know why Barry treated Rowland that way," she said. "At least he was an educated person." Joan said, "All that weekend we were in Chatham, Rowland would go racing to Barry and Mary as if he were a child. He would say the worst things about Edie and Barry Junior and he was literally tattling. I once heard him say something like, 'Mary, you should have heard the way Edie got after Rob when he left a towel on the floor!' " But again, Mary Bingham seemed never to have said to her new son-in-law, "I don't want to hear about it."

For years Mary Bingham ran the *Courier-Journal* book page. She assigned reviews to local writers and turned out a good page. By the late 1970's an editor named Shirley Williams had taken over. In the winter of 1981 Shirley Williams became ill. As it happened, Sallie Bingham and Shirley Williams were good friends as well as neighbors—they lived across the street from each other in Louisville. When Shirley Williams told Sallie that she would have to take a leave of absence from the newspaper because she needed an operation, Sallie asked her if she would mind if she took over her job temporarily. Innocently, Shirley Williams told Sallie she would be delighted. Then Sallie and Shirley Williams told Barry Junior their plan. At that time he had no objection, perhaps reasoning that if Sallie ran the book page she would leave him alone.

"At first, I was terrified to be the book editor," Sallie said. "I had hardly ever been in that building before." Nevertheless, she began to make changes. "My aim was to get half of the books reviewed by women. I also wanted to do a lot more obscure feminist books and books that were controversial, like Ben Bagdikian's book on the press which is very critical." Sallie had theme pages: children's books, regional books, feminist books. She tightened up on the reviewers' deadlines and word counts, and each week wrote a column of publishing news. "I filled in for two months and loved it. It was loads of fun," she said.

That November Harvey Sloane had declared again for the mayor's race. By this time Edie Bingham was fed up with Kathy Sloane and could no longer stand hearing at the country club what good friends they were. Edie wrote Kathy Sloane a letter:

Dear Kathy,
With the onset of a political campaign for Harvey and you, Barry has decided that the best policy for us is to refrain from entertaining or being entertained by political candidates or politicians in office. Otherwise, news staff (and doubtless others) can be seriously misled regarding the in-

dependence of political coverage by the papers. . . . Therefore, we must send our regrets for your caroling party on
December 23rd, and I have to tell you not to expect an
invitation to our upcoming square dance. Although at arms
length, we extend wishes to the family for a happy Christmas season.

Kathy Sloane was furious when she got Edie's letter. "I called
Mary Bingham and said, 'I am so upset. How can they do this
to my daughter, Abigail, who loves their square dance? Mrs.
Bingham was just as shocked as I was," she said. "She said to
me, 'I cannot figure them out.' "

Mary could have taken her son's side out of pure maternal
loyalty, saying something to Harvey and Kathy Sloane such as
"Please do not criticize my children to me." Again, Barry Junior never heard a word of criticism from his parents about Edie's
letter. "I didn't expect my mother to take my side," Barry said.
"But when someone is criticizing me constantly, the least she
could have done would have been to say, 'I have been hearing
this about you.' " However, Mary was discussing the situation
with Sallie and Eleanor, who were friendly with the Sloanes.

In May Harvey Sloane won the primary, and by autumn he
was running for mayor against a Republican named George
Clark, a local businessman who had founded a chain of fast-
food restaurants. At a meeting the newspaper editors interviewed the candidates. "Harvey Sloane was the more lackluster
and colorless of the two men," Barry Junior said. "He didn't
have one decent idea. Clark was a businessman and Louisville
was in a terrible decline. We thought he was the better candidate."

For one of the few times in history, the *Courier-Journal* endorsed a Republican, George Clark. "We were shocked," said
Kathy Sloane. "And so were Mary and Barry Bingham." The
family was outraged that Barry had done this—here was yet another assault on their way of life. Eleanor was especially furious
and wore a large Harvey Sloane button around town. "My
brother and I disagree," she said. Sallie, as if she were her
mother, wrote a letter to the *Courier-Journal* to attack Barry
Junior's Republican choice.

Almost immediately, the *Wall Street Journal* picked up on the
coming feud and quoted Sallie's letter to the editor, which said
that the Clark endorsement "betrayed" the newspaper's reputation. Barry Junior remained oblivious. Although they had lunch
together once a week, his father never once took Barry Junior
to task for endorsing Clark. Not a word was said about how
disappointed he was. "I think he thought that would have been
interfering," Barry Junior said. But despite the *Courier-*

Journal's endorsement of George Clark, Harvey Sloane won the election with ease. Later, Barry Junior would wonder if the Clark endorsement "tore the veil with my father." He said, "I thought I had the authority to endorse who I wanted to. Maybe I simply did not notice that my father might have been upset."

Soon, Shirley Williams recovered from her operation and wanted to come back to her job as book editor, but it was not to be. Significantly, one day after the election Barry Senior called his son, according to Barry Junior: "Sallie wants to stay on as book editor. You will have to move Shirley Williams to the magazine." Barry Junior was horrified by his sister's attempt to enlist her father to help her take her friends's job. "I cannot do that," Barry said. "We have procedures. If a job is available we have to post it for the Equal Employment Opportunity Commission." There was a pause on the telephone, Barry Junior remembered, and then his father said, "Sallie is going to be book editor." Barry Junior went into the newsroom to tell Paul Janensch what had happened. "This is what my father wants. . . . He is the chairman of the board," Barry said. Barry was beginning to understand that for all his father's promises, he was not really running the newspaper.

32

Winter, 1982. Despite the resentment at the newspaper for the manner in which she was made book editor, Sallie was doing a decent job, but even better, she had fallen in love. This time her new hope was different from any man she had been with before. Tim Peters was tall and dark with rough movie-star good looks; he wasn't rich, he wasn't social, but he was filled with confidence and genuinely kind. Peters was a building contractor, the kind of man who could lay a floor and who rarely wore a tie. He paid little attention to Sallie's moods and artistic pretensions, and Sallie was kittenish with him. For the first time in years Sallie seemed content. Tim was the exact opposite of the kind of man Sallie had been reared to marry. He was, as Mary Bingham said, "hardly Sallie's equal intellectually." Barry Senior described Tim Peters as "a man who spent a great deal of time in the military." The first time Peters ate dinner at the Little House he turned a gold plate over to look at it, Sallie's mother told a friend. "I have no idea what commonality of interests she has with him," Mary said.

But Sallie was relatively happy. She and Tim had settled into a large yellow Victorian house near Cherokee Park, which Sallie kept fastidiously. Her dining room was lined with bookshelves; her drawing room had peach-colored walls, a chintz sofa and a portrait of her aunt Henrietta. From the living room a visitor could see into Sallie's kitchen, where each pot was organized by shape and color, as if she could permit no disorder in her life. "I suppose I learned this obsessive behavior from my mother," she said. Certainly, Sallie still maintained her stringent writing schedule. In the mornings she would awaken early and drive twenty minutes up the River Road to work in a small studio that had no telephone. Sallie often entertained her friends, however, and seemed to relax in their company. She would hover over her guests "plying us with food and wine," a friend said, as tireless a hostess as she had once been organizing activities for her small children, as her mother had done. "When we saw Sallie relaxed and laughing we would think to ourselves, Thank heavens, let her be,'' a friend said.

Sallie and Tim had met each other shortly after Sallie came back to Louisville when Sallie bought two large run-down Victorian houses and hired Peters to restore them. About the time Sallie took over the book page she sent a card to her friends and family that said in effect, ''Tim Peters and Sallie Bingham have amalgamated their households.'' Mary Bingham was shocked by this gesture, but she tried to be philosophical. In any event, she was now extremely worried about one of Sallie's sons.

Although Sallie seemed more relaxed, one of her sons was having severe problems, perhaps because he had been separated from his father so abruptly. As a young teenager, the child became involved with drugs. Mary Bingham said, ''I am sorry to say that he is a menace.'' A few years after he moved to Louisville with his mother, Sallie told friends that he stole her car and was picked up in Dallas. ''Our real problems with Sallie began over this boy. . . . We thought he might be dangerous and we did not know what to do,'' Barry Senior said. He was so agitated, according to Barry Junior, that he called Harvey Sloane, at City Hall, to see that his grandson did not get put in jail. As if she were imitating her mother's own refusal to take responsibility for her maternal shortcomings, Sallie at first denied that the boy was troubled and that perhaps she was not doing enough to help him. She refused to get help for her son and told family members who urged her at least to get him to a psychiatrist, ''Why? Psychiatrists ruined my life.'' However, soon enough, the situation became so worrisome that Sallie did arrange for psychiatric help.

Sallie was anguished. One day Sallie had lunch in the cafeteria with Elaine Corn, the food editor. ''I just don't know what I am going to do,'' she said. ''I have always been so pusillanimous with the boys, given them anything they wanted.'' ''She tried Toughlove, she tried psychiatrists, she tried no psychiatrists. She was beside herself,'' Edie Bingham said. Her teenage son was allowed to live at home with Sallie and Tim Peters, who was, as a family member said, ''unbelievably good at bringing this boy around.'' Still, the boy's problems were well known in Louisville, and Mary and Barry, upset about their grandson, began to investigate schools all over the country for him—a move that would later infuriate Sallie, who would bitterly resent her parents' interference with her attempt to bring up her children.

Perhaps because she was trying to become more concerned with her son's activities, in the spring of 1982 Sallie joined a committee to help raise taxes for the Louisville schools. Belonging to a political committee was in direct violation of Barry's ethics guidelines, so he told Paul Janensch to tell Sallie to resign from this group. Janensch walked into Sallie's cubicle and said, "Look, Sallie, I agree with you . . ." but, he told her, she was not allowed to be on any political committees. Sallie said, "Those silly rules do not apply to me. I am the book editor." Janensch said, "You will have to make a choice." The clear implication was that her job was at stake. Sallie, furious, resigned from the committee but was so angry she sent another letter to the newspaper attacking Barry Junior's ethics policies, a letter that he published. At the next board meeting, Mary Bingham asked Barry Junior to review the ethics guidelines. "I thought he was carrying it a bit too far," she said.

The tension was building. That autumn the paper published a critical series on the Humana hospital corporation. Barry Junior and Paul Janensch "were summoned" to Humana headquarters to hear the management's complaints. They went willingly and met with the public relations officer who had a long list of grievances to go over with them: misleading headlines, mistakes and so on. "At first the tone was businesslike," Barry Junior said. "But after we had been sitting there for fifteen minutes, the door flew open and David Jones and Wendell Cherry, who ran Humana, started screaming at us about the reporter. They called him 'a crook' and were yelling at the top of their lungs with the worst profanity about the newspaper as if they were trying to intimidate us." Later, Cherry and Jones complained to Barry Senior about the newspaper, but he once again did not repeat a word to his son. Barry Junior was bitter about this and learned of Cherry's remarks to his father thirdhand. "There was no closing of the loop. The problem was always people saying things behind my back. My father never once told me a negative word that was said," Barry Junior said.

Barry was now desperate to do something about his problems with his board of directors. He was irritated with his sisters. He didn't like the fact that Edie did her needlepoint during meetings and that Eleanor wrote out Christmas cards. "I wanted to get some people with real management skills into the company," he said. And so, in early 1983, one of the paper's executives called a management consultant named Léon Danco, the founder and head of the Center for Family Business, based in Cleveland. He had helped over three hundred companies improve their boards. Danco was sixty years old, a Harvard graduate, but, he later said, he was not up to the Binghams socially. "My father was a Catholic immigrant, although they came over first class on the ship," he said.

Before going to Louisville to meet with the Binghams, he studied a videotape of Sallie reviewing a book on Louisville television. "There was no question in my mind that she was a viper . . . a second-rate intellectual with too much money and a big house," he said. "She seemed like so many people I meet in my business, a spoiled, wealthy child." Sallie had refused to meet with the Dancos because Danco and his wife, who was also his partner, had written books for women in family companies. "The chapters were called things like 'Pillow Talk' or 'How to Win the Game,' " she said. "I thought they were revolting, and I told them I wasn't going to spend any time with them."

But Mary and Barry, Eleanor and Rowland, and Barry and Edie met with the Dancos. At lunch at the Little House, Mary laid out three forks and fingerbowls. "I got the clear impression that Mrs. Bingham was watching my table manners," Danco said. But after several sessions with the Binghams, Danco refused to involve himself anymore. "The situation was impossible. There were these yo-yos on the board who would not let the directors do their work," he said. "Barry Junior was a tough kid. He was admired by his troops, who liked working with him. Eleanor was pleasant enough, but her husband was the classic son-in-law. There are competents and there are incompetents. He seemed to want a place to do his architecture. Sallie, I consider, was the malevolent spirit. She was a vicious woman having a marvelous time."

During his last visit to Louisville, Danco met with Mary and Barry Bingham. "The old man was impressive, but he was nostalgic for the past, like a lot of eighty-year-olds are, and didn't know anything about business," Danco said. "I never could get through to his wife, who was brilliant but very reserved. She seemed to be in control of the situation." Danco said that he advised Barry Bingham Senior to buy Sallie out. "I said to him, 'There will be no peace in this family until you tell your daughter Sallie to buzz off.' I said to him, 'You must not be swayed by a fifteen percent opinion.' " When Barry Senior heard this, Danco said, his eyes shone with tears. "I cannot bear to see my family broken up," he said to Léon Danco. "We cannot have this as a matter of public discussion. I will do everything in my power to preserve this family." Danco replied, "Mr. Bingham, I am sorry to tell you that there will be no limit to the price you are going to be asked to pay." Danco went back to Cleveland with a very bad feeling about the family. "Sallie Bingham seemed to have nonnegotiable malevolence for her brother. He was in her craw and she was in his craw. I believed there was no way to compromise."

That summer the entire family attended Sallie and Tim Peters's wedding reception. It had been Barry Senior's idea to give the reception on a small boat called *Bonnie Belle*, which could hold about one hundred fifty guests. "We catered it from Ken-

tucky Fried Chicken,'' Sallie said. ''It really was a nice party.''
It was a lovely day and the family seemed content. ''You would
never have known there was any hostility between them,'' the
Courier-Journal writer John Ed Pearce said.

33

Eleanor reveled in her marriage to Rowland. As if she had been inspired by her mother's example, she devoted herself to her husband and seemed not to resent his frequent presence at family meetings or his opinions about the newspaper. "Mother always said to me, 'Your husband is more important than your children,' " Eleanor admitted. Mary and Barry were not cold or dismissive to Rowland as they had once been to Edie and Joan, nor did they condescend to him as they did to Tim Peters, Sallie's new husband. Edie believed that Mary and Barry would "tolerate anything from Rowland. They were determined to make sure that Eleanor's marriage worked."

Eleanor and Rowland were living in Glenview in a gray house that overlooked the Glenview hills of her childhood. The house had the atmosphere of a charming country retreat and was filled with whimsical objects, such as architectural drawings of fantasy buildings and a post-modern tea service under glass. But in her own way Eleanor was as purposeful as Sallie, and her discipline was evident on the second floor, where she kept a proper office with double desks and bulletin boards clogged with reminders and announcements. Her executive ability and her need to organize her time would be apparent even in the notes she later wrote to her household help. "Mrs. Granny Miller will pick up Rollie at 2:30 P.M. He will need his bottle at 2:00 P.M.," she once wrote in an even hand.

Having spent less time with their youngest child as she was growing up, Mary and Barry now showered her with attention. Mary's bias was obvious. "She is such a considerate girl with such flair," Mary said. Hardly a day went by when Eleanor did not visit her parents or arrange to see them. Eleanor was not withdrawn and puritanical like her brother, nor was she as artistic or self-absorbed as her sister.

Mary and Barry were delighted to see that their younger daughter was part of the new Louisville, where the daughters of the old families were changing the town with their nouvelle cuisine, appreciation of Kentucky crafts, and eagerness to have Louisville shed its reputation for civic laziness. The new governor, John Y. Brown, had advertised the state in the *Wall Street Journal*: "Kentucky & Co.: the State That's Run Like a Business." The new First Lady of Kentucky, Phyllis George, merchandised Kentucky products around America. The well-bred Louisvillians often referred to Phyllis George, the former beauty queen, with contempt, but there was no question that she was getting the state the attention her predecessors hadn't. As Phyllis George sent blue-and-white stoneware to Bloomingdale's for their "Oh Kentucky!" boutique, Eleanor and her friends scoured Appalachia for nineteenth-century quilts. Eleanor produced the Olmsted Festival, which was a tribute to the distinguished landscape architect Frederick Law Olmsted's Louisville parks. Her exhibition of Kentucky quilts attracted 22,000 people in six weeks at a local museum. She served on the board of the Bingham Enterprises Foundation, which donated several million dollars a year to Louisville, and like her father, she was active in the local museums and art councils as well as the family's special charity, the Crusade for Children, Inc. "Eleanor's nature is to take on far too much public service," her father said proudly.

Unlike Sallie, Eleanor did not blame her parents for neglecting her when she was a child. "Well, they weren't around a lot, so what?" she said. "Sallie was the one who took care of my emotional needs." Now she basked in their attention. "It was as if Mary and Barry were trying to make up for all the years they left her alone," a family member said. Eleanor took them to the movies, had them to dinner, entertained them with her activities, and was, as her father said, "a constant delight." She served on boards and foundations around town, as did her close friends Wendell Cherry, the chairman of Humana, and Kathy Sloane. Cherry hired Rowland to do some interior work on the new Humana headquarters. In the summers she rented expensive houses in the Hamptons, where she often saw her friend the painter Larry Rivers and, later, the novelist Kurt Vonnegut. Her friends from the East would be invited to Louisville for the Derby and taken to dinner with Mary and Barry, who thought, as her mother said, "that Eleanor has the most delightful social way."

Even better, after a difficult miscarriage, Eleanor and Rowland now had a baby named Rowland Junior, whom they nicknamed Rollie. Mary and Barry were thrilled with this child, as much as they had once been with Barry Ellsworth, the first boy baby in the family. Barry's future adversary, Wendell Cherry, was named Rollie's godfather. All of Mary's strictness about child-rearing evaporated when it came to Eleanor's son. Mary, who had once told a daughter-in-law that her children's behavior at the dinner table was like "the participants in a nig funeral," seemed to ignore her new grandson's unruly ways. "Eleanor just feeds him little bits of peanut butter a lot of the time," Mary said. "She said, 'The doctors now say that babies eat too much.' " Almost every day Eleanor took the baby to her mother's for a long visit.

While Sallie suffered from her own son's problems her view of Eleanor became more clear-eyed. Although they were still close friends and soon would be allies, Sallie saw the more political side of Eleanor's behavior. "Eleanor is determined to be the good girl," she said. "She would drive the parents everywhere all the time and then complain about it. She would say, 'Oh God, I have to do this again.' She was trying as always to please everybody. And then Rowland said to me, 'I don't want Eleanor to be rated the bad one like you are.' It makes me so mad!"

Eleanor was not shy about letting her parents know she was annoyed that her brother did not respect her opinions. Later, Barry Junior believed that Rowland repeated every nasty remark to Mary and Barry that Wendell Cherry had to say about the *Courier-Journal.* "I would always hear later what had been said behind my back," he said.

For months Eleanor had been concerned about money. Eleanor's income from the Louisville *Courier-Journal* was close to three hundred thousand dollars a year, but she and Rowland had bought two buildings to renovate in downtown Louisville, only to find that they could not sell or rent them, so she worried about what she called "my capital base." "You might say we got off to a slow start," Rowland said. Later, she asked her brother in a memo about loans from the company at low interest rates. Barry had answered her memo tartly: There could be no low-interest loans for directors without making the same privilege available to every employee of the newspaper. "We were concerned. And we wanted to have enough capital to make sure everything was taken care of," Rowland said.

Eleanor and Barry Junior, who had once been close friends, were now on a collision course. Their friendship had eroded as Eleanor and Rowland had tried to have more of a voice in the company. She wrote Barry memos suggesting that the Bingham station fund a documentary unit and let her do feature films. Barry refused. She told Barry she did not think she needed any business training to take over WHAS. "I thought my two years doing public relations was training enough to run it," she said. In fact Eleanor was ambivalent about working. She had days when she thought she wanted to have complete power at WHAS. Other days she wanted to stay home with her son and not think about the pressure of work. Her ambivalence was entirely understandable, but her strong lack of commitment was not reassuring to her brother. "I never thought running a TV station was an adequate career for Eleanor," her father said. "She is more creative." According to Edie, "Eleanor did not know what she wanted. She flip-flopped and drove everyone wild."

Just before Rollie was born, the new Standard Gravure plant opened in Tennessee. All the directors and their husbands and wives were invited, but Eleanor declined because she was a month away from giving birth. Barry did not send Rowland a separate invitation. "An oversight," he said. "Who would have dreamed he would have wanted to come with Eleanor not going?" Months later, Rowland complained to his mother-in-law about this, and she became angry with her son, accusing him of "a mean-spirited little plot."

The inability to communicate directly made everything so much worse. Barry did not soothe Eleanor by giving her the attention she wanted or finding a proper place in the company for her. He did not have his father's ability to be gracious to people he didn't like. Instead, he bristled and pulled within himself and resented his sister's frequent complaints about the editorial policy of the newspaper. "If Barry had made any effort to be a friend to me, we never would have had our problems," Eleanor later said.

On paper, the family debated "the role" of board members. Letters were traded, lengthy memos, more paper about a subject that should never have had to be raised, and tiresome documents about the family's "place." But no amount of paper could camouflage an inability to talk plainly with one another. A dozen memos could not instill familial bonds and trust. Everything Barry Junior did was wrong, Eleanor believed. She was angry that she was getting little response from him. So there were more complaints to her parents: *Why doesn't Barry like Rowland? Why won't he pay attention to me?* As if they were lost souls desperate for spiritual guidance, the family and the board members now addressed themselves to the notion of "personal goals." The newspaper's general manager at that time, George Gill, spent hours writing a list of goals, which were published in the newspaper's *Intercom* magazine. "Maintain and improve the quality of products"; "Retain and preserve Bingham family ownership"; "Continue active civic leadership and involvement." Mary Bingham dismissed Gill's family goals. "They are generic," Mary said at a family meeting.

On the first of December 1983 Eleanor Miller sent her brother a ten-page single-spaced memo called "Family goals-setting project." On the first page, she defined her battleground and stressed her mother's influence on her memo. "The enclosed papers contain . . . goals for the companies as defined by me

with comments and inclusions from Mother, who most generously allowed me to bounce my rough draft off her during the
past few months." She cited her mother at length. "To quote
Mother on this issue: . . . The Conflict of Interest Policy is
inhibiting here. It is perhaps too stringent. If we had it [in Lou-
isville], I do not think the Guild would put up with it."

Eleanor's memo covered newspaper goals, ethics questions and
WHAS. She called for a restructuring of the board with committees, outside consultants and workshop sessions. It was a plea
to Barry Junior to take her seriously, but he viewed it as impertinent criticism and an attempt to set policy for areas at the
newspaper that were none of her business.

Eleanor's memo opened briskly, with a threat of the possibility
of "subverted or abandoned ownership" if the goals she was
submitting were not followed. Besides setting up the goal for a
fifty-fifty ratio for advertising and news, she suggested that family members be allowed to borrow money at low interest rates,
that family internships be available to anyone up to age thirty,
that Pulitzer prizes and being in the top ten newspapers in the
country be an expectation. Ten pages of demands and complaints
were delivered to the publisher's office almost two weeks before
the next board meeting, which was scheduled for December 12,
1983. Later, Barry Junior would say, "Eleanor's memo read like
the constitution of the State of Kentucky."

The family meeting following the board meeting was held in
the conference room at the Junior League in downtown Louisville. Halfway through the meeting, Barry Junior said, "I have
something to say that is off the agenda." Eleanor took notes, as
she always did, and was astonished by what was on her brother's
mind. "According to my notes, Barry did have something ready
to say, for a change. He said that he felt the confidence of the
family was lacking. He had three points to make. Edie, Mary,
Joan, Sallie and I had to get off the board because we were not
professionals. Sallie had to sign the buy-back agreement, which
said that no stock in the company would be offered to an outsider
before it was offered to the family. . . . Then he said, 'If you
don't do these two things, I am leaving.' " He had been provoked by Eleanor's memo, but everyone in the family knew that
the real reason for his decision was Sallie.

"My pencil was dropping off," Eleanor said. "This was the
biggest bombshell that had ever been dropped in the world."

Sallie was at the meeting at the Junior League, and after it
was over, she called Eleanor. "I am so thrilled," she said. "Now
let's have another meeting to talk about who Barry Junior's successor might be!" Eleanor later told the reporter Joe Ward from
the *Courier-Journal*, "Sometimes it eases the transition to the
fourth generation to have an outsider come in for a period of

time.'' But Barry Senior stood up to his daughters and said he would not consider an outsider running the Bingham companies—this was a shared dream—and with some reluctance, Mary and Barry took their son's side. Barry Senior reportedly said that if there was no family leadership, they might as well sell the newspapers. ''There can only be one person running a newspaper,'' Mary said. Barry Senior said he would sell the newspapers rather than let an outsider run them. ''Getting off the board was pretty much the obvious choice,'' Eleanor later said. Sallie violently disagreed.

In private, Mary in particular begged her son not to force his sisters off the board. ''Couldn't you just add some professional business people to the board?'' she said. ''No,'' he said. As if he were trying to settle a childhood score, Barry Junior was compelled to move against Sallie in particular. Edie told him it was a ''dangerous'' idea. So did Joan. His parents warned him of Sallie's vengeful nature, but he was not to be deterred. For three months the family met at the Little House to try to work things out. ''I was the one that everybody was dumping on,'' Sallie said. ''It was too much. Mother would say things like, 'Are you trying to destroy your brother?' Or she would get angry later and say that I had broken some confidence, that I had discussed something with someone at the paper that I shouldn't have discussed. It was real bad. It was very much like going back to being a small child. 'Why did you behave that way?' . . . If I had been a stronger person, I would have decided to put up with it. . . . It was just too devastating. At first I used to cry a lot.''

Every few weeks the family would meet at the Little House. At first the atmosphere would be polite. Hors d'oeuvres would be passed. Sallie remembered, ''It was only a question of time before someone would bring up something. Usually my mother. My mother is more aggressive than my father. He chooses not to be. He would never scold. He would never criticize. He would never discipline.''

Mary and Barry, however, began to tell their three children, ''Make peace between you or we are going to sell the newspaper,'' a threat Eleanor said ''that none of us took seriously.'' At one meeting at the Little House, Tim Peters, Sallie's new husband, even volunteered to be the peacemaker. ''Let us try to think of the things that bind us together, not those that tear us apart,'' Edie said, who remembered the strain and the pretense in the room that afternoon. But it was not to be. Sallie interpreted her mother's behavior as a dreadful repetition of the pattern of her childhood: boys over girls. ''Whenever I went into Barry Junior's office it was perfectly clear to me after a few minutes that he would literally freeze, as if to say, 'Get out of here before I lose it,' " Sallie said. In the boardroom she became Sallie the princess of Melcombe, who knew she was smarter than Barry Junior. "I think my children lack confidence in each other. Their lack of faith is terribly sad," Barry Senior said. Later Sallie told reporters that her mother was trying to protect her "only remaining son." Sallie interpreted her mother's bias as "a feminist issue," as if her mother's specific pathology was political. Sallie could never view Barry's decision to ask her to leave the board as having anything to do with the question of whether or not she was competent. She began to see her life in feminist terms, and complicated problems were reduced to a fashionable ideology. In Louisville, Sallie began to talk about "raising my consciousness" by visiting "spouse abuse" centers. She propped up her own specific problems into a public issue. *My family has always mistreated women*, she said. *My brother is bothered by what he considers ridiculous questions*, she said. Sallie's women friends nodded their heads sympathetically. *Poor Sallie*. "The woolly-minded will always think Sallie's arguments are logical," her cousin James Callahan said.

Sallie's feminist argument disguised yet another rupture in the family, which was the continuing controversy over her troubled son. "There had been a bitter division on the subject of the boy," Mary said. There had been little improvement in his behavior. After a court hearing a local judge recommended that he be placed in an institution under psychiatric care. His father and his grandparents wanted him sent to a luxurious place for troubled children called the Brown School in Austin, Texas. The tuition was $75,000 a year. "His father was going to pay half and we were going to pay half," Barry Senior said. "And Sallie was furious about this and said she would never ever send him there." Sallie saw her parents' relationship with her former husband as yet another betrayal. But even Sallie's current husband, Tim Peters, would sometimes call Barry and Mary to discuss Sallie's stubbornness about her son. "I am calling from a pay phone because my phone may be tapped," he would say, according to a family member. "Sallie would become impossible to live with if she thought I was speaking to you."

"It is my belief," her father told me sometime later, "that we can never understand Sallie's mind unless we understand how troubled she is about her son. She is angry and blamed us. She was determined to cause as much hurt as possible." Mary and Barry could not understand why she would not accept their help or even discuss her son's problems with them. Now Sallie had her own taboo subjects. "He is fine," she said to anyone who asked. Or, if pressed, "I don't want to get into that."

"Sallie's fury is entirely with me," her father said. "Not her brother."

* * *

In March 1984 Mary and Edie Bingham left the board of directors, but Sallie refused to resign. "At the climactic meeting in March, the family and I and the secretary of the company sat down in one windowless room and they all had to cast their votes for the other directors and not cast their votes for me. . . . I cast all my votes for me, but since I only owned four percent or five percent of the voting stock, it wasn't enough," Sallie said. "It was traumatic." To Paul Janensch "this was a fight for the very soul of the newspaper." An investment banker who specialized in newspaper companies remarked, "I saw this all the time. The business could be healthy, but the third generation would use the newspaper's editorial policies as their dueling ground for the real problems between them."

Yet it was still important for Mary and Barry to keep the illusion of closeness, so a week or two later Mary called Sallie and asked her and Tim to go to the movies. But Sallie declined saying, "I don't see how we can just go on as if nothing has happened, Mother." Soon thereafter, Mary received a note from her daughter. "She wrote and said that she thought it would be better if we didn't see each other anymore," Mary said. "I am used to telling the children when I think they are wrong. I am their mother." But Mary made no attempt to call Sallie, to demand a further explanation, or even, as some mothers would have, drive to her house, cry and plead for a reconciliation. "Why should I have?" Mary said. "When you get a letter from someone saying that they don't want to see you anymore, I consider that to be something I can't do anything about . . . so much so that I wouldn't run the risk of being rejected. I would fear that." "That is so pitiful," Sallie later said. "I think that is what she has dreaded all along. A rebuff from anybody."

Barry Senior, however, was deeply upset about the rift with his daughter. That spring he wrote to friends in Connecticut who were close to Sallie and asked them to mediate. He also asked Norman Isaacs to talk to her. "I would call her and write to her and say, 'You know that I love you and always loved you. Let's talk things through.' At that point she made it clear that it was useless to try to have contact with me until her newspaper stock was sold," Barry Senior said.

Easter, 1984. Edie Bingham thought it would be a wonderful idea to get everyone in the family together for Easter lunch. Easter was always glorious in Louisville; the tulips bloomed along the banks of the Ohio River and the dogwood would be just beginning to flower. She called Mary and invited her to the River Valley Club for lunch, but Mary said, "Eleanor and Rowland will be with Rowland's parents." Edie responded by say-

ing, "Fine. We'll invite them too. I'll get a big table." Mary
said, "Let me take care of it. I will do the place cards."

On Easter morning Mary telephoned Edie to say, "I am terribly sorry to tell you this, but we have to disinvite you from the
Easter lunch." She sounded very upset, Edie said, and told her
that Rowland did not want to be with Barry for Easter because
he felt that Barry "humiliated" Eleanor by not paying enough
attention to her ideas. "We are going to the River Valley anyway," Edie said. "I am terribly sorry that Rowland cannot bring
himself to be with the family at least on Easter." Edie told her
mother-in-law that she would instruct the captain to place her
table on the porch at the club. "We would be delighted to sit
separately," she said.

After church, Edie arrived at the River Valley Club to discover
that the long table was already set and their place cards were
still there. "It was so awkward," Edie said. "When Mary arrived she kept us at the table but put us far away from Eleanor
and Rowland. I don't think she wanted the other people at the
club talking about this petty scene." Edie remembered how
mortified Barry Senior seemed to be. "He kept rushing from
one to the other of the family being overly charming, so conversational, trying to make everything be all right," Edie said.
Later, Barry Junior and Edie would be bitter about this Easter
lunch. Mary and Barry had never once blamed Rowland for his
role. "It was as if my parents would put up with any amount of
agitation just to make sure Eleanor's marriage would not have
any problems," Barry Junior said.

Summer, 1984. Now that Sallie was off the board of the company, she thought it might be a good idea to see if she could sell
her stock. "I told my parents that I would have a relationship
with them again after we had concluded our business together,"
Sallie said. Sallie went to the company lawyers and asked them
to prepare a list of investment bankers who could evaluate her
stock's worth. She owned 4 percent of the voting stock of a
privately held company, but if she survived her parents, she
would ultimately have 14.6 percent of the vote. Sallie studied
each company and chose Shearson Lehman Brothers because
"they had the most women working there." She told her brother
and the financial officers of the company that she would abide
by whatever Shearson Lehman said. "Let them name the price,"
she said.

Sallie's husband, Tim, told a friend that he had advised Sallie
to be very careful: "If you put your stock on the market, it could
bring the entire company down." Sallie's answer was brusque:
I don't care, I'll get my money out. Now that her family had
forced her off the board, she began to tell reporters, "I've taught

myself to stop saying, 'Daddy.' I've given up being approved by my ex-family. If I had to see them every day it would be very painful. They really tried to ruin me. Every few weeks there is some new instance of something really nasty, so I feel as though that justified me.'' She added, ''And I am hoping [Eleanor] is going to join me.''

Sallie began to meet with Stephen Schwarzman, an energetic Shearson Lehman Brothers managing director. Schwarzman liked Sallie and spent a great deal of time with her. ''She was reasonable at first. She believed the company should have expanded. She believed her brother was mired in his mistakes, such as the expansion of Standard Gravure. I kept telling her that was a minor part of the company. He was really running a Tiffany operation that was very valuable. I told her that Barry was content, like many family owners, to run a quality regional operation,'' Schwarzman said, and left his meetings with Sallie with the clear idea that there was more than money involved. ''She didn't like her brother. She thought he was self-indulgent and a bad businessman.''

The Shearson Lehman Brothers group tried to explain to Sallie that there were two market prices for her stock. The first was what she could potentially receive if the company was liquidated or sold completely: a minimum of $40 million. The second was what she would get if the company stayed in private hands. ''Very few buyers want five percent of a company, Sallie,'' Schwarzman said he told her. ''Sallie would answer, 'I know I am being irrational but I want forty million.' ''

In private, Stephen Schwarzman counseled George Gill, the general manager of the newspaper. ''I said to him, 'Your company can afford forty million in the great scope of things. What do you care? It is just money. You can earn it back.' And he would say, 'I cannot deliver that money.' '' It was clear to Schwarzman that Barry Bingham Junior was not about to give his sister her way. ''Well,'' said Schwarzman, echoing Léon Danco's sentiments, ''something bad is going to happen. You really have to settle with her. Just give her what she wants and get rid of her.''

That August, Joan, Eleanor, and Rowland decided to rent a house together on Nantucket. Eleanor and Rowland were pleased that their best friend, Wendell Cherry, the chairman of Humana, lent them the corporate plane to take their baby furniture to the island. Eleanor knew that the Cherrys thought the newspaper did not cover Humana properly, and in the past Wendell Cherry had called Barry Senior when he thought the reporters were asking too many questions about Humana's hospital procedures. ''I repeated to him that I thought it was Barry's responsibility,'' Barry Senior said.

Wendell Cherry and David Jones, his partner, might have been angry with Barry Junior for another reason, however. He had refused to use Humana health insurance for the employees. Humana had bid on the Bingham business and had drawn up a package that would give the newspaper companies a complete range of benefits, but only at Humana hospitals. Barry turned it down. Wendell Cherry then called Mary Bingham, according to Barry Junior. "Your son is costing the *Courier-Journal* an extra million dollars not taking our insurance plan," he said.

The Cherrys were now powerful in Louisville, stars in the social orbit. They funded the Actors Theatre's annual playwriting festival, which was now renamed the Humana Festival. They were constructing a distinguished new headquarters in downtown Louisville and had invited the finest architects in the world. The quality of architecture was to be so splendid that ultimately a book would be written about the competition. Michael Graves was eventually chosen to design the new headquarters, which was to be directly across the street from the new Kentucky Center for the Arts, for which Barry Bingham Senior and Wendell Cherry raised $6 million. Wendell Cherry, like Barry Senior, was now considered a premier citizen, a philanthropist, a man who believed in serving the commonweal. Only later would Barry Senior admit to reporters—but never to his own son—how much it distressed him that Cherry disliked how Barry Junior ran the *Courier-Journal*.

That summer of 1984 at the summer house, there were endless conversations about the family's problems: Sallie and Mary's fight; Barry Junior's decision about the board; why Barry Junior was cold to Rowland; what would happen if Sallie sold her stock. However strained the relationship was between Barry Junior and Rowland, that summer Eleanor was very much involved, at Barry's request, in searching for outside directors for the company. "Eleanor was getting ready to fly off to Chicago to interview directors," Joan said. "She seemed very busy working with Barry Junior."

On the first day they were all together, Rowland made an off-color remark to Joan's new beau, a diplomat. Joan was mortified. The visit did not start well. "This was the summer that I realized Joan was not the friend to us I thought she was," Rowland said. "Living together was a disaster," Joan said. Everything went wrong in the house that could possibly go wrong. All those family members under one Nantucket roof was, in hindsight, a serious mistake. The tension of the past months, the divided loyalties, the missed communications played out in the pettiest of arguments. Who was going to clean dishes? Who was going to sleep in which room of the house? It was a claustrophobic nightmare, and by the time the summer was over it was clear that the family had begun to take sides.

Barry and Edie had been looking forward to September of 1984 for years. Even though the family was tense, they planned to leave Louisville for nine months so that Edie could finish her college degree at Smith. Edie had dropped out of college in her senior year when she married for the first time. Now Smith had a program to accommodate women who hadn't finished their original degrees. Edie and Barry rented a small apartment in Northampton. However myopic it would later seem, they believed that the autumn of 1984 was a good time to leave Louisville.

Everything seemed to be in place at the newspaper. The profits were up to 12 percent, which was still only half of the industry norm, but an improvement nonetheless. Barry was testing out yet another plan called the Regency, to see how the newspapers would run without the top man. He left Paul Janensch and George Gill in charge of the papers, despite Janensch's unpopularity in the family. With Emily and Molly in boarding school near Boston, Edie and Barry arrived in Northampton with a U-Haul truck filled with skis, a computer and two printers, a silver coffee pot, sugar and creamer, two chain saws and their bikes. Their new apartment had only two bedrooms, but they loved being away from the family turbulence, the ghosts of the Big House and the pressure of the newspaper business. During the day Edie and Barry took courses together and audited a course on Shakespeare. "Shakespeare is surprisingly good family therapy!" Edie later wrote.

It had been months since they had seen Mary and Barry, who had spent the summer in Chatham. "On the surface they seemed pleased that we were taking nine months off," Edie said, "but looking back, I realized there was an undercurrent, 'Why wasn't Barry working?' " Edie thought it odd that Mary and Barry hardly acknowledged her detailed letters about "the pleasures of our intellectual exercise." She tried not to think about how much their relationship had deteriorated. Edie now knew that Mary thought she was dreary and entertained poorly. "I always got the feeling that she felt there was something inadequate about being served a casserole or a salad and French bread in the kitchen if I asked them to come over for dinner," Edie said. "We just weren't grand enough. . . . We didn't cultivate enough celebrities."

In Northampton, Barry was in touch with the office on the telephone and on a computer hookup, but he was out of the fray of the family struggle. Edie and Barry did not even feel compelled to come home for Christmas. Instead, they took their daughters trekking in Nepal. It was just after they returned that George Gill sent them an ominous message via Barry's computer hookup: "Sallie is going to sell her stock outside the company."

A month earlier Barry had met with Stephen Schwarzman and his associates from Shearson Lehman Brothers at the Ramada Inn near the Hartford, Connecticut, airport. "Barry seemed as reasonable as Sallie," Schwarzman said. "He seemed like a man who was happy to be alive. He was very controlled, thoughtful, orderly." But Schwarzman left the meeting feeling that Barry Junior's tactics were all wrong where Sallie was concerned. "There were no real dividends to make them feel as rich as they were. The values of media properties were skyrocketing. The capital gains taxes were low. I said to him, 'If you let her stay out on the Street long enough with her stock, eventually someone is going to pay the price.'" Once again, Barry paid no attention to Schwarzman's shrewd advice.

Sallie was not shy about going public. In January 1985 she announced her intentions in the *New York Times*. "Share Offered in Louisville Newspaper Company," the small story in the business section was headlined. The piece was short—711 words, to be exact, but it got the point across. She said that she was selling out because she had been "removed as a director" and was "uncertain about future management." Her father told the *Times* that his daughter's announcement was "premature."

For a brief time the family tried to unite against Sallie. In February the agenda of the family meeting was to discuss various methods—what Wall Street calls "shark repellents"—to ward off outside buyers for Sallie's stock. Barry Senior agreed to put all the voting stock in a trust that he would control. The voting trust gave Barry Senior 95 percent of the voting stock, but it led to even more discussion about Eleanor's future role in the companies. Eleanor had made it clear to her father that she wanted a voice in the newspapers. In the meantime, Eleanor had hired a prominent local lawyer named Rucker Todd to represent her interests. Todd was known for his encyclopedic understanding of the law and his nitpicking on contracts. "He would argue over the meaning of commas," a banker said. He also had a keen idea of what his client's stock was worth and he wanted to protect her at all costs, the more so perhaps because of his long-standing competition of sorts with the newspaper's attorney, Gordon Davidson.

In the midst of this turmoil, Sallie resigned as book editor. The newspaper gave her a going-away party, and everyone came, including her father. "They served wine. Barry Senior came up and kissed her on the cheek. They congratulated her on what a great job she had done," the reporter Joe Ward said. Sallie was the very image of a refined Bingham daughter. Later, when Joe

Ward asked her why her relationship with her brother was so bad, she said, "It's not bad. We like each other. We just have no relationship whatsoever." As Sallie packed her possessions a columnist named Elinor Brecher walked past Sallie's cubicle. "There was a Bachrach portrait of her parents in the trash can," she said. "Upside down."

March 1985. It had been nine months since Barry and Edie had seen Mary and Barry Senior, but now it was time to go home to Louisville for a visit. A board meeting was scheduled for March 18 and there would be much to discuss. Family tension had become unbearable. Sallie had gone back on an agreement to accept the Shearson Lehman Brothers' evaluation of her stock. Shearson Lehman Brothers had told her that her 14.6 percent share in the company was worth at most between $21 million and $29 million if the company was not liquidated. "I thought that was too low," she said. Furthermore, she asked, Why shouldn't I get my money out of the company? She explained to her two oldest sons, Chris Iovenko and Barry Ellsworth, that there were so many grandchildren in the family that they would never have enough stock to have any real voice in the running of the newspaper.

The Shearson Lehman Brothers' bill for evaluating Sallie's stock was more than one hundred thousand dollars, and Barry Junior instructed George Gill to pay it. Then Sallie announced that she had asked the firm of Henry Ansbacher Inc., which specialized in media companies, for another evaluation. Ansbacher was far less conservative than Lehman and told Sallie that her stock was worth between $82 million and $92 million. Sallie named her price in February of 1985: $42 million. "The telephone rings all the time with investment bankers. Someone will buy my stock," Sallie said at the time.

She had entered the marketplace at an opportune moment. Media companies were bringing astronomical amounts of money as many third-generation newspaper families were breaking up. The Detroit *News* empire sold for $717 million; the $170 million Des Moines *Register* sale was double what anyone thought it was worth. The statistics were grim for family newspapers. Over 70 percent of the newspapers in the country were now owned by groups such as the $2 billion Gannett Company, which had bought the Detroit *News* and Des Moines *Register* and published *USA Today*.

If the Bingham family had truly wanted to preserve the newspaper, it would have been easy enough to buy Sallie out, as Shearson Lehman Brothers had advised them to do. So had Léon Danco. Sallie would have been content and felt she had scored a psychological victory. But Barry Junior could not bring himself

to give in to his sister's demands. He said, "Our profit margin
was too low. We could never have replaced our equipment in the
future. And if we had a bad year the papers would have been in
serious shape." That wasn't exactly right. In fact there was am-
ple money in the company. The *Courier-Journal* had little debt.
Wall Street bankers "ran numbers," as they called it, and wrote
spread sheets for Barry that proved the company could easily
afford the debt. But Barry had a rationale for not wanting to pay
Sallie off. He said he was worried about his credit rating. He
didn't want to drop to a "BB," which meant a credit risk.
He would always think of the worst-case syndrome: what
if the newspapers made no money and they had to replace all
the equipment in one year and his parents died at the same time?
"There was enough money, so that the risk he was taking on
was only to be for a year in the life of a debt-free company," a
banker said. "He was worrying about estate taxes and replacing
the equipment, when all of those expenses could have been
spread out over years."

There was more to it than that. Barry felt that Sallie was trying
to take advantage of him and the company, and felt her demands
were unreasonable. Later, the bankers from Goldman, Sachs
who negotiated the final sale of the newspaper said that Barry
Junior did not understand how to steer the *Courier-Journal* out
of possible future debt, and that his resistance to Sallie was a
product of his "insecurity." But Barry said he felt very much
alone in the midst of this fight, that his parents did not back him
up, and he was right. Mary and Barry appeared unhappy about
Barry Junior's style, which they saw an antithetical to their own.
"He doesn't even have any fun," his mother told Sallie. For his
part, Barry Junior was as moralistic and stubborn as the rest of
the family, maybe more so. He was not the kind of man to
submit to Sallie's demands, no matter what the cost. The bankers
all said privately that Sallie would be willing to settle for $32
million. Barry said no to that as well. During this period, Sydney Gruson, a director of the *New York Times,* visited Mary and
Barry Senior: "I said to him, 'You can't let this company go
down the drain.' " Barry Senior responded, according to Gruson, "I promised my son I wouldn't interfere and I won't. It is
a matter of principle." But Barry Bingham made it clear to Gruson that if he was forced to sell the newspapers, he certainly
hoped the buyer would be either the *Washington Post* or the
Times.

When Barry Junior and Edie came home to Louisville that
March, they knew there had been a dangerous sea change. Edie
believed that Mary was not happy to see them. It was as if the
months of complaints she had heard about her son from Eleanor
and Rowland, the Sloanes and the Cherrys had finally worn her

down. Later Kathy Sloane would be particularly upset because the newspapers published several articles accusing her of improprieties such as using her husband's political connections to further her real estate business; using a city sanitation employee for her personal chauffeur; charging to the city an airline ticket to Alaska and so forth. Kathy Sloane denied all the accusations and, as a family member said, "muled into Mary's ear about how Barry Junior was trying to ruin her." Soon Mary began to say that she was convinced that Barry had "changed." She blamed his cancer. "He was the most overweight and amusing child," she said. "Now he is very inflexible. I know it's the cancer. He makes up his mind about people and cannot be dissuaded. I have never been able to get to the bottom of his coldness about certain people," Mary later said.

"Everything was different when we got home," Barry Junior said. "It was obvious that the drumbeat of criticism had rained on my parents' head. We were never in Louisville to defend ourselves. And naturally, no one had ever said a critical word to us when we were away." In March, when Barry and Edie arrived at the family meeting, they were handed a document with a threatening title: "13 Commandments." The last commandment on the list was that Barry Junior and Eleanor would have to get along with each other. The implication was that if they didn't, their father would sell the company altogether. "All Eleanor had to do was keep stirring up dissension and it was guaranteed that the newspaper would go," Barry said. However calm Barry was when he came home, after a week he was as tense as when he had left. Mary was harsh at the meeting about Barry's relationship with Eleanor and Rowland, so much so that when Edie got home she wrote her mother-in-law another earnest letter trying to make peace.

Dear, dear Mary,

Our leave taking on Thursday afternoon was so abrupt and uncharacteristic (after nine months separation) that I am deeply disturbed and alarmed. The bitterness and hostility which I sensed were all the more cutting because I simply do not understand their provenance. If trespasses of mine have offended you, I must fervently state that I do not know what they could be. My loyalty to your family is as strong now as it has been for over twenty years, and I have no wish nor ever have in the past to estrange myself from your affection and respect which I treasure.

Even though I place so little hope in the power of my words to enlighten your views, I must convey to you the sincerity of my efforts over many years to foster normal and loving relationships in the family. This desire and effort has

never been withdrawn on my part; in fact I have repeatedly
extended my love despite discouraging reception at times.
(Mothers learn to do that, I think you'll agree!)

I write this because I see a genuine and hopeful possibility to put the past behind us and begin to build relationships
based on shared kinship and people values.

Eleanor was now fed up with her brother and she had her own
bombshell to drop. "I don't want my family's shares in any
company that Barry would run," she said. Nevertheless, she had
agreed to place her voting stock in the trust that her father established until the problems between her and her brother could
be worked out, if they could ever be worked out. Her mother's
sentiments were obvious: "Eleanor has tried to keep all the
friendships going in the family," Mary said. "Eleanor and Rowland have a flair that Edie and Barry do not like. It is so absurd.
There they are in that huge house saying that Rowland and Eleanor should live more simply. Eleanor is daring, casual and non-
judgmental."

From Northampton, Barry Junior had written his father a long
and heartbreaking letter. "I know that you don't agree with everything that I do but as long as you don't suspect my motives
we have a relationship which I find both loving and construc-
tive."

A week earlier Mary had sent Barry Junior a tough letter accusing him of bad faith in his relationship with Rowland. She
accused him of plotting against his brother-in-law and was incensed that Barry Junior was not going to create a role for Rowland in the company. But Barry, once again, saw the question
of Rowland as a violation of his authority at the newspaper. He
wrote his father pages about this problem. "I harbor no hostile
feelings toward Rowland. I won't pretend that he is my best
friend but I am certainly capable of being civil to him despite
Mother's characterizations which, in my opinion, do nothing to
improve the situation." Barry pleaded with his father for support, for a sign that he was not sitting, as usual, on the fence of
good manners and good intentions. "Let me ask you how I
should respond to Mother's letter of the 4th? . . . I think it brings
up many of the old canards which I really don't know how to
answer. Rather than making her angry with answers which she
will feel are impertinent, let me try them on you for your good
advice. . . ." He listed all the reasons that he believed the company should not give Rowland an architectural assignment: What
if his designs were unacceptable? What if the employees complained? What if no other architect would bid against him?
Wouldn't this give Sallie's husband, Tim Peters, the right to special treatment too? The Bingham family was dissolving into a

war over patronage. "It was tragic that a family this intelligent and public-minded should have been reduced to these stinking, minor squabbles," Edie said.

In May the newspaper ran another eight-part series on the Humana hospital corporation. For months the reporters had been working on it, and David Jones, the chief executive officer of Humana, Inc., took the occasion to attack the *Courier-Journal* in public. At a Rotary Club lunch, Jones said that the *Courier-Journal* reporters' relentless questions were a sign that they "look for evil motives, and when they can't find them, they sometimes invent them." He went on to say that dourness often seems to be "a requirement for working at that place." The newspaper published Jones's remarks under the headline: "Humana Chairman Calls C-J a 'Problem.' " Mary and Barry Bingham were very upset about the newspaper's position on Humana and said publicly that they were opposed to the paper's policies.

Sallie Bingham was beginning to enjoy herself. Now, in May, she was scheduling interviews with newspapers and magazines to discuss her desire to sell her stock. "Breaking Away: Sallie Bingham Aims for Top Bid," the *Lexington Herald-Leader* headlined. Sallie was photographed in front of her large Victorian house in Louisville. "I asked questions and never got answers," Sallie told the reporter. "It took about six months before I realized there was no other solution." A local writer named Alanna Nash spent hours with Sallie interviewing her for *Working Woman.* Sallie told her all about her childhood, that she had been raised by the servants, that Nursie was more a mother to her than Mary had been, that her brothers were favored, that her writing career was a disaster, that she felt compelled to help women when she saw "a battered wife" go into a shelter in Louisville. She attacked the policies of the newspaper on minority hiring and lambasted the newspaper's editor, Paul Janensch. "I dislike Paul Janensch intensely. . . . Oh God, he is awful. He's terrible," she told Nash.

Finally, Sallie was getting the attention she had always wanted. Her mother was furious, and perhaps a bit envious. "Sallie is having the best time she has ever had giving all these interviews," her mother said. Sallie used the opportunity to announce what she intended to do with her new riches. She would start a foundation to help the women artists of Kentucky. Could anything have sounded more like a Bingham? In fact, Sallie had already rented a suite of offices in a distinguished downtown building two blocks from her brother's office at the newspaper. The offices were plush, painted in shades of pale blue and taupe. Sallie's every move became "an announcement," an opportunity for more press. She announced that she was hiring a black woman from Indiana named Maxine Brown to run the Kentucky Foundation for Women and an editor to put out a literary quarterly with a suitably grand name, the *American Voice*. Though Sallie had criticized her brother viciously for using nonunion labor for Standard Gravure, the *American Voice* would be printed in a nonunion shop as well. "Why didn't anyone tell me how much cheaper it was?" Sallie reportedly asked friends. Soon the phones would be ringing constantly with more requests for interviews from the new head of the Kentucky Foundation for Women. Sallie had already decided what her first grant would be: $25,000 for a tapestry about menstruation, which a Louisville artist was doing with the feminist painter Judy Chicago. "I am afraid Sallie will be preyed upon by all sorts of people looking for money for rather absurd projects," Barry Senior said.

That June it was muggy in Louisville and a hot wind was blowing off the Ohio River. The Bingham family problems were now public. "It is mortifying," Eleanor said then. Rowland was home a great deal because, as he said, "With all this business going on in the family, I can't get any work done." Barry Junior and Edie were home from Smith in time for another family meeting, but this time Barry Junior had an idea that he believed would make everyone happy. He told his parents he could not run the newspaper "with Eleanor and Rowland pecking at me all the time," so why didn't they trade stock? He would give Eleanor his television shares, she would give him the newspaper shares, they would figure out the numbers to make it financially equitable and then Eleanor would have complete control of the Bingham television and radio properties. Joan agreed with this plan and wanted to cast her lot with Barry Junior. Mary Bingham exploded, according to Barry Junior. "Do you think Eleanor would be happy with a mere sop like WHAS? That is pure blackmail," she said.

Barry Junior was astonished by this outburst and was as angry about his mother's remark as he had been in 1962, when he had been forced home from Washington to run the family stations. "That 'mere sop,' as Mother called it, was for what I gave up a great job in network television which I loved to work for this family," he said. Once again he felt himself in the same inferior position he had been in as a small child. However thin, rigid and disciplined he had become, here he was, fat, lazy and vague in his mother's eyes, the dull boy who had played the mellophone, being shown once again that his parents had no regard for his passion, television and radio, which they considered intellectually inferior to the printed word. "It was shocking," he said. "Besides the psychological argument, the television property was worth close to a hundred million."

Eleanor was in turmoil. She was beginning to think that Barry junior might be right. WHAS was valuable. She could run it, she believed, with ease. She began to talk about accepting the idea of her brother's "stock swap" as they were now calling the plan, if only Barry Junior would agree to pay Sallie the money she wanted. But Eleanor waffled. She was pregnant. Rowland did not want her to work so hard. Barry was being stubborn about meeting Sallie's price. Lawyers were calling constantly. Harvey Sloane was on the phone from Alaska, where he was on business. Eleanor's lawyer, Rucker Todd, had no doubt made it clear to her and Rowland exactly how rich they would be if the companies were sold. Mary and Barry Bingham, Eleanor said, were "beside themselves with anguish," while she said she was trying to be a good daughter, carrying messages to Sallie from her parents.

In Eleanor's bedroom was a shelf displaying a group of pictures. One showed a teenaged Sallie dressed like a princess clutching four-year-old Eleanor to her chest. "I won't do anything in this matter that is going to upset my sister," Eleanor told me that June in Louisville. "You know I am now convinced that Sallie and Barry Junior are exactly alike. They are both stubborn moralists convinced that they are right. They would die to think that they were similar to each other."

Barry Senior was agonized that the struggles in his family were about to be made public. Here was what he had always feared: scandal, public disclosure emerging from beneath the smooth façade. "My family is in an uproar," he said. "The lid is coming off now," a family member said. "And God knows where it will end."

The Bingham family problems were talked about all over Louisville that summer of 1985. Here was a scandal to rival what must have plagued Judge Bingham in the summer of 1917. The national newspapers picked it up, as they had once picked up the Kenan family allegations against the Judge. Barry Senior tried to appear jaunty and unruffled but he was obviously agitated. The other fine Louisville families sympathized with the Binghams, lauded their remarkable achievements and couldn't understand why such splendid people had to suffer such terrible distress. It was impossible to tell whether Sallie's decision to sell her stock was an act of liberation or of revenge. "I think after she was kicked off the board, Sallie decided that she could not forgive her father and was determined to cause him pain any way she could," Kathy Sloane said. The Louisville Country Club set could talk of little else. "This rupture is a cause célèbre in town," Sallie said happily.

Theories abounded. Paul Janensch talked about King Lear and speculated that the daughters were plotting to do in their father.

Sallie adhered to her version of events, the feminist argument that women in the family are mistreated. Eleanor blamed the problems in the family on what she called "the decline of the newspaper," a theory that reportedly was backed up by the Cherrys and the Sloanes. Friends speculated that Mary and Barry were unwilling to have the newspaper run by anyone except themselves and that they wanted their dream to die with them. "It is a peculiar family in which there seems to be no love," John Ed Pearce said. "Sallie seems to have resented her parents ever since I've known her. Apparently because she thought they neglected her. But the average person looking on from the outside world could not imagine two more ideal parents."

At the Little House, Mary and Barry tried to go on as usual. They read *Hay Fever* at their play-reading group. They took off for Chatham for several weeks to get away from the gossip and the speculation, and tried to stay as regal and impassive as they had always been. "It was just shredding to have the children in such disarray," Mary later said. As always, as a powerful family began to split apart there was a great deal of secret pleasure in the community. *All that money and power and they still couldn't get along. Thank God it wasn't us.* The local Republicans began to make comments about old Judge Bingham and how bad stock finally begins to show. "You know what they say," Kathy Sloane later told Joan Bingham. "The closer the parents, the more orphaned the children."

In July another family meeting was scheduled at the Seelbach Hotel. Mary and Barry were away in Chatham and missed this session. How odd it was, Joan remembered. The hotel was dark and gloomy, deserted in the summer heat, and the dark paneling with ancient photographs of Derby racehorses added to the eeriness. Almost seventy years before, Mary Lily Bingham had once suffered in this same setting, and now, as if she were exacting her revenge, three generations of Binghams gathered to decide the fate of the Judge's dream.

At the family meeting there was now a slight chance for a settlement. Eleanor had decided that she would agree to the stock swap, and that she would run WHAS. "We were thrilled," Joan said. "We called the parents to tell them and they said, 'Wait just a minute. You have not thought this through.'" Mary and Barry said they would come right home.

There would be considerable trust problems involved. "Trust 9" had been set up by the Judge for "M. C. Bingham et al." It held about 18 percent of the voting stock, but it was a crucial percentage. Mary and Barry had 51 percent of the vote, and Barry Junior and Sallie owned most of the remainder. If there was not a unanimous agreement to break Trust 9 by Sallie, Barry Junior, Joan, as guardian for Worth's children, and Eleanor, the

Binghams would have to petition the court to break the trust. The stock swap could not be negotiated unless the trust was terminated. "Daddy was terrified of having to make a public statement about what was going on in the family," Eleanor said. "He just could not bear the idea of a scandal." The lawyers drew up a model—how the shares would be traded, how capital gains taxes could be avoided. More pages of legal documents assaulted the family. But Mary and Barry were unsure that Eleanor could run WHAS. Barry Junior spent weeks working with his financial officers trying to come up with an offer to make Sallie for her stock. "I wanted to offer her something really low like ten million," Barry Junior said, "then she would have settled for twenty-five million. But my mother would not allow it and said, 'That is disreputable.' " And so an offer was made to Sallie for $25 million, which she immediately refused.

On the eighth of July Edie had a combined birthday party at the Big House for her younger daughter, Molly, and Eleanor. It was very humid that night, and Edie served a cold salmon outside on a terrace. She was in festive spirits because that very day Barry Senior and Junior had worked on a press release to announce the stock swap. Eleanor had been at the meeting but, characteristically, announced she had to go home before the draft was finished. Barry Junior said, "Eleanor did not say to us, 'Let me check the press release when we meet tonight.' " Eleanor had seemed content at the meeting to leave everything to her father and brother, but that night at the Big House she was angry, Edie remembered. "She said, 'Why wasn't I consulted about this?' It was as if she were backing out again." Clara, Robbie, Molly and Emily all said, "But you said you were going to run WHAS, Aunt Eleanor," Edie remembered. At dinner, even Mary Bingham seemed in a fit of pique at her daughter, according to Edie Bingham. "You said you were going to do this, Eleanor," she said. Eleanor pouted in front of some of Molly's school friends and said, "Why do I always have to sacrifice?" The party was a disaster. Rowland was belligerent. "How can you insult Eleanor by putting out a press release without consulting her?" Rowland said, according to Edie. "WHAS would have been the booby prize," Rowland later said. But the announcement of a tentative agreement to swap stock was made.

The day after the birthday party Edie wrote an earnest letter to her sister-in-law:

Dear Eleanor,
    . . . I think you should feel self-confident about your decision, and rely on your instinct and judgment and ability to listen and learn. You can *do* it well. . . . I think it is a serious mistake to enter this undertaking feeling you are

making a "sacrifice" as was mentioned several times last
night. . . . To view your efforts to manage an awesome responsibility to yourself, the community and the family in
any such context belittles and degrades the task and the
purpose and reasons for your decision. Stand tall, learn, and
go for it—with love,

                                                        Edie

Eleanor, however, would not be inspired by Edie's note. A
few weeks later she confided in Joan that she was "terrified"
about running WHAS because of her belief that she would not
do an adequate job. "I don't think I can do a good enough job
to please Barry," she said. "Don't worry about him, do it for
yourself," Joan told Eleanor, who paid no attention to this fine
advice.

34

Throughout the crisis in their family, Mary and Barry Bingham seemed almost ageless, still in love and as locked together as they had been when they would rise at dawn to watch the horses working out at Churchill Downs. But now, in addition to their love, they also shared their anguish over the struggle in the family and were deeply mortified by Sallie's interviews in the press. They could control the *Courier-Journal* through their stock, but they could not control their children. The Bingham ownership of the newspaper had begun as the redemption of Barry's father's reputation. Now it was ending in greed and rage that was going to bring the family down. All civility had evaporated. Now raw emotions ruled the family.

In the end, the family would not fade with dignity. There would be no privacy and no discretion. Barry Junior, Sallie and Eleanor each spoke of their "morals" and their individual principles, and each was desperate for Mary and Barry's approval. There could be no peace between the three surviving children as Mary and Barry had wished.

That autumn, Mary and Barry burrowed in at the Little House as their three children surrounded themselves with lawyers and attempted to define "positions." Sallie was hardly speaking to Mary and Barry, and was closeted with her own lawyer, Rebecca Westerfield, a prominent local feminist. Barry Junior was cold, but still polite. All through the autumn he continued to have strained lunches with his father once a week. Later his father would complain that Barry Junior never talked to him directly about what was going on in the company. "You can't have it both ways. He told me he didn't want to know," Barry Junior later said. Only Eleanor and Rowland lavished attention on Mary and Barry. "We took Rollie over every day to see that their spirits stayed up," Eleanor said. Mary suffered from insomnia, and railed against Sallie to Eleanor, blaming her for bringing on all the problems. Eleanor was just about to give birth to her second child, and her mother hovered over her. "Poor Eleanor had had such a tough time of it before Rollie was born, we were worried about her," Mary later said.

In October Sallie made a counteroffer to Barry Junior. She would accept $32 million for her stock. Barry Junior said, "Absolutely not," and said he would "counter" her counteroffer. Meanwhile Eleanor and Barry Junior could not agree about the stock swap because he would still be in control of the newspaper. "I could not trust Barry with my dividend income," she said. Barry and Eleanor disagreed about what Barry should offer to pay Sallie for her stock. In the meantime, Sallie told local reporters that she was convinced her brother wanted to be relieved of his burden and wanted the newspapers to be sold.

In October there was cause for celebration. A new baby came into the family. Eleanor called her new son Robert Worth Miller. She had given him the same name as his cousin Rob, the son of his uncle Worth, the descendant of his great-grandfather (the Judge, the original North Carolina colonel).

In the end, everyone had his or her own good reasons for refusing to change positions. The reasons were "rational," they made perfect sense, and expensive lawyers had spent months drafting position papers for each camp. Eleanor had now decided definitively: she would not take WHAS. She sent a memo to the family in which she said that she wanted the companies completely sold. It stated that it would be "a mistake" for her to run WHAS. Her reasons, as always, appeared logical. She listed legal minutiae, such as potential problems with the Internal Revenue Service, the Federal Communications Commission and Trust 9. She said that she felt the stock swap would be impossible, that Louisville was not a potentially viable economy for television and that she didn't want to be mired in a poor investment. Her husband, Rowland, backed her completely. Like all Binghams, she hid her real feelings behind an apparently rational surface. "I did not want Barry Junior to have the newspaper," she finally said. "That would mean that he had won."

Barry's stock-swap proposal had become seventy pages of legal documents by early November. Mary and Barry told their son they would not break open the trust agreements to effect the stock swap. To add to their woes, the family was now drowning in legal paperwork. Barry Junior was desperate now to save the newspapers, and had a new idea that he called the Wednesday Plan. He would sell WHAS Inc. and Standard Gravure, buy out Eleanor and Sallie, and keep the newspapers for his family and for Joan's. With the proceeds of the sale, Joan and Barry Junior could well afford to buy out Eleanor and Sallie. That proposal, he believed, would give Sallie and Eleanor each a minimum of $37 million, $5 million more than Sallie's asking price. Through their lawyers, Barry had shown the Wednesday Plan to his father, who at first thought it was the ideal solution. He told George Gill that he would announce it at the next family meeting scheduled for November 20.

The meeting was held in the boardroom of the *Courier-Journal,* and that day Barry Senior was angry. It was remarkable, Joan remembered, that there wasn't a hint of his usual civility. "I am going to run this meeting," he said in a tone that defied challenge, Eleanor later remembered. "Daddy said, 'Before we start this meeting, I don't want a lot of recrimination and slanging.' He said this to me and Rowland, Edie, Barry and Joan." At that point, Gordon Davidson stood up and handed out a sheet of paper that proposed to sell WHAS and Standard Gravure. The Wednesday Plan was Barry Junior's last best hope.

But when Eleanor read the plan, she could not restrain herself. "If this plan is approved, Rowland and I will have to leave Louisville," she said.

Mary looked stricken at Eleanor's outburst. Later Eleanor explained, "I felt I was being forced out of the company and that I would not be able to live in Louisville under these circumstances." Rowland said it was "a punitive action," and the meeting broke up. But Barry Senior insisted that he thought the Wednesday Plan was workable and the best idea so far.

Rowland and Eleanor later attempted to rationalize their outburst at the meeting. "Eleanor was trying to make it easier for her parents to do what she thought they wanted to do," Rowland said. "The thing I was working for was family unity," Eleanor added. That was hardly the case, however. Eleanor was violently opposed to the Wednesday Plan because she perceived it as an attempt by her brother to shut her and Sallie out of the newspaper. "He would have at last gotten rid of me and Sallie, which was his number one priority," Eleanor said. Eleanor said her lawyer pointed out other flaws in the plan: she could make twice the money if the companies were completely sold; Barry Junior and Joan would be taking on a tremendous load of debt—how could they pay estate taxes after Mary and Barry died, when they could be as much as $24 million if media stocks kept booming? "The other aspect of the Wednesday Plan which was bad was that Eleanor's parents would get nothing then, and they had many things they wanted to do before they died. They wanted to fund Louisville charities and give money to Harvard. This way they would be sacrificing once again for Barry Junior," Rowland Miller said. "It's not like my parents ever had an extra nickel to give to charity," Eleanor said. But Eleanor and Rowland were wrong. If the Wednesday Plan had been approved, the sale of WHAS alone would have brought Mary and Barry

Bingham over $10 million, enough to fund any cause they wanted to.

No doubt Rowland and Eleanor conveyed their feelings to Mary and Barry over the next few weeks. At the same time Eleanor was agitating with her brother about an alternative idea for the Wednesday Plan: "Offer Sallie $28 million for her stock." Eleanor later said that she put a note under Sallie's door begging her to accept that price. In the meantime, Sallie had heard, of course, about the Wednesday Plan from her lawyers. Barry Junior believed that there was collusion between the sisters. "All Eleanor had to do was to keep making trouble and she could force the sale of the company," Barry Junior said. "Barry is a paranoid," Eleanor said. "And Edie is power-mad all the way. It is very hidden. It's wear the plain clothes and hide the diamonds and rubies in the vault." Eleanor and Sallie did not like the Wednesday Plan because it had no "look-back." Eleanor said, "If the *Courier-Journal* were sold in five years, there was no way we could get a reevaluation of our price and our stock. It just seemed that I was being tossed out."

With all this dissension, Mary and Barry soon changed their minds and told their son that the Wednesday Plan would cripple their estate. "There would be two very heavy death duties and many things that needed replacing at the newspaper," Mary said. Barry Junior violently disagreed and thought his parents were being condescending and, once again, taking his sister's side. He believed they they disliked what he was doing at the newspaper, his aloofness from the political people, his attacks on Harvey Sloane and Humana. He had heard they disliked his editor, Paul Janensch, as did many of their friends. But wasn't he the person who had been able to budget the newspaper and get the profits up? They begged him to increase his offer to Sallie for her stock. He refused. Goldman, Sachs had now been hired by the company to discuss the sale of Standard Gravure and WHAS. The Goldman, Sachs bankers ran up numbers for Barry Junior at least a dozen times with different variables, what the company could afford the pay Sallie if the profits dropped to 5 percent, 4 percent, what would happen if ever there was zero growth. It all worked out the same: the *Courier-Journal* could afford to pay Sallie a minimum of $28 million and would not even be crippled by giving her exactly what she wanted—$32 million. Now a new plan, Project Ambassador, was being discussed by the lawyers. Project Ambassador was the code name for the eventual sale of the newspapers, should it come to that. "That has to have been named by the sickest mind in Louisville," Barry Junior later said. In fact it was Barry's own lawyer, Gordon Davidson, and the Goldman, Sachs bankers who had come up with the name.

Barry Junior's final offer was $26.3 million, which Sallie and her lawyers rejected as "not being in good faith." Eleanor said, "After all, they had come down millions from their original $42 million asking price, which was what Sallie always wanted." Two weeks before Mary Bingham's eighty-first birthday Barry Senior made his announcement, "We will have Christmas as usual and then I will decide what I am going to do with these companies." Since Barry Senior controlled the voting stock of the company, he could decide to sell the entire empire, but tragically and paradoxically, he could not force his children to settle among themselves. Furthermore, he seemed determined not to overrule Barry Junior by insisting that he give Sallie her final price of $32 million, a move that would have kept the company in Bingham hands. "We would no longer have been a Cadillac operation," Mary later explained, meaning that the newspaper would have a cash shortage and would not be able to afford the lavish news staff. Barry Junior and Joan told Mary, "Who cares if the newspaper is a Chevrolet? At least it would be our Chevrolet." For his part, Barry Junior wanted his father to decide in favor of his new idea: the Wednesday Plan. In December, Barry Junior said to his father, "If you decide that you are going to sell the *Courier-Journal,* then I am going public with my feelings that it is a betrayal of what this family has always stood for."

Christmas, 1985. There was no use pretending anymore, or to let the dance of manners go on. That Christmas, Edie and Barry had a dinner as usual at the Big House, but Roland and Eleanor did not attend. "I hadn't felt welcome in their house for a long time," Rowland said. On Christmas day, however, Eleanor took her children for a short visit. She was turning out to be as skilled a diplomat as her father, very much like him, in fact— the same warm façade, the same charm. Eleanor's new baby, who was called Worth, was to be christened two days before Christmas, the day before her mother's birthday. "It was not without considerable thought that one of Sallie's children and one of Barry's children were made godparents to Worth," she said. The christening was held at St. Francis in the Fields, the arena of so many previous Bingham events. Barry and Edie were there, but not Sallie. "She didn't want to see Barry Junior and Daddy," Eleanor said. "But she did allow Chris to be the godfather of Worth."

Just after the new year Barry Bingham called his son and younger daughter and told them to be at the Little House on January 8, 1986, at 10:00 A.M. He left a message for Sallie, but she did not return his call. Joan was in the Orient. That morning of January 8, when he awakened he "felt like I had a black cloud over my head," he later said. At last the horrible morning

had arrived when Barry Senior would announce his "dread decision" to sell his newspaper empire, even though he would later
explain to a grandson that he knew the sale would "wound the
heart" of Barry Junior. Sixty-eight years of Bingham dreams
were about to come down to this gray morning at the Little
House when Barry Senior would tell Barry Junior and Eleanor
that he was going to sell everything—the newspapers, the television station, Standard Gravure.

As Barry Junior and Eleanor sat in the library with its editions
of Faulkner and Marquand, Mary and Barry Senior stood before
them. Barry Senior said he had his own good reasons for the
sale, that his behavior was not directed at his son. He said he
wanted peace for the family and to put an end to the public
scandal. As Barry Junior took in the enormity of his father's
words he could not stop himself from blurting out, "This is a
complete betrayal of everything this family stands for." Barry's
outburst shocked Eleanor. Binghams did not talk that way. All
his life Barry Junior had done his parents' bidding. He had taken
the miserable reading drills; suffered pituitary shots for the sake
of his mother's phobias; he had given up his dreams of Africa
and, far more important, he had turned his back on something
he loved, network television, to be a good Bingham son. He had
worked through his radiation treatments, his problems with his
stepchildren, his parents' refusal to search out a first-class editor
to help him run the newspaper. And this was where it had
brought him, to the Little House that cold, dank January morning when he drank coffee in his parents' jewel of a library and
waited to be fired by his father—in effect, to find himself in mid-
life without a newspaper and a job.

The next day, when they met to exchange public statements,
Eleanor remembered her father's words to her brother: "There
is no point in your pointing a finger at me. Everyone in town is
going to stand by me, not you." Later, Eleanor said, "There is
no point in opposing that man. He is one of the great movers
and shakers of the community. For a child or anyone else to go
around and say ugly things about him is just asking for it."

That day Eleanor took her parents out to lunch and offered to
call all the grandchildren. "I will do it myself," her father said.
He reached Joan, Clara and Rob in Hong Kong, where they were
spending the Christmas holidays. It was 5:00 A.M. Hong Kong
time. Rob answered the telephone. "It was very eerie," Rob
said later. "I cried a little bit. It was like the end of a dream."
Such was Barry Senior's state of mind that he had detached himself completely from his usual façade of consideration for others
and did not even ask to speak to Joan. "Please tell your mother,"
he said. Barry Junior and Edie found Joan in Hong Kong too.

"None of this would have happened if Worth hadn't been killed," Edie said, her voice breaking on the telephone.

That day Barry Bingham Senior posted his announcement on the bulletin board at the *Courier-Journal*. Barry Junior's statement was directly next to it, calling his father's decision "a betrayal" and "irrational." The two sheets of paper appeared at 1:00 P.M. Sallie, who had no idea what had gone on in the Little House the day before, was having lunch with two friends when she was called to the telephone. It was Elinor Brecher from the *Courier-Journal*. "Your father has just posted an announcement that the newspapers are going to be sold," Brecher told her. "Oh my God," Sallie cried into the phone as if she had been told of a death in the family, "I never wanted this to happen."

But it was too late now. When Sallie got back to the table she was shaken, one of the women later told Elinor Brecher. But her maneuvers, her anger, her notes, had set in motion an inexorable process. Later that day she was composed enough to go on the radio and make a statement. "It is for the best," she said. "There is no inherent virtue in a family ownership."

The next day both Barry Junior's and Barry Senior's announcements ran in the *Courier-Journal*. "Sale by Binghams Marks End of Era in Kentucky Journalism," the *New York Times* headlined its coverage, and reprinted both statements. Barry Senior said he hoped this sale would effect "healing" in the family; and was astonished that "every major newspaper and magazine in this country has called me." Barry Senior sent a copy of the *Courier-Journal* with the announcement of the sale to the reporter Theodore White, a friend from the Marshall Plan days.

The publicity could have ended at that moment. Barry Senior might have said enough was enough, that he would not discuss family matters with reporters. After all, the Binghams were sophisticated about the press. They were discreet. They knew how to say "No comment," which would have stopped many stories from ever being written. But the Binghams did not say "No comment." Instead, they scheduled interview after interview. "The only way we can communicate with each other is through journalists. Because reporters are impersonal. Reporters will not scream if we say what is on our mind. Reporters will not tell us that we have no right to think the things we do. It is just easier to let messengers take our words back and forth," Sallie said. As Mary said, "We all have our separate pride."

Why do you hate your mother? the reporters asked Sallie. Why did you throw your brother's cat in the fire? They asked his parents, Did Jonathan take drugs? Did Jonathan commit suicide? What was wrong with the Wednesday Plan? Did the Judge really murder Mrs. Flagler? One reporter asked Barry to re-create the day his mother was killed. What was it like when Henrietta had breakdowns? With these reporters, the senior Binghams had no taboo subjects. Everything was fair. Mary cried sometimes. But she never said to the reporters, "We have no comment to make."

For the record, Mary was determined that Sallie "not speak for this family." Mary was furious that Sallie had publicly accused her of neglect. She did not know what she had done to bring this nightmare to her family and was forced to confide in total strangers. Every time her daughter said, "My mother was too busy with her correspondence to spend time with me," Mary had to answer, "Sallie is a creature of her fantasies. She was a beloved child." It was demeaning, humiliating, this public point and counterpoint. What was worse, at any moment Mary or Barry could have said, *Stop! This vulgar behavior cannot go on.* But they didn't. However anguished Mary and Barry were, they seemed to welcome the attention they were now getting. The reporters flattered them. They called them heroic. They marveled at their grace and dignity in the face of their overwhelming tragedies. Mary and Barry could hardly speak directly with Barry Junior and Sallie, but they had no reservations about discussing them with national reporters. "We are shredded. But it is my unwelcome duty to speak to the press," Mary said.

Late afternoon, Louisville. A New York photographer was setting up his shades and lights in the Binghams' living room. He had been sent down to Louisville by a national magazine to take the photographs for an upcoming story on the Binghams and their problems. For the photographer it was just another magazine assignment—Go shoot the Binghams for the May issue—a quick trip down to Louisville on US Air, a hamburger at the Seelbach, making sure the releases for the pictures were signed properly. "I love these decline-and-fall stories," he said in the car. "Let's hope we can wrap it up by tomorrow and get back to New York."

As the photographer set up his equipment his assistant stared at a Foujita nude over the mantel that Barry and Mary had bought so many years ago in Paris in the glory of their youth. He marveled at the realism and the sexuality of Foujita's model, unaware, of course, that for part of her childhood, Eleanor Bingham was convinced the nude was a portrait of her mother, such was the aura of sensuality in her home.

Only a few weeks had passed since Barry Senior had announced the sale of his family's newspaper, but he seemed jaunty, almost eager to be of help. "Isn't that picture lovely?" he said. "It is our very favorite. Mary found it when we were in Paris with the Marshall Plan." At interviews he had spoken with the same cool detachment about his children's individual and collective anguish, about Sallie's "deep distress" over the drug problems of her son and Eleanor's hippie days. He mentioned Barry Junior's reading problems and his rage over the sale of the newspaper. "I don't see how my son can expect me not to change my mind about a decision to let him run these newspapers that I made over fifteen years ago," he said.

This day in the Little House, he told stories about the war, and how he took the press around then too, as if his own family's turmoil was another war, another press opportunity that he must mastermind. The distinguished chairman of the *Courier-Journal*, a titan of American journalism, did his duty for the fourth estate. Nothing was too personal. This was another form of public service, after all. He was pleased to talk about how Mary found the Foujita nude at the Salon des Indépendants, "lo, so many years ago."

Mary was not in the living room. She was sitting in the tiny library with the picture of Sallie with Barry Ellsworth as a baby still in place on the mantel, as were the wedding pictures of Worth and Barry Junior and their innocent young brides. At that moment Mary Bingham, who had once come to Melcombe with such high hopes, was crying. Her cheeks glistened with tears. She had just learned, she explained, that Sallie said that she had every intention of writing a book about the family. Sallie had told a friend of Mary's that she intended to say everything, even the ultimate horror, about her grandfather's role in the death of Mary Lily. And so Mary Bingham wept. "Sallie's book will be filled with lies, half-truths, distortions. Why would she do this to us? Doesn't she know that anything she could say would break her father's heart? The idea of this book sends my blood running cold."

The photographer waited in the living room. Finally, he walked down the hall to the library, passing the picture of Franklin Roosevelt that had been on the table for years. "We are ready, Mrs. Bingham," he said. "All right," she said. Mary Bingham stood and walked very slowly toward her yellow sitting room to pose in front of the fireplace. She had stopped crying, but she was grave. "Doesn't my daughter care about my grandchildren? What kind of legacy will it be for us to leave?" she asked me as she walked into the room.

"Mrs. Bingham, will you please sit in front of the fireplace on the bench with your husband?" the photographer asked. "Of course," she said, then Barry took his wife's arm gently and steered her to the wooden bench, as carefully and with as much love as he had escorted her everywhere for almost sixty years. But he seemed oblivious to her mood, as if he was unaware that she had been weeping moments before. Barry Senior bantered

with the English photographer about the origins of his name.
Mary's eyes were red from weeping and she did not laugh at
Barry's jokes.

"Shall we start now?" the photographer said.

"By all means," Barry Senior said.

"May I look at Barry now?" Mary said.

"Of course," the photographer said.

"That's good," Mary said, and with those words, she turned
toward the love of her life and took his hand. "Thank God, one
does not have the powers of Cassandra in this life. I am afraid
I don't know what I would have done so many years ago if I had
known how my lovely family would turn out," she said very
quietly. Her audience for this remark was strangers, a reporter
and a photographer, both of whom tried to contain their tears.

The decision to sell the newspapers should have been, as Mary
and Barry hoped, the beginning of the healing process for the
family. It was hardly that. Within days of the announcement the
family had a new dilemma, which was how to respond to one
another's remarks in the press. The story of the Binghams' tra-
vails was written about in *Time*, the *Washington Post*, the *New
York Times*, the *Los Angeles Times* and dozens of other newspapers around the country. The newspaper stories, for the most
part, were laudatory and detailed the rich history of the *Courier-
Journal*, the splendor of Melcombe, the tragedies of the sons. If
there were hints of the Mary Lily Flagler scandal, the references
were vague. It might have been mentioned that the Judge inherited $5 million of Mary Lily's money when she died eight months
after they were married, but there was only the faintest sugges-
tion that there might have been foul play.

In any event, Barry Senior was preoccupied with the sale of
the newspaper and had hired Goldman, Sachs to represent the
family at the sale. He was convinced, he told his family, that
they would make a "quality" sale and would never sell to a
buyer that wasn't suitable. He hoped that the *Washington Post*
or the *New York Times* would be the ultimate publisher of the
Courier-Journal and would maintain the same high standards he
had sought for the papers his whole life. A sale to the *Post* or
the *Times* would be a fitting end to the Bingham ownership, he
truly believed. It would be another type of award, another cer-
tification of the family's liberal ideals. After all, as he said to
his family, Punch and Kay, as he called Punch Sulzberger of the
Times and Katharine Graham of the *Washington Post*, were old
friends. They knew how distinguished his newspaper was. He
felt he would not be forced to sell to Gannett or to any of the
other faceless publishing conglomerates. "I wouldn't consider a
sale where they do not keep up the quality of the paper," he

said. Goldman, Sachs began to work on a list of "covenants" that a new owner would be expected to adhere to: The promise to maintain the 5 percent tithing to Louisville charities, to keep the day-care facilities and the *Courier-Journal* gym, and to continue the support of the Binghams' projects, Save a Tree and the Crusade for Children. At the first meeting, when one of the young bankers addressed Barry Senior as "Barry," Gordon Davidson pulled him aside. "No one addresses Mr. Bingham that way," he said.

From Brown University, Rob Bingham sent his grandfather a long letter asking him not to sell the family newspaper to friends who might not pay the proper price, such as Katharine Graham of the *Washington Post* or the Sulzberger family of the *Times*. Rob's letter was heartfelt, and his grandfather used it as another opportunity for a semipublic forum. He distributed Rob's letter to everyone in the family, then wrote him back a three-page single-spaced response and sent copies to ten family members. In the letter, Barry Senior apologized for not consulting his grandchildren about the sale as he had promised to do, and described how he and Mary had wrestled with their "dreadful dilemma." He said that he hoped that the next generation of Binghams would not be as torn with hatred and dissension as his own children were, and he expressed regret for "wounding the heart" of Barry Junior. He said that he would not argue his position, for he disliked the fact that the family was taking sides. And he reminisced about his own days as a publisher in an "easier time" when he could have influence and access, factors that more than offset the accusations that he was "a Communist," a "war monger before World War II" and "a nigger lover" over the telephone at 2:00 A.M. He told his grandchildren that he did not want any response to his letter because he did not want to become another source of dissension, but later his granddaughters Emily and Molly would say that this was another example of their grandfather refusing to continue a dialogue he had begun. Edie was angry about this letter, and wrote Clara, Rob, Emily and Molly a two-page letter in which she sought to clarify the points she found "offensive and/or confusing" in "Grandy's recent letter to Rob."

Grandy made a decision *for* Uncle Barry, that he 'could not see it as a way of life for him that could bring satisfaction. . . .' It is a cruel and patronizing attitude to assume decisive power over a mature adult's future life without consulting him in any way or discussing the circumstances which persuade one to take such a drastic step. . . .

Granny and Grandy have suffered terribly through this, but until they and all of us ask ourselves why, and are will-

ing to hear and give candid answers, I am afraid that the
peace that has been bought for us will be elusive and beyond
purchase. . . .

For weeks Barry Junior kept his distance from his father as
he debated what to do: should he stay on as publisher to help
his father effect the sale? "I don't know why Barry Junior can't
reconcile himself to our dilemma," Mary said repeatedly. Finally, Barry Junior decided he would do his duty, and another
announcement was made in the press: he would stay through the
sale.

Just before Barry Senior's eightieth birthday, a reporter from
People made an appointment to see the chairman of the board.
The writer, David Chandler, was a friend of Sallie's, and had
written several books, including a biography of Henry Flagler,
the railroad magnate and Standard Oil tycoon. He had once been
on a news team at a Florida paper that had won a Pulitzer for
public-service reporting. Bingham was pleased to greet him—a
Pulitzer Prize winner—but was upset when he left. Although
Chandler and his wife were ostensibly in Louisville to report on
the family collapse for *People,* they informed Barry Senior that
they were deep into research on a book about his father. And
according to Barry Senior, they began to ask him some tough
reporter's questions: Did Judge Bingham murder Mary Lily
Flagler? Who were the nurses that took care of Mrs. Flagler at
the end? Why was the codicil written by hand? How did she
become addicted to morphine?

The interview was followed by a five-page letter from the
Chandlers with more questions about the murder allegations.
Barry Senior told his family that he was astonished and horrified
by this document and immediately turned it over to his lawyers
to draft a response. He told his daughter Eleanor that these
journalists' questions "sounded like pure blackmail." He had
come to his eightieth birthday having blotted out the central
incident of his adolescence, and he knew no answers to most of
Chandler's questions, but he was soon to be as agitated by the
questions as he must have been in 1917 by the events themselves.
He instructed Gordon Davidson to draft a lengthy answer to
Chandler, as if to remove himself from the process altogether,
in the same way he might have removed himself as a child. As
the months passed Chandler's biography would grow to haunt
Barry Bingham's days.

But that was yet to come. All through the spring of 1986 Barry
Senior was involved with lawyers and the Goldman, Sachs representatives who were trying to organize the sale. The bankers
were Gary Gensler, a vice president, and Bob Thornton, his

associate. They were young, but they did a splendid job. Gensler
was appalled by the number of stories being written about he
family and told the Binghams firmly that the media circus was
going to have to stop. "What if someone in the family decided
to tell the press who was bidding?" Gensler said. "It could have
badly affected the sale." They insisted that the family sign a
confidentiality agreement because of the amount of attention the
Bingham feud was getting. Barry Junior was opposed to this.
"I'm a journalist," he said. "If I know it I am going to tell it."

Barry Senior had spent the morning a few days after his eightieth birthday watching Sallie on the *Phil Donahue Show.* By now
Sallie was able to deliver her public statements professionally:
how the family believed in "smoothness"; how her brother had
a traditional Kentucky attitude toward women. Sallie looked good
on television; her head thrown back nodding, her answers to Phil
Donahue appeared marvelously spontaneous. She had a new forum and she excelled at using it, basking in the attention. But
the audience wasn't taken with Sallie, and some of her question-
ers appeared to think she was greedy. "The Lady from Kentucky," a woman in the audience called out. "Do you realize
what it's like to roll pennies?" a caller asked. "The question
here has to do with fairness," Sallie said.

On the show Donahue asked her, "The point is that wealth
alters everything, doesn't it?" She answered, "It does make it
harder to develop a value system." When a woman asked,
"When you were children did you ever wish you were just like
everyone else?" Sallie said, "No, I loved it." And she said she
thought her parents loved all of them, in their own way. Later
that morning, Barry Senior, ever the optimist, said about her
appearance, "I was glad to see that kind of gesture . . . because
I would love to see a reconciliation. . . . I think she wants it to
happen."

Mary was horrified by her daughter's performance; she said,
"She craves recognition and this is very important to her. And
I think she has never enjoyed anything so much as this episode
in her life," and added that she believed Sallie was a hypocrite.
"She told her son Chris that she wasn't going to leave him any
money. She said, 'You are a man and you can make your own
way.' " Mary was particularly upset about this because "darling
Chrissie," as she called him, had been told by his mother that
the reason she wanted to sell her stock in the newspapers was
that he would never be given "a proper voice." And now that
the papers were sold, she was cutting him off. "I don't know
what has come over Sallie," her mother said. "Perhaps her behavior has been brought on by her analysis."

Diane Sawyer then brought the *60 Minutes* camera crew to
Louisville. The family had debated whether or not to appear.

"Our friends can't imagine what on earth we were thinking of," Mary later said. Sawyer filmed for hours, and her first question to Barry Junior was, "Do you still love your mother?" At the end of the interview she put her arms around her old friend and said, "I feel so sorry for you." The *60 Minutes* camera was relentless. Mary described Jonathan's death. She said her daughter Sallie "lives in a world of fantasy." Eleanor said her own family reminded her of *Dallas*, and Barry Junior said he felt that he had "failed." Sallie talked about the specialness and the smoothness of their life and what the cost had been. When Diane Sawyer came back to New York, she felt strangely out of sorts. "They were all so clinical and cold," she told me. "I felt as if I were being used as a messenger. When I was growing up in Louisville, the Binghams represented dignity. I was seared seeing them behave this way."

Just after the filming, Edie Bingham wrote her parents-in-law another earnest letter, trying to make peace. "This is to test the waters ever so tentatively to see how we can all relate to each other in the future," Edie wrote. Barry Bingham wrote a note back which said that he and Mary would have to wait and see how *60 Minutes* turned out.

What was even stranger than Barry Senior's letter was that Barry Junior assigned a reporter to write a full magazine supplement about the family. "Why is it important to publish it now?" his father said. "Why not?" Barry Junior said, as if to exercise his final power as publisher. "The *New York Times* had an article. The *Wall Street Journal* had an article. The *Boston Globe* had an article. When is the *Courier-Journal* going to have the quintessential article on the Bingham family? You ought to be able to read the *Courier-Journal* and get the best-informed article on this that you're going to read anywhere." "Why now?" his father said. "Why not?" Barry Junior said. Barry Senior showed a proof copy of the *Courier-Journal* piece to Eleanor and Rowland, who reportedly were angry that Ward had described their "glitzy" life-style. Gordon Davidson, the *Courier-Journal*'s own lawyer, then wrote Barry Junior a letter saying the magazine supplement could be injurious to the sale. "Talk about a betrayal," Barry Junior said. "There was Gordon Davidson doing my father's bidding, as always. All our liberal principles vanished into hypocrisy," Barry Junior said.

Soon a promotion for the family radio station called Bingham Bucks Sweepstakes was playing on WHAS. Bingham Bucks featured a series of TV spots that imitated the opening credits of *Dallas*. One scene had the actual pillars at the entrance to the road that led to Melcombe. The narrator said, "The Binghams! The epic tale of a family empire built and sold—but not before the 84-WHAS family gives away the family fortune!" Mary

Bingham complained about "the obscene vulgarity of this promotion. . . . The sale of these properties is not a joke to us. It's far from it." Mary was so angry about this campaign that she called Barry Junior in Massachusetts, told him to take it off the air and then hung up on him.

By April Goldman, Sachs had drawn up a list of potential buyers and the family's convenants. All the Binghams were required to sign the contract for sale before a buyer could see it so that there could be no disputes after the process began. Newspaper companies began to visit Louisville. Sydney Gruson, who had courted Barry Senior for so many years, arrived with the delegation from the *Times*. As Barry Senior began to talk about hopes for the newspaper, Gruson reportedly said, "We know how to run newspapers, let's just have a look at the printing plant." Ben Bradlee came from the *Washington Post* and toured the newsroom. Allen Neuharth, the chairman of Gannett, came to Louisville, and three limousines were parked outside the modest *Courier-Journal* building. Neuharth wore his little-finger ring and his trademark black-and-white suit. He strolled through the lobby as if he were a conquistador. "It was such an incredible contrast, new money versus old money," a Bingham executive said. All through the process, the bankers remembered, Barry Bingham Senior did not reveal a shred of ambivalence. "He seemed intensely relieved," one said. Barry Junior, who was after all the newspaper's publisher, did not participate in the lunches and the meetings with the buyers. "It was very odd," one banker said. But it wasn't odd at all. Barry Bingham Senior had simply decided to eliminate all pretense that his son was running the newspaper.

The bids for the newspaper came in from the *Washington Post*, from Jack Kent Cooke, who owned the Washington Redskins and the *Los Angeles Daily News*, and from Gannett. In the end, the *New York Times* refused even to bid for the Louisville *Courier-Journal*. The executives said it was a dinosaur, the town wasn't prosperous and the newspaper was much too expensive to run. However humiliating it was, Barry Senior asked his bankers to call Kay Graham and Ben Bradlee at the *Washington Post* to up their bid so that at least the *Courier-Journal* could stay in elitist hands. But the *Washington Post* refused, despite the years of friendships and dinner parties. After all, money was at stake. In the end, the family had to decide to sell to the highest bidder, which was, of course, Gannett.

On Friday, May 6, the family met at the Brown hotel in Louisville to review the bids. Gary Gensler led the discussion. There was tremendous tension in the room. The family members were separated by their lawyers, although Barry Junior and Joan sat together. When Mary saw Sallie come into the room, she put her cheek up and received a chilly kiss. "Hello, Mother," Sallie said, as if she had seen her the day before, though in fact the two had not seen each other for months. There were no surprises at the meeting, and the Gannett jets were already landing at Standiford Field.

That night Mary gave a dinner at the Little House for the entire family. Sallie and Tim Peters came, as did Joan and her son, Rob. Barry and Edie were there, as was Eleanor, but Rowland did not come. He said he had "an allergy attack." It was clear to Rob Bingham that his aunt Eleanor was angry with Rowland for not showing up, but Mary tried to make light of it and prepared some food for Eleanor to take him, as if nothing in the world was wrong. The years of breeding shone mightily that Friday night. Mary looked elegant in a floral chiffon hostess gown that Barry Senior had bought for her at Bergdorf Goodman. The evening was cool and correct, Mary later said. Edie sat next to Barry Senior. Joan sat between Tim Peters and Barry Junior. At dinner the subject of Emily Bingham's Harvard thesis came up. "She is studying a group of post–Civil War poets," Edie said. "Why isn't she writing about Renaissance writers?" Mary said. "Because she is majoring in American history, Mother," Barry Junior said.

All that weekend, Barry Bingham Junior brooded: What did I do, what should I have done? On Saturday Barry Senior walked over to the Big House, where Joan, Edie and Barry Junior were playing tennis. "This is my press release about the Gannett sale," he said. "It is flat," his son said. On Sunday night, workmen built a platform so that Neuharth could address the newsroom. Although the official announcement of the sale wasn't scheduled until Monday morning, there was no doubt who the buyer would be. The price was $307 million for the Louisville *Courier-Journal* and the *Louisville Times*. The family was selling their other companies separately. From the newspapers alone Mary and Barry would receive almost $100 million, Sallie and Eleanor approximately $40 million each, and Barry Junior and Joan and her children close to $29 million. In the newsroom, Al Neuharth said how happy he was to have completed his triple crown, the acquisition of the Des Moines *Register,* the Detroit *News* and now the "sparkling jewel," the *Courier-Journal.* Barry Senior said, "There is a time to sow and a time to reap." Barry Junior said, "This is a day I had hoped never to live to see."

That night Mary and Barry Bingham flew to Washington on the Gannett jet for a party at Gannett headquarters. Barry Junior chose not to attend. Eleanor and Rowland were making plans to take off for East Hampton, where they had leased Ben Bradlee's house for the month of July. Sallie gave a party at her new million-dollar farm, Wolf Pen, to "celebrate" the sale. She called it the "shout" party because, as a friend said, "It's all over but the shouting." Clara Bingham arrived from Hong Kong and went to see her grandmother. "I don't know why Barry Junior cannot reconcile himself to our dilemma. Doesn't he realize that he will now have a fortune and can do anything he wants?" Mary told her granddaughter. Joan and Mary had tea at the Little House and Joan began to cry: "This is the end of my children's patrimony." Mary wept as well, Joan remembered. "At least it was an honest emotional exchange," Joan later said. Soon after, WHAS-TV was sold to the Providence Journal Company for $85.7 million; Standard Gravure, to an Atlanta businessman named John Shea for $20 million; and WHAS-AM and WAMZ-FM, to Clear Channel Communications of San Antonio for $20 million.

And two days after the sale of the newspaper was announced, an odd and inappropriate letter Mary Bingham had written to the editor of the *Courier-Journal* was published in the newspaper. As if she had retreated into the same obsession that had taken her mind off Jonathan's death, Mary's letter concerned the modernization of the Book of Common Prayer and an upcoming visit to Kentucky by Queen Elizabeth:

> The news that Queen Elizabeth II will attend the 11:15 service at St. John's Episcopal Church in Versailles [Kentucky] . . . raises some interesting questions. Will the service follow Rite I or Rite II or perhaps the unadulterated liturgy of the 1928 Book of Common Prayer? . . . For at a point in the service when the "Peace" is passed, it is now customary for members of the congregation to embrace everybody within reach, including perfect strangers. Indeed, I have been shrinkingly present when the priest, in an excess of bold and fervent zeal, advances down the aisle hugging and kissing all hapless and accessible parishioners. Will her Majesty be thus affronted?

In the end, it was over as it had begun, with Mary and Barry Bingham acting in concert, as they always had. The fighting in their family had not separated them as it might have done to other parents as they sought to assign the blame for their children's misdeeds. Instead, it drew them even closer as they prepared a long list of ways to spend the $85 million they would realize from the sale of their companies. They would give $4 million to the University of Louisville. They would give $1 million to the Presbyterian Seminary of Louisville for new headquarters, $100,000 to the archdiocese of Louisville and to the Speed Museum. Mary and Barry contributed an average of $272,500 each to seventy-two different organizations, including

Mary's Richmond girls' school, Radcliffe, the English Speaking
Union, the Louisville Ballet, the Bar Foundation, the Louisville
Deaf Oral School, the Kentucky Quilt Project and the National
Alliance for Research on Schizophrenia and Depression. By Sep-
tember of 1987 they had given away approximately $18 million,
$17 million of which was spent in Kentucky. They were lionized
for their generosity around Louisville, and gave a reading of *The
Tempest* for charity to a full audience.

That summer, Mary lost heart with Barry Junior, Edie and
Sallie, in particular, for she blamed her older daughter for making a scandal of the family's anguish. "You just have to retire in
a kind of shell and hope that sometime there will be a change,"
Mary said. All of Edie's attempts to reconcile with Mary and
Barry Senior were futile. In June, Sallie appeared on the cover
of *Ms.* magazine under the headline "The Woman Who Overturned an Empire." Sallie looked as out of place on that slick
magazine cover as Lillian Hellman once did in her "What becomes a legend most?" Blackglama ad, as vain and self-satisfied
as the playwright had looked. In *Ms.* Sallie wrote that her brothers had walked away with some of the good jewelry. "The slave
mentality abounds in the palaces of the rich, even when the slave
is decked in precious attire. We are dependent, after all, on the
fickle good will of those who will never proclaim us their
heirs. . . . We are not taught skill, self-discipline, or self-
nurturing. . . . And in the end, we may find ourselves totally
dependent on our male relatives, for friendship, status, affection,
a role in life—and financial support."

Sallie's article in *Ms.* enraged her sister and her mother, who
were appalled by "what would appear to be sinister logic," as
her mother said. Eleanor was livid because Sallie said she had
no jewels. "She got all the jewelry!" Eleanor said. Mary was
furious that Sallie had said she had no stocks and bonds, when
she had been living off her *Courier-Journal* shares since she was
in her twenties. Although there were plenty of justifiable arguments she could have made about her own specific family—that
her father was detached, that her mother was intimidating—
Sallie generalized her personal experience to provoke sympathy
for a new breed of heroine—her perennial favorite—the needy
heiress. "We are captives as poor women are captives. . . . The
jewels must not be too big, nor the furs too obvious," she wrote.
Shortly after her cover story was published, *Ms.* announced that
Sallie Bingham's foundation had donated $1 million to the Ms.
Foundation, saving the magazine from collapse. She also do-
nated $1 million to the Women's Project of the American Place
Theatre, the company in New York that had staged her plays,
Milk of Paradise and *Paducah*. A short time later, to save money,
Sallie's foundation eliminated three people from the staff—in-

cluding the black woman director—and Sallie's husband, Tim Peters, announced in the press that from now on a man would run her foundation for women.

Just after the article in *Ms.* was published, Sallie wrote her mother a note and asked her and Barry Senior to come to Wolf Pen for "a nature walk." It was clear that Sallie wanted to resume some kind of relationship after two years of relative silence, but Sallie was forced to invent an event as artificial as Edie's Month of Mondays, Edie's way for the Binghams to get together with different groups of grandchildren every Monday.

Mary pondered what to do about her daughter's invitation. "I do not want to go," she said. "I cannot find it in my heart to forgive Sallie very easily for all the trouble she has caused." But she said that Barry was determined to go and be with his older daughter, whom he had so loved. She was angry about this, she said and her pale eyes gleamed when she said her daughter's name. At age eighty-one, after all the glorious years of passion and power Mary had shared with the love of her life, she appeared worried about adversaries. "Why don't you allow Mr. Bingham to go without you?" I asked her as we said goodbye. "Go without me?" she asked incredulously. "Do you think I would allow Sallie to believe she could come between Barry and me? We will go together, of course."

Epilogue

There would never be healing in the family—only the barest gestures of civility that were the Binghams' stock-in-trade. At Christmas, Barry and Mary left Louisville for the first time in years and went to the Homestead with their closest friends, Mary and Edward Warburg of New York. Joan had moved to Paris the autumn before, and that Christmas she received a side of salmon from Sallie, who was so oblivious to her sister-in-law's whereabouts that she first sent the present to her Washington home. A few days before Christmas, Edie and Barry, along with their cousin James Callahan, delivered wine to the Little House and stayed for about forty minutes for a drink. There was one safe area of discussion at that pre-Christmas visit and that was Sallie. Mary and Barry were now both united in their frustration with Sallie because she had told their closest friends that she was convinced her grandfather had murdered Mary Lily Flagler. Even worse, she had established a new award, as if she was trying to torture her father, and named it the Mary Flagler Bingham award.

Although his family had collapsed, Barry Senior's primary concern that Christmas was the projected publication of David Chandler's book. He had learned that Chandler was going to speculate that his dear father not only had killed Mary Lily but had infected her with syphilis. There was no conclusive proof of any of this, but the traumatic effect on Barry Senior was overwhelming. Although he was a liberal publisher, he could not let this go. His life had come full circle: the father whom he worshiped would be tainted by these sordid "falsehoods," as he called them. The trauma of his childhood had come back to haunt his old age.

Later, in the winter of 1987, Barry Bingham blamed Sallie for cooperating with David Chandler's research. Mary took Sallie out to lunch to discuss her father's anguish and was astonished by her response. "Why does Father care so much?" she said, according to Mary. "Sallie, he loved his father. You never knew the Judge. You are not aware that these charges were not true.'' Sallie then said, ''Oh, Mother, there are many different truths.''

The Binghams now attempted to move against the Macmillan Company, the publisher of Chandler's book. Sam Thomas, the Binghams' former historian, was hired to check Chandler's galleys for errors. He and the lawyers believed they found 160 major errors, and turned them over to Wyatt, Tarrant & Combs, the Bingham lawyers. A young lawyer, Mark Wilson, was sent by the law firm to Asheville, to Johns Hopkins Hospital in Baltimore, to Wilmington, North Carolina, where Mary Lily was buried to try to disprove Chandler's thesis. Curiously, Wilson did not travel to Palm Beach and the Flagler Museum, where the docents regularly discuss the mysterious circumstances of her death as a standard part of their tour. Elaborate folders of historical documents were given to two other Bingham biographers, Alex Jones of the *New York Times* and me. In Louisville the lawyers began to talk to their friends about the allegations in Chandler's book, and soon enough Joe Ward, who had covered the sale of the newspaper for the *Courier-Journal*, got the galleys of the book and bannered the allegations in the former Bingham newspaper. The next day George Gill ran into Eleanor Bingham at a cocktail party. ''She began to chastise me and said I had no right to do that to her father,'' Gill said.

Just before the 1987 Kentucky Derby, Barry Bingham Senior came to New York and told his family he would see Thomas Mellon Evans, the father of the chairman of Macmillan, Inc. Evans was a social acquaintance and was reportedly pleased to receive the former *Courier-Journal* chairman in his office. Bingham presented Evans with five volumes of legal data challenging Chandler's book. Libel was not an issue because it is impossible under the laws to malign the dead. But the Davidson law firm had spent months analyzing what they believed were factual errors to try to convince Macmillan that they should stop the book. An accompanying memorandum to the five volumes of documents read:

. . . Chandler's explanations of Judge Bingham's marriage to Mary Lily and her death rest on unsupported assertions, erroneous suppositions and fabrications. He too often cites material that he has not examined or material that fails to support the proposition for which it is cited. These errors are compounded by mistaken or misleading quotations and the omission of materials that contradict his theories, . . . Chandler's reference to some materials possibly violates the copyright laws. . . .

The five volumes of legal memoranda weighed fourteen pounds, and no doubt earned huge legal fees for Gordon Davidson, who seemed to believe that the challenging of a book would generate praise for his client.

Barry Senior had been unable to prevent his family's collapse, but he was determined to save his father's reputation. His plan was to wait until the book was in the warehouse about to be shipped. The Binghams appeared to believe that Macmillan would not spend the money necessary to correct the text and would simply pulp the book. The Binghams also knew that they must not appear to be trying to stop the book—the impression must be that they were only trying to correct it. The precedent for this had been set by Katharine Graham, who had moved against a biographer called Deborah Davis and had prevailed upon Harcourt, Brace to recall her book. The case ended in a suit that Harcourt, Brace lost and in which the author received a hundred thousand dollars in damages.

> The . . . examination of Chandler's story in light of the facts [the memorandum stated] should in no way be construed as a threat to initiate litigation or as reflective of any intent to coerce a particular result. To the contrary, these materials represent only an earnest, good faith attempt to communicate the facts and expose the inaccuracies in Chandler's book. As a leading publisher, Macmillan should be as concerned as I am about preserving editorial integrity and protecting society from the propagation of unjustified attacks and factual errors.

The Binghams of Louisville was set for publication for June of 1987. "My father stood for freedom of the press and free speech his whole life," Barry Bingham Junior said. "And now this. It really is a disgrace." Barry Senior was clever. When Chandler's book was in galleys, he copyrighted all of his father's documents at the Filson Club, which meant that Chandler would have to obtain his permission to publish them. David Chandler, however, was ill and could not comply; he had had open heart surgery in St. Louis that very month. Joe Ward called him for comment. "I have everything wrong with it except a stake driven through it," he said.

Sallie Bingham, whom David Chandler had described as "a blond, blue-eyed Athena . . . warring against perceived sexism," publicly attacked her father for trying to stop Chandler's book. Sallie had written "about thirty" prominent book review editors and the head of the Censorship Committee of the American Civil Liberties Union about her father's attempt "to suppress" David Chandler's book:

David Chandler's book on my family, called *The Binghams of Louisville,* was scheduled for publication by Macmillan in June of 1987. After galleys were sent out two months ago, my father hired a team of lawyers to repudiate Chandler's opinion (expressed as an opinion only) that my step-grandmother, Mary Flagler Bingham, was killed through collusion between my grandfather and an unscrupulous doctor. . . . An eighteen-inch-high stack of legal documents was sent to Ned Chase at Macmillan a month ago, purporting to detail other factual inaccuracies in the Chandler book. . . . Through legal intimidation, this document seeks to chill a publisher's interest in a book which has already been favorably reviewed by *Publishers Weekly* and *Virginia Kirkus Review.* Through suppression of a book, powerful people are able to deprive a professional writer of his livelihood. MACMILLAN HAS JUST WAREHOUSED DAVID CHANDLER'S BOOK.

Immediately, the press picked up the accusations. "Daughter Charges Bingham Coverup," the *New York Post* headlined. "Binghams on Hold: Book on Louisville Publishers Postponed," the *Washington Post* reported in a lengthy story on the front page of the Style section. Sallie's letter was persuasive, and, for the uninformed, had the same logic as her piece in *Ms.*: "The only factual basis for a different interpretation has been concealed for years in an autopsy which the family refuses to reveal." But as David Chandler and Sallie well knew, this was wrong. If it existed at all, the Binghams did not have the autopsy report; the Kenan family did. In July Macmillan announced it had canceled Chandler's book. By October, however, Crown had announced it would publish *The Binghams of Louisville* in January of 1988.

Certainly, Barry Senior and Mary were enjoying their new riches. Barry Senior traded in Mary's small blue Ford for a large Mercedes. He announced that the Mary and Barry Bingham, Sr., Fund was giving $2.6 million to the city of Louisville to build in the middle of the Ohio River the world's tallest floating fountain, which would spray water up to 375 feet—as high as the nearby Humana building—in the shape of a fleur-de-lis, the *Courier-Journal* reported. He said that he had been fascinated by such fountains when he saw a water jet in Lake Geneva in Switzerland twenty years ago. Governor Martha Layne Collins said the fountain will be a "great stimulus" for economic development and a "major boost" for Louisville's riverfront. Earlier, Barry Senior and Mary left for Europe with Eleanor, Rowland and their boys. They traveled on the *QE II* and stopped at the Connaught in London, and then Eleanor and Rowland went to the Bristol Hotel in Paris, one of the most expensive hotels in the world. When Mary and Barry Senior joined them in Paris, he was jubilant about Macmillan's deliberations. The family had dinner with Joan and her daughter, Clara. "How are Uncle Barry and Aunt Edie?" Clara asked Rowland. "No one has seen them in a year," Rowland said.

Barry Senior, Eleanor and Rowland now shared office space in downtown Louisville, and Eleanor had returned to her career of making documentaries. That summer, Eleanor and Rowland produced a video called *Baby Massage*, which they planned to advertise in *Child* magazine.

Although there had been dire predictions about how the Gannett ownership would affect the *Courier-Journal*, the newspaper in fact became more profitable. Paul Janensch was sent to work at Gannett headquarters, and a new editor, the tough-minded Michael Gartner, was brought in for thirteen months. Gartner had been an editor of the *Wall Street Journal* and the Des Moines *Register*, and even owned a small newspaper in Iowa. When he arrived in Louisville in July, he spent months reorganizing the paper's structure, which was "top-heavy with mid-level managers," the *Washington Journalism Review* reported. With Irene Nolan, the managing editor, he wrote a 199-page blueprint for the paper. "We wanted a paper that looked like the C-J and incorporated the spirit, sparkle, and liveliness of the [Louisville] *Times,*" Gartner told the *Washington Journalism Review*. It was his intention to have an expanded news hole and somewhat shorter stories, to try to maintain the statewide coverage, to take the advertisements off the op-ed pages, and increase the business and sports reporting. To do this, however, the *Louisville Times* had to shut down. It did on February 14, 1987. Two days later the "all new" *Courier-Journal* appeared. The first year Gannett ran the newspaper the profits were 20 percent, and Gannett made plans to drastically cut back the statewide circulation that was costing the newspaper $1 million per year. At the end of his year at the *Courier-Journal* Michael Gartner went back to his own newspaper in Iowa, and David Hawpe was named editor.

In Louisville during the summer of 1987 Barry Junior wrote his father a letter asking for a meeting: "I had seen several consultants who told me that I needed to have an 'exit interview' with the chairman to have a heart-to-heart talk about my mistakes. And so I wrote that to my father, who said, 'Let's have lunch.' Barry Junior eagerly anticipated the lunch and the chance at last to have an honest conversation with his father, but it was not to be. At the table, when Barry Junior said, "Well, you know why I am here," he was astonished to hear his father say, "Barry, you didn't make any mistakes. You did a wonderful job." Barry Junior responded incredulously, "Then why don't I have my newspaper?" He said, "My father just kept repeating to me, "You've done a wonderful job." Finally Barry Junior grew impatient with this pretense. "Well, I guess I will have to wait until the books are published to find out what really happened, " he said. "The bottom line of this entire family tragedy is the failure of communication."

Before Barry and Mary left for Europe, they received a phone call from Sallie. According to a close family friend, Sallie asked her father if he would meet her for lunch. Barry Senior was elated at the prospect of some kind of tentative reconciliation. "This is the phone call I have been waiting for," he told a friend. He arrived early and waited, but Sallie never appeared. When he returned home, he called his friend to tell him what had happened. "These things take time," his friend said to him. Barry Senior paused and his voice broke on the telephone. "I don't have any time left," he said.

In November, Barry Senior began to have peculiar symptoms: his vision blurred and his balance was off. His Louisville doctors suspected he might have a brain tumor. Immediately, Barry Senior and Mary left for Boston and Massachusetts General Hospital for more tests. Before he left, he wrote Sallie a letter and asked Eleanor to deliver it. Sallie, unaware of her father's condition, at first refused to open it, according to family members, saying, in effect, "If Daddy wants to talk to me he can call me directly." It was only when Eleanor told her about the contents of the letter that she agreed to read it. Her parents were already in Boston, where Barry had checked into a grand room with a fireplace at the Phillips House at Mass. General when Sallie called him. She was "all peaches and cream," Mary told members of the family, but curiously she did not immediately fly to Boston to be with her parents. Neither did Barry Junior and Edie. "We weren't asked if we wanted to be part of the consultation process," Edie said. Instead, Mary and Barry Senior consulted with Harvey and Kathy Sloane. Eleanor, however, did go to Boston. Worth and Joan's daughter, Clara, working in Boston at Harvard's Kennedy School, did not wait for an invitation to come to the hospital either, but just called her grandmother and informed her she was on her way. Barry Senior, as always, was amazingly cheerful, determined not to inconvenience anyone in the family, eager to talk on any subject, such as the upcoming presidential campaign, except his health. He told his grandchildren that he did not want his suite at the Phillips House to resemble "a room at an Indian hospital," but his grandchildren, including Sallie's sons, Barry Ellsworth and Chris Iovenko, ignored him and came anyway. The day Barry Senior was admitted to Mass. General

the *Courier-Journal* reported his condition in the second section:
"Barry Bingham Sr. Found to Have a Brain Tumor."

His tests were inconclusive. The tumor seemed lodged in his
cerebellum, which would make it inoperable, but there was no
other evidence of malignancy in his body, which was highly
unusual with this form of cancer. Some doctors suggested he
take radiation, and other family members suggested laser surgery in Sweden—a new experimental method of removing tu-
mors. After a week in the hospital, Barry Senior came out for
an afternoon and took his grandchildren to lunch at the Ritz.
Mary was dressed beautifully and was, one said, "articulate and
brilliant" as she explained Barry's condition in minute and sci-
entific detail; Barry "wanted to make all of us feel comfortable," the grandchild said, and avoided all unpleasant
conversations.

After lunch the five Bingham grandchildren went off to "really
talk," as one said. The next generation of Binghams gathered at
the Ritz to analyze their family. In the room that day were Barry
Junior and Edie's daughter, Molly; Worth and Joan's children,
Clara and Robbie; and Barry Ellsworth and Chris Iovenko. They
spoke of their own parents' reactions to their grandfather's condition. Sallie's sons gave the impression that they believed their
mother was still so hurt by her father that his illness would do
nothing to help reconcile the family. "That's what my parents
say too," Molly Bingham said, according to a family member.

A few days later, Barry Senior and Mary left for Louisville,
where tests would continue. Before they left for the holidays,
Barry Junior and Edie visited Barry and Mary at the Little
House. It had been months since Edie had seen Barry Senior,
and she was astonished that he continued to sustain the perpetual
good spirits and fine manners that had seen him through every
personal crisis of his long life. "He was still keeping up that
wonderful façade," Edie said. Mary hovered protectively, determined, as she had always been, to protect her dearest love
from any stress. "Is it possible that Barry Senior's condition
could cause the family to come back together?" I asked Edie
Bingham on the morning that she and Barry Junior were taking
off to spend Christmas abroad. "How can we ever reconcile if
all we ever do is smooth things over?" Edie said, with immense
sadness and resignation in her voice.

Notes

KEY TO ABBREVIATIONS

BB   Barry Bingham Senior
MB   Mary Bingham
SL   Schlesinger Library, Radcliffe College, Mary (Caperton) Bingham and
          Barry Bingham Papers, Ascension no.:81–M262

PROLOGUE

PAGE
3   "When I was growing up in Louisville": Telephone interview, Diane Sawyer
         with author, spring 1987.
4   "The Binghams were supremely elegant": Interview, Ann Arensberg with au-
         thor, New York, March 1986.

CHAPTER ONE

5ff.   Information about Paris in June of 1949 was drawn from the letters of BB to
         MB, SL.
6ff.   "champagne supply": BB to MB, June 26, 1949, SL.
6f.   "the convenience of the house": Interview, BB with author, Louisville, Jan-
         uary 17, 1986.
7   "wouldn't dream of": BB to family members.
7   *"silhouette elegante et sportive"*: BB to MB, June 26, 1949, SL.
8   "The whole countryside": BB to MB, June 11, 1949, SL.
8   "that it hurts physically": BB to MB, June 26, 1949, SL.
8   "a bluestocking": Interview, MB with author, Louisville, January 24, 1986.
8   "terribly well-born but living in rather reduced circumstances": Ibid.
9   "arriviste": Interview, MB with author, Louisville, February 5, 1987.
9   "the colored lady": Interview, MB with author, Louisville, January 24, 1986.
9   "midnight feasts": MB to BB, various dates, SL.
10   "I can't believe your grandparents": Interview, Rob Bingham with author,
         New York, May 27, 1987.
10   "We called our coloreds": Interview, MB with author, Louisville, February
         5, 1987.
10   "limousine liberals": Interview, Barry Bingham Junior with author, Louis-
         ville, February 6, 1987.

PAGE
10   "a doll-like blonde": Internal *Time* memo from W. S. Howland to David
        Hulburd, February 21, 1946.
10f.   "pretty horrifying" and "Those with dark hair": BB to MB, June 8, 1949,
        SL.
11   "a delightful old boy": BB to MB, June 11, 1949, SL.
11   "still strangely interested": BB to MB, June 19, 1949, SL.
11   "was always quite good about family": Interview, MB with author, Louisville,
        January 24, 1986.
12   "I don't want to spend the next twenty years": BB to MB, July 15, 1945, SL.
12   "insouciance" and ". . . His good humor in the face": BB to MB, June 11,
        1949, SL.
12f.   "Wallis was floating around": BB to MB, June 26, 1949, SL.
13   "I've got a lot to learn": "Barry Bingham: A Profile," *Eureca,* June 28, 1949,
        Paris.
14   "Worthless": Interview, Joan Bingham with author, Washington, January 21,
        1986.
14   "optimistic": BB to MB, June 11, 1949, SL.
14   "lazy, fatter and vague": MB to BB, May 5, 1943, SL.
15   "Do you really think a girl who puts a spoon": Interview, Barry Bingham
        Junior with author, Louisville, February 6, 1987.
15   "I have always regarded": Joe Creason, 1868–1968, *The Courier-Journal Cen-
        tennial, Mirror of a Century* (Louisville Courier-Journal, 1968), p. 19.
15   "a boogery": BB to MB, June 26, 1949, SL.
15f.   "Take some advice": Interview, MB with author, Louisville, January 24, 1986.

CHAPTER TWO

17   *"We must let"*: Interview, BB with author, Louisville, January 17, 1986.
18   "It will take time": Ibid.
18   "Sale by Binghams Marks End of Era in Kentucky Journalism": *New York
        Times,* January 13, 1986.
18   "I worked for the Bingham papers": Interview, Hunt Helm with author, Lou-
        isville, June 1986.
18   "I thought my father": Interview, Barry Bingham Junior with author, Louis-
        ville, January 17, 1986.
18   "Mary and I will get through": Interview, BB and MB with author, Louisville,
        January 17, 1986.
19   "God knows what would happen": Interview, Eleanor Bingham Miller with
        author, East Hampton, N.Y., July 29, 1986.
20   "I was not telling her": Interview, BB with author, Louisville, February 5,
        1987.
20   "My heavens, the tulips": Interview, BB with author, Louisville, January 17,
        1986.
21   "judgmental": Neil R. Peirce and Jerry Hagstrom, *The Book of America,
        Inside 50 States Today* (New York: W. W. Norton, 1983), p. 388.
21   "We tried to convey": Interview, MB with author, Louisville, January 24,
        1986.

PAGE

21   ''You will be governor'': Interview, John Ed Pearce with author, New York, summer 1987.

22   ''had a finger in saving everything'': Interview, Lois Mateus Musselman with author, Louisville, June 6, 1986.

22   ''A fine, ugly, intelligent woman'': BB to MB, June 19, 1941, SL.

22f. ''This town, from its beginnings'': Fred Powledge, ''City in Transition,'' *New Yorker*, September 9, 1974.

23   Louisville's 1974 economy: Ibid.

23   ''I am so tired'': Interview, MB with author, Louisville, February 5, 1987.

23   ''I just want you to know that I am thinking Fair'': Telephone interview, Bill Cox with author, July 6, 1987.

24   ''the Commie Binghams'': Interview, Edie Bingham with author, Louisville, February 6, 1987.

25   ''Mother and Daddy just lived too long'': Telephone interview, Barry Bingham Junior with author, spring 1987.

25   ''Those things are meant for my daughter'': Interview, Clara Bingham with author, New York, May 27, 1987.

26   ''You could come in here in the middle'': Interview, Barry Bingham Junior with author, Louisville, February 6, 1987.

26   ''My daughters and I wouldn't think of'': Interview, Edie Bingham with author, Louisville, February 6, 1987.

27   ''The Kennedys actually push each other about'': Interview, Clara Bingham with author, New York, summer 1986.

27   ''We vied with each other'': Interview, Eleanor Bingham Miller with author, East Hampton, N.Y., July 29, 1986.

27   ''Sallie looked at our profit and loss statement'': Interview, Barry Bingham Junior with author, February 6, 1987.

27   ''My brother is a terrible businessman'': Interview, Sallie Bingham with author, Louisville, January 23, 1986.

27   ''I could not live in Louisville'': Interview, Eleanor Bingham Miller with author, Louisville, January 24, 1986.

27   ''I don't know why I couldn't'': Interview, Rowland Miller with author, Louisville, January 24, 1986.

28   ''Edie is a cloth-coat moralist'': Interview, Eleanor Bingham Miller with author.

28   ''We will have Christmas'': Interview, Eleanor Bingham Miller with author, Louisville, winter 1986.

29   ''as if he were going to jump'': Ibid.

29   ''A terrible rigidity'': Telephone interview, MB with author.

29   ''I don't believe in hyperbole'': Interview, Barry Bingham Junior with author, Louisville, January 17, 1986.

30   ''Eleanor wants everybody to love her'': Interview, Sallie Bingham with author, Louisville, January 25, 1986.

30   ''To think we almost didn't even want to have her!'': Interview, BB with author, Louisville, January 1986.

PAGE

30   "You couldn't get away from it": Interview, Barry Bingham Junior with author, Louisville, winter 1986.

30   "an utter phantasm": Interview, MB with author, Louisville, January 17, 1986.

31   Letter from Sallie Bingham to book editors, dated May 29, 1987.

31   "After we are gone": Interview, BB with author.

31   Sallie Bingham's appearance on *60 Minutes*, April 13, 1986.

31f.   "This is the hardest decision": Interview, Eleanor Bingham Miller with author, Louisville, January 24, 1986.

32   "How dare you say I am irrational?": Interview, Barry Bingham Junior with author, Louisville, February 6, 1987.

32f.   "My father spoke of": Statements published in *Courier-Journal*, January 10, 1986.

33   "that working at the *Courier-Journal*": Interview, Norman Isaacs with author, Dobbs Ferry, March 10, 1986.

34   "I will not allow Sallie": Interview, Sallie Bingham with author, Louisville, January 24, 1986.

34   "I think we all decided": Interview, Sallie Bingham with author, Louisville, January 25, 1986.

34   Profile: Joe Ward, "The Binghams: Twilight of a Tradition," published in Louisville *Courier-Journal Magazine*, April 20, 1986.

34   "It was so damn subtle": Interview with a person close to the family.

34   "It is a question of pride": Interview, MB with author, June 9, 1986.

35   "How will I ever be able?": Interview, Joan Bingham with author, June 1987.

35   "Our children may resent": Interview, MB and BB with author, Louisville, January 17, 1986.

35   "There never has been a question": Ibid.

CHAPTER THREE

36   "I can remember at just what point": MB to BB, November 19, 1942, SL.

36   "Barry was so striking": Telephone interview, Constance Greene with author.

36   "We all drank so much": Interview, MB with author, Louisville, February 5, 1987.

37   "Like Christopher Robin": BB, "Editorial Notebook," Louisville *Courier-Journal*, June 26, 1966.

38   "Wouldn't you like to be in this?": Interview, Barry Bingham Junior with author, Louisville, February 6, 1987.

38   "a Giotto Madonna": Dora [Doric] Carrington, *Letters and Extracts from Her Diaries* (New York: Holt, Rinehart & Winston, 1970), p. 254.

38   "on top of a piano": John Houseman, *Run-through: A Memoir* (New York: Simon & Schuster, 1972) p. 46.

38   "Distant Work": Interview, MB with author, Louisville, January 24, 1986.

39   "came from a West Virginia": Ibid.

39   "the cabbage patch" and "a small Pekinese dog": Interviews, Helen Cronley, Michael Ballentine and Mrs. Leslie Cheek with author, Richmond, June 13, 1986.

39   "One must marry rich": Telephone interview, James Callahan with author.

PAGE

39   "florid thrillers": BB to MB, July 12, 1943, SL.

39   "That was always considered": Interview, Helen Cronley with author, Richmond, June 13, 1986.

40   "the only nice thing Dottie ever did in her life": MB to BB, SL.

40   "These are curious tales": Helena Lefroy Caperton, *Like a Falcon Flying* (Richmond: Garrett & Massie, 1943), p. ix.

40   "All the voyage he sat beside": Ibid., p. 19.

40   "the handling of the Negro problem": BB to MB, July 12, 1943, SL.

40   "My mother would throw up her hands": Interview, MB with author, Louisville, January 24, 1986.

40   "insistent and pious reference to the Latin roots": MB, "Ten O'Clock, Mary Dear," *Harvard Alumni Gazette*, June 1987.

40   "The dead hand of the Civil War": Interview, MB with author, Louisville, January 24, 1986.

41   "on the sidewalk": Telephone interview, General Frank McCarthy with author, June 30, 1986.

41   "accomplishing a boy": MB to BB, SL.

41   "I was stopped": Interview, MB with author, Louisville, January 24, 1986.

41   "I believe I was rather deeply upset": MB to BB, December 10, 1944, SL.

41   "He was almost never there": Telephone interview, General Frank McCarthy with author.

41   "The theory in Mother's family": Interview, Barry Bingham Junior with author, Louisville, February 6, 1987.

42   "The Judge could not believe": Interview, Joan Bingham with author, Washington, January 21, 1986.

42   "American history": Interview, MB with author, Louisville, January 24, 1986.

42   "I feel deeply that [Barry] might": to BB, September 9, 1943, SL.

42   "Who is the greatest man?" Interview, Mrs. Thomas B. Scott with author, Richmond, June 14, 1986.

42   "We were taught to be tremendously thoughtful": Interview, Mrs. Leslie Cheek, Richmond, June 13, 1986.

43   "covers" and "consciousness of kind" as well as Southern background drawn in part from Florence King, *Confessions of a Failed Southern Lady* (New York; St. Martin's/Marek, 1985).

43f. "I imagine there can be no greater": Helena Lefroy Caperton, "Care and Feeding of Sons-in-Law," *Ladies' Home Journal*, November 1933.

44   "I have sent off the printed silk": MB to BB, May 3, 1944, SL.

44   "In all contacts encourage the best": Caperton, "Care and Feeding."

45   "I had no part of club life at Harvard": Interview, BB with author, Louisville, February 5, 1987.

45   "hip flasks passed behind the scenes": BB, "Too Good to Last," *Harvard Alumni Gazette*, June 1987.

46   "the orchestra leader, Ruby Newman": MB, "Ten O'Clock, Mary Dear."

46   ". . . the late afternoon": BB to MB, October 1942, SL.

46   "These were among the happiest years": MB, "Ten O'Clock, Mary Dear."

PAGE

46   "anyone who can choose": Interview, Rob Bingham, New York, May 27, 1987.

47   Information about the relationship between Edie Callahan and Henrietta Bingham was derived from interviews with John Ed Pearce and members of the Bingham family.

47   "I was brought onto the houseboat": Interview, MB with author, Louisville, June 9, 1986.

47   "In Paris": Interview, BB with author.

48   "Both these girls were beautiful": Frances Partridge, *Love in Bloomsbury. Memories* (Boston: Little, Brown, 1981), p. 99.

48   ". . . sang exquisite songs": Carrington, *Letters and Extracts*.

48   "hardly an intellect": Interview, BB with author, January 17, 1986.

48   "engulfed in her father and brothers": Carrington, *Letters and Extracts*, pp 299, 294.

48   "[I] could get along": Interview, BB for "Oral History of The Courier-Journal," Marlow Cook Papers, University of Louisville.

49   "Do we have to talk about her?": Interview, MB with author, Louisville, June 9, 1986.

49   "curious glamor" and Garnett "the perfect oval of a Buddha . . .": Houseman, pp. 56, 61, 134, 313.

49f. "I have tried hard to examine": MB to BB, May 20, 1945, SL.

50   "into an awful sodden state of drunkenness": Interview, MB with author, Louisville, June 9, 1986.

50   *Milk of Paradise* performed at American Place Theater in New York, March 1980.

CHAPTER FOUR

51   "I wanted you too badly then": MB to BB, April 28, 1944, SL.

51   "Did my father wait years": Interview, Barry Bingham Junior with author, Louisville, February 6, 1987.

51   "She was hardly much of a chaperone": Interview, MB with author, Louisville, June 1986.

52   "I just poured everything into it": Interview, BB for "Oral History of the Courier-Journal," Marlow Cook Papers, University of Louisville.

52   "I suppose": Interview, BB with author, Louisville, January 17, 1986.

52   "a strong station": Interview, William Paley with author, New York, winter 1987.

52   "we wrote a lot of letters": Interview, MB with author, Louisville, June 6 1986.

52f. "Mistress Constance Templeton": MB to BB, December 29, 1929, SL.

53f. "crowded into a cell-like room": BB to MB, February 1, 1930, SL.

54   "I'm in such a swivet": MB to BB, May 9, 1930, SL.

55   "flowed in torrents": BB to MB, May 8, 1930, SL.

55f. "The Derby weekend": BB to MB, May 29, 1930, SL.

56   "brains are addled": BB to MB, July 1, 1930, SL.

56   "Barry was just young": Interview, MB with author, Louisville, June 9, 1986

PAGE
56   "My dearest M., I've just been": BB to MB, August 19, 1930, SL.
57   "Barry dearest, I have just cabled": MB to BB, October 30, 1930, SL.
57   "I don't know what to say": BB to MB, November 2, 1930, SL.
58   "The reporters themselves are a race apart": BB to MB, November 1930, SL.
58f. "Darling . . . I am so glad": MB to BB, November 18, 1930, SL.
59   "wanted to do something with my French": Interview, MB with author, Lou-
     isville, June 9, 1986.
59   "in the queer, pearly gray cold weather": MB to BB, October 4, 1944, SL.
59   "Francis was my first friend": Interview, BB with author, Louisville, Febru-
     ary 5, 1987.
59f. "I have had so many ideas": Francis Parks to BB, SL.
60   "lugubrious luncheon" and "I feel very queer": BB to MB, December 2,
     1930, SL.
61   "I will not allow Sallie": Interview, MB with author, Louisville, June 1986.
61   "wouldn't hear a word against her": Interview, Lee Segal with author, New
     York, winter 1987.
61   "opened a bottle": Interview, MB with author, Louisville, January 24, 1986
     and June 1986.
61   "It is so obvious that life for me": BB to MB, March 10, 1931, SL.
61   "I continue to be amazed": BB to MB, 1931 (undated), SL.
61   "roe herring": BB to MB, March 10, 1931, SL.
62   "I feel an even greater": BB to MB, March 31, 1931, SL.
62   "in his frenzy of heat-driven": MB to BB, June 24, 1944, SL.
62   "nigger Lizzie": BB to MB, March 31, 1931, SL.
62   "Doesn't the phrase": BB to MB, March 8, 1931, SL.
63   "I want you": BB to MB, March 31, 1931, SL.
63   "wore a white satin gown": "The Personal Side," (wedding announcement),
     Courier-Journal, June 10, 1931, p. 8.

CHAPTER FIVE

64   "lovely bed": MB to BB, September 9, 1943, SL.
64   "St. Paul's passionate puritanism": MB to BB, August 30, 1943, SL.
64f. "the greatest joy in life": MB to BB, January 31, 1944, SL.
65   "She told me": Interview, BB with author, Louisville, February 5, 1987.
65   "Why does Father": Interview, MB with author, Louisville, February 5, 1987.
66   ". . . if this intimidation": Letter from Sallie Bingham to book review editors,
     May 29, 1987.
66   "Barry Senior is more outwardly concerned": Interview, Gordon Davidson
     with author, Louisville, February 6, 1987.
66   "What my father has done is shocking": Telephone interview, Barry Bingham
     Junior with author.
66   "It was clear": Telephone interview, Richard Harwood with author.
66   "My father never once spoke to me": Interview, BB with author, Louisville,
     February 5, 1986.
66   "marvelous man" and "He was a most proper": Interview, MB and BB with
     author, Louisville, February 5, 1987.

PAGE

67   "I don't know how to account": Ibid., BB with author.

67   "weeded out": Legal dossier, "Relevant Documents Concerning Mary Lily
     Flagler Bingham," prepared by GD; memo from JAD to GD dated April 24
     1986, given to author February 1987.

68   "My father was the most wonderful man": Interview, BB with author, Lou
     isville, February 1987.

68   "the drama reminds me of Papa on the defensive": BB to MB, September 8
     1944, SL.

69   "I am very proud of having such friends": Bingham Family Scrapbook, date
     June 26, 1974, Woodrow Wilson to Major Robert W. Bingham, January 1
     1922.

69   "That was a very beautiful picture": Ibid., Josephus Daniels to Judge Bing
     ham, July 13, 1933.

69   "Jack is far from being a well boy": Ibid., Joseph Kennedy to Judge Bingham
     November 12, 1935.

69   "to own a newspaper": Interview, Sallie Bingham with author, January 25
     1986.

70   "Dear Mrs. Mitchell, . . . the peak of my rejoicing": Scrapbook, letter from
     Judge Bingham to Margaret Mitchell, February 16, 1937.

71   "raised many suspicions about the Judge": Telephone interview, Thomas Kena
     with author, December 18, 1986.

CHAPTER SIX

72   "lungers" and "No Consumptives Taken" and general Asheville background
     David Herbert Donald, *Look Homeward, A Life of Thomas Wolfe* (Boston
     Little, Brown, 1987), p. 21.

72   Information about the Bingham family in the nineteenth century was draw
     from *Bingham Family Genealogy,* "Descendants of James Bingham of Count
     Down," Northern Ireland, compiled by James Barry Bingham (Baltimore
     Gateway Press, Inc., 1980), "The Bingham Family: From the Old South t
     the New South and Beyond," by William E. Ellis *(Filson Club Historic*
     Quarterly, January 1987) as well as the Filson Club Archives, Louisville.

73   "On the football team": Hugh Young, *Hugh Young: A Surgeon's Autobiogra*
     phy (New York: Harcourt, Brace, 1940), pp. 148–49.

73   The first Bingham family member in America had been William Bingham, wh
     arrived from Northern Ireland in 1789. He was a graduate of the University
     Glasgow who came to Wilmington, North Carolina, to a teaching job. H
     opened his own school, which was to change locations several times durin
     the next century. His son, William, Bob's grandfather, was born in 1802. Th
     school was rigorous and emphasized Greek, Latin, mathematics and histo
     and eventually attracted cadets from all over the country, but primarily fro
     the South. There were "Bingham boys" who fought in the War of 1812. Th
     Bingham School was the prep school of choice unofficially affiliated with th
     University of North Carolina, a center of progressive thinking in the Sout
     David Herbert Donald wrote. Often, the "Bingham boys" earned the highe

PAGE

honors and praised the school for its "stern discipline and rigorous examinations" (Ellis, "The Bingham Family," p. 8).

By May of 1861 North Carolina, following Virginia's lead, had voted for secession. William's son, Robert, joined the 44th Regiment. The Binghams turned their school into a military academy, trained officers and struggled all through the war. Robert was taken prisoner, and he kept a diary of his experiences in which he wrote, "The Yankee nation is the most infamously mean race that blights God's green earth." It was in prison that he hardened his views about white superiority and the divine mandate that would surely be coming to the South (Ellis, "The Bingham Family," pp. 11–14).

73f.   ". . . hundreds of his fellow prisoners": Bingham Family Scrapbook, dated June 26, 1974, Judge Bingham to Margaret Mitchell, February 16, 1937.

74   Comparison of Colonel Bingham to Theodore Joyner and Robert Worth Bingham to "Silk" Joyner suggested by Ellis, "The Bingham Family," p. 27.

74 .   Before he attended Harvard, Thomas Wolfe was offered a job at the Bingham School but turned it down because he was sure he would become "a sour, dyspeptic small-town pedant" (Donald, "Look Homeward," p. 63).

74f.   "When he first decided": Thomas Wolfe, The Hills Beyond (New York: Harper & Brothers, 1941), pp. 274–75.

75   "a kind of elegant country club": Ibid., p. 280.

75f.   Information on Mary Lily Kenan drawn in part from David Chandler, "Seed Money, The Birth of Kentucky's Bingham Dynasty": The Binghams of Louisville, as excerpted in Southern Magazine, June 1987, p. 58.

76   "It is awfully hard": Interview, BB with author, Louisville, February 5, 1987.

76   "She was by no means a tramp": Telephone interview, Thomas Kenan with author, December 18, 1986.

76   "We had what could be called": New York Evening Journal, November 6, 1916.

77   "Even when I was growing up": Interview, MB with author, Louisville, February 5, 1986.

77   Information on the meeting of Mary Lily and Flagler was drawn in part from the Henry Morrison Flagler Museum archives, Palm Beach, Florida, as well as from David Leon Chandler, Henry Flagler: The Astonishing Life and Times of the Visionary Robber Baron Who Founded Florida (New York: Macmillan, 1986).

78   "Obviously he cared a great deal": Telephone interview, Thomas Kenan with author, December 18, 1986.

79   "a piquant face" and "My father and grandmother": Interview, BB with author, February 5, 1986.

79f.   ". . . was attended by": Courier-Journal, May 21, 1896.

PAGE

CHAPTER SEVEN

81   Information about turn-of-the-century Louisville was drawn in part from George
        H. Yater, *Two Hundred Years at the Falls of the Ohio: A History of Louisville
        and Jefferson County* (Louisville: Heritage Corporation, 1979), pp. 143–46.

81f.   Information about Henry Watterson was drawn from Clara Bingham, "Henry
        Watterson," thesis for Harvard, 1986; "Mirror of a Century," *Courier-
        Journal,* November 10, 1968, pp. 8–11; Arthur Krock, *Memoirs: Sixty years
        on the Firing Line* (New York: Funk & Wagnalls, 1968), pp. 36–37.

81   "I remember being taken to see him": Interview, BB for "Oral History of the
        Courier-Journal," Marlow Cook Papers, University of Louisville.

82   "Everyone assumed that he was the owner": Interview, BB with author, Lou-
        isville.

82f.   "The bathtub, rearing its massive bulk": BB, "Barry Bingham's Louisville,
        Kentucky," *Courier-Journal,* May 3, 1976.

83   "To call my father a politician": Interview, BB with author, Louisville, Feb-
        ruary 5, 1987.

83f.   Information on Louisville politics and Boss Whallen machine at the turn of the
        century drawn in part from William E. Ellis, "Robert Worth Bingham and
        Louisville Progressivism, 1901–1905," *Filson Club History Quarterly,* 1980,
        pp. 169–173; and Chandler, "Seed Money," *Southern Magazine.*

84   "Come on now": *Courier-Journal,* June 29, 1907.

84   "This fight here must be made": Ellis, "Robert Worth Bingham," p. 189.

85   "pro-Southern politics and sympathy": Ellis, "Robert Worth Bingham," p.
        190.

85   Mary Lily marriage, Palm Beach, and Whitehall information drawn from Flag-
        ler Museum archives: Chandler, *Henry Flagler*; Wilmington *Star-News,* May
        1, 1906.

CHAPTER EIGHT

86   "If anything happens to me": Chandler, "Seed Money," *Southern Magazine,*
        p. 60.

86f.   "In the dim past": Sadie Bingham Grinnan to BB, October 2, 1942, SL.

87   "Here I come lowly": Interview, MB with author, Louisville, February 5,
        1987.

87   "like a heavy animal risen from its wallow": BB, "Editorial Notebook,"
        Courier-Journal, February 6, 1957.

87   "Lizzie has been puttering around": MB to BB, January 21, 1944, SL.

88   "having my mother and father come to kiss me": BB, "Editorial Notebook,"
        Courier-Journal, February 14, 1967.

88f.   Information about Eleanor Miller Bingham's death was drawn from the
        Courier-Journal, April 27–28, 1913, and from interviews with BB.

88   "I heard my mother scream": Interview, BB with author, Louisville, February
        1986.

PAGE

89   "It was terrible": Interview, Eleanor Bingham Miller with author, East Hampton, N.Y., July 1986.

89   "My sister was crying uncontrollably": Interview, BB with author, January 24, 1986.

90   "I wish you could have known her": BB to MB, March 10, 1931, SL.

90   "because his mother had just been killed": Interview, Sophie Alpert with Sam Thomas, Louisville, June 24, 1986.

90f.   ". . . all the kids": Interview, BB with author, January 1986, and Aloha Club background drawn from BB, "Editorial Notebook," *Courier-Journal*, August 1, 1962.

91   "I think he had no heart": Interview, BB with author, February 5, 1987.

91   "Latest Photograph of Dying Millionaire": Louisville *Herald*, April 11, 1913.

91   Owen Kenan and Mary Lily Flagler, *West Palm Beach Weekly News*, May 14, 1915, courtesy Henry Flagler Museum archives.

91f.   "My niece, Louise Wise": New York *Herald*, November 6, 1916, courtesy Henry Flagler Museum archives.

92   "She was so lonely": Telephone interview, Thomas Kenan with author.

92   "Mary Lily came to Asheville": Interview, BB with author, February 5, 1987.

92   "I remember lots": Interview, Carolyn Drautman with Sam Thomas, Louisville, January 19, 1986.

92   "shiver when I beheld it": BB, "Editorial Notebook," *Courier-Journal*, February 17, 1961.

93f.   "Mrs. Flagler's Romance": New York *Herald*, November 6, 1916.

CHAPTER NINE

96   "Their marriage went sour": Telephone interview, Thomas Kenan with author.

96   "I just don't know how to account": Interview, BB with author, Louisville, February 5, 1987.

97   "Aleen always acted": Telephone conversation, Helen Jacobs with author. (Miss Jacobs refused to be formally interviewed but spoke briefly with the author on the telephone from her home in Weston, Conn.)

97   "The letters started coming": Telephone interview, Thomas Kenan with author.

97   "I was the first person": Interview, Sophie Alpert with Sam Thomas, Louisville, June 24, 1986.

97f.   "I was eleven years old": Interview, BB with author, February 5, 1987.

98   "filled with pink Killarney roses": Louisville *Courier-Journal*, December 31, 1916.

98   "Henrietta was thoroughly unappreciative": Interview, Ellen Barret Wood with Sam Thomas, Louisville, April 12, 1982.

98   "a drunk and a drug addict": David Leon Chandler, "The Binghams of Louisville" (Macmillan version), bound galleys.

98   "There is not a word": Interview, MB with author, February 5, 1987.

98   "I don't think anybody": Interview, BB with author, Louisville, February 5, 1987.

PAGE

99   "He didn't want her money": Ibid.

100   "They were remarkable": Telephone interview, Thomas Kenan with author.

100   "She was a sad case": Interview, BB with author, Louisville.

100   Lincliffe house party described in the *Courier-Journal*, June 10, 1917, and house described in Jefferson County Office of Historic Preservation and Archives.

101   Walter Boggess obituary, *Courier-Journal*, July 2, 1934; Sol Steinberg obituary, *Courier-Journal*, January 15, 1925.

101   "You wonder why her family": Interview, BB with author, Louisville, February 5, 1987.

101   "Everybody knew Dr. Ravitch left town": Interview, Carolyn Drautman with Sam Thomas; Louisville, January 19, 1986.

101f.   "I give and bequeath to my husband": Mary Lily Bingham, codicil written June 19, 1917, exact replica published in Chicago *Daily Tribune*, September 21, 1917.

102   "As I have always been told": Interview, BB with author, Louisville, February 5, 1987.

102   "that he was overdosing Mary Lily on morphine": Telephone interview, Thomas Kenan with author.

103   "Would it do any good": Rev. George Ward to Judge Bingham, July 19, 1917, Louisville Filson Club archives.

103   "It seems to me that my childhood": BB to MB, October 1943, SL.

103   "I heard about it from my aunt": Interview, BB with author, Louisville, February 5, 1987.

103   Henry Flagler bequest, reported in *New York Times*, July 28, 1917, and probate of codicil, August 28, 1917.

104   "The story of their sudden departure": Louisville *Times*, August 27, 1917.

104   "So many of our family's fine acquaintances": Telephone interview, Thomas Kenan with author.

105   "There was no question in any of our minds": Telephone conversation with Lawrence Lewis, December 1986. Mr. Lewis refused to be formally interviewed by the author but recommended that she contact his cousin Thomas Kenan, the family historian.

105   "was the most suspicious about Mary Lily": Telephone interview, Thomas Kenan with author.

105   "At the time": Interview, BB with author, February 5, 1987.

105f.   "He said, 'Before you hear this . . .' ": Interview, Barry Bingham Junior with author, Louisville, February 6, 1987.

106   "Now this may seem incredible": Interview, BB with author, Louisville, February 5, 1987.

106   "on his vacation in Maine": Transcript of probate hearing of Mary Lily Bingham's will, Louisville, September 1917, reported in *New York Times*, September 21, 1917.

106   Judge Bingham's location reported in Lexington *Herald*, September 21, 1917.

108   "If I had been the Judge": Interview, Gordon Davidson with author, Louisville, February 6, 1987.

PAGE
108   "It was reported": Louisville news clip, September 22, 1917, and *New York Times*, September 22, 1917.

109   "That car belonged to my father": Interview, BB with author, Louisville, February 5, 1987.

109   "Body Secretly Exhumed": *Courier-Journal*, September 24, 1917. This story was also reported in the *New York Times*, September 21, 22, 24, 1917.

109   "Mrs. Bingham Was Drugged": New York *American*, September 21, 1917.

109   "Husband Given No Chance": *Courier-Journal*, September 24, 1917.

CHAPTER TEN

111   he "was never even aware": Interview, BB with author, Louisville, February 5, 1987.

112   "The heirs of the Flagler fortune": Louisville *Evening Post*, September 26, 1917.

112   Haldeman family background drawn from David Cusick, "Déjà Vu," *Louisville Magazine*, March 1986.

113   "he walked to a window": Arthur Krock, *Memoirs: Sixty Years on the Firing Line* (New York: Funk & Wagnalls, 1968), p. 47.

113f. "might be in a vault": Telephone interview, Thomas Kenan with author.

114f. "About six months after his marriage": Dr. Hugh Young memo from research material about Judge Bingham and Mary Lily Flagler Bingham; legal dossier prepared by Gordon Davidson, February 1987.

115   "This statement makes it clear": Interview, Gordon Davidson with author, February 1987.

115   "to take Judge Bingham": Dr. Hugh Young, memorandum from BB to Macmillan & Co., April 12, 1987.

115   "The slight impairment": Edwin A. Weinstein, *Woodrow Wilson: A Medical and Psychological Biography* (Princeton: Princeton University Press, 1981), p. 365. Daniel's criticism of Wilson's doctors included Dr. Cary Grayson as well as Hugh Young, as detailed in Gene Smith, *When the Cheering Stopped* (New York: William Morrow, 1964), p. 111.

116   "As requested by you": Dr. Hugh Young to Aleen Bingham, February 14, 1940, from Davidson research papers about Judge Bingham and Mary Lily Flagler Bingham.

116   "I had just written": MB to BB, November 26, 1945, SL.

117   "I feel dreadful": Telephone interview, BB with author, March 1987.

117   "The Kenan brothers": Interview, BB with author, Louisville, February 5, 1987.

117   "Barry managed to sublimate": Interview, MB with author, Louisville, June 1986.

CHAPTER ELEVEN

118   "I have always regarded": "Mirror of a Century," *Courier-Journal*, November 10, 1968.

PAGE

119 Information about Arthur Krock and the Judge drawn from Krock's *Memoirs* (New York: Funk & Wagnalls, 1968), pp. 48–49.

119 "a globe-trotter and a friend of prime ministers and presidents" and "convinced that Negroes": Llewellyn White, "Papers of Paradox: The Louisville Courier-Journal and Times Confounds Critics of Press Monopolies," *Reporter,* January 31, 1950, p. 23.

119 "unfair and unsavory": Krock, *Memoirs,* p. 49.

119 "fell into the extreme": Krock, *Memoirs,* p. 28.

120 Information about James Brown drawn from Michael Lesy, *Real Life: Louisville in the Twenties* (New York: Pantheon Books, 1976) pp. 68–69; White, "Papers of Paradox," p. 24; George Yater, *Flappers, Prohibition and All that Jazz: Louisville Remembers the Twenties* (Louisville: Museum of History and Science), pp. 26–27.

121 "the somehow hopeful": BB to MB, September 24, 1944, SL.

121 "unAmerican and unpatriotic": "Mirror of a Century," p. 11.

121 "They were extremely plain people": Interview, Sophie Alpert with Sam Thomas, Louisville, June 24, 1986.

121 "the Presence": Aleen Bingham to Margaret Norton, June 1933.

121 "and slaughtered every young girl's reputation": Interview, Sophie Alpert with Sam Thomas.

121f. "In view of my upcoming marriage": Codicil, dated August 20, 1924.

122 "He was kicked out of Princeton": Interview, Elsie Hilliard Chambers with Sam Thomas, Louisville, August 11, 1986.

122 "He was most courtly": "Mirror of a Century," p. 11.

122 "Oh Lord": Interview, BB with author, Louisville, January 17, 1986.

123 "Flossy flirt": "Mirror of a Century," p. 12.

123 "My father wanted": Interview, BB with author, Louisville, January 17, 1986.

CHAPTER TWELVE

125 "Barry invited her": Interview, MB with author, June 1986.

125 "I was a lot less Southern": Ibid.

126 "In Louisville like everywhere else": Interview, Suzanne Browder Hamlin with author, New York, March 1986.

127 "Enlist in the War Against Depression" and Louisville during the Depression drawn in part from Yater, *Flappers, Prohibition and All that Jazz,* pp. 194–195.

128 "girls together" and "I didn't play bridge": Interview, MB with author, Louisville, June 1986.

128 "her ornate feminine tastes": Interview, MB with author, Louisville, February 5, 1987.

128 "Mother dressed us in coat and tie": Interview, Barry Bingham Junior with author, Louisville, February 6, 1987.

128f. "How We Raised Our Six Daughters": Helena Lefroy Caperton, *The Woman's Home Companion,* December 1930.

129 "implant the seed": Helena Lefroy Caperton, *Ladies' Home Journal,* November 1933.

PAGE

129   ''My mother used to say'': Interview, Suzanne Browder Hamlin with author.

129f.   ''The red-haired concierge'': BB to MB, September 16, 1944, SL.

130   ''At first, they thought it was pneumonia'': Interview, BB with author, Louisville, February 5, 1987.

130   ''what a fine one'': MB to BB, May 7, 1944, SL.

130   ''My anxiety about you sharpened'': MB to BB, March 28, 1945, SL.

130   ''I have been thinking back'': MB to BB, May 7, 1944, SL.

130   ''darby'': Interview, MB with author, Louisville, June 1986.

130f.   Information on the Chicago convention of 1932 drawn from Ted Morgan, *FDR: A Biography* (New York: Simon & Schuster, 1985), p. 351.

131   ''I saw Roosevelt'': Interview, BB with author, Louisville, February 5, 1987.

132   ''There were probably four thousand people'': Telephone interview, Kenneth Davis with author.

132   ''stiff dose for the international bankers'': Raymond Moley, *After Seven Years* (New York: Harper & Brothers, 1939), p. 112.

132   ''a swivel chair Colonel'': *Congressional Record*, March 15, 1933, pp. 377–78.

133   ''May was out to get my father'': Interview, BB with author, Louisville, February 5, 1987.

133   ''We gathered around'': Interview, BB for ''Oral History of the Courier-Journal,'' Marlow Cook Papers, University of Louisville.

CHAPTER THIRTEEN

134   ''a pleasant conformist'': *New York Times*, December 9, 1937.

134   ''The Duke of Windsor'': *Franklin D. Roosevelt and Foreign Affairs* (Cambridge: Belknap Press of Harvard University, 1969), vol. III, Judge Bingham to Franklin Roosevelt, January 5, 1937.

134   ''dangerous and menacing possibilities'': Ibid, Bingham to FDR, September 4, 1936.

134   ''latent fever'': *New York Times*, December 19, 1937

135   ''Bob has been quite ill'': Aleen Bingham to Margaret Norton, April 25, 1933.

135   ''battery of cameras'': *New York Times*, May 11, 1933.

135   ''Bob looked too sweet'': Aleen Bingham to Margaret Norton, May 26, 1933.

136   ''the vanity and pomposity'': *Franklin D. Roosevelt and Foreign Affairs*, Judge Bingham to FDR, December 4, 1933.

136   ''I remember so vividly'': BB to MB, September 24, 1943, SL.

136f.   ''My father discussed'': BB for ''Oral History of the Courier-Journal,'' Marlow Cook Papers, University of Louisville.

137   ''The whole time the Judge'': Interview, BB with author, Louisville, June 1986.

137   ''I think his happiest times'': Interview, Barry Bingham Junior with author, Louisville, February 6, 1987.

138   ''I began to hear'': Interview, BB for ''Oral History of the Courier-Journal.''

138   ''a liberal firebrand'': Interview, John Ed Pearce with author, Louisville, February 1986.

138   ''My father'': Telephone interview, David Ethridge with author.

PAGE
138 "sit all night": Interview, Barry Bingham Junior with author, Louisville, February 6, 1987.

138 "We kind of took": Interview, BB for "Oral History of the Courier-Journal."

138 "Please come to Louisville": Interview, Lee Segal with author. New York, spring 1987.

138f. "the beginning of the unique": "Mirror of a Century," p. 13.

139 "English journalistic practice": Internal *Time* memo, December 12, 1946.

139 "During that period": Interview, John Ed Pearce with author.

140 "The old propaganda story": Joseph P. Lash, *Eleanor and Franklin* (New York: W. W. Norton, 1971), pp. 519–20, letter from BB to Eleanor Roosevelt, August 1934.

140 "a perfect replica": Young, *A Surgeon's Autobiography,* p. 514.

141 "poor Bob was unconscious": Ibid., p. 515.

142 "My son Barry": *New York Times,* December 21, 1937.

142 "We just don't have enough": Interview, Lee Segal with author.

CHAPTER FOURTEEN

144 "serious and deep joy" and "The hope and belief": MB to BB, January 31, 1944, SL.

144 "We were very committed to the idea": Interview, MB with author, Louisville, June 9, 1986.

144 "seems to have decided": BB to MB, July 26, 1940, SL.

144f. "Worth came to me in despair": Interview, MB with author, Louisville, June 9, 1986.

145 "He asked me if": BB to MB, July 26, 1940, SL.

145 "It seemed to me that it was essential": Interview, BB for "Oral History of the Courier-Journal," Marlow Cook Papers, University of Louisville.

145 "the whole atmosphere" and "old trouts": BB to MB, May 19, 1941, June 19, 1941, SL.

146 "the deplorable Chatham episode": BB to MB, August 16, 1944, SL.

146 "The moment of his making": BB to MB, February 15, 1943, SL.

146f. "I think he is the greatest solace": Helena Caperton to BB, July 30, 1943, SL.

147 "a very, very courtly gentleman": Interview, BB for "Oral History of the Courier-Journal."

147 "embarrassing": BB to MB, January 12, 1942, SL.

147 "forty other Americans": BB to MB, January 18, 1942, SL.

147 "whipped cream": BB to MB, February 8, 1942, SL.

148 "Nancy Tree's taste": Interview, William Paley with author, New York.

148 "a baboonery beyond compare": BB to MB, February 8, 1942, SL.

148 "the old school friend": BB to MB, February 15, 1942, SL.

148 "the exact yellow": BB to MB, March 8, 1942, SL.

149 "no tendency to sit among the ruins": Copy of BB's speech attached to letter of April 17, 1942, BB to MB, SL.

149 "The Morning Star": BB to MB, March 15, 1942, SL.

149 "elected captain by his own men": BB to MB, February 8, 1942, SL.

PAGE

149   "Thank God, I did not prevent": BB to MB, February 15, 1943, SL.

150   "Am thinking constantly of the Swannanoa Club": BB to MB, June 9, 1942,
       SL.

CHAPTER FIFTEEN

151   "I won't dwell on that": BB to MB, August 30, 1942, SL.

151   "I imagine the children": BB to MB, January 18, 1942, SL.

151   "the same copy of War and Peace": BB to MB, August 30, 1942, SL.

151   "If you didn't understand the South": Telephone interview, Gay Talese with
       author.

152   "a bomber's moon": Interview, BB for "Oral History of the Courier-
       Journal," Marlow Cook Papers, University of Louisville.

152   "crowded but cheerful office": BB to MB, August 6, 1942, SL.

152   "cheerful and diplomatic liaison": Courier-Journal, November 4, 1944.

152f. "of Jonathan kicking his feet": BB to MB, August 6, 1942, SL.

154   "I take great comfort": MB to BB, November 29, 1944, SL.

155   "Is that your house?": BB to MB, February 15, 1943, SL.

155   "those capitalistic dream clothes": BB to MB, March 18, 1943, SL.

155   "clean shirts": MB to BB, September 27, 1942, SL.

156   "great-eyed country boy act": MB to BB, September 9, 1942, SL.

156   "the latch-key children": Courier-Journal, October 21, 1944.

156   "his tacky host . . .": MB to BB, October 8, 1942, SL.

156   "pure virtue": MB to BB, August 23, 1944, SL.

156   ". . . the children got themselves suitably dressed": MB to BB, October 8,
       1942, SL.

157   "with the queerest nightmare": MB to BB, December 16, 1942, SL.

157f. "with much surreptitious": MB to BB, December 25, 1942, SL.

158   "I am afraid I am": MB to BB, June 13, 1945, SL.

158   "Original sin": MB to BB, April 5, 1943, SL, and interview, MB with author,
       Louisville, June 9, 1986.

158   "Focus on your husband": Interview, Eleanor Bingham Miller with author,
       East Hampton, N.Y., July 29, 1986.

159   "Not that the dear children": MB to BB, May 7, 1977, SL.

159   "Miss Priss": Interview, MB with author, Louisville, June 9, 1986.

159   "responsible," "conventional," "original," and "affectionate": various let-
       ters MB to BB, 1/4/45, 5/15/43, 9/5/43, 10/28/44, 12/2/42, 8/3/43, 9/30/43
       etc., SL.

159   "The little girls": MB to BB, December 3, 1944, SL.

160   "I will never understand": Interview, MB with author, Louisville, June 9,
       1986.

160   "I thought of her as my real mother": Interview, Sallie Bingham with author,
       Louisville, January 23, 1986.

160   "I have a weakness in that area": Helena Caperton to BB, October 22, 1942,
       SL.

160   "Her very quickness": Ibid., July 29, 1943.

PAGE

160 "Small children are not capable": Interview, MB with author, Louisville, June 9, 1986.

160 "Your being away from him now": MB to BB, SL.

161 "Barry and I were so in love with each other": Ibid.

161 "Surely we know": MB to BB, winter 1942, SL.

161 "filled with charm": MB to BB, November 8, 1942, SL.

161 "They were expendable": MB to BB, November 4, 1942, SL.

161 "a prissy companion": MB to BB, December 12, 1942, SL.

161 "that will delight": MB to BB, December 6, 1942, SL.

161 "hoards up everything": MB to BB, December 2, 1942, SL.

161 "Dear father": Worth Bingham to BB, June 11, 1945, SL.

161f. "Dear Mother": Barry Bingham Junior to MB, November 28, 1944, SL.

162 "Dear Mother, I have decided": Worth Bingham to MB, undated, SL.

162 "Dear Father": Worth Bingham to BB, May 5, 1943, SL.

162 "This sort of innocent": MB to BB, May 1945, SL.

163 "what was happening to liberal arts": MB to BB, November 23, 1942, SL.

163 "There are a good many newspaper men": BB to MB, winter 1943, SL.

163 "bright and wealthy young people": BB to MB, July 1, 1945, SL.

163 "those children": MB to BB, July 22, 1945, SL.

164 "moving the clientele of 21 to Glenview": MB to BB, June 13, 1945, SL.

164 "Clearly Arthur": Interview, MB with author, February 1987.

164 "highly congenial": MB to BB, April 19, 1944, SL.

164 "I always believed": Interview, Barry Bingham Junior with author, February 1987.

164 "Did you ever hear": MB to BB, December 15, 1944, SL.

164 "Afterward I took Sybil": BB to MB, September 2, 1944, SL.

165 "burning up the cables": BB to MB, August 14, 1944, SL.

165 "may provide an occasion": BB to MB, August 14, 1944, SL.

165 "a pretty, red-haired": BB to MB, December 20, 1942, SL.

165 "He put me off a little": BB to MB, June 14, 1944, SL.

165 "a la Maria": BB to MB, June 4, 1944, SL.

165 "terrible racism": BB to MB, January 20, 1943, SL.

166 "Cantabrigian": MB to BB, November 22, 1944, SL.

166 "I am sending you": MB to BB, December 3, 1944, SL.

167 "It has to do with": MB to BB, October 17, 1943, SL.

167 "I don't want to exercise": Telephone interview, MB with author.

167 "Too bad the libel laws": Telephone interview, Bill Cox with author, July 6, 1987.

167 "could feel the blood rise": MB to BB, October 30, 1944, SL.

167 "I do wish": BB to MB, November 1, 1942, SL.

167f. "I have always wanted": BB to MB, January 20, 1943, SL.

168 "My own opinion": MB to BB, October 28, 1943, SL.

169 ". . . the tag line": MB to BB, July 22, 1945, SL.

169 ". . . what a stinking": BB to MB, July 1, 1945, SL.

169 "the advisability": MB to BB, December 1944, SL.

170 "I imagine there is already": BB to MB, July 1, 1945, SL.

PAGE

CHAPTER SIXTEEN

171   "I get a nightmarish feeling": BB to MB, August 3, 1943, SL.
171   "awakened at 7:45 A.M.": MB to BB, November 1944, SL.
172   "one of the very nicest little boys": MB to BB, September 9, 1943, SL.
172   "I thought he was going to kiss me": Interview, Helen Hammon Jones with Sam Thomas, Louisville, August 5, 1986.
172   "very erect and handsome": MB to BB, spring 1943, SL.
172   "Streams of little boys": MB to BB, March 26, 1945, SL.
172   "The poor darling child": BB to MB, August 3, 1943, SL.
173   "the best adjusted": MB to BB, April 8, 1943, SL.
173   "best informed child": MB to BB, May 5, 1943, SL.
173f. "suffers by contrast": MB to BB, July 20, 1943, SL.
174   "I'm afraid he": MB to BB, May 1943, SL.
174   "of course such a place": MB to BB, February 8 (no year noted), SL.
174   "fear of not being able": MB to BB, June 18, 1945, SL.
174   "boy who doesn't really learn anything": BB to MB, July 1943(?), SL.
174   "merry little boy": Telephone interview, MB with author.
174   "He was such a pathetic thing": Interview, Sallie Bingham with author, Louisville, January 25, 1986.
175   "Sallie had, of course": MB to BB, June 8, 1945, SL.
175   "She . . . became so engrossed": MB to BB, April 18, 1945, SL.
175   "They were like a family to me": Interview, Sallie Bingham with author, Louisville, January 23, 1986.
175   "I believe blue stockingness": MB to BB, August 15, 1944, SL.
175   "The only time": Interview, Sallie Bingham with author, January 25, 1986.
175   "It was terrifying": Interview, BB with author, February 6, 1987.
175f. "Her verse": BB to MB, May 2, 1943, SL.
176   ". . . when I read": MB to BB, May 7, 1945, SL.
176   "a stranger": BB to MB, August 9, 1943, SL.
176   "agreeable Irish face": MB to BB, September 24, 1943, SL.
176   "I'm sorry to say": MB to BB, November 27, 1944, SL.
176   "Eat this": MB to BB, October 25, 1944, SL.
176   "Dear, dear Mama": MB to BB, December 18, 1944, SL.
176f. "I didn't rise as quickly": MB to BB, December 17, 1944, SL.
177   "He is much more": MB to BB, June 13, 1945, SL.
177   "hag-ridden . . .": MB to BB, September 7, 1943, SL.
177   "I do wish": MB to BB, June 22, 1945, SL.
177   "glandular exuberances": MB to BB, June 22, 1945, SL.
177f. "Worth, in one": MB to BB, May 1944, SL.
178   "Mother": MB to BB, October 28, 1944, SL.
178   "there was a sudden swish": MB to BB, September 23, 1944, SL.
178   "Oh Lord": MB to BB, September 1944, SL.

CHAPTER SEVENTEEN

179   C. MacKenzie, "Absent Fathers," *New York Times Magazine*, April 9, 1944, p. 9; J. Danziger, "Fathers in the Army," *New York Times Magazine*, October 10, 1943, p. 36; C. MacKenzie, "Fathers Home from War," *New York Times Magazine*, February 4, 1945, p. 33; "Children's Reaction to Temporary Loss of the Father," *American Journal of Psychiatry* 130:7, July 1973, footnotes.

179   "My father loves": Interview with longtime intimate of Bingham family.

180   "We thought Father": Interview, Barry Bingham Junior with author, Louisville, February 6, 1987.

180   "How could I understand": BB to MB, September 9, 1943, SL.

181   "hustle and bustle": BB to MB, October 25, 1942, SL.

181   "parable of the talents": BB to Worth Bingham, July 18, 1955, SL.

181   "Toughie": BB to Barry Bingham Junior, March 22, 1943, SL.

181f.   "I have just come back": BB to MB, May 2, 1943, SL.

CHAPTER EIGHTEEN

183   "It makes me blush and wriggle": BB to MB, May 2, 1944, SL.

184   "kinky-headed niggers": MB to BB, June 24, 1944, SL.

185   "I have never in my life been more moved": MB to BB, July 22, 1944, SL.

185   "in his queer dark": MB to BB, August 23, 1944, SL.

185   "Dear Mrs. Roosevelt": MB to Eleanor Roosevelt, July 25, 1944, SL.

186   Letter from Mark Ethridge to Franklin Roosevelt, July 25, 1944, SL.

187   ". . . and I must say": MB to BB, August 20, 1944, SL.

187   "Being in the same room": MB to BB, August 30, 1944, SL.

188   "Getting into bed": BB to MB, September 1944, SL.

188   "if you and I": BB to MB, September 16, 1944, SL.

188f.   "I seem to detect": MB to BB, August 2, 1944, SL.

189   "We will have . . .": BB to MB, August 18, 1944, SL.

189f.   "I can hardly express to you": MB to BB, December 14, 1944, SL.

190   "I suppose it is fundamentally": BB to MB, June 1944, SL.

190   "Our happiness together": BB to MB, August 20, 1944, SL.

190   "The only real thing": MB to BB, March 13, 1945, SL.

190   "tiresome": MB to BB, April 4, 1945, SL.

191   "too sharp at cards": MB to BB, March 21, 1945, SL.

191   "their new DePinna": MB to BB, November 15, 1943, SL.

191   "I have sometimes wondered": MB to BB, December 21, 1944, SL.

191   "I would not call Sallie": MB to BB, October 4, 1944, SL.

191   "It is very queer": MB to BB, October 1, 1944, SL.

191   "Your father was so horrible": Interview, Clara Bingham with author, New York, May 27, 1987.

192   "It was the first time": Interview, Sallie Bingham with author, Louisville, January 1986.

PAGE

192   "I have just heard": MB to BB, April 12, 1945, SL.
192   "I feel sorrier": MB to BB, April 15, 1945, SL.
192   "This tragic thing": MB to BB, April 12, 1945, SL.
192f. "I could hardly believe it": Worth Bingham to MB, April 21, 1945, SL.

CHAPTER NINETEEN

194   "stunned, lost and empty feeling": BB to MB, April 23, 1945, SL.
194   "to keep the correspondents": BB to MB, April 16, 1945, SL.
194f. "the narrowing of Natt's life": MB to BB, April 21, 1945, SL.
195   "We thought she was dead": Interview, Barry Bingham Junior with author, Louisville, February 6, 1987.
195   "I sometimes think": MB to BB, December 16, 1942, SL.
195   "Dr. Sprague's": BB to MB, July 20, 1943, SL.
195   "simply baffled": MB to BB, June 22, 1945, SL.
195   "Aunt Henrietta was": Interview, Barry Bingham Junior with author, Louisville, February 6, 1987.
195   "I suppose, poor dear": MB to BB, April 26, 1944, SL.
195f. "In the unreal world": BB to MB, July 1945, SL.
196   "solitude": MB to BB, August 1944, SL.
196   "bottles safely hidden": BB to MB, March 7, 25, 1944, SL.
196   "extremely hazardous situation": MB to BB, August 6, 1944, SL.
196   "the inability to admit": Interview, MB with author, Louisville, February 5, 1987.
197   "Isn't it nice": MB to BB, March 6, 1944, SL.
197   "murky Freudian assumptions": MB to BB, April 21, 1945, SL.
197   "psychotic": MB to BB, April 21, 1945, SL.
197   "The Lost Weekend": MB to BB, February 8, 1944, SL.
197   "had a hauntingly": BB to MB, March 7, 1944, SL.
197   "It was so boring": MB to BB, spring 1944, SL.
197   "I have given the electric": Henrietta Bingham to BB, April 1944, SL.
197   "I shall not": MB to BB, April 21, 1945, SL.
198   "This is just the minute": MB to BB, April 16, 1944, SL.
198   "She never would know anything": Interview, MB with author, Louisville, June 9, 1986.
198   "In general narcissists": MB to BB, April 21, 1945, SL.
198   "every five months": Dr. Spafford Ackerly to BB, August 8, 1944, SL.
198f. ". . . t199chance that": BB to MB, June 4, 1945, SL.
199   "good works": MB to BB, May 20, 1945, SL.
199f. "She was always": Interview, MB with author, Louisville, June 9, 1986.
200   "My sister": Interview, BB with author, Louisville, February 6, 1986.
200   "remorse": MB to BB, June 9, 1945, SL.
200   "He was": Interview, BB with author, Louisville, February 6, 1986.
200   "Uncle Robert": Interview, Barry Bingham Junior with author, February 6, 1987.
200f. "is convinced that": MB to BB, July 4, 1944, SL.
201   "neurotic indecision": MB to BB, September 24, 1944, SL.

PAGE
201   "midnight feasts": MB to BB, August 25, 1944, SL.

201   ". . . I still feel": MB to BB, December 14, 1944, SL.

201   "I don't know why": MB to BB, June 6, 1945, SL.

202   "Mother screamed at us": Interview, Barry Bingham Junior with author, Lou-
      isville, February 6, 1987.

202   "This was a most": Interview, MB with author, Louisville, January 24, 1986.

202   "My own darling": MB to BB, July 14, 1945, SL.

203   Mary Bingham's assessment of George Retter's character proved to be wrong.
      Retter remained in Louisville and became a successful businessman, running
      the George Retter Lawn Service. He declined to be interviewed about the
      Bingham family.

204   "of dubious habits": BB to MB, July 29, 1945, SL.

204   ". . . I would not": BB to MB, July 1945, SL.

204   "I had to go to Loubelle": Interview, MB with author, Louisville, January
      24, 1986.

204f. "with his clarinet": MB to BB, August 22, 1945, SL.

205   "outcry from the": BB to MB, August 12, 1945, SL.

205   "I've paid $20": Interview, Thomas Guinzburg with author, New York.

206   "tawdry, cheap and tasteless": BB to MB, September 1945, SL.

206   "I will not try": BB to MB, September 7, 1945, SL.

206f. "Worth and Barry": MB to BB, September 1945, SL.

207   "I want to be somewhere": MB to BB, September 4, 1945, SL.

207   "get caught up in": MB to BB, July 29, 1945, SL.

207f. "You know, I can hardly": MB to BB, July 14, 1945, SL.

CHAPTER TWENTY

209   "Mark Ethridge will never give": Internal *Time* memo, February 28, 1946.

209   "would not miss a committee meeting": Interview, Joan Bingham with author,
      Washington, January 21, 1987.

210   "Mother's role was very much": Interview, Sallie Bingham with author, Lou-
      isville, January 23, 1986.

210   "the most sincerely liberal": Internal *Time* memo, February 28, 1946.

210   *Courier-Journal* "Editorial Notebook," dated January 2, 1959, December 30,
      1959, March 22, 1963, January 19, 1963.

210   "wide grass-meadows": "Editorial Notebook," *Courier-Journal*, November
      17, 1961.

211   "When Mark Ethridge": Interview, John Ed Pearce with author, Louisville,
      February 1986.

211   "quite sure we should": Interview, BB with author, Louisville, January 17,
      1986.

211   "was really the person": Interview, Eleanor Bingham Miller with author, Lou-
      isville, January 24, 1986.

211   "for someone to take care of": Interview, Sallie Bingham with author, Lou-
      isville, January 25, 1986.

211   "job jar": Interview, Eleanor Bingham Miller with author, Louisville, January
      24, 1986.

PAGE

211   "It was logical": Interview, Barry Bingham Junior with author, February 6, 1987.

211f.   *Milk of Paradise:* performed at the American Place Theater, March 1980, in New York.

212   "a bad sinking spell": BB to MB, June 8, 1949, SL.

212   "very tired and strung up": BB to MB, June 11, 1949, SL.

213   "nervous and brittle as Robert": BB to MB, June 26, 1949, SL.

213   "Are All Mission Chiefs": *Eureca,* June 1949.

213   "a disaster": Interview, Barry Bingham Junior with author, Louisville, February 6, 1987.

213   "He resented my return": Interview, BB with author, Louisville, February 5, 1987.

213   "If you're coming": Interview, Barry Bingham Junior with author, February 6, 1987.

214   "I can't help": BB to MB, June 11, 1949, SL.

214f.   "Moral Rearmament": Interview, Barry Bingham Junior with author, February 6, 1987.

215   "marched Worth down the road": Telephone interview, Joan Bingham with author.

215   "I'm not learning anything": Interview, MB with author, Louisville, January 23, 1986.

215   "watch as the models": Interview, Barry Bingham Junior with author, Louisville, February 6, 1987.

216   "were out every night": Interview, Eleanor Bingham Miller with author, Louisville, January 24, 1986.

CHAPTER TWENTY-ONE

217   "Compared to the Binghams": Telephone interview, Katharine Johnson with author.

217   "We'll run it on page one": Interview, MB with author, Louisville, June 9, 1986.

218   "It was psychedelic": Interview, Eleanor Bingham Miller with author, Louisville, January 24, 1986.

218   The anecdote about the Windsors appeared in J. Bryan III and Charles J. V. Murphy, *The Windsor Story* (New York: William Morrow, 1979), p. 549.

218   "They were the king and queen": Telephone interview, Suzanne Browder Hamlin with author, September 1987.

218   "I only pleaded that he . . .": Kenneth Davis, A *Prophet in his Own Country* (New York: Doubleday, 1957), p. 393.

218   "to get Stevenson": Interview, Wilson Wyatt with author, Louisville, February 7, 1986.

219   "exhaustive study": *New York Times,* November 10, 1952.

220   "We went to every": Interview, MB with author, Louisville, January 24, 1986.

220   "wrecked": Interview, John Ed Pearce with author, Louisville, February 1986.

220   "forbidden parks": Anne Braden, *The Wall Between* (New York: Monthly Review Press, 1958), p. 8.

PAGE

220   "If it sounded Russian": Telephone interview, Anne Braden with author, spring
      1987.

221   "I'm going to tell them": Telephone interview, Richard Harwood with author.

221   "Why don't you?": Telephone interview, Anne Braden with author, spring
      1987.

221   "advocating sedition": New York Times, December 11, 1954.

221   "Sedition is Communism": Braden, The Wall Between, p. 271. (Mrs. Braden
      dedicated her book to her children "and all the other white children in the
      South, who today may have the opportunity my generation never had—to grow
      up with out the blight of segregation on their souls.")

221   "Carl Braden's employment": New York Times, December 11, 1954.

222   "I can remember": Interview, Stewart Bryan with author, Richmond, June
      1986.

222   "I taught him lessons": Interview, Norma Isaacs with author, Dobbs Ferry
      N.Y., March 10, 1986.

222f. Information about Worth Bingham at Harvard drawn from interviews from his
      friends and classmates John Macrae, Ward Just, John Wagley, David Halber-
      stam.

223f. "They were all very sophisticated": Interview, Helen Hammon Jones with
      Sam Thomas, Louisville, August 5, 1986.

224   "It was unbelievable": Interview, Barry Bingham Junior with author, Louis-
      ville, February 6, 1987.

224   "absolutely fabulous": Interview, Barry Bingham Junior with author, Louis-
      ville, January 17, 1986.

225   "I fear he is a gourmand": BB to MB, March 5, 1953, SL.

225   "My impression is confirmed": BB to MB, March 28, 1953, SL.

225   "but on the night": Interview, Joan Bingham with author, Washington, Janu-
      ary 1986.

225   "The four years of Harvard": BB to MB, April 16, 1953, SL.

226   "dodged an invitation": BB to MB, May 5, 1953, SL.

226   "She was particularly": Interview, MB with author, Louisville, June 9, 1986.

226   "determined to be an oddball": Interview, Louise Duncan with author, New
      York, March 8, 1986.

226   "I didn't go out on a date": Interview, Sallie Bingham with author, Louisville
      January 1986.

227   "has a tongue": Alex Jones, "Fall of the House of Bingham," New York
      Times, January 19, 1986.

227   "You get out of that car": Telephone interview, David Ethridge with author
      July 2, 1987.

227   "How dare you!": Interview, Lee Segal with author, New York, spring 1987

CHAPTER TWENTY-TWO

229   "When we went anywhere": Interview, Sallie Bingham with Diane Sawyer on
      60 Minutes.

229   "I had never seen": Interview, Fred Seidel with author, New York, May 12
      1987.

PAGE
229 "more of a Bingham": Interview, Louise Duncan with author, New York,
     March 8, 1986.
230 "They were madly in love": Interview, Ward Just with author, Boston, March
     11, 1986.
230 "wasn't worth": Internal *Time* memo, undated.
230 "which read him the riot act": Interview, Norma Isaacs with author, Dobbs
     Ferry, N.Y., March 10, 1986.
230 "Smith threw his stories": Internal *Time* memo, undated.
230 "It was amazing": Telephone interview, David Halberstam with author.
231 "I loved what I was doing": Interview, Barry Bingham Junior with author,
     Louisville, February 6, 1987.
231 "dressed beautifully": Interview, Ann Arensberg with author, New York,
     spring 1986.
231 "apathy": Telephone interview, David Halberstam with author, spring 1986.
231 "The Radcliffe dean": Interview, Sallie Bingham with author, Louisville, Jan-
     uary 1986.
232 "women": Interview, MB with author, Louisville, January 1986.
232 "Unhappiness": Interview, Fred Seidel with author.
232 "Jonathan was": Interview, BB with author, Louisville, January 17, 1986.
232 "a wounded animal": Telephone interview, Diane Sawyer with author.
232 "He seemed to always be dressed": Telephone interview, Suzanne Browder
     Hamlin, with author.
232 "Europe is very nice": Interview, Lee Segal with author.
232 "Eleanor is now 'fat' ": Telephone interview, James Callahan with author,
     January 1987.
233f. "totally out of my depth": Interview, Joan Bingham with author, Washington,
     January 21, 1986.
234 "It was a great opportunity": Interview, Barry Bingham Junior with author,
     Louisville, January 23, 1986.
235 "Send a telegram": Interview, Joan Bingham with author.
235 "He was profane": Interview, Alanna Nash with Sallie Bingham, Louisville,
     summer, 1985.
235 "You can have the moon": "Fall of the House of Bingham," *New York Times*.
235 "This was ridiculous": Interview, Barry Bingham Junior with author, Louis-
     ville, February 6, 1987.
236 "so highly favored": Interview, Sallie Bingham with author, Louisville, Jan-
     uary 1986.
236 "He liked her": Interview, Joan Bingham with author.
236 "They were such different personalities": Interview, Norman Isaacs with
     author.
237 "put aside": Telephone interview, Jay Iselin with author.
237 "I didn't want to get married": Interview, Joan Bingham with author.
237 "personally asked": Interview, Joan Bingham with author.

PAGE

CHAPTER TWENTY-THREE

239   "He loved to thumb": Interview, Ward Just with author, Boston, March 11, 1986.

239   "You've got to bring": Interview, Barry Bingham Junior with author, Louisville, February 6, 1987.

239   "literally thousands of thank-you notes": Interview, Joan Bingham with author.

240   "I wanted Worth": Interview, BB for "Oral History of the Courier-Journal," Marlow Cook Papers, University of Louisville.

240   "He had a great eye for a con": Interview, Ward Just with author.

241   "Worth demanded his birthright": Interview, Joan Bingham with author.

241   "I knew he was fine": Interview, Norman Isaacs with author.

241   "Isn't it about time?": Interview, Barry Bingham Junior with author, Louisville, February 6, 1987.

241   "I like to do the correct thing": Interview, Edie Bingham with author, Louisville, February 6, 1987.

242   "curious": Interview, Joan Bingham with author.

CHAPTER TWENTY-FOUR

243   "I thought he was": Interview, Sallie Bingham with author, Louisville, January 23, 1986.

243   "Jonathan did not know": Interview, Suzanne Browder Hamlin with author.

244   "Do you have": Interview, Louise Duncan with author.

244   "We knew everyone": Interview, Suzanne Browder Hamlin with author, New York, March 1986.

244   "It was a terrible tragedy because it was as if": Conversation, George Plimpton with author, East Hampton, N.Y., September 6, 1987.

244   "opalescent eyes": Interview, Louise Duncan with author.

245   "extra-enthusiastic undergraduates": Telephone interview, Richard Alpert with author, April 28, 1987.

245   "he had been": Interview, Louise Duncan with author.

245   "maybe two or three": Telephone interview, Richard Alpert with author.

246   "Something terrible": Interview, Sallie Bingham with author, Louisville, January 25, 1986.

246   "Jonathan followed": Telephone interview, Louise Duncan with author.

246   "Peter wants me": Diary of Louise Duncan, 1963–64.

246   "It was always Peter": Interview, Louise Duncan with author.

246   "Jonathan wants to pursue": Interview, BB with author, Louisville, January 17, 1986.

246   "asked to leave": Interview, Louise Duncan with author.

246   "Maybe he was schizophrenic": Interview, Sallie Bingham with author, January 1986.

247   "was deeply involved": Interview, BB with author, Louisville, January 1986.

PAGE

247   "We let out": Interview, Eleanor Bingham Miller with author, Louisville, January 24, 1986.

247ff. Information on Jonathan Bingham's death drawn from interviews with Norman Isaacs, Eleanor Bingham Miller, Joan Bingham, Louise Duncan and MB and BB.

248   "My mother simply fell apart": Interview, Eleanor Bingham Miller, Louisville, June 13, 1985.

249   "You have never": Interview, Joan Bingham with author, Washington, January 1986.

249   "would never be able": Telephone interview, James Callahan with author.

249   "I don't believe": Interview with intimate of Bingham family.

249   "It was grotesque": Telephone interview, Barry Bingham Junior with author, spring 1987.

249   "For God's sake": Ibid.

250   "We were going to hide": Interview, Louise Duncan with author, New York, March 8, 1986.

250   "to put away": Interview, Sallie Bingham with author, Louisville, January 25, 1986.

251   "We all appreciate . . .": Sallie Bingham, *The Way It Is Now* (New York: Viking, 1970), "Mourning," pp. 41–53.

251   "Sallie's writing": Interview, MB with author, Louisville, June 9, 1986.

251   "Was I close": Interview, Sallie Bingham with author, Louisville, January 25, 1986.

CHAPTER TWENTY-FIVE

253   "I asked them about": Interview, Eleanor Bingham Miller with author, East Hampton, N.Y., July 29, 1986.

253   "My father literally said": Interview, Barry Bingham Junior with author, Louisville, February 6, 1987.

253   "What do I need": Interview, BB with author, Louisville, January 1986.

253   "One must always": Interview, Tania Vartan with author, New York, March 8, 1986.

253   "Their stoicism": Interview, Wilson Wyatt with author, Louisville, February 7, 1987.

253f. "If you ever talk": Interview, Barry Bingham Junior with author, Louisville, February 6, 1987.

254   "Mary had a certain darkening": Interview, BB with author, Louisville, January 1986.

254   "We heard that Johnson": Telephone interview, Joan Bingham with author. (Whatever the Bingham family believed about Lyndon Johnson and Earle Clements, there is some evidence that Lyndon Johnson and Earle Clements had had a serious break in their relationship by the time Johnson was elected president in 1964.)

254   "Worth would get up at five A.M.": Interview, Joan Bingham with author, Washington, January 1986.

PAGE

257   ''very much at loose ends'': Interview, Sallie Bingham with author, Louisville,
      January 25, 1986.

257   ''It was terrible'': Interview, Eleanor Bingham Miller with author, Louisville,
      June 13, 1985.

257f. ''Good morning, Father'': Telephone interview, James Callahan with author.

258   ''Eleanor was certainly'': Interview, MB and BB with author, Louisville, Jan-
      uary 17, 1986.

258   ''We invited him back again'': Eleanor Bingham to Michael Kirkhorn, ''The
      Bingham Black Sheep,'' Louisville Today, June 1979, p. 39.

258   ''She would come here'': Interview, Barry Bingham Junior with author, Lou-
      isville, February 6, 1987.

258   ''Eleanor has seen'': Interview, MB with author, Louisville, June 9, 1986.

258   ''You would always see something'': Interview, Ann Arensberg with author,
      New York, February 1986.

258f. ''They needed somebody'': Interview, Sallie Bingham with Alanna Nash.

259   ''Sallie just seemed miserable'': Interview, Fred Seidel with author, New York,
      May 12, 1986.

259   ''Worth and Whitney'': Interview, Joan Bingham with author, Washington,
      January 21, 1986.

259f. ''I didn't know what to do'': Interview, Fred Seidel with author.

260   ''She would look at you'': Interview, Ann Arsensberg with author, New York.

260   ''Sallie's entire problem'': Interview, MB with author.

260   ''She was a lovely'': Telephone interview, Barbara Epstein with author.

261   ''It was as if'': Interview, Joan Bingham with author.

261   ''We are going'': Sallie Bingham, The Way it is Now, ''The Visit,'' pp. 151-
      56.

261   ''You know who'': Interview, Sallie Bingham with Alanna Nash.

261   ''bring myself'': Interview, MB with author, Louisville, January 17, 24, 1986.

262   ''no willingness to spar'': Interview, MB with author.

CHAPTER TWENTY-SIX

263   ''He told me'': Telephone interview, Richard Harwood with author.

263   ''The weather here'': Norman Isaacs, Courier-Journal, July 13, 1966.

264   ''It was an old wood station wagon'': Telephone interview, Joan Bingham with
      author, winter 1987.

264ff. Information about Worth Bingham's death was also drawn from interviews
      from John Wagley, Joan Bingham and Norman Isaacs.

264   ''We called the ambulance'': Telephone interview, Joan Bingham with author.

264   ''The phone buzzed'': Interview, Norman Isaacs with author, Dobbs Ferry,
      March 10, 1986.

265   ''Oh my God, Edie'': Telephone interview, Joan Bingham with author.

265   ''The plane was a DC-3'': Interview, Barry Bingham Junior with author,
      Louisville, January 17, 1986.

265f. ''He was a big'': Norman Isaacs, Courier-Journal, July 13, 1966.

266   ''Worth has been killed . . .'': Interview, Ward Just with author, Boston, March
      11, 1986.

PAGE

266 "His death is a terrible tragedy": Telephone interview, Joan Bingham with author.

266 "was the closest person": Interview, Barry Bingham Junior with author, Louisville, January 23, 1986.

266 "a beastly hot day": Telephone interview, John Wagley with author.

267 "I know how devastated": Interview, Joan Bingham with author.

267 "as a brawl": Telephone interview, Richard Harwood with author.

267 "He sobbed and cried": Sallie Bingham to Alex Jones, *New York Times*, January 19, 1986.

267 "What would you like to do?": Interview, BB with author, Louisville, January 1986.

267 "He could have told me anything" and "When Barry told me": Interview, Barry Bingham Junior and Edie Bingham with author, Louisville, January 23, 1986.

CHAPTER TWENTY-SEVEN

269 "Television will replace newspapers": Interview, John Ed Pearce with author.

270 "We simply did not know": Interview, BB with author, Louisville, January 1986.

270 "We knew Louisville": Interview, Barry Bingham Junior with author, Louisville, January 1986.

271 "She thought journalism": Ibid.

271 "I took one look": Interview, Edie Bingham with author, Louisville, February 6, 1986.

271 "Why can't we use the one?": Interview, Barry Bingham Junior and Edie Bingham with author, Louisville, January 23, 1986 and February 6, 1987.

273 "Sallie was very brave": Interview, Ann Arensberg with author, New York, spring 1987.

273 ". . . Her remarkable virtuosity": *New York Times*, April 23, 1972.

274f. "I wanted him to do things": Interview, BB with author, Louisville, January 17, 1986.

275 "dazzled by the Binghams": Interview, Kathy Sloane with author, New York, May 6, 1987.

275 "We thought it was odd": Interview, Edie Bingham with author, Louisville, February 6, 1987.

275 "Barry was just stoic": Interview, Kathy Sloane with author.

275 "If you had to think of": Telephone interview, Edie Bingham with author, spring 1987.

276 "I said to everyone, 'I am sorry that' ": Telephone interview, Barry Bingham Junior with author, spring 1987.

276 "I loved every minute": Interview, Kathy Sloane with author.

276 "In his acceptance speech . . .": Telephone interview, Barry Bingham Junior with author.

276 "He was such a social publisher": Interview, Ben Bradlee with author, East Hampton, N.Y., August 1986.

276 "Do you think Barry is too rigid": Interview, Wilson Wyatt with author.

PAGE

276 "Louisville Newspapers Cherish": *Wall Street Journal*, July 1, 1974.

277 "If there is a book published": Interview, Lee Segal with author.

277 "I thought Kathy would": Interview, Edie Bingham with author, Louisville, February 6, 1987.

278 "We were a small city": Telephone interview, MB with author.

278 "There was so much to be done": Interview, Kathy Sloane with author.

278 "Many people": Interview, Edie Bingham with author.

278 "a million gallons of gas": Telephone interview, Barry Bingham Junior with author, September 1987.

278 "two hundred fifty": Interview, Donald Towles for "Oral History of the Courier-Journal," Marlow Cook Papers, University of Louisville.

278 "No new": Telephone interview, Barry Bingham Junior with author.

278 "We thought it was the Hodgkin's disease": Interview, Carol Sutton for "Oral History of the Courier-Journal."

279 "The newspapers were": Interview, Barry Bingham Junior with author, Louisville, February 6, 1987.

280 "Somewhere along the line": Wendell Cherry to Fred Powledge, as reported in "City in Transition": *New Yorker*, September 9, 1974. (Wendell Cherry refused to be interviewed by the author.)

CHAPTER TWENTY-EIGHT

281 "Confiding in Sallie": Interview, Bingham family member with author.

281 "Her knowledge of everything": Interview, Edie Bingham, Louisville, January 23, 1986.

281f. "I always felt": Interview, Edie Bingham with author, Louisville, February 6, 1987.

282 "Are you the father?": Interview, Barry Bingham Junior with author, Louisville, February 6, 1987.

282 "You don't know anything": Interview, Edie Bingham with author.

283 "Why did he memorize": Interview, Joan Bingham with author, New York, January 19, 1987.

283 "My agent dumped me": Interview, Sallie Bingham with Alanna Nash.

283 "Sallie was slowly": Interview, Thomas Lipscomb with author, New York, June 1987.

284 "she would get in a rage": Interview, Joan Bingham with author, Louisville, January 21, 1986.

284 "Marriage is a dreadful institution": Interview, Clara Bingham with author, New York, May 27, 1987.

284 "She was showing some grainy video": Interview, Thomas Lipscomb with author.

284 "What is it that Sallie": Interview, MB and BB with author, Louisville, January 17, 1986.

284f. "The spring in Louisville": Interview, Sallie Bingham with author, Louisville, January 23, 1986.

285 "a perfectly reasonable": Interview, MB with author.

285 "He thought it would be better": Interview, Sallie Bingham with author.

PAGE
285 "I believe": Interview, MB with author, Louisville, January 24, 1986.
285 "There were endless complaints": Interview, Sallie Bingham with author,
     Louisville, January 1986.

CHAPTER TWENTY-NINE

287 "It was almost as if": Interview, Bingham family member with author.
287 "Mother and Daddy really wanted": Telephone interview, Eleanor Bingham
     Miller with author, October 1, 1987.
288 "How does Punch": Interview, BB, Louisville, February 19, 1986. (Ruth
     Golden Holmberg is the publisher of the Chattanooga *Times* and a member of
     the board of the New York Times company.)
288 "This newspaper is for them": Interview, Barry Bingham Junior with author,
     Louisville, January 17, 1986.
288f. "I said to my father": Interview, Barry Bingham Junior with author, Louis-
     ville, February 6, 1987.
289 "After the war": Interview, MB with author, Louisville, June 9, 1986.
289 "It was a natural instinct": Interview, Eleanor Bingham Miller with author,
     Louisville, January 24, 1986.
289 "an expert on . . . foreign relations": Interview, Cyrus MacKinnon for "Oral
     History of the Courier-Journal," Marlow Cook Papers, University of Louis-
     ville.
290 "I knew everything": Telephone interview, Barry Bingham Junior with author,
     spring 1987.
290 "Sallie made us all so nervous": Interview, MB with author, Louisville, Jan-
     uary 17, 1986.
290f. "John Ed, I know I will be": Telephone interview, George Gill with author,
     spring 1987.
291 "a hippie": Interview, Hunt Helm with author.
291 "Rowland kept everyone": Interview, Bingham family member with author.
291 "were delighted when": Interview, Barry Bingham Junior with author, Lou-
     isville, February 6, 1987.
291 "where we used to ride": Letter, Barry Bingham Junior to Eleanor Bingham,
     July 25, 1975, and July 29, 1975.
291f. "It was my job": Interview, Eleanor Bingham with author, Louisville, January
     24, 1986.
292 "I could serve as a link": Interview, Paul Janensch with author, Louisville,
     February 19, 1986.
292 "to be doing some kind of penance": Interview, Sallie Bingham with author,
     Louisville, January 25, 1986.
292 "Eleanor really was": Interview, BB with author, Louisville, January 17, 1986.

CHAPTER THIRTY

294f. The *Courier-Journal* moved to another location during the Depression at Third
     Street and Liberty before occupying its current building in 1947.
295 "Mary and Barry never once disagreed": Interview, Barry Bingham Junior
     and Edie Bingham with author, Louisville, February 6, 1987.

PAGE

295 "Edie was always so stiff-necked": Interview, Kathy Sloane with author, New
     York, May 6, 1987.

296 "To the Editor of the Courier-Journal": *Courier-Journal,* October 15, 1979.

296 "I thought, 'All right' ": Interview, Edie Bingham with author.

296 "I had every right": Interview, MB with author, Louisville, February 5, 1987.

296 "It is pretty horrible": Interview, Barry Bingham Junior with author.

296 "Dear Mary, I realize also that . . .": Edie Bingham to MB, October 17, 1979.

297 "I said to her, 'I would like' ": Interview, Edie Bingham with author.

CHAPTER THIRTY-ONE

298 "Sallie was always": Interview, Barry Bingham Junior with author, Louisville,
     February 6, 1987.

299 "He was really doing nothing": Telephone interview, Sydney Gruson with
     author.

299 "Computers are the handiwork": Interview, Barry Bingham Junior with au-
     thor.

299 "People would say": Interview, Sallie Bingham with Alanna Nash.

299 "repressive gentility": Sallie Bingham to Michael Kirkhorn, "The Bingham
     Black Sheep," *Louisville Today,* June 1979, pp. 36–41.

300 "Your moves are gutting" and "Surely we do not intend": Eleanor and Sallie
     Bingham to Joe Ward, "The Binghams" in *Courier-Journal* supplement, April
     20, 1986, pp. 29–30.

300 "since the dividends": Interview, Barry Bingham Junior with author, Louis-
     ville, February 6, 1987.

300 "Barry was paranoid": Interview, Sallie Bingham with author, Louisville,
     January 23, 1986.

300 "We had listed one woman": Interview, Barry Bingham Junior with author.

300f. "We had a thousand pages": Interview, Barry Bingham Junior with author.

301 "Mother would always say": Interview, Sallie Bingham with author.

301f. Information on the buy-back drawn from Gordon Davidson and Barry Bingham
     Junior.

302 "You cannot fault [my parents]": Interview, Barry Bingham Junior with au-
     thor, Louisville, February 6, 1987.

302 "What is this?": Interview, Sallie Bingham with author.

302 "It was sheer perversity": Interview, Edie Bingham with author, Louisville,
     February 6, 1987.

302 "What would you advise me to": Interview, Barry Bingham Junior with au-
     thor.

302f. "Dear Sallie": Memos from Barry Bingham Junior dated July 11, 16, 22,
     1980.

303 "One summer in Patmos": Interview, Clara Bingham with author, New York,
     May 27, 1987.

303 "Barry, could we have": Interview, Barry Bingham Junior with author.

303 "Oh, come on, Barry": Interview, Rowland Miller with author, Louisville,
     January 24, 1986.

304 "I don't know why": Telephone interview, MB with author, spring 1987.

PAGE

304 "All that weekend": Interview, Joan Bingham with author, New York, January 19, 1987.

304 "At first, I was terrified": Interview, Sallie Bingham with author, Louisville, January 25, 1986.

304f. "Dear Kathy": Letter from Edie Bingham to Kathy Sloane, Louisville, December 1, 1980.

305 "I called Mary Bingham": Interview, Kathy Sloane with author, New York, May 6, 1987.

305 "I didn't expect my mother": Interview, Barry Bingham Junior with author.

305 "My brother and I disagree": Interview, Eleanor Bingham Miller with author, Louisville, January 24, 1986.

305 "betrayed": *Wall Street Journal,* October 21, 1981.

305f. "I think he thought": Interview, Barry Bingham Junior with author and telephone interviews, spring 1987, October 1987.

CHAPTER THIRTY-TWO

307 "hardly Sallie's equal": Telephone interview, MB, spring 1987.

307 "I suppose I learned": Interview, Sallie Bingham with author, Louisville, January 25, 1986.

307 "plying us with food and wine": Telephone interview, Elaine Corn with author.

308 "Sallie Bingham and Tim Peters": Interview, Ann Arensberg with author, spring 1986.

308 "I am sorry to say": Interview, MB and BB with author, Louisville, January 17, 1986.

308 "Why? Psychiatrists ruined": Telephone interview, Edie Bingham with author.

308 "I just don't know": Telephone interview, Elaine Corn with author.

309 "Look, Sallie, I agree with you . . .": Interview, Paul Janensch with author, Louisville, February 19, 1986.

309 "At first the tone was": Interview, Barry Bingham Junior with author, Louisville, February 6, 1987.

309f. "My father was a": Telephone interview, Léon Danco with author, spring 1987.

310 "The chapters were called things like": Interview, Sallie Bingham with author, Louisville, January 25, 1986.

310 "I got the clear impression": Interview, Léon Danco with author.

310f. "We catered it from": Interview, Sallie Bingham with author.

311 "You would never have known": Interview, John Ed Pearce with author.

CHAPTER THIRTY-THREE

312 "Mother always said to me": Interview, Eleanor Bingham Miller with author, East Hampton, N.Y., July 29, 1985.

312 "She is such a considerate": Interview, MB with author, Louisville, January 24, 1986.

313 "Eleanor's nature": Interview, BB with author, Louisville, January 1986.

PAGE

313   ''Well, they weren't around a lot'': Interview, Eleanor Bingham Miller with
      author.

313   ''It was as if'': Interview with an intimate of the Bingham family.

313   ''that Eleanor has the'': Interview, MB with author.

314   ''Eleanor is determined'': Interview, Sallie Bingham with author, Louisville,
      January 23, 1986.

314   ''I would always hear later'': Interview, Barry Bingham Junior with author,
      Louisville, February 6, 1987.

314   ''You might say'' and ''We were concerned'': Interview, Rowland Miller with
      author, Louisville, January 24, 1986, and telephone interview.

314   ''I thought my two years'': Interview, Eleanor Bingham Miller with author.

315   ''I never thought'': Interview, BB with author, Louisville, January 1986.

315   ''Eleanor did not know'': Interview, Edie Bingham with author, Louisville,
      February 6, 1986.

315   ''An oversight'': Interview, Barry Bingham Junior with author.

315   ''Maintain and improve the quality of products'': Intercom, March 1981.

315   ''They are generic'': Interview, Eleanor Bingham Miller with author.

315f. ''Family goals-setting project'': Memo to Barry Bingham Junior dated Decem-
      ber 1, 1983.

316   ''Eleanor's memo'': Telephone interview, Barry Bingham Junior with author.

316   ''I have something to say'': Interview, Eleanor Bingham Miller with author.

316   ''Sometimes it eases'': Eleanor Bingham Miller to Joe Ward, as reported in
      ''The Binghams: Twilight of a Tradition,'' Courier-Journal, April 20, 1987,
      p. 36.

317   ''There can only be one person'': Interview, MB with author.

317   ''Getting off the board'': Interview, Eleanor Bingham Miller with author.

317   ''Couldn't you just add'': Interview, Barry Bingham Junior with author.

317f. ''Whenever I went into'': Interview, Sallie Bingham with author, Louisville,
      January 25, 1986.

318   ''I think my children'': Interview, BB with author, Louisville, January 24,
      1986.

318   ''only remaining son'': Interview, Sallie Bingham with Alanna Nash.

318   ''The woolly-minded will'': Telephone interview, James Callahan with author.

318   ''There had been a bitter division'': Interview, MB with author, Louisville,
      January 17, 1986.

318   ''His father was'': Interview, BB with author, Louisville, January 17, 1986.

318   ''I am calling'': Telephone interview, Joan Bingham with author.

318   ''It is my belief'': Interview, BB with author.

318   ''He is fine'': Interview, Sallie Bingham with author, January 23, 1986.

318   ''I don't want to'': Interview, Sallie Bingham with Alanna Nash.

318   ''Sallie's fury'': Interview, BB with author.

319   ''At the climactic meeting'': Interview, Sallie Bingham with Alanna Nash.

319   ''this was a fight'': Interview, Paul Janensch with author, Louisville, February
      19, 1986.

319   ''I don't see how'': Interview, Sallie Bingham with author, Louisville, January
      17, 1986.

PAGE

319   "She wrote and said": Interview, MB with author, Louisville, January 24, 1986.

319   "That is so pitiful": Interview, Sallie Bingham with author, Louisville, January 25, 1986.

319   "I would call her": Interview, BB with author.

319f.   Information about the Easter lunch of 1984 drawn from interviews with Edie Bingham and Barry Bingham Junior.

320   "I told my parents": Interview, Sallie Bingham with author, January 1986.

320   "They had the most women": Telephone interview, Barry Bingham Junior with author.

320   "If you put your stock on the market": Interview, John Ed Pearce with Alanna Nash.

320f.   "I've taught myself to stop saying, 'Daddy' ": Interview, Sallie Bingham with author.

321   "I've given up being approved": Interview, Sallie Bingham with Alanna Nash.

321   "She was reasonable": Telephone interview, Stephen Schwarzman with author, spring 1987.

321   "I repeated to him": Interview, BB with author.

322   "Your son is costing": Interview, Barry Bingham Junior with author, Louisville, February 6, 1987.

322   "Eleanor was getting ready": Telephone interview, Joan Bingham with author.

322   "This was the summer": Interview, Rowland Miller with author, Louisville, January 24, 1986.

322f.   "Living together was a disaster": Interview, Joan Bingham with author.

323   "the Regency": Interview, Barry Bingham Junior with author, Louisville, January 17, 1986.

323   "Shakespeare is": *Smith Alumnae Quarterly,* Summer 1985, p. 11.

323   "On the surface": Interview, Edie Bingham and Barry Bingham Junior with author, Louisville, February 6, 1987.

324   "Barry seemed as reasonable": Telephone interview, Stephen Schwarzman with author.

324   "Share Offered in Louisville Newspaper Company," *New York Times,* January 14, 1985.

324f.   "They served wine": Interview, Joe Ward with Alanna Nash.

325   "There was a Bachrach": Interview, Elinor Brecher with author, Louisville, January 1986.

325   "I thought that was too low": Interview, Sallie Bingham with Joe Ward in "The Binghams: Twilight of a Tradition," *Courier-Journal,* supplement, August 20, 1986, p. 33.

325   "The telephone rings all the time": Interview, Sallie Bingham with Alanna Nash.

326   "Our profit margin was too low": Interview, Barry Bingham Junior with author.

326   "There was enough money": Interview, author with anonymous source involved with the final sale of the newspaper.

326   "He doesn't have any fun": Interview, Sallie Bingham with author.

PAGE

326 "I said to him": Telephone interview, Sydney Gruson with author.

327 "muled into Mary's ear": Interview, an intimate of the Bingham family wit author.

327 "He was the most overweight": Telephone interview, MB with author.

327 "Everything was different when we got home": Interview, Barry Bingham Junior with author, Louisville, February 6, 1986.

327 "13 Commandments": *Courier-Journal*, April 20, 1986, supplement, p. 34.

327 "All Eleanor had to do": Interview, Barry Bingham Junior with author, Lou isville, February 6, 1986.

327 "Dear, dear Mary, Our leave taking": Letter from Edie Bingham to MB March 1985.

328 "I don't want": Interview, Eleanor Bingham Miller with author, Louisville January 24, 1986.

328 "Eleanor has tried": Interview, MB with author, Louisville, January 24, 1986

328 "I know that you don't": Letter from Barry Bingham Junior to BB, April 10 1985.

329 "It was tragic": Telephone interview, Edie Bingham with author.

329 "look for evil motives": *Courier-Journal*, April 19, 1985.

329 "Breaking Away: Sallie Bingham": *Lexington Herald-Leader*, May 13 1985.

329 "I dislike Paul Janensch": Interview, Sallie Bingham with Alanna Nash.

329 "Sallie is having": Interview, MB with author, Louisville, June 9, 1986.

330 "Why didn't anyone": Interview, Barry Bingham Junior with author, Louis ville, February 6, 1987.

330 "I am afraid": Interview, BB with author, Louisville, January 17, 1986.

330 "It is mortifying" and "With all this business": Interview, Eleanor and Row land Miller with author, Louisville, June 1985.

330 "with Eleanor and Rowland pecking": Interview, Barry Bingham Junior with author, Louisville, February 6, 1986.

330 "Do you think Eleanor": Ibid.

331 "beside themselves with anguish": Interview, Eleanor Bingham Miller with author.

331 "My family is in an uproar": Telephone interview, BB with author, June 1985.

331 "The lid is coming off now": Interview with an intimate of the Bingham family.

331 "I think after": Interview, Kathy Sloane with author, New York, May 6, 1987.

331 "This rupture is": Telephone interview, Sallie Bingham with author, June 1985.

332 "the decline of the newspaper": Interview, Eleanor Bingham Miller with au thor, Louisville, January 24, 1986.

332 "It is a peculiar family": Telephone interview, John Ed Pearce with author.

332 "It was just shredding": Interview, MB with author, Louisville, January 17, 1986.

332 "You know what they say": Telephone interview, Kathy Sloane with author.

PAGE
332   "We were thrilled": Interview, Joan Bingham with author, Louisville, January 21, 1986.

333   "Daddy was terrified": Interview, Eleanor Bingham Miler with author.

333   "I wanted to offer her something": Interview, Barry Bingham Junior and Edie Bingham with author, Louisville, February 6, 1987.

333   "WHAS would have been": Interview, Rowland Miller with author, Louisville, January 24, 1986.

333f.   "Dear Eleanor, I think you should feel": Letter from Edie Bingham to Eleanor Bingham Miller, July 9, 1985.

334   "I don't think I can do": Telephone interview, Joan Bingham with author.

CHAPTER THIRTY-FOUR

335   "You can't have it both ways": Interview, Barry Bingham Junior with author.

335   "We took Rollie": Interview, Eleanor Bingham Miller with author, Louisville, January 24, 1986.

335f.   "Poor Eleanor": Interview, MB with author, Louisville, January 17, 1986.

336   "I could not trust Barry": Interview, Eleanor Bingham Miller with author.

336   "a mistake": Memo from Eleanor Bingham Miller, November 19, 1985.

336   "I did not want Barry Junior": Interview, Eleanor Bingham Miller with author, Louisville, January 24, 1986.

338   "All Eleanor had to do": Interview, Barry Bingham Junior with author.

338   "Barry is a paranoid": Interview, Eleanor Bingham Miller with author.

338   "There would be two": Interview, MB with author, Louisville, January 24, 1986.

338   "That has to be named": Interview, Barry Bingham Junior with author, Louisville, February 6, 1986.

339   "After all": Interview, Eleanor Bingham Miller with author.

339   "We would no longer have been": Interview, MB with author.

339   "Who cares if the newspaper": Telephone interview, Joan Bingham with author.

339   "If you decide that you are going to sell": Interview, Barry Bingham Junior with author, Louisville, February 6, 1987.

339   "I hadn't felt welcome": Interview, Rowland Miler with author, Louisville, January 24, 1986.

339   "It was not without considerable thought": Interview, Eleanor Bingham Miller with author.

339   "felt like I had": Interview, BB with author, Louisville, February 19, 1986.

340   "This is a complete betrayal": Interview, Barry Bingham Junior and Eleanor Bingham Miller with author.

340   "There is no point": Interview, Eleanor Bingham Miller, Louisville, January 24, 1986.

340   "It was very eerie": Rob Bingham to Joe Ward, "The Binghams: Twilight of a Tradition," *Courier-Journal,* supplement, April 20, 1986.

340   "Please tell your mother": Interview, Joan Bingham with author, Washington, January 21, 1986.

341   "a betrayal" and "irrational": *Courier-Journal,* January 10, 1986.

PAGE
341 "Your father has just posted": Interview, Elinor Brecher with author, Louis-
     ville, February 1986.

341 "Sale by Binghams": *New York Times,* January 13, 1986.

341 "every major newspaper": Interview, BB with author, Louisville, January 17,
     1986.

341 "The only way we can communicate": Interview, Sallie Bingham with author,
     Louisville, January 23, 1986.

341 "We all have our separate pride": Interview, MB with author, Louisville,
     January, February 1986.

342 "Isn't that picture lovely?": BB to author, Louisville, February 5, 1986.

343 "I don't see how my son": Interview, BB with author, Louisville, January
     1986.

343 "Sallie's book will be filled": MB and BB at *Vanity Fair* photo session, Feb-
     ruary 5, 1986, with author and Neil Selkirk, photographer.

344 "I wouldn't consider": Interview, BB with author, Louisville, January 1986.

345 "Barry": Interview, anonymous source with author.

345 "offensive and confusing": Letter from Edie Bingham to Clara, Rob, Emily
     and Molly Bingham, February 5, 1986.

346 "I don't know why Barry": Interview, MB with author, Louisville, June 5,
     1986.

346 "sounded like pure blackmail": Telephone interview, Eleanor Bingham Miller
     with author, February 26, 1986.

347 "What if someone": Interview, Gary Gensler with author, New York, spring
     1987.

347 "I'm a journalist": Telephone interview, Barry Bingham Junior with author,
     spring 1987.

347 "The lady from Kentucky": *Phil Donahue Show,* February 20, 1986.

347 "I was glad to see": Interview, BB with author, February 20, 1987.

347 "She told her son Chris": Interview, MB with author, Louisville, June 5,
     1986.

348 "I feel so sorry for you": Telephone interview, Diane Sawyer with author.

348 "This is to test the waters": Letter, Edie Bingham to Mary Bingham.

348 "see how *60 Minutes*": Interview, Edie Bingham with author.

348 "Why is it important to publish": Interview, Barry Bingham Junior with au-
     thor.

348f. "Bingham Bucks Sweepstakes": *Louisville Times,* April 12, 1986: *New York,*
     April 28, 1986; interview, Barry Bingham Junior with author.

349 "It was such an incredible contrast": Interview, anonymous source with au-
     thor.

350 "Hello, Mother": Interview, Joan Bingham with author, New York, September
     1986.

350 "She is studying a group of post–Civil War poets": Interview, Edie Bingham
     and Barry Bingham Junior with author.

350 "the sparkling jewel" and "There is a time to sow": *Courier-Journal,* May
     20, 1986.

351 "It's all over but the shouting": *Courier-Journal,* June 2, 1986.

PAGE

351   "I don't know why": Interview, Clara Bingham with author, New York, summer 1986.

351   "The news that Queen Elizabeth II: *Courier-Journal*, May 21, 1986.

352   "The Woman Who Overturned an Empire": Sallie Bingham, *Ms.*, June 1986.

352   "what would appear to be sinister logic": Interview, MB with author, Louisville, June 9, 1986.

352   "She got all the jewelry": Interview, Eleanor Bingham Miller with author, East Hampton, N.Y., July 29, 1986.

353   "a nature walk": Interview, MB with author, Louisville, June 9, 1986.

EPILOGUE

354f.   "Why does Father care so much?": Interview, MB and BB with author, Louisville, February 6, 1987.

355   ". . . Chandler's explanations of Judge Bingham's marriage": Memorandum to Macmillan Publishing Co. entitled "The Binghams of Louisville," April 1987.

356   "My father stood for": Telephone interview, Barry Bingham Junior with author, May 1987.

356   "I have everything wrong with it": David Chandler to Joe Ward, from telephone interview, Joe Ward with author.

357   "David Chandler's book": Sallie Bingham to book editors, May 29, 1987.

357   "Daughter Charges Bingham": *New York Post*, June 8, 1987; "Binghams on Hold," *Washington Post*, June 3, 1987.

357   "The only factual basis": Letter from Sallie Bingham to book editors, May 29, 1987.

357   "a water-jet in Lake Geneva": *Courier-Journal*, August 18, 1987.

358   "How are Uncle Barry": Interview, Clara Bingham with author, New York, June 1987.

358   "top-heavy with mid-level managers": Maria Braden, "New Workout for an Old Thoroughbred," *Washington Journalism Review*, July–August 1987, pp. 12–15.

358f.   "I had seen several consultants": Telephone interview, Barry Bingham Junior with author, Louisville, September 25, 1987.

Author's Note

I began work on this book in June of 1985. The first signs of trouble in the Bingham family had been mentioned in the *New York Times* and the *Wall Street Journal*: an announcement that Sallie wanted to sell her stock in the company; a small story about the dissension in the family over Barry Bingham Junior's editorial policies at the *Courier-Journal*. However minor these items appeared, they were startling. The Binghams had always represented greatness, a family that was united in its desire to do good for the world, seemingly impervious to occasional criticism of their some-times sanctimonious, sometimes imperial manner. Despite the tragedies they had endured, they had always seemed united. At that point I was looking for a new magazine assignment at *Vanity Fair* and my editor, Tina Brown, sent me to Louisville, the first of many trips she generously encouraged. I was not a stranger to Kentucky or to Louisville, having spent time a few years earlier crossing the state with its governor, John Y. Brown, on assignment for *New York* magazine. Then as now, I was fascinated by the charm of Louisville and the city's mores symbolized by its informal slogan "Politeness before progress." It was a town of hidden rules and social camouflage, controlled by a hundred or so old families. I had been reared in such a town, San Antonio, Texas, and so I felt comfortable there.

In Louisville no family was grander, more worldly or patrician than the Binghams, I was, of course, well aware of their immense importance to the city and to the state. But beyond this, I believed, however high-flown it sounds, that the Binghams repre-sented the best of America. Their newspaper was the dominant liberal voice in the South. They had set the highest standards for their children, and their children had lived up to them. They lived and acted old money. They had reared their children to help others and to think of themselves as citizens of the world. Any split in this family would be tragic for the newspaper, as well as for Louisville and Kentucky. The Bing-hams *were* different; their story was not a story of spoiled monsters. Understandably, at first no one in the family was happy to be interviewed. This was a family matter and certainly not to be discussed with a reporter for a national magazine.

Before I arrived in Louisville that muggy June, Barry Bingham Senior called me on the telephone. Although we did not know each other, for some moments he made the pleasantest small talk, as if he wanted nothing so much in the world but to chat me up that summer day. And then with no warning, his voice suddenly turned cold. "I am speaking now for all of us. We will not greet you at this time. I have spoken to Sallie, Eleanor and Barry Junior and we are all in agreement," he said. "Our family is in turmoil." Later that day, Sallie called me. "My father does not speak for me," she said. "He is trying to control everything."

But I believed Barry Senior was right not to see me that summer of 1985—why should he talk about his own family to a reporter? Later I wondered why he had bothered to waste so many minutes on small talk before saying no. Why not a direct

400

answer? Why the need for the façade and the grace? The chill underneath the charm was eerie. I remember wondering if that was how he might have dealt with his children.

That autumn the dissension grew louder. Stories began to appear frequently in the national press. I began to fill notebooks. Although there are many American families that have decided to sell their businesses and have quarreled bitterly among themselves, the Binghams' plight seemed singular. Why couldn't the members of this splendid family play straight with one another? As a Southerner, I sensed that there were some powerful reasons that might go back a generation or more.

Just after the announcement in January 1986 that the newspaper empire was going to be sold the Binghams inexplicably became more cooperative about being interviewed. Although it was odd for a family this high-minded to talk about one another in such intimate detail, I believe they were as mystified about what had happened to them as I, a virtual stranger, was. Perhaps they wanted to talk about their problems with reporters as a way to understand what had happened to them. Communication had broken down completely between them. Perhaps they reasoned that these interviews would become an alternative way of communicating.

Hearing each member of the family talk was a little like staring at Chinese puzzle boxes. In each person I saw a totally different pattern. Each sounded absolutely correct and rational about the situation, although no one agreed on who was to blame or why. There were no real villains of the piece. Each person, in his or her own way, was sympathetic and intelligent. And yet, despite their intelligence and high-mindedness—or perhaps because of them—their relationships with one another had collapsed. Any one of them at any point in the collapse could have compromised and saved the newspapers and the legacy for the family and ensured that the Bingham family dynasty would go on for the next generation. But there was to be no compromise.

I continued to be mystified and I kept going down to Louisville from New York City, promising Tina Brown she would get her ten thousand words for *Vanity Fair*. I began interviewing dozens of the Binghams' friends, relatives and acquaintances, not all of them so enamored of this fascinating clan. The deadline was pushed further and further back.

Barry and Mary Bingham were no longer cold to me. I was invited to lunch. Mary spent hours with me. Sometimes she wept. Even at age eighty-one Mary Bingham was extraordinary. She used Latin phrases when she spoke and had a subtle way of pausing for just a beat to make sure that you had understood her reference. A faint line of judgment and even of contempt would cross her brow when it was clear that a phrase had not been understood, a book not read, a play not seen, a Shakespearean reference not remarked upon. Here was another clue: I wondered if these same judgments were regularly passed upon her children of if they were reserved for strangers.

In one of our conversations Barry Senior mentioned an interview he had once given to an oral history project at the University of Louisville. In that interview, he mentioned letters that Mary had donated to Radcliffe. *Letters*. I flew to Boston the next day. I discovered that the Bingham papers were housed in a small private library at Radcliffe devoted to women's studies where the security was so tight one had to check all belongings in a locker outside the door. The librarian said, "There are *crates* here. Do you want to see all of them?"

Crates there were. The letters were astonishing. Hundreds of letters spanning decades, thousands of pages written by Mary to Barry or Barry to Mary, sometimes five thousand words a letter, years and years of family secrets, revelations, passions, intimacy, beautifully written as if for posterity. What were they doing at Radcliffe? Why would anyone give such personal documents to a library where anyone could read them, letters their children had never seen? What began as a ten-thousand-word magazine article I knew had to be expanded into a full-length study of a family.

Although I was not chosen to be the Binghams' "authorized" biographer—that role was given to Alex Jones, of the *New York Times*, who won a Pulitzer Prize for his reportage on the sale of the newspaper and the family—the Binghams continued to grant me interviews and allowed me the use of their letters without any restrictions. The thousands of pages of Bingham family papers finally began to explain what months in Louisville never could.

Over a hundred people were interviewed for this book. I am grateful to all those friends and acquaintances of the various members of the Bingham family who shared their memories and experiences with me. I will not list their names because in some cases they requested anonymity. However, I have cited dozens of my sources in the Notes. I tried as much as possible to omit references to the younger generation of Binghams—the children of Joan and Worth, of Barry Junior and Edie, and of Sallie and her former husbands, Whitney Ellsworth and Michael Iovenko. Eleanor and Rowland Miller's children are babies. I felt that the story belonged to their parents, grandparents and great-grandfather, the old Judge, Robert Worth Bingham. The cousins are for the most part good friends and seemed determined not to allow their parents' feelings about one another affect their own future relationships. I tried only to use their words or actions where it directly related to the larger story.

I am indebted to many people. I am particularly grateful to Tina Brown, the editor of *Vanity Fair*, who encouraged me to expand what she had imagined to be a magazine piece into a lengthy book and then generously gave me the time to complete it. Along the way, she read parts of the manuscript and her suggestions were inevitably helpful and insightful. My own editor, Jason Epstein at Random House, was enthusiastic about the book from our first meetings and nurtured it with his strong support and ability to bring out the best in a writer through his rigorous attention. His sense of the book and his wisdom guided me through a lengthy and difficult process, and I will always be grateful to him.

In Louisville, I was helped in my interviewing by Sam Thomas, a local historian, who was particularly helpful in gathering information about Judge Bingham, the controversial family patriarch. Additionally, Alanna Nash, a Louisville writer, shared her own interviews with me. And Elinor Brecher, a columnist at the *Courier-Journal*, now a Nieman Fellow at Harvard, was extraordinarily helpful by explaining to me the inner workings of the newspaper. In Richmond, Michael and Mary Ballou Ballentine and Mary Stuart Stettinius assisted in my research of Mary's family, the Amazing Capertons, as they were called. I am grateful to Lacy Dick and Gregg Kimball at the Valentine Museum in Richmond; the Henry Morrison Flagler Museum in Palm Beach; the University of Louisville *Courier-Journal* oral history project; the Filson Club; and, above all, to Pat King and Diane Hamer at the Schlesinger Collection at Radcliffe College for their wonderful support and encouragement. In San Antonio, my mother, Thelma Brenner, spent weeks in the University of Texas library researching for me, and I am grateful for her love and support and that of my father, Milton Brenner. In New York, my researcher, Lisa Cohen, worked diligently for months on the manuscript, as did Della Roland and Donna Ruskavage.

Among many others who have helped me are Wayne Lawson at *Vanity Fair*; Joni Evans, Sono Rosenberg, Kassie Evashevski, Leslie Oelsner, and Sarah Timberman at Random House; my agent, Owen Laster at William Morris. Before he left Random House, Howard Kaminsky was generous with his time and encouragement. I am especially indebted to my friends and family who have encouraged me through these last few years and particularly to Ann Arensberg and Richard Grossman, Carl and Barbara Brenner, Sarah Lewis, Judith Green, Susanna Moore, Amanda Urban and Ken Auletta, Nick Pileggi, Nora Ephron, Katharine Johnson, Edward Kosner, Nima Isham, Barbara Liberman, John Leo and Jackie McCord Leo, Jane Hitchcock, Sharon Hoge, Jesse Kornbluth, Dominick Dunne, Andrew Tobias, Jonathan Schwartz, Katherine Schwartz, Justin Pomerantz, Diane Sokolow, Patti Kenner, Liz Smith, Shirley

Clurman, Helen Bransford, Robert Ascheim and Lidia Martinez. But most of all I am grateful to my husband, Ernie Pomerantz, who encouraged me with his love and patience and spent countless hours discussing the book with me over these last few years.

—MARIE BRENNER
November 1987

Index